AURIC LIVING

AURIC LIVING

Happiness Is Counting on You

LEE MARIE JACOBS

Waterside Productions

Copyright © 2022 by Lee Marie Jacobs

www.auricliving.com

All rights reserved. This book or any portion thereof may not be reproduced or used in any manner whatsoever without the express written permission of the publisher except for the use of brief quotations in articles and book reviews.

The information presented is the author's opinion and does not constitute any health or medical advice. The content of this book is for informational purposes only and is not intended to diagnose, treat, cure, or prevent any condition or disease. Prior to starting any new health, wellness, or nutritional program, consult with your primary healthcare practitioner.

First Printing, 2022

ISBN-13: 978-1-958848-32-6 print edition
ISBN-13: 978-1-958848-33-3 e-book edition

Auric Living, an imprint of:

Waterside Productions
2055 Oxford Ave
Cardiff, CA 92007
www.waterside.com

"Don't try to not be yourself, just be yourself"
—Jaks Jacobs

Table of Contents

Chapter 1: An Invitation · 1
Chapter 2: Auric Breath · 29
Chapter 3: Auric Mind · 45
Chapter 4: Auric Heart · 79
Chapter 5: Auric Body · 133
Chapter 6: Auric Health · 166
Chapter 7: Auric Nutrition · 240
Chapter 8: Auric Beauty · 298
Chapter 9: Auric Home · 330
Chapter 10: Auric Wealth · 365

References · 387

Chapter 1: An Invitation

"If prayer is you talking to God, then intuition is God talking to you"
-Dr. Wayne Dyer

Auric Living: The weaving of art, heart, nature, spirituality, and intuition. Auric Living is a way of life that promotes and maintains continuous communication with your heart, your soul, with nature and with the divine. Auric Living is a path of integration promoting order, healing, wholeness, integrity, and rhythm throughout the physical and energy body.

Throughout my life, books have often mysteriously landed on my lap. Sometimes they have literally fallen off the shelf at a bookstore, while others were left behind at hostels and retreats during my travels abroad. My intuition has always alerted me when a book is a worthy read, and I have come to listen with great attention. Some of the books that have entered my auric field have even mysteriously and spontaneously surfaced at just the perfect time. I hope this book has entered your auric field with divine timing and synched to your very own cosmic clock. The source of all the chaos, struggle, and disfunction in life today is a lost connection with soul. Auric Living is the reintegration and reordering of individual life with nature, spirituality, rhythm, soul, simplicity, beauty, and love. Consider the concept of Auric Living to be a cosmic reset in your life where you have full permission to reorder everything that doesn't integrous and true. This book will guide you through a transformational shift where spiritual truth and order take precedent over the material and physical world. Your inner world is prioritized over your outer one. This doesn't mean you don't embrace the outer world, but you are no longer emotionally and mentally swept away by it. You become anchored in peace and joy. This book is truly a guide to transitioning from human *doing* to human *being*. The inner question now becomes "who am I going to be?" rather than "What am I going to do?" or "What am I going to be?" Consider the experience of reading this book to be a temporary yet profound cosmic "time-out" where you give yourself full permission to contemplate, explore, expand, and awaken.

If you're reading this book, you may have animated and activated the energy flow from higher dimensions and realms. You may be shifting from career to calling or surrendering just a little deeper to your soul. You may sense a strange shift in your physical world right now, even though everything looks pretty much the same. You may wake up more mornings that not, wondering what day it is, what time it is, and what the heck your purpose is.

If you're reading this book, you're ready to experience depth, dimension, and destiny in this life. You're being intuitively guided to prepare yourself for spiritual initiation so that you can navigate the great change and awakening that is taking place on the planet. For many, awakening to cosmic memory is also taking place. Memories of past lives are coming to light as well as ancient wisdom and truths that were long forgotten. High clairvoyance is also entering our body and being as we begin to hear, see, and feel invisible truths. You may not have all the details, but deep within your soul, you know something big is coming and you must now prepare for it. Something bigger than yourself is guiding you now to pivot, prepare, release, surrender, and pray. You're becoming more enticed by divine law and spiritual truths than you are seduced into keeping up the fancy and the fake. You have finally come to understand, that happiness cannot be fully realized, unless there is unobstructed communication with your soul.

This is what we will accomplish throughout this book. Get ready to feel an intense soul-charge and a spiritually activation as you progress through each chapter. We will uncover the reason for life's chaos and the journey back to whole. Once you understand the bigger cosmic picture, you are able to more deeply surrender to simpleness. We have lost the uncomplicated, the gentle, and the kind. Our bodies have been conditioned with untruths and unnatural modes of being. What may have been true for you at the beginning of this book could quickly become a lie in your life upon completion. The wisdom that carries cosmically correct truth is yearning to enter your being. Throughout this book, you will discover that cosmic truth has been kept out of schools, churches, workplaces and institutions. This has resulted in mass addiction, dis-ease, and unrest.

This book is for the creatively curious and spiritually strong.

You surely feel something serious going on in your soul right now. Your physical world might seem to look fairly similar, but energetically, everything feels strange. That is because, throughout your body, portals and energetic floodgates are opening, and cosmic wisdom is pouring in. From now on, healing will only happen through the heart. We must remember that what we actually see through the eyes is only 10% of the actual picture. The non-physical and invisible realms are the true architects of our reality. We must now learn to live more of our day present and protected in our interior castle—in the seat of our soul.

As you move through these pages, you will come to understand how we become frail through fear. Fear is, by far, the number one reason for body breakdown, and we have been swimming in it since before birth. The most devastating consequence of this is that fear has become our comfort zone. Because fear is such a "normal" and subtle state in everyday life, most people aren't even aware they have been programmed to vibe low. When you vibe low for long enough, you forget there is a high. In this book, you will learn how to dance with fear as it comes in and sing it a lullaby as it goes out. Your work throughout this book will be to redirect your day from lower vibrational linear time, to synchronistic soul time. This is when all the high vibes will shine for you!

From a young age, I could perceive the energy fields of others. It was like I could sense what they were thinking and feeling. I was not aware of auras at the time, but it was very clear to me that although I couldn't *see* auras, I could *feel* them. As a child, I obviously knew nothing of energy and biofield medicine, but I was keenly aware that my nervous system was highly sensitive. I could feel stored trauma in others and often gain insights into the details of their traumas. I have also always had an ability to feel what others are thinking. This can come in handy in many situations, but also create havoc on my own body when energetic boundaries are not clearly set.

My method for managing this anxious energy was to stay focused, organized, and orderly as a means of controlling my environment, which allowed me to convince myself that I was fully in charge. Eating was also a grounding practice I used—not so much to feed my body but as an attempt to fuel my soul and calm my nervous system. Food was used in an attempt to ground my energy body to the earth. When I felt too frazzled in my nervous system, eating was a way for me to ground my highly sensitive energy body. It was if food were the anchor I needed to keep the ship from drifting away. What I later realized was that self-nurturing was desperately needed and that I was responsible for loving and nurturing the child within. Storing other people's energy systems in my own body became almost like a part-time job as I tried to manage everyone around me. I wasn't aware I was doing this, but I was very aware that I always felt heavy and dense inside. It wasn't until decades later that I realized I was literally being weighed down by the energetic and emotional bodies of other people. In many cases, food issues have to do with boundary issues. As a result, I often "ate my feelings" and surrendered to what appeared to be my destiny: feeling restricted and limited in all dimensions of life even as I wanted desperately to live to my fullest potential. I had all the creativity and the will but neglected to strengthen self-love. I often felt as if there were some invisible cage around me keeping me trapped on an energetic hamster wheel of busy and of stress. I felt like a genie in a bottle just waiting to explode out and experience the magic of life. I felt restrained by the boundaries, constraints, and limitations put on me by others and by society, and I was too spiritually immature at the time to truly understand the mountain I was climbing. I hadn't yet taken full responsibility for my journey, nor had I developed the spiritual maturity to fully harmonize my personality with my soul.

On top of feeling inauthentic in my own body as I moved through life and taking on the energies of others while people-pleasing in order to fit in, I also struggled with a deeper problem. I felt completely misaligned with most of the information that was being taught to me. It is my belief that stuffing children with as much information as possible, regardless of their needs or interest level, leads to a form of trauma. The amount of fear children are exposed to from a very young age is also deeply traumatic for them. This creates a false fortress around their soul and keeps them caged in a fear-based environment where security and safety become the daily mission and mandate. Visionary living outside have to be processed, as many of us are experiencing at this very moment in time. What children need now more than ever is the freedom to play, to receive, to express, and to love. They must be given full permission to be themselves, to listen to their hearts, and to express and process their feelings. They must be encouraged to be truly, madly, and deeply *authentic*.

As I progressed through high school, university, post-grad work, and the beginnings of a career, I unconsciously overfilled my schedule and my life as a means of keeping my spongy energy system under wraps. The stuffing including shopping, eating, running, rushing, and keeping chronically busy. Little did I realize that with practice and care, my highly intuitive nature would actually become my greatest gift. It was thanks to Dr. Judith Orloff, MD, a prominent psychiatrist and the author of *The Empath's Survival Guide*, that I could finally make sense of the emotional weight I had been carrying for so long. I strongly related to the characteristics and behaviors of what she describes as an "intuitive empath"—that is, someone who is deeply sensitive and intuitive and who experiences heightened emotions and perceptions. An intuitive empath also emotionally takes on the feelings of others and stores them in his or her own emotional body. This is where the chronic feeling of heaviness comes in because intuitive empaths are carrying the addition emotional burdens of other people.

Unsure of how to rise above this buffet of energies in my body, I soothed myself by emotional eating, which I counterbalanced by obsessing over physique and physical fitness and by staying extremely busy. I found myself saying "Yes" to every demand for my time while also energetically inviting the auras of everyone around me for a piggy-back ride. Every day seemed to be strangely similar: the same drives, the same foods, the same people, the same experiences. Although details differed each day, the pattern was the same. It was like the movie *Groundhog Day*, where the main character finds himself trapped in the same day, destined to repeat it over and over without any kind of escape in sight. This isn't a far stretch from the reality of many of us.

This was my Groundhog Day:

Morning	*Day*	*Evening*
Alarm clock wake-up	Worry + Guilt all day	Eat my feelings
Inhale food without chewing	People Please	Rush and do more
Stress over overfilled day	Answer the need and call of others	Avoid stillness
Worry about many things	Ignore intuition because of responsibility	Stress over next day
Feel guilty about many things	Manage monkey mind	Rush or limit self-care
Skip self-care	Be good, liked and nice	Feel anxious
Panic over to-do list	Take on too much	

I struggled to understand how decades of schooling, a master's degree, and growing professional credentials in my field could result in such uninspiring, lifeless, and robotic living. How could someone with degrees, intelligence, and talent fall slave to an existence void of lifeforce and creativity? Of course there were many joyful experiences and heaps to be grateful for, but a key question kept playing in my brain: *Is this really what I incarnated for? Am I the only one who feels something is very off about the structures and systems of society?* I was blessed with the most loving family and friends, but for the most part, I was living each day with a big question mark: When does life begin? And, more privately, *Is there not a greater purpose than this?* When was it time to authentically spread my wings?

As I perfected being a highly functional intuitive empath, I got the job, the marriage, the house, the fast-paced weekend-warrior schedule, and all other assets that I was supposed to want and need. And yet, the more I tried, the more inauthentic I felt. I had become extraordinary at being ordinary. I perfected small talk, being nice, social smiles, and adulting. I mastered Stephen Covey's seven habits and being a "human doing," but in all of that accomplishment, I had neglected to master the most relevant and meaningful practices in life. I had lost touch with mindfulness and with the moment. I had graduated from multiple educational institutes without learning how to authentically *be*. For anyone going through this experience right now, it is deeply important that you give yourself full permission to grieve, to cry and to break down. This experience is a necessary step on the journey to self-awakening and spiritual initiation.

As I began to develop self-awareness and observe my life rather than get entangled within it, I realize that not being enough was a belief I carried that became a crack in the very foundation of my being. If I wasn't doing, I felt less than enough. If I wasn't busy achieving or doing, I wasn't enough. Nothing was really ever enough. Being present was absolutely not enough. These thoughts haunted me day in day out. I got a temporary snooze when I was engaged in business, projects, or a busy schedule. It wasn't until my children were born that I was exhausted enough not to fight the lesson. I was finally ready to deal with it—at my most vulnerable, raw, and exhausted state as a new mom of three boys under three. My ability to face the challenge was probably because I was too exhausted to think, which was actually a great blessing. As my children got older, I did have a few setbacks in busyness, but what I later realized was that sometimes a little step back in consciousness is exactly what is necessary before taking a big leap forward.

This included a short stint in medical school along with a few other holistic schools until I recalibrated back to center and recognized those old busy tricks were trying to throw me off course. What I did learn from my time in medical school was that there is a great void and emphasis on self-care, self-compassion, and self-love. In all of my intake forms, I wish the following would have been included:

Do you understand how to be well?
Do you feel deeply connected to nature?
Do you know how to be still?
Do you know how to quiet the mind?
Do you practice meditation and breathwork?
Do you feel and listen to your intuition?
Do you understand your aura?
Do you know how to create healthy boundaries for yourself?
Do you know your deeper purpose?
Do you know how to eat for optimal radiance and energy?
Do you fully express your creativity?
Do you live intuitively and authentically?
Do you have daily heart-opener exercises?
Do you know how to optimally breath?
Do you mindfully and gently move your body?
Do you deeply love yourself?
Are you flexible, stable and strong?
Do you feel harmonious in your body and being?

Do you know how to not think?
Do you have a strong and balanced mind?
Do you understand the difference between intellect and awareness?
Do you understand how to live well?
Do you have an understanding of universal laws?
Do you have practices for developing higher senses?
Do you know how to prioritize calm over chaos?
Do you lead every day with heart?
Do you feel inspired every day?
Do you forgive yourself and others easily?
Does your soul feel nourished and free?
How easily do you let go in your life?
Who are you not forgiving right now?

If you've read *Beautiful Money*, you have an intimate understanding of how my drive to be perceived as nice, liked, and socially acceptable impacted both my personal and professional journey; I was hemmed in by my own limitations, defined by other people's opinions and boundaries for my life. It took another eight years or so find answers to many of my questions. I am still exploring many of my questions to this day.

Creating connection to your higher-self and authentic voice—especially when you have been trained from all dimensions of life to fit in and avoid feather-ruffling—can seem impossible. The secret, I found, is to start asking the right questions in the right direction. Begin to question everything. Become the observer of your own play and watch yourself navigate through the day. If you're up for it, it's a fascinating experience—and one that is incredibly *un*complicated. Simply observe yourself navigate each moment of the day. With compassion and kindness, watch yourself maneuver each experience in a day. Observe the repetitive patterns, emotional triggers, emotional roller-coasting, and autopilot behaviors that seem automated beyond belief.

> **AURIC ACTION**
>
> For one full day, observe yourself navigating through the day. Without judgement or attachment, take one day just to enjoy yourself in observation.

My first life-class mentor was the therapist I visited when I was 27 years old. She shared with me that the questions and feelings I had were more common in women in their 50s and 60s. Apparently, I'm an old soul! I took this as a compliment and a sign that I was heading down the right track for finding truth. It was during that very therapy session that I began my own unschooling curriculum. Little did I know that this curriculum had no end date and would probably stretch into future lifetimes. The hidden wisdom in this unschooling process is that we are so deeply intuitive that blocking intuition is what creates all the chaos and conflict in our lives. We are given guidance and answers at every moment that we don't act upon out of fear—fear that we won't fit in, we won't get into the club, we won't get the job, we won't get invited. We have been mind-conditioned through fear, guilt, and shame to not trust our inner knowing and to go against our very intuitive nature, all in the name of fitting a broken mold.

I invite you to come along with me as we unlearn together and keep much of this gorgeous mental, emotional, and cellular space as, well, *space*. As you unfold, unravel, and release, I invite you to deeply cherish and mindfully keep this sacred space in your mind, heart, and body. Take gentle notice of the addiction we all have to filling this space. I invite you to use this moment to speak to your soul and vow to prioritize space over silliness. When I speak of silliness, I mean all the things in our social structure today that really don't matter much: the clock, the job, the party, the to-do list, the home renovation. I'm not saying that they aren't part of the human experience, but if our bodies and beings are not alive and flowing with life force energy, how authentic is the smile at the party? Take some time to feel the deliciousness of emptiness, of peace, and of simplicity; also, take time to grieve. For me, the unlearning process brought with it a significant grieving process—for all the lost time, play, energy, and wing-clipping that went into living inauthenticity. We are all weighted down by society to some degree, but the intuitive empaths tend to carry more of this resistance in their energy bodies. Those feelings are real, and allowing yourself to hold space for them is part of the process of releasing inauthenticity. Love them for the purpose they served and gracefully let them go. Breathwork is magic for this!

There is collective grieving that also needs to take place right now in order for us to release lifetimes of heaviness, conditioning and density. This is our work! On the cosmic clock, it's time to recalibrate and realign as individuals to our spiritual truths, cherished values, and authentic nature. We have been living for other people for far too long. It's time to do you!

As the grieving process takes place, much resistance will be released from the body. This is why a cosmic approach to healing is so very important. Cosmic healing is a deeply personal and deeply spiritual experience—there is no one-size-fits-all. What I can tell you is that you will be guided every step of the way and given clues as to what to do next. You are your own master healer. You can seek outside help and guidance, but true healing happens within. When you heart is open and your mind is flexible, your soul can speak. Dr. Edward Bach, the great British doctor, bacteriologist, and homeopath, reminds us that what happens to the physical body is a manifestation of our mental, spiritual, and emotional inner movement. The human body is a temple for the spirit. As we grieve, reorder, and heal as individuals, collective healing will naturally begin to gain beautiful momentum. We will witness incredible transformation on this planet as each one of us commits to focusing on our own healing journey instead of trying to fix and change others. Projecting our unhappiness onto other people may feel therapeutic for a while, but eventually, an awakening happens and rising above projecting just feels so much better.

Through my own healing journey, I have learned to use my body (especially my nervous system), as a compass for how close to spiritual home I am. Spiritual home is your place of deep alignment, truth, flexibility, grace, authenticity, truth, and peace. When you are spiritually home, you lead with your heart in every moment and ask for nothing in return. In this house, deep compassion carries you through each day and an inner sense of safety and security is always present. I have also come to understand that knowing home, finding home, and getting back to home are three separate journeys that all carry wisdom. Today, I intuitively feel throughout my body when something is true and authentic to my soul, and when it is not. One of my favorite quotes is by the medieval Persian poet Hafiz: "Love sometimes wants to do us a great favor: hold us upside down and shake all of the nonsense out."

Now is the time to return to simple, peaceful living—to return home to truth. Now is the time to shake the nonsense out.

Auric Living is a cosmic perspective on daily life and a resource for spiritual maturation. This is a very sacred and divinely timed nodal point for humanity calling many to begin spiritual activation and initiation. If you are being called to have a more intimate, powerful, and daily relationship with the divine right now, you are not alone. The rate of spiritual awakening is higher and faster than ever before in human history. It's a truly quantum awakening for humanity; planetary ascension is happening at lightning speed.

To sort divine truth from mere noise is no easy task. Many humans are now also awakening to the very reality that what has been pitched to us throughout history is a manipulated version of actual truth. This is a very difficult reality to wake up to and one that takes much compassion and love for all (including ourselves). Auric Living is a way of life that promotes total integration and harmony. From the moment you wake up in the morning, you focus on a feeling of wholeness, wellness, and joy. You speak to your body with love and grace and keep in continuous contact with your soul. Auric Living promotes the mental muscle-building that supports and trains how to truly think. With this methodology, you think and feel your way to truth. As we transition through the 4th dimension (which I will speak about later), we must more deeply ground to earth's intelligence as well as more expansively spread our spiritual wings. This is no easy task, and we have been cut off from much of the ancient spiritual wisdom that was once widely practiced and understood. The tools and techniques for happiness and joy are available, you just need to be creatively curious enough to access higher truth. Our work here is to continue spiritually ascending individually as well as collectively while keeping our feet firmly planted to the ground. We must learn how to navigate the spiritual realm while running a business, raising a family, taking care of our health, and engaging in relationships. We must also remember that the earth is also evolving and ascending as we do, which can make for a bumpy ride. This ride may feel dark at times, but it will be filled with richness and revelation that will feed and fuel your soul. As intense as it seems, having a daily practice for presence, peace, and play will soften the journey. Fully embrace all layers of your being each day, the light and the dark. The beauty of this time is that we are all coming back to whole, and we are doing it together. Auric Living is a spiritual lifestyle guide for heart-centered, highest-vibrational living. This book teaches how one rebuilds integrity in the auric field, which results in a gorgeous glow that cannot be found or attained through physical beauty tools. You will learn how to consciously expand your aura and shine your rays everywhere you go.

Seeking a job or a career is an important step in the developmental process, but we are graduating beyond jobs and careers. We are spiritually maturing into *callings*. We are learning not only to discover our archetypes but to understand which ones are activated when, and which ones are leading the way at different times throughout our lives. You may have a season in your life where your warrior is meant to take the lead only to pass the torch to the mystic for the next season. As we become more familiar with our own archetypes, we can then work with them as we flow into our highest calling in this lifetime. As you open your heart and release resistance (fear and shame being big ones) from the body, space opens up for divine will and higher calling to flow in. As we break free from the old, we create space for only the highest of possibilities. We have an opportunity to get clear and create our greatest version of reality. My intention for this book is to open a portal for you—to help you realize that for your entire life, you have been conditioned how to think, choose, and behave in a very predictable way. Even when you feel your rebellious side take the lead, it is still usually within the boundaries of predictable behavior. When you suppress your light, your body will eventually break down. There's a high probability that you are feeling the effects of this lifelong suppression right now, but trust me, you're so ready to burst your gorgeous rays of light.

Auric Living is about giving yourself permission to express who you truly are with great love and appreciation for your own sacredness. You are an expression of divine light; it's time for you to own and embody this truth. If you feel like you've been living beneath your potential or light, this is your loving wake-up call. It's time to fully embrace and own your divinity. Life is not a rehearsal; you are here for great purpose, great awakening, and great possibility. "Highest vibrational choices only" has been my vow over the past two years, and it is incredible the difference that has made in my own life. With all of my heart, I want you to experience the power of your own extraordinary inner light. Through practice, pivots, and pursuits, you will learn how to bring your being into greater harmony with capital-t Truth. You are sunshine within. Have great compassion for yourself, and you will have great compassion for all of life. Give yourself a moment to exhale the stored, stale energies trapped inside; you carry lifetimes with you. Your work is to continuously release the stale to make room for the sun.

Auric Living is also a daily practice for prioritizing simplicity, spirituality, and play. Much of this book has been written from

Nosara, Costa Rica—a region where play is the way. When I first arrived in Nosara, I actually felt guilty committing to play every day. I had arrived at a place in my life where health and harmony were prioritized, but play was still uncomfortable for me. Most of my life up to that point had been about productivity, responsibility, and achievement. How often do you experience pure play? I was inspired by the residents in Nosara who surf in the morning, go to yoga over lunch, and meet up with friends in the evening for sunset. Living playful and free here is as important for adults as it is for children. If quantum healing is a priority, this way of life is a treasure. We underestimate how important unstructured play is for the soul. In an overly systemized and structured world, when you observe a child or adult deep in unstructured play, there is nothing more blissful.

Over the past decade, motherhood had also brought a dose of worry, fear, and guilt. Feelings of not being enough easily creep into a mom-mind, and I believe new moms especially can be easy prey for lower vibrational energies that hang around in fourth dimension consciousness. A very wise spiritual teacher, Simon Calnan, shared with me that there is never a time in a woman's life where she is more closely connected to the realms of birth and death than early motherhood. This is a very vulnerable time for women, and they aren't often trained on the spiritual side of the childbirth gateway. Because of this, they overly focus on every detail of every minute of pregnancy and forget to prepare the soul. Many energetic portals open during childbirth, and we simply don't educate women enough on how to manage and protect their energy fields during this sacred time. When the baby comes out, so does the stored trauma. The flood of unintegrated trauma and grief from the past is overwhelming for a new mom. This is why many women find the first year of motherhood so deeply difficult. The emotional body has not been prepared for motherhood the way the physical body has. The good news is that the regular outburst of emotions and tears is a mother's natural grief work. Healing happens without much effort during this period. It may take some time, but it eventually happens. How, you ask? New moms are exhausted and drained. When the heart portal is open and you're too exhausted to cling to your ego, healing just happens. It doesn't always happen overnight, but it does happen.

A mother is typically so exhausted juggling way too many balls that the only thing she can do is bawl. "Shouldn't this be the happiest time ever?" she asks. It would be so helpful for soon-to-be moms to know this information before giving birth—to know that all the crying and emotional outbursts are a sign that harmonious healing is taking place. To see the light, we must first pass through the dark. There are very few heart-opening experiences as profound as having a child. Since healing happens through the heart, the whole heart-opening experience of childbirth can do nothing less than release stored grief and integrate trauma. Trauma doesn't have to be big in size to take up big residence in the body.

Throughout this book, you will learn how to design your day so that it is infused with spiritual strength, present moments, and heart-opening experiences. You will also learn how to design your nights to be restful, refueling, and filled with insight and guidance. This is how to feed and fuel the soul.

My intention in writing *Auric Living* is to invite you to close your eyes and leap into vitality. It's time to commit to a new daily code of conduct where time warps and synchronicity dominates—one where simplicity, spirituality, creativity, self-expression, play, and authentic joy rule the day. When this becomes our new normal, much less time and effort are needed to get the results your heart truly desires. The universe hears the desires of your heart, but the portal (the heart) must be activated and opened for them to manifest in this reality. This book is an invitation to begin an all-access intuitive life. In all dimensions of your life, unleash that intuitive power today. Bring it to your eating, learning, parenting, working, loving, interacting, building, training, teaching, behaving, and nurturing. It is uncomfortable and a little frightening in the beginning, but with practice and patience, true intuitive living becomes unconditionally non-negotiable. Every time you block an intuitive nudge, you mess with your reality. We have been programmed to ignore, suppress, and delay intuition which is detrimental to health and wellbeing. Our world is in chaos because we are in chaos. We have lost connection with our very souls. Soul communication has become a rare occurrence instead of a continuous flow. It's time to reconnect our cosmic wiring and gear up for instantaneous intuition ALWAYS.

What *Auric Living* will offer you:

- A cosmic perspective on reality
- How fear imprisons and harms
- How to eat for cosmic health
- Why spiritual nutrition is so powerful
- Why we struggle for stillness
- How to transform your body into a beam of light
- How to heal through the heart
- The role of the sun in healing
- How to manifest auric wealth
- How to align with your inner master-healer
- How to self-heal
- How to think
- How to free yourself from labels
- The power of "Present-Moment Awareness"
- How to live intuitively every day
- The importance of rhythm for health and happiness
- How and why to ground daily
- Why authenticity is so important for you
- How to set boundaries with ease and grace
- How to release resistance from the body

As you begin your Auric Living journey, there are a few questions you are invited to ask yourself, without judgement or force, to see how you intuitively respond. Try to observe your responses from a place of love, compassion, and slight detachment. (Should you have no answers to some of the questions, don't worry about it. Everything divinely timed, and you will get there eventually—when it's time for you to do so.)

- Why do I wake up each morning?
- Why do I do what I do?
- How open is my heart?
- How easy is it for me to let go and let God?
- How easily do I get attached to thoughts and things?
- How often do I gossip in my life?
- How much do I question what I am taught?
- How easy is it for me to forgive?
- How much do I value integrity and purity in my life?
- Where are the energetic blocks stored throughout my body?
- Do I hold anger, hate, or resentment in my body?
- Is my thinking aligned with highest vibrational living?
- How free do I feel? Where in my life do I not feel free?
- Is my life filled with purpose, clarity, and joy?
- Do I honor my body as my greatest tool for feedback and alignment?
- Do I live intuitively or from conditioning and social norms?
- How often in a day do I question my behaviors, actions, and thoughts?
- How much of my life is owned by other people (their expectations, opinions, etc.)?
- Who controls my thinking?
- How many addictions circulate in my life? Which ones?
- How do I program my mind?
- Am I following a path of light, life-force, and love in my life?
- Do I have complete faith in the greater unfolding of things?
- How spiritually strong and mature am I?
- How often do I attach to a victim mindset in my life?
- How often to I blame others for my current reality?
- Do I make choices from fear or faith?
- How much fear do I have stored in my body?

* How much resistance is stored in my body (fear, anger, resentment, envy, guilt, shame, grief)?
* Do I release resistance built up in my body on a daily basis or let it store up?
* How quickly do I act on intuitive nudges and creative downloads?
* How often do I go against intuition in my decisions and choices?

It is time for humanity, as a whole, to realize that spiritual maturation is at work at this stage in our evolutionary process. We must have the deeper conversations with ourselves about what we stand for, what we believe in, and what feels in alignment with our very soul. With technology quickly gaining more power than ever before, we must consider and clarify what boundaries we want to set for our lives and for our children. As you gain clarity on your value system and lifestyle priorities, you get creative! It's not just about what house you want to raise your family in and what school you want them to attend (or not attend), but what you want daily living for them to look like. For my husband and me, it is important that we spend our days together as a family with health and freedom as our priorities.

As our hearts soften and old paradigms crumble, we will enhance and activate higher chakras and spiritual strengths. It will become much more common for us to see auras, feel the feelings of others, and hear the thoughts of others. Remote viewing, spontaneous healing, and astral projection will become our new normal. This is already happening, but the speed at which this will accelerate is significant. We begin again to look to trees for answers and plants for healing. We master our five senses in order to live a divinely guided life. We learn that we have universes within us that we haven't even begun to explore.

With this level of spiritual maturation taking place, our awareness is heightened, and we see things from a quantum perspective—and this is when it becomes obvious that we have not been well trained on how to think. Were quantum physics and collective consciousness ever discussed when you were growing up? They certainly weren't for me. If we train our children not only how to think, but also the very laws of nature and spirituality, they probably won't be in such a state of confusion and chaos as adults. It took me until the age of 34 to find a book that outlined spiritual laws and sub-laws, and it is my belief we should all be taught this as children. (That book was *The Light Shall Set You Free* by Dr. Norma J. Milanovich and Dr. Shirley D. McCune). If we balance our attention more between body fitness and mental fitness, we will come to understand that a mind makeover is often much more powerful than a body one. When the mind is healthy, the body follows. When the mind is healthy, the body wants to move, express, and create. When the mind is healthy, the body is destined to thrive.

A few years ago, I realized that it wasn't my body that needed my attention, it was my mind. My mental muscles had atrophied. Through my child-bearing and early parenting years, I got lazy with my mind. I am deeply compassionate with myself for these times, but I had forgotten to train my mind on a daily basis. I let my exhaustion get the best of me. Regardless of the conditions that led to my "stinking thinking," I had developed some habits that were not worthy of my soul and that were actually dulling my aura. I knew I did not incarnate to settle for low-vibrational thinking! I took the next year to retrain my mind and rewire my thoughts. Be very, very cautious about who and what you allow into your cranial castle. Your mind is just as much of a temple as your body, and I could even argue that it should be prioritized *over* your body. Body care is essential, but it counts for very little if one neglects mind care.

In these unprecedented times, we *need* a new lifestyle resource for cosmic living and spiritual growth. We are conditioned to focus more on the job, the house, and the school than we are on happiness, health and whole. Did anyone ever ask you, when you were a child, to write out the greatest vision you have for your life? If they did, I'm sure working 10 hours a day, stuffing in stand-up meals, hoarding goods from big box stores, and being at the mercy by a cell phone were not part of the dream you imagined.

Have you ever taken a moment to evaluate your daily mode of operation? Isn't it curious that money and career management remain at the top of the list even if daily life is miserable? It is now crystal clear to many that we have been trained to be highly functional dysfunctional.

Much of humanity is seeking tools, resources, and a rhythm that is more in line with nature, consciousness, heart, and deep peace. As we progress and evolve, spiritual leadership will become even more valued than academic leadership. Integrity, a moral compass, and spiritual values will indeed find their way back into society. *Auric Living* provides you with the rhythm and resources for living in alignment and integrity with higher truths and realities. As we practice pivoting back to presence, we relearn what came naturally to us as children. The more present you are, the more peaceful you feel. As you progress through the book, you will be guided to make simple shifts that result in less superficial and more spiritual sweetness. This book will guide you on how to prioritize your spiritual practice while still enjoying this physical incarnation.

It is my heartfelt hope that *Auric Living* supports you and your family in better navigating choices. I hope this book provides a clearer understanding of how our daily choices impact not only our physical health but also our entire physical reality. We must all be trained on how to practice "Cosmically-Connected Living" if we want to break free from the chaos, constraints, and conditioning to which we have all been chronically exposed. For the sake of the children on this planet today and all future generations, we must get started RIGHT NOW.

For the sake of simplicity, here is a summary of the priorities that must now become policy: Our health and spiritual wellbeing must be a daily priority. Spiritual leadership must become a daily practice. We must value rest as much as we value aligned action. We must give ourselves permission to grieve. We must cleanse our bodies and beings of all that no longer serves the higher self. We must rebuild our bodies with an "energy first, matter second" approach. We must learn how to think. We must prioritize the teaching of spiritual and natural laws to our children. We must command integrity, truth, authenticity, and a moral compass back into society. We must heal our relationship with nature and make earthing the order of the day. We must do this together. We must create conscious communities.

We are outgrowing traditional time management programs, nutrition programs, health programs, education programs, and financial programs. It's time for a revolutionary new approach to living in alignment with higher states of consciousness, deeper inner peace, pure integrity. The cosmos are calling us; we must reorder our lives this very instant in order to get even a glimpse at the magic that we were meant for.

As you read through this book, you will begin to reprioritize, release, and relax into higher realms of being. Your days will no longer be consumed with trivial matters but will be filled with creative expression and light like never before. You will say goodbye to time management and embrace cosmic fluidity. You will develop a heightened ability to morph time through creative expression and present moment awareness. At the end of this book, with an exhale and a smile, you will say to yourself "I can see clearly now."

Auric Living consists of six simple practices that will become the most important daily dos. Instead of holding back on these offerings until later in the book, I want to share them here so you can begin to contemplate, consider, and implement—starting today.

The Six Spiritual Practices for Auric Living

Everything we are experiencing today is heightened. Body symptoms, emotional ups and downs, confusion, limbo, and fear are all surfacing up in our lives like never before. The most important and foundational teaching that this book can offer is the critical nature of starting a spiritual practice at this very moment in time. From this moment on, having a daily spiritual practice will be necessary and take precedence over external world chasing and spinning.

Not only are these six spiritual practices beneficial for restoring order, health, mental clarity, and harmony to your life, but they will also awaken your soul. Don't worry so much about doing everything perfectly or stressing about the time. These exercises are the actual practices that will help you warp time, manifest magic, and experience healing and happiness *continuously*. Implementing these spiritual practices daily will support the transformational experience from human body to Light Body and eventually to Superlight body. With every day, the individual human aura will become more and more expansive until one becomes an absolute being of light on earth. These activities are simple and don't require much time. I suggest that you start with the first activity and create consistency with it before introducing the second. Should that take a week or a month, there is no rush. The goal then is to build upon Practice 1 by adding Practices 2-6 once Practice 1 is consistent. The order of these practices is important, and I suggest that you follow them sequentially until they all become consistent and natural; then it will be possible to do them out in the world as needed in the midst of the chaos that is daily life. These practices will support the most miraculous glow to your aura and transform your being into a manifesting magnet for all the beauty your desire in your life. They are indeed aura shiners.

1. *Auric Meditation and Prayer*
   It is often said that prayer is you speaking to God and that meditation is God speaking to you. Both meditation and prayer are essential activities for Auric Living. Prayer is a practice wherein you communicate with God, a loved one, your guardian angel, a saint, or an ascended master, depending on what feels true to you. Both meditation and prayer are powerful spiritual practices, but I do believe that prayer will take on an even more significant role in the years ahead. Spending at least five minutes every day in stillness and silence will revolutionize your life. There

are many forms of meditation and of prayer and you may already have a favorite practice. You may choose to practice both meditation and prayer each day or to start off by alternating between them. You might also consider starting your day with meditation and ending your day with prayer. This practice is deeply personal and should feel intuitive and right.

As we will discuss shortly, your meditation practice is your own and may take on many forms, including; walking meditation, passive meditation, guided meditation or active meditation. Visualization exercises are forms of active meditation. Learning to intuitively meditate means that your meditation practice will best suit the moment and the mood. In an active meditation practice, instead of directing your energy out of the body, practice holding your life force and your light within the body (it can be helpful to visualize a bubble or shield around you). What is most important is that you find a rhythm that works right and feels right for you. As you work through this book, you may wish to select a mantra to support this meditation practice in which the space between the thoughts is the stillness to seek. In the beginning, it may be difficult to keep the monkey mind still. "Monkey mind" is the term I like to use for the part of your brain that is untrained, easily distracted and always busy. It loves to wander and think and deeply craves distraction. It is, of course, helpful to deepen and develop both a meditation and prayer practice over time, which will result in a longer practice. But in the beginning, focus less on the time and more on the moment.

2. *Auric Visualization*

    Consider Auric Visualization to be a more active form of meditation. It is still meditation, per se, but the goal is to create imagery with your miraculous mind. Music (or even a guide) is absolutely okay. The beautiful thing about Auric

Visualization is that it also develops motivation, will, and clarity in one's life. Without a regular visualization practice, life can feel colorless, lifeless, and dull. Make the movie in your mind first (energy first) and watch it unfold in your physical world with purpose, clarity, and power (matter second). Even a few minutes of intentional visualization daily will revolutionize your reality. Visualization opens you up to highest vibrational possibilities for yourself and shows you your true power as a creator. It is an essential daily practice for Auric Living.

3. *Auric Breathwork*

    A daily breathwork practice will transform every aspect of life. Although there are many different breathwork practices to choose from, a basic diaphragmatic breathing exercise done daily will open channels and portals throughout the body. A daily breathwork practice will enhance conscious awareness, mindfulness, healing, and vital lifeforce. A five-minute practice each day is encouraged as consistency is key. We will discuss several breathing practices shortly. I invite you to also visit AuricLiving.com for some guided breathwork practices.

4. *Auric Action*

    Spiritual activation and initiation require not only spiritual awareness but a strong spiritual will. There is a time for rest but also a time for action. In many cases, when we swing too far toward spiritual practices such as meditation and prayer, we can neglect the importance of developing and strengthening will with aligned action. To keep things simple, when you wake up every morning, pick one simple action that you commit to for the day. Practice acting on intuition more often than not. As you commit to living more intuitively, you will be guided when an auric action is ideal as well as instructions on what to do. What becomes important is to take notice of when your intuition tells you to act but your mind talks you out of it. When we pause or wait too long to act, the mind often talks us out of taking any auric action in life.

5. *Auric Movement*

    Having a mindful movement practice is sacred for Auric Living. Not only is it important for lymphatic movement but for spiritual movement, as well. Auric Movement is spiritual movement, which means that it must bring you to present moment awareness, awaken your soul, and invigorate your spirit. This may include a labyrinth walk, a nature walk, a surf, a yoga class, a dance class, mindful stretching, etc. The added benefit to Auric Movement is that it detoxifies the body by invigorating the lymphatic system and strengthening the cardiovascular system. Auric Movement weaves together strength, balance, and flexibility in the body and in the mind.

6. *Auric Love*

    This practice is simple but not always easy. The intention with this practice is to center in on and open the heart chakra a little more every day- and directing this love towards yourself. You cannot be an expression of love in the world unless you love and care for yourself first. Fundamentally, auric love is the practice of showering yourself with love, grace, compassion, and kindness throughout the day. Think of your heart as a flower; throughout the day, feel the petals of your heart either opening or closing. You will begin to be highly attuned when the petals begin to close throughout the day. With patience, time, and practice, you will begin to be able to consciously open the heart petals when you feel them closing. You will become particularly aware of how the heart petals close when you are hard on yourself, unkind with yourself or when you neglect to self-nurture yourself. You will also feel the heart petals close when your actions or words are unkind, or when you project your fears onto others. As I often tell my children, when you are mad, your heart is really just feeling sad. It can sometimes be healing to feel the mad, but it is also important to feel the sad. Your soul is calling you to deeply nurture yourself right now. This is when miracles begin to occur. This is a practice to bring you back to your heart space. When done daily, this practice builds the love muscle of your being so strongly that you are able to gracefully forgive, let go, surrender, love, and serve. Holding on to grudges will be a thing of the past and trying to control others to make yourself feel better will feel less than worthy of your greatness. You will find that judging and gossiping about others simply falls out of your reality and although it may creep in from time to time, it will bring a tear to your eye. My favorite Auric Love practice is to sit quietly with my hand on my heart as I slow down and deepen my breath. As my body calms and my breath gains rhythm, I visualize a beautiful pink aura surrounding my heart. With every deep breath, this pink light becomes larger and brighter until it is surrounding my entire body. As an alternative, I have also created a Heart Harmonics Breathing Practice available at AuricLiving.com as well as on Insight Timer (insightTimer.com).

This book will provide further insight and exploration into the dynamics of each practice as we move along, but I believe it is important to offer these six practices right from the start so that you can begin to think about them and how they might be integrated as divine daily rituals.

As a final offering, this book will support the most integrous work for spiritual initiation. Even the act of working through these pages with intentionality is a spiritual practice that supports pure alignment of thoughts, words, action, habits, and character.

> ## *AURIC ACTION*
>
> Take notice without judgement today on moments when there is disharmony in your thoughts, actions, words, habits, and character. These moments represent powerful opportunities to become more self-aware as they light up a gateway to pursue a more integrous and authentic path with your soul. When all of these elements move in a spiritually ascending direction together, you experience Auric Living—a life guided by the soul. When these elements are not all moving in a spiritually-ascended direction, addiction of any kind (work, food, substance, sex, people-pleasing, gossip, busyness, fitness, etc.) is just one signal that spiritual shifting is needed. The soul may be suffocating.

Having a spiritual practice each and every day must now be a priority. Humanity is experiencing, at quantum speeds, the chaos that sets in without one. May this book be a guide and a deeply loving resource for you as find your way back soul-home.

Welcome to Auric Living!

Chapter 2: Auric Breath

"There is one way of breathing that is shameful and constricted. Then, there's another way: a breath of love that takes you all the way to infinity."

-Rumi

Auric Breath is conscious, circulating, cosmic essence. All healing forces are housed in the human breathing system. What is the very first thing we should do as we rebirth during this new cosmic time? We must rebuild a spiritual relationship with our breath, rewiring our bodies and our minds via the way we breathe. Not only do we charge our body through breath, but we can physically rewire our body that way as well. Breathing efficiently and deeply creates a harmonious tonal pattern throughout the body. These healing tones created by deep breath resonate throughout the body in ways that are nothing less than symphonic. The physical carbon structures throughout our bodies can literally be morphed through the air we breathe. This is why many people who practice daily breathwork begin to physically look younger and brighter. Many of us have never had a sacred relationship with our breath. We must all now accept that order and harmony cannot be restored in the world unless we reunite with conscious breath, both individually and as a collective. We must teach our children how to effectively breath not only for body health but in order to spiritually thrive. Conscious breathing as a sacred ritual on a daily basis for children and adults must become as common as eating. Asking our children how their breathing went today needs to be a normal thing! Before anything else, breathing must be restored to the purity and perfection we had as infants. Think about it—birth and breathing are inextricably linked. In the same way, breathwork is the path to restoring cosmic essence to the energy body which then rejuvenates, revitalizes, and rebirths the physical body. If the circumstances of your life have left you feeling fatigued, exhausted and aged, breathwork is the most powerful restorative practice.

As we develop a rhythmic relationship with our breath, we awaken the soul and revolutionize the body. When we practice auric breathing, we activate the continuous and conscious circulation of vital lifeforce throughout the body. Auric breath, therefore, is every breath you take that is conscious, creative, and cosmic. Unlike unconscious, every day breathing that tends to be shallow, quick, and filled with stress, an auric breath is one that is slow, deep, diaphragmatic, and fully conscious. The goal is to have more and more auric breaths every day, which means that more of the breaths that you take throughout the day are conscious, creative, and cosmic. As you increase the number of auric breaths in your day, not only will your body transform into a temple, your entire being will develop a consciousness that was previously just a dream. You will radically transform yourself into a being of peace, joy, and mindfulness— all by way of breath.

One of my favorite spiritual teachers once told me that all dysfunction in life begins with dysfunction in breath. Our breath is the basis for the quality of our life. Breathing should be a dimension of life that we are directed to come back to every single day. As we breath deeper, we are more effectively able to connect to Source (to God), plug into lifeforce and activate the heart portal. As we begin to fully embrace the cosmic power of breath, we gain a better understanding of how deep and direct the relationship is between breath and love. Obsessions with time, control, and perfection are typical indications of dysfunctional breath. When shallow breathing and holding breath become chronic, stress and anxiety becomes a "norm storm." This leads to higher acidity within the body. We often overly focus on acidic foods being the cause of our body disfunction, but an even greater cause of this is a dysfunctional breath. Max Strom, author of *A Life Worth Breathing*, shares that when breathing is highly functional, our body's "rest and digest" mode switches on while "fight or flight" switches off. Dan Brulé, author of *Just Breathe*, shares that when it comes to breath, control is about power, while surrender is about peace. As we let go with every exhale, we are breathed by the breath. It's as if source energy takes care of us and simply does its thing. This is a deeply nurturing experience both physically and spiritually. This can be deeply uncomfortable at first but as we learn to let go and surrender, we are given what we asked for in the first place: peace.

Aside from how incredible my body feels after my yoga practice, I also use daily yoga to retrain my breathing and remind myself of how unstuck and light I feel after 75-90 minutes of functional and optimal breathing. When my breathing is shallow or held, I tackle my day with more force, frustration, fear, and freak-outs. When my breathing is beneath my potential, I pick up stray energies, almost like psychic hitchhikers, and revert back to fight or flight behaviors. For many, depression can be exacerbated by dysfunctional breathing, while others experience chronic anxiety. When it comes to breathing, the intention is to pick up on what happens in your own reality when you don't breathe deeply and purposefully. All kinds of lower vibrational frequencies are welcomed into your field unless breathing is beautiful.

The very meaning of respiration is "reconnection to spirit." As we discussed in Chapter 1, this book is an invitation to have a heart-to-heart talk with your soul. You are likely waking up to the more meaningful layers of your existence and your reality. You may even be feeling emotional on a more regular basis right now as grieving becomes a regular practice. It's time to more intimately meet your soul—perhaps for the very first time. The first and most effective way to begin to a spiritual romance with your soul is through your breath.

> ### *AURIC ACTION*
>
> Take a few minutes today to sit in silence and observe your breath. How does it feel? How deep is your breath? How alive do you feel when you breathe deeply? How long or short is your inhale? How powerful or soft is your exhale? Feel your breath and its impact on your body as you take air in and release air out. Experiment with how different your body feels when you hold your breath, take a few shallow breaths, and then take deep breaths. How activated does your belly feel with a shallow breath vs a deep breath?

When I look back on the busiest years of my life, I can say with confidence that not only were they the most chaotic, but they were also the most dysfunctional in terms of how I breathed. There are entire books, even mystical volumes, written about breath and breathwork that you may now be inspired to read. The stories within the Upanishads (a body of Vedic Sanskrit texts) often explore the mystical beauty of breath. Sacred texts have always drawn me in but the stories and myths in Vedic traditions simply speak to my soul. I was also introduced The Transformational Breath Foundation and the work of Dr. Judith Kravitz decades ago. This began my fascination with the breathing as both a healing and a spiritual practice.

The challenge I faced throughout my personal breathwork journey was that the more techniques I added to my spiritual toolbelt, the more confused I got. Even transitioning from teaching Pilates to teaching yoga threw me for a loop, as the breathing techniques are different. How do you know what breathing technique is best? Should you breathe out through the nose or out through the mouth? Why do some prefer breathing out through the mouth over breathing out through the nose? How long should you hold the inhalation?

The purpose of this chapter is not to go through all of the methodologies behind breathwork or introduce you to every technique, but to remind you that the more attention you give to your breath, the more beautifully your life will unfold. This doesn't mean that you won't have challenges and turbulent times, but it does mean that the layers of your being will work in such harmony together that your aura will expand beyond your wildest dreams.

Let's take a closer look at our breath. When we breath in, we draw pure lifeforce energy into our bodies. We are inhaling spiritual power. As we take in this lifeforce, the motion towards us comes in a clockwise spiraling motion. When this force comes into our lungs, we put order into it through the shape of the lungs. Our lungs give shape to lifeforce energy. Shaping the lifeforce on the inhale gives it a certain pattern and function. This is a brilliant example of divine order and sacred forming. When you shape energy, you get function. As the oxygen is inhaled and given function by the lungs, it can then make all sorts of miracles happen within the body. When you breath out, you lose the shape and the order that is now being released. The incoming and exiting spirals of energy are in perfect balance and span multiple dimensions. Just one breath impacts everything in the cosmos. The balance of lifeforce energy through breath is the key to physical life. If reality is offering less-than-ideal emotional conditions, the answer is to reconnect with breath.

We have forgotten to give ourselves permission to intuitively and consciously breathe, but we don't need a great master to show us how. While I do believe that many gifted individuals are destined to support humanity through teaching breathwork, I also believe that simply starting a daily breathwork practice is all you need. A daily practice will absolutely transform your reality. As you get regular with your practice, you can explore different techniques available and powerfully enhance your practice.

Just remember that your master healer within already knows how to breath perfectly for you. You've got this! My advice is to keep it simple, stay safe, and trust your inner guide. I prefer to do my breathwork in a seated position, but an advanced or therapeutic session may be done lying down. I prefer to breathe in through the nose, while others prefer to breathe in through the mouth. (You may come across several breathwork facilitators that require a specific technique.) My usual Pranayama breathing practice simply feels right to me, which keeps me breathing in through the nose and out through the nose for the most part. When I feel there is emotional energy that wants to be released, I will then switch to exhaling through the mouth. This is where Lion Breath comes in handy! (I'll cover both of these techniques in detail below.) In summary, much of my breathwork is in through the nose and out through the nose, but I include exhales through the mouth when I feel there is stale and stuck energy that needs to leave my body. It is an intuitive thing, and as you practice more, you will know when a good exhale through the mouth will serve you well. This may not be the way for all breathwork practitioners, but it works perfectly for me for right now. I have several friends who make Tummo Breathing (another technique we will explore shortly) a daily practice to really get things moving. The most important thing is to just get started. Take a few minutes every day to focus on your breath and consciously deepen and slow down your breath. Feel your entire body get showered with life force as your core gets expansive and strong. Feel vibrant lifeforce energy expand and brighten your aura in 360 degrees with every inhale. Feel your entire body soften and release with every exhale. Should you be interested in joining me in my own *Heart Harmonics Breathing Technique*, it is up on both our website and through Insight Timer (insighttimer.com).

    Getting fancy with breathwork can become deeply transformative, but simply returning to breath is the greatest gift. My yoga practice is a breathing practice first. I am reminded daily that the breathing is the leader of the movement. I use my breath first and then my movement to release resistance from my body. If you are considering committing to a regular meditation practice, it can be helpful to get a conscious breathing practice going first.

    A regular practice I do with myself and my children is a simple Lion's Breath. We all inhale deeply through our nose and powerfully exhale with our tongues sticking out through our mouth. Lion Breath is one of my favorite practices to release stored tension and any built up stress. Dr. Belisa Vranich, author of *Breathe*, shares that young children five and under tend to breathe perfectly already but tend to develop less optimal breathing habits after the age of five. To functionally breath again, she explains, we should expand our body in a 360° fashion as we inhale, just like animals do.

The challenge with shallow and quick breaths is oxygen transport. It's all about balance! Along with getting enough oxygen, we want that oxygen to efficiently travel to tissues and organs for lifeforce oxygenation, for which we need carbon dioxide. When we perform shallow quick breaths, we end up with too much oxygen and not enough carbon dioxide. This causes imbalance and disharmony.

Dysfunctional breathing impacts virtually every part of our physical reality, including:

* Blood chemistry
* Body acidity
* Adrenals
* Immune system
* Bowel function
* Kidney function
* Sleep
* Weight
* Flexibility
* Spine mobility and posture
* Pelvic floor
* Esophagus
* Digestion
* Gut health
* Nervous system response
* Anxiety and depression
* Self-regulation
* Mental health

* Eating habits
* Memory
* Connection to our higher self/soul
* Heart and lung function
* Circulation
* Lymphatic system

Keeping your aura glowing with grace requires beautiful breathing. When you meet someone who has a special lifeforce glow about them, you can be sure their breathing is impeccable. There is no aura-dulling where these angelic beings are concerned. Aura-dulling happens when mouth breathing is dominant, which results in a person taking in cold, dry, and high-particulate air into their body. This narrows the airways and puts chronic stress on the body and the mind. Over the years, these constricted airways end up significantly impacting our lifeforce energy and dulling our aura. When mouth breathing is dominant, an individual tends to be held in a pattern of fight or flight on a continuous bases, as if on autopilot. Mouth breathing leads to shallow chest breathing while nose breathing results in deeper more powerful breathing supporting the entire body.

If you are a parent, it would be lifelong gift to your child to teach them how to breathe properly. I was a mouth breather as a child, and this habit has stuck with me. If I am not consciously coming back to my breath, I default to mouth breathing. My oldest son has inherited many of my personality traits, including mouth breathing. Over the years, I contemplated that his higher aptitude for worry may stem from his mouth breathing. Imagine with just a simple lesson on proper breathing, worry can become a thing of the past. I believe that with proper breathing, lower vibrational frequencies are well and divinely shielded from entering the aura. When breathing is highly functional, communication with the divine is also highly functional.

Breath is the most important tool we have on the planet. You can change your entire body chemistry through your breath. We usually speak about increasing alkalinity in your body through food, but one of the most effective ways to increase alkalinity is through breath. The spine is the cosmic axis of the body. As cosmic energy freely moves up and down this cosmic axis, it can then radiate out to all components of the body, much like sun rays of cosmic light. When movement up and down the cosmic axis is hindered or stagnant, the body begins to lose its light. This is why so many traditions discuss the importance of the movement of vital lifeforce up and down the main axis of the body. Breathwork is one of the most important practices for working with this energy of light and distributing it throughout the entire body by way of this cosmic axis.

> ### *AURIC ACTION FOR PARENTS*
>
> Take 15 minutes today to provide a simple overview on how proper breathing impacts health, mood, and behavior. Teach your child the benefits of deeply breathing in, slowing down the breath, and consciously breathing out. Teach them the benefits of deep belly breathing and how proper breathing increases strength, resilience, and happiness.

Kriya yoga is also a beautiful practice for experiencing internal alchemy, which includes kriya pranayama breathing. It is an ancient method of enhancing human spiritual evolution but requires deep commitment and readiness. Kriya yoga typically enters your consciousness at just the right time on your own spiritual path.

Your breathwork practice should be sacred and intuitive to you. As you learn and layer on more and more breathing techniques, the key objective is to experience full, expansive, and diaphragmatic breathing. Filling the belly with the inhale as well as learning how to fully expand through the entire solar plexus is key but takes practice. As you find your own rhythm, you will likely alternate between different breathing exercises depending on your desired goal and emotional state. It is important to note that some breathing techniques (such as Kumbhaka) should not be done during heightened states of anxiety, stress, or physical distress. In the beginning stages of any breathwork practice, taking it slow and at your own pace is very important. I recommend that you do breathwork exercises in a seated position, but if relaxing is a struggle, doing the practice lying down is fine.

As you begin your breathwork exercise, take a comfortable seated position as you reconnect with your breath. You can start with your hands laying on the top of your knees or place one hand on your belly and the other hand on your heart. Always take a few moments to connect with breath. Slow and deepen your breathing until you feel calm and centered.

Here are just a few breathwork techniques that are among my favorites:

Belly Breathing (Diaphragmatic): **In this simple exercise, the goal is to breathe deeply into the belly through the nose and out through the mouth or nose. As you breathe in, observe the belly expanding as the diaphragm moves down. The downward pressure of the diaphragm causes the belly to move outward. As you breath out, the diaphragm moves up to its original dome position, and the belly moves back inward. In this exercise, breathing should be deep, smooth, even, continuous, and flowing. As you practice 10-20 rounds of belly breathing, notice that the body becomes the breather, and you have a greater sense of what it means to be the observer of the breathing. This is a perfect breathing exercise as a starting point.**

Bee Breath (Bhramari) **: This is a beautiful technique for calming the nervous system and grounding yourself in times of anxiousness or stress. In your seated position, take a moment to inhale deeply through the nose and exhale through the nose as well. On** the next round, inhale deeply through the nose but on the exhale, make a humming bee sound as you exhale through the nose. Once you have a rhythm going with the deep inhale and humming bee exhale, place the palms of your hands on your ears to silence out the external world. Continue the slow inhale and humming exhale with your palms placed on your ears. Repeat this exercise for 5-9 cycles.

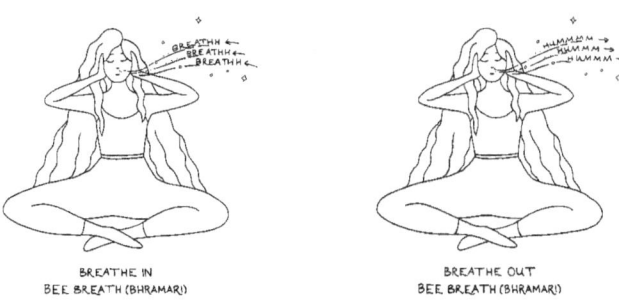

BREATHE IN
BEE BREATH (BHRAMARI)

BREATHE OUT
BEE BREATH (BHRAMARI)

Auric Breathing: This very simple breathing technique is a perfect way to get started with a regular breathing practice. In a comfortable seated position, take a few moments to get grounded and centered. Place your hands on your knees or, as an alternative, place one hand on your belly and one hand on your heart. Slow down and deepen your breath. As you inhale through the nose, visualize your rib cage and belly expanding to their fullest potential. At the top of the inhale, hold your breath for a few seconds (as long as feels comfortable). As you exhale through the mouth, soften your shoulders, jaw, and chest. Release and surrender all of the air out of your body until you reach stillness and void. Tune into the feeling of this emptiness and surrender. Repeat the cycle 5-7 times.

Skull Shining Breath (Kapalabhati): This breathing exercise is a fabulous detoxifier as it enhances the mind, improves circulation, and gets the lymphatic system moving throughout the body. This is a cleansing practice that leaves you with a gorgeous glow when done regularly. Kapalabhati breathing incorporates more passive inhalation and forceful exhalations. Seated in a comfortable position, place your hands on your knees or alternatively place one hand on your belly. Take a few slow, deep breaths in through the nose and out through the nose or mouth. Then take a gentle inhale through the mouth as you fill the lungs and belly with breath. Once the belly is expanded and filled with breath, forcefully push air out of the body through the nose in short bursts using the belly. For every inhale, you can work up to a count of 50-100 exhales as your practice advances. In the beginning, a count of 10-20 exhales for every inhale is a good place to start.

Alternate Nostril Breathing (Nadhi Shodhana): This breathing exercise is an energy body cleansing practice with the goal of cleansing all of the energy channels throughout the body. This practice balances the physical and mental body as well as supports the release of emotional blockages. In a comfortable seated position, place both hands on your knees. Prior to starting, fully empty the lungs by taking a deep inhale into the belly through the nose, and a fully exhale through the nose or mouth. Now take your right hand and position your fingers so you thumb, ring and pinky finger are extended while your index and middle finger are bent. Starting with this breathwork through your left nostril, you will first use your right thumb to close the right nostril. Inhale into the chest and belly through your left nostril. At the top of the inhale, use the ring finger to close the left nostril as the thumb continues to close the right nostril. Hold the breath here for as long as you are able. Once you cannot hold the breath any longer, release the thumb from the right nostril and exhale fully through the right nostril. When your exhale is complete, inhale fully through the right nostril. At the top of the inhale, close the right nostril with the thumb and hold the breath for as long as you can. Once you cannot hold the breath any longer, release the ring finger from the left nostril and fully exhale through the left nostril. This cycle can be repeated 10-20 times. Traditionally, the ratio for the inhale, hold and exhale was said to be 1-4-2. In counts, an advanced practitioner would inhale for 12, hold for 48 and exhale for 24. This is of course an advanced practice. When beginning, always trust your body and perform counts that are comfortable and non-strenuous.

Joy Breathing (Chedvah): The first time I experienced Chedvah, I cried. The grace and beauty in this breathing practice is a mystical experience. Rabbi Ginsburg first introduced me to this technique, and I have been hooked ever since. The technique is based on a 4-step process consisting of *inhale, hold, exhale, release.* The counts for these steps are 8, 4, 6, and 5. The sacred coding behind these chosen numbers are part of the mystical experience. The full inhalation to the count of 8 was something I had to work up to, but with practice, lung capacity improves. The premise of the practice is "To breath joy is to experience joy." You cannot experience this breathing practice without getting goosebumps and a thirst to learn more about Kabbalah.

Lion's Breath: This practice is one I do often during my daily life while driving or when I need a moment to release tension or density from the body. Although breathwork is usually best done while seated, Lion's breath is the one technique I tend to incorporate into any regular activity I am doing. This is a beautiful breathing practice for relieving anxiety and stress. I also do this practice often with my kids. To begin this practice, inhale fully and deeply through the nose. As you exhale, open your mouth, stick out your tongue, and make a strong "ha" sound. This is the stress-buster breath! Repeat for 5-7 cycles.

Breath Retention (Kumbhaka): Kumbhaka is the holding of breath. There are many variations of Kumbhaka breathing, but I found I prefer to do it with a ratio of 1-2-1-1/2. For example, if you inhale through the nose for a count of 6, you would then hold your breath at the top of the inhale for a count of 12, exhale through the nose for a count of 6, and hold the breath at the bottom of the exhale for a count of 3. This is a powerful exercise and should not be done while pregnant, during times of high stress or anxiety, or if you have a heart condition. This is a more advanced practice that also requires an intuitive understanding of how the holds feel within the body. Often there is a fear of the void of emptiness at the bottom of the exhale, which is why it is only held for a half count. An experienced yoga or pranayama teacher is always beneficial to guide you through this practice in the beginner stages.

Bellows Breath (Bhastrika): There is nothing that invigorates and energizes the body like bellows breath. In a seated position, with a straight spine, raise the arms above the head on the inhale, with hands open wide (palms facing front). As you exhale, bring the elbows down to touch the sides of the rib cage as the hands make a fist. This breathing exercise is typically done with charge and energy. This means that as your elbows come down to touch the sides of your rib cage on the exhale, you are using force to drive the exhale out of the body as you touch the sides of your ribs. Both the inhale and exhale are powerful and charged. Advanced Bhastrika partitioners will often do up to 50 rounds of bellows breath, which I found to be very challenging in the beginning. This practice can leave you feeling dizzy, so practice caution and mindfulness as you do this exercise. It is best to start small and work up to a number of rounds that feels effective yet comfortable. If five rounds are where you start, that is a beautiful practice.

BREATHE IN
BELLOWS BREATH (BASTRIKA)

BREATHE OUT
BELLOWS BREATH (BASTRIKA)

Inner Fire Breathing (Tummo): In Tibetan Buddhism, Tummo is the goddess of heat and passion. Tummo is primordial, rising energy often associated with fire and purification. This ancient practice was used by Tibetan Monks to develop heat in icy caves and was shown to produce visible steam off of their robes. This ancient practice brings about bliss and happiness and when performed regularly, fills the body with vital lifeforce. The practice includes three steps. The first step is visualizing yourself as a large, hollow balloon containing a burning flame lying just below the navel. The balloon is an illustration of the sphere being the primal container for the energy in consciousness. The second step is the breathing practice, where you place your right hand on the belly and your left hand on top of the right. This enables you to feel the fire being generated by this energy anchor point (the *tan tien* or *hara*) located about 2-3 inches below the navel. With your hands resting on the *tan tien*, take a deep inhale through the nose as you slightly arch your body back, enabling a full invigoration of oxygen into the chest and belly. In this step you really want to feel the expansion of the rib cage, which is facilitated by a slight arch back to allow the breath to fully enter the chest. As you exhale fully through the mouth, slightly round your body forward in order to release all of the air out of the chest and belly through the mouth. This can be repeated for 5 cycles as you begin. The last step occurs on the fifth and final breath of the cycle. As you inhale on the fifth breath, hold the breath at the top of the inhalation. As you hold this breath, swallow while at the same time contracting your Kegel muscles (lifting your pelvic floor). Hold your breath at the top of the inhale for as long as you are able. When you are ready, perform a slow exhale as if you are breathing out into a straw.

    The most important thing to remember where breathwork is concerned is to not take on too much, too aggressively in the beginning. Your breath is sacred, and your breathing practice must also be sacred. The most important principle is that your breath work practice leaves you feeling full of life and resilience. In the beginning, some of the practices may leave you feeling light-headed or dizzy, which is why listening to your intuitive body is so important. Remember that a regular breathwork practice can radically transform the physical makeup of the body. It not only acts to alkalize the body, but through its ability to rebuild and revitalize the vital body, your physical body is completely rebuilt. Many of the ancient mystery schools discuss how breathwork restructures the carbon blueprint of the body, and because carbon is the primary element found in the human body, it holds the power to grow a new physical body. Breathwork has both a mystical and magical ability to transform the carbon in your body. Physical reordering and restructuring are therefore highly possible and even likely through regular practice. You can and will reshape your body through breathwork. The more breath you take in, the more light you carry. As you carry more light, it will take form within you.

Chapter 3: Auric Mind

"Mind extends everywhere throughout infinite. Mind is the ocean in which everything is formed."

-Daskalos

The Auric Mind is the ordered and individualized manifestation of the ever-eternal cosmic mind. Your mind is a divine carving of universal mind. For Auric Living, you can lovingly makeover your mind through inspirational thought.

As children, teens, or even adults, we are simply not trained how to think. We are not trained to wake up in the morning and align our thinking with highest vibrational living. We are not trained to direct thought, redirect thought, or stop thought. We are simply guided to obey and repeat. We are given zero instruction on how to handle or train the very monkey mind that keeps us coiled up like a slinky for most of our lives. Chaos, conflict, drama, and trauma seem to be normalized and even encouraged in our society. We think we're fully living when we are actually just trying to keep our head above water. This chapter is a guide to reordering the mind and understanding how to teleport ourselves from surviving to thriving.

This is a sacred time in human history where we are being guided and given permission to leverage the power of the heart to completely makeover the mind. The way we thought, analyzed, and behaved yesterday will no longer be the way of the future. Through the heart, we are being guided to commit to a mind makeover that will bring us in closer resonance with the soul. The key for unlocking this new higher mind is the heart. Without the power of the heart, the mind remains imprisoned by patterning, subconscious programming, and soul dis-resonance. The way we were trained to think is more closely associated with *not* thinking. We were taught to memorize, cram, and follow along, but not to truly and divinely think for ourselves. This is why society has a tendency to favor academic success and fancy appearances over integrous and whole living. It is as if the further away from your true divine soul you stray, the more success in society you achieve. Consider this for a moment as you scan the energy of the planet today.

In the physical realm, everything is constructed from the mind at varying frequencies of vibration. Because we have never really been taught how to truly think, nor have we been taught how to order the mind, we live in a constant and chaotic state of monkey mind for the majority of our life. This results in a life that is constantly filled with upswings and downswings, distractions, constant thinking, chaos, conflict, and confusion. For today, consider how different life would be if the mind was optimally fit, positive, resilient, and well ordered. When the mind is well, the body is well, the emotional body is well, and the mental body is (of course) well. As we learn to fully understand and appreciate the interconnectedness between our individual mind and the God mind, we are then able to shape and order our individual minds into cosmic consciousness carpenters—workshops of creation and innovation.

I want you to become a master of thought who honors and cares for your mind with great care and mindfulness. Visualization, creativity, intuition, insight, positivity, and stillness are all sacred skills that soar when the mind is ordered and trained. This is the most cosmic time for you to become the master of your mind. Without an aware master, the untrained mind gladly wanders throughout life, distracted by anything and everything that activates and stimulates. We eat this and that, speak anything and everything, chase material fancy, and do all we can to avoid being still. We are seduced by the senses for our entire lives until we cave from exhaustion. Even with many cues and hints, we neglect to enter and explore the very inner sanctuary of mind and soul. This is the truest and most worthy work in our lives, yet most of us avoid it until just before death.

"The human mind is a mirror of the entire universe that mirrors the human mind. There are no one way streets in creation," explains Douglas Hofstadter in his book *Gödel, Escher, Bach: an Eternal Golden Braid*.

At this very moment, you are existing in many different dimensions in a unified quantum field, in an ever-expanding universe. If this isn't perplexing enough, many researchers believe that time might actually be speeding up alongside this expansion. If everything is quantumly connected, when you have a thought, you are influencing reality and influencing everything in the cosmos. In his book *Science and the Akashic Field*, Ervin Laszlo explains that all things in the world have materiality and interiority. Matter and mind are not separate, distinct realities; they are complimentary aspects of a much more expansive cosmic reality.

The new frontiers are mind and heart. How to unify them with great synergy and cohesion becomes the cosmic question as this is where peak human performance takes place. We have arrived at our time in history to more deeply understand the mind in both its waking and sleep states. Everything begins in the mind. As quantum physics progresses and measures its progress, we are becoming keenly aware that what we held so strongly as truth is curiously false. We have been trained that we are matter first and foremost. For most of our educational lives, we have studied matter, periodic tables, material, and all that can be seen. We build our lives around matter and even hold on to jobs we dislike in order to pay for that matter. But our entire world has been built around false or incomplete knowledge. As an example, throughout my entire educational career, I was never taught that there were actually four states of matter: solid, liquids, gas, and plasma. When you heat gases high enough, they transform into plasma. Why was plasma always left out? The mystery and intrigue surrounding plasma is just beginning to reach mainstream, but it has already revolutionized the scientific world, and it just starting to be granted center stage. Watch what unfolds in the world over the next decade when it comes to plasma research and technology.

We should be building our lives around energy first, matter second. As children, this information should be fundamental knowledge taught in schools. In this chapter, you will get a simple and clear understanding of how the mind works and how you can use your days and your nights to maximize greatest possibilities for yourself. Today is the most perfect time to create your next level reality, flooding with joy, creativity, inspiration, and vibrance. This is Auric Living at its finest! Your most important work is taming that monkey mind and consciously training your new Auric Mind.

> ## *AURIC ACTION*
>
> Take time today to surrender to all judgement as you observe your thought patterns and the monkey mind. We all have one! With a light heart and a smile, observe the fluctuations in your thinking throughout the day and how difficult it can be to silence the mind. Take notice of the more drastic swings in positive and negative thoughts. Gain clarity in just how successful powerful thoughts can be in talking us out of intuitive wisdom. Observe the patterns and thoughts that go in the opposite direction of your dreams and desires. Getting to know your monkey mind is essential before mind mastery can take place.

So much of our daily vital energy is exhausted and hemorrhaged by the swinging pendulum of our thoughts. The ups and downs of thinking is exhausting when one isn't properly trained on *how* to think. Image how many times our mind swings up and down in one day, and how much energy it takes to fuel this roller coaster. Imagine if all of this wasted energy could be consciously used for deeply meaningful work such as unfolding your dreams and healing your body. Instead, most people surrender in quiet desperation to the untrained monkey mind and accept the chaos and disorder that comes from chasing their own tail. When we leave the five senses in charge of our life without training them, the monkey mind has an endless heyday. Although lifeforce energy is exerted by the physical body every day, much more is exerted by the mind—especially the monkey mind. The untrained mind is every bit as exhausting, if not more so, than any physical exertion. Freedom in our outer world results from first finding freedom in our inner world. The more stillness we can find in the mental realm, the more peace, joy, and security we can experience in the physical realm. (And let's always remember that for this to happen, breath must be deeply functional. This is why breathwork and meditation are both essential.)

What the Upanishads taught me was not only to rein in the five senses but to train them. We must learn to direct our attention to our interior castle and make our choices from within. Of course we must use our five senses in our daily life, but they should not be in full control of our choices. Inner truth and inner wisdom should lead the way.

We have radically underestimated how important training the mind is. It is far more significant than training the body, because as you enhance that mind into tip-top shape, the body will effortlessly follow. We are moving away from hustle and into heightened flow. It has been proven that you actually can think your way to better health. If fitness is your passion, keep the good vibes going, but remember your mind is just as powerful at getting your body into optimal shape as your physical activity and dietary choices. I tested this out when I had an injury that lingered for a few years. Finally, I decided to test this theory on myself. All day long I would think: "I am in the best shape of my life." I was in my forties, had given birth three times, and hadn't worked out in years. I complimented my thinking with a cleansing lifestyle including juicing, colon hydrotherapy, supplements, herbs, and gentle yoga that was limited to supported postures and gentle poses that helped me enhance flow. At the same time I was limited in the physical realm,

I was expansive and free in the mental one. It took time to break down my old belief systems but eventually, a new truth took shape: We are what we think about, and anything really is possible. I have met countless yoga masters who have rebounded from life threatening injuries and into their most physically fit and flexible selves. One of my teachers shattered both knees but trained his body and mind (through yoga and meditation) to surpass any level of health he had experienced prior. Anything is possible with clarity and commitment.

And while it is true that we create our own reality, it is more like we co-create (or co-co-create) our reality. There are actually three forces at play here: us (and our state of consciousness), the divine (highest order), and the free will of others. It therefore makes sense that we do tend to repeat patterns and manifest based on our own field of consciousness, but we don't always have control over what choices and possibilities others may choose. It is also important to remember the divine order of all things and the role it plays in our physical reality.

Consciousness

There is one original formless substance from which all things are made, and this substance is consciousness. It was Wallace Wattles, author of *The Science of Getting Rich,* who wrote that this original substance moves according to its thoughts. This is why thoughts are things. As lifeforce flows into our field and fills our body, our mind gives form to this energy, called "thought form." Our mind gives order to Source energy. Similar to the lungs giving form to the air we breathe, our minds give form to the thoughts we think. Our reality then, is a visible expression of a thought made from this original substance. It moves according to the thought. This very moment, you are projecting your very consciousness across the entire universe. Every thought links up with collective thought, which links up with the earth, which links up with the cosmos, which links up with the entire universe. This is why even a basic understanding of quantum physics is powerful. We do influence the entire universe with just one thought. We must become mindful about every thought we have because every thought has an effect. Exploring the work of quantum physicist and author of *The Quantum Doctor,* Amit Goswami, PhD, will open your eyes to the absolute connectivity of all things. Greg Braden also explores the interconnectedness of everything (including thought) in his book *The Divine Matrix.* It's difficult to fully grasp the expansive and spiritual nature of how interconnected everything really is, but as we ascend in consciousness ourselves, we will begin to feel this interconnectedness more often as we activate and ascend through the heart. In the 4th dimension of the quantum (which we will discuss shortly), we begin to navigate through the interconnected field and understand it by way of the mind. As we then ascend further into the 5th dimension and the realm of the heart, we will finally be able to truly turn this knowledge into wisdom. We will, for the very first time, sense the feeling of interconnectedness at the highest level. Some have already started to experience occasional states of this interconnectivity by engaging in mind training techniques, meditation, prayer, and even through a near death experience. As we activate the portal through the heart, we will come to better understand this concept through feeling. As we move closer towards the experience of unconditional love, the interconnectivity of all things (the so-called Law of One) will be understood and felt more deeply by humanity. It's a slow ride, but we're getting there.

Consciousness is distributed throughout the entire body. To keep things simple, I like to visualize the fascia (the meshy, protective covering that surrounds our tissues and organs throughout the body) as being the consciousness connectivity highway throughout the body. This is how brain consciousness connects to body consciousness. In perfect harmony, brain and body consciousness mutually inform and condition each other. This unity creates complete coherence of brain and body. This is also why, in my opinion, body work techniques that reorder the fascia also have the ability to support a rise in consciousness. I like to consider the pineal gland as the gateway to consciousness and the fascia as the network that distributes it around the body. The heart then acts as the activator switch that opens the pineal portal gateway. This is why an open heart plays a crucial role in ordering and optimizing the mind.

So, what exactly are we? Are we physical beings, astral beings, or spiritual beings? Simply put, we are a physical expression of pure consciousness. We are energy first, matter second. We are spiritual beings having a physical experience. When we overly identify with our physical bodies, leave an untrained mind in control, and let our five senses run the show, we run into trouble. In today's fast paced and media run world, it's easy to become entangled and overly attached to the physical body and physical experiences. The trouble is that this rarely results in a happy and joyful life. We are not physical first, but we live that way. Here lies the dilemma.

Consciousness is the cause and the substance of the entire world. Consciousness is the secret of creation and is the only reality. All things evolve out of consciousness. Through our power to imagine, feel, and choose the idea we seek to express, we have control over creation and our very reality. We must learn how to think. We must activate the heart portal. We must continuously imagine. We must powerfully visualize. We must creatively express.

As Bob Proctor, author of *You Were Born Rich*, put it so beautifully, "the beginning of creation starts in your marvelous mind". The conductor of reality lies in the heart, but it is through the mind that we pull our greatest desires into the physical realm. The mind makes the music.

The Conscious, Subconscious and Superconscious

I have been studying the layers of the mind for decades, and I am fascinated by my own behaviors that seem to sometimes spin in counterproductive directions. One of the best little audio books on the workings of the mind is *Feeling is the Secret* by Neville Goddard.

As above, so below and as within, so without. This is universal law. The external world mirrors the internal one. Nothing comes from without, all things come from within. You, by way of your very feeling, determine creation. You are divinity within, and as soon as you embrace the great magnitude of this light, you become a master creator. Denying our divinity dulls our very reality. To seek on the outside for that which you don't feel you are on the inside is an endless maze. Neville Goddard shares that "we never find that which we want, we only find that which we are." Embracing the wish as already fulfilled is the road to a new reality.

Consciousness is divided into three main streams:

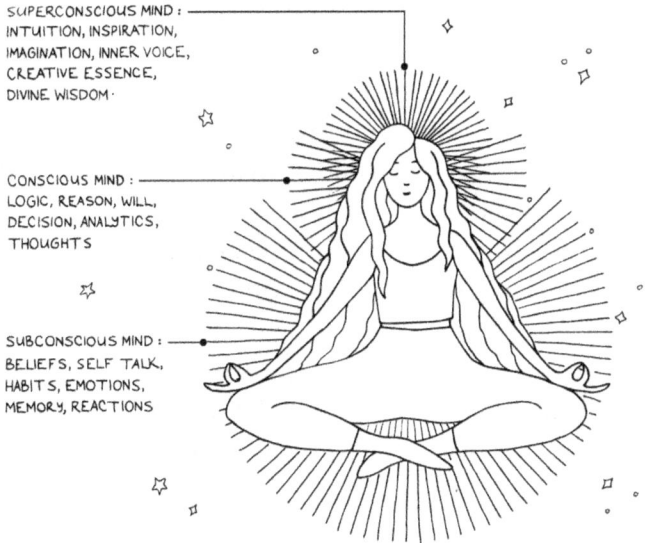

SUPERCONSCIOUS MIND: INTUITION, INSPIRATION, IMAGINATION, INNER VOICE, CREATIVE ESSENCE, DIVINE WISDOM

CONSCIOUS MIND: LOGIC, REASON, WILL, DECISION, ANALYTICS, THOUGHTS

SUBCONSCIOUS MIND: BELIEFS, SELF TALK, HABITS, EMOTIONS, MEMORY, REACTIONS

The Conscious Mind is your thinking mind. This analytical mind is responsible for thinking, analyzing, deciding, and reasoning. The conscious mind is personal and selective. The conscious mind is the realm of effects and the male aspect of consciousness. This thinking mind generates ideas and then imprints them on the subconscious by way of feeling. We are not trained how to effectively think, so we leave our minds wide open to programming and conditioning that eventually turns on the autopilot button in our life. We then surrender to the "whatever" of life and let everything and everyone around us do our thinking. Eventually, our very conditioning is in complete control of our reality, and we decline free will. As Bob Proctor often said, "If you don't like what's happening in your life, change your thinking. It's not her, it's not him, it's not them—it's you." I'll admit I didn't fully embrace this when he first shared it with me, but I now know it to be completely true. You are a thinking center that is drawing in the lifeforce energy that is swirling around you at all times, and then giving order to it through thought. Anything that has a center creates a vortex. You are a divine creator at the center of your most magnificent vortex. You have worlds within you just waiting to be fully expressed. Don't settle for less! As you unlock the portal through the heart, the life force energies pour in. These energies are then given form through thought. When you understand this, you begin to *consciously* think. You learn how to direct your mind and carefully craft your thoughts at each and every moment.

The Strangest Secret by Earl Nightingale is a must-read. In short, if you think in negative terms, you will get negative results. If you think in positive terms, you will achieve positive results. Always think of how you can create what you truly desire and not on why you can't. Most people let everyone else shape their thinking, but don't invest in the knowledge and resources to learn to think for themselves.

The Subconscious Mind. The subconscious mind is our memory bank. Below the surface level of the conscious mind lies the hidden secrets of the mind! The deepest levels of subconscious are beyond our awareness but are the reservoirs of our conflicts, traumas, emotional wounds, and past-life memory.

Our deep-seated fears and hostilities, cravings, beliefs, conflicts, and emotions are also stored here. The subconscious mind cannot reject input and must always accept what it is programmed with; it receives ideas and gives order, form, and express to them through the body. This is why the body is the physical expression of subconscious mind. Subconscious impressions create the conditions of your reality. The conflicts that are stored here can prevent us from experiencing joy and harmony in our life. These conflicts can make it difficult to concentrate, focus, and align our life with our deepest values. This is illustrated when our heart desires for us to live in pure health and light, but our subconscious conflicts keep us trapped in an addictive cycle of emotional eating, alcohol consumption, and television. We want to be in vibrant health and light with all of our heart, but we can't seem to break the cycle we have become trapped in. In many cases, these conflicts are also at the root of physical ailments. Current life trauma and past-life trauma are the common causes of conflict in the subconscious mind. Remember that trauma doesn't have to be big to cause these issues either. Being shamed as a child could have been stored as conflict in the subconscious if there was feeling attached to the event (which there almost always is).

Remember that the subconscious mind is impersonal and non-selective. The subconscious is the realm of cause and is the female aspect of consciousness. It is not concerned with the truth or falsity of a feeling. What you feel to be true is what *is* true for the subconscious. The subconscious expresses all that is impressed upon it. The subconscious mind takes feeling as fact. It does not originate any ideas and is therefore programmed by way of the conscious mind through feeling. Mastery of the mind happens when you demonstrate spiritual leadership over your thoughts and feelings. This does not mean you suppress feelings but instead learn how to dance with them and navigate the emotional scale with awareness and care. Every feeling makes a subconscious impression. Once a thought has been impressed onto the subconscious mind, it must be expressed in one way or another. The subconscious therefore works to express the conditions of whatever dominant feeling it has been impressed with. The dominant of two feelings will be the one that is expressed, which is why we must carefully and consciously choose our feelings. This is how the creative process works. First thought, then feeling, then expression. This is why affirmations that include *I AM* are much more powerful than affirmations that include *I will be*.

To impress the subconscious with a desired state, you must assume the feeling as if that state has already happened. If you dwell on difficulties, fears, and challenges, the subconscious will accept these states as fact and works on expressing them in physical reality. What you feel you are always dominates what you feel you would like to be. When we cut ourselves off from creative expression, the female energy system of the body gets thrown out of balance. Once felt, it must be expressed. Feeling is the one and only medium through which ideas are conveyed to the subconscious. We must practice and entertain only feelings that contribute to our happiness. Although feelings of fear, regret, and worry may arise, we must learn not to entertain and attach them. Neville Goddard teaches that one should never entertain an undesirable feeling nor should we dwell on the imperfections of self or others. Understanding the vibrational resonance of feeling will be discussed in a later chapter. Training the mind takes patience, practice, and persistence, but it will be worth every mindful moment.

The Superconscious Mind. The superconscious mind is the highest level of consciousness. The superconscious mind is where intuition, divine wisdom, inspiration, and imagination are held. A mind in this state provides the answers to the bigger questions in life such as "What is my purpose?" and "Why am I here?" This is also the problem-solving state. The subconscious mind "sees" the interconnectivity of all things. A mind in the superconscious state experience divine love and bliss. At this level of consciousness, we attract only highest vibrational energies, which will be drawn into our energy body and will be given highest order thought form. In order to access the superconscious, a consistent and regular spiritual practice is necessary. Chanting, breathwork, meditation, affirmations, and prayer are all great practices for connecting with the superconscious.

In many cases, it is the mind that needs a makeover with greater priority than the body. This is because the cause of an out-of-harmony body is rooted in the subconscious mind. When our thinking is pure, our body is pure. We often forget to incorporate the mind when we're doing cleanses, detoxes, or body programs, but we must! We must work on our mind-muscles alongside any physical cleansing or fitness program. This is why my spiritual nutrition programs and courses always include discussions about the crucial nature of mind-body-heart coherence.

The great mystics teach us to still or calm the mind through mantras, meditation, and reflection. They seek to bring the mind and every mental process under their complete control (both conscious and subconscious).

Schumann Resonances and Rhythm

The Schumann resonance is also referred to as the heartbeat of Mother Earth. Although there is a range, 7.83 Hz is usually considered to be the foundational Schumann resonance. Schumann resonance waves interconnect and interlink with our brain waves. The brain operates entirely by resonance and forms pictures in the same way. Many of the frequency bands emitted by the brain match up with those of Mother Earth. We are finely tuned in more ways than one to the vitality and vibration of the earth. If we want to link ourselves with the cadence of life, we must be in resonance and harmony with nature. Similar to sound waves, the brain has its own set of vibrations that it uses to communicate. We cannot hear extremely low frequencies, but our bodies perceive them as rhythmic. The brain is a giant source of extremely low frequency signals that get transmitted through the body via the nervous system. This nervous system is sensitive to magnetic fields, which is one of the reasons grounding our bodies to this field of the earth is so important for brain health.

When we spend too much time indoors or neglect to walk barefoot in nature, we hinder brain performance. When the brain is linked up with the extremely low frequency signals of the earth (the Schumann resonances), we experience a harmonic life. When we are deeply connected with Mother Earth, we are pitch perfect and can ride the cadence of life.

There is a harmonic relationship between the earth and our mind. The magnetic field of the earth and the electrostatic field emitted by the brain and body are cosmically interconnected. Our internal rhythms interact with external rhythms, which is why barefoot walking is absolutely good for the brain.

The rhythms and pulses of the human brain mirror those of the crystal core of the earth. This is why rhythm plays such an integral role in optimal brain function as well as physical health. The most important rhythm is the daily rhythm, which the pineal gland senses and controls though changes of light. These daily rhythms are known as circadian rhythms. When we synch up our brain waves to foundational Schumann resonances, we richly benefit from the vibrations emitted by the earth's own magnetic field. When we do this, we synch up to nature and experience body and mind harmonization.

There are four major biological rhythms that are important to honor and appreciate. They are gentle reminders that nature loves rhythm, and that losing rhythm is a sure way to throw everything out of balance and out of wellness. Here are the four major biological rhythms:

1. *Circadian rhythm:* the 24-hour cycle that includes physiological and behavioral rhythms such as the sleep and wake cycle
2. *Diurnal rhythm:* the circadian rhythm synched with day and night
3. *Ultradian:* biological rhythms that are shorter than 24 hours and of higher frequency
4. *Infradian:* biological rhythms that last longer than a 24-hour period, such as a menstrual cycle

It is likely that there are some intuitive nudges coming right now as to what dimensions of daily living in your own life may benefit from a little more rhythmic love. Morning and evening rhythms are typically the easier ones to set through daily wellness rituals.

Creating rhythm around sleep, movement, and mealtimes is a great place to start.

Human Brainwaves

Brainwave patterns create portals and gateways to higher realms of consciousness. As young children, we function in brain wave patterns that keep us connected to this higher consciousness and to Source. This is often why children can tap into the invisible realm with more ease than parents and teens.

Delta waves (0.5-4 Hz) are the slowest but highest in amplitude. These brainwaves are associated with deep and dreamless restorative sleep. In waking states, these waves are associated with the personal unconscious mind. These brainwaves are associated with the vital (etheric) body layer of the aura. From about the age of 0-2, children are functioning almost entirely in delta brain wave patterns.

Theta waves (4-8 Hz) mean "slow" activity and are associated with creativity, insight, intuition, daydreaming, and spiritual awareness. Your body is in rest, but your mind is awake. An extended Shavasana pose in yoga can produce theta activity. Focus is internal in this state between waking and sleep. Under stress, it may manifest as distraction or lack of focus. In theta state, you can connect with present-life and past-life memories and get insights on how to heal. This is also the repository of long-term memory. Long meditation can result in extended phases of theta brain wave activity. These brainwaves are associated with the emotional body layer of the aura. From about the ages between 2 and 6, children function mostly in theta brain wave patterns. They are in the subconscious state and place all of their attention on their inner world.

Alpha waves (9-13 Hz) support relaxation, imagination, mental coordination, calmness, alertness, inner awareness, mind/body integration, and learning. This is the major rhythm of a functional adult in a state of relaxation. In alpha state, your inner world is more of a reality than your outer one. These brainwaves act as a bridge between the conscious and subconscious mind. This frequency is associated with the mental body layer of the aura. Between the ages of 6 and 12, children function primarily in alpha brain wave patterns. They pretend, play, interact, and develop a heightened awareness with their external world.

Beta waves (13-32 Hz) are fast thinking activity waves during waking consciousness. They present when we are alert or even anxious, and they facilitate problem-solving, judgment, decision-making, processing information, mental activity, and focus. When you wake up in the morning and your pineal gland detects light, serotonin is produced and fast-acting daily activities start to happen. Beta waves are associated with the causal body layer of the aura. After the age of 12, brain waves move into beta more consistently. In beta, the outer world is more real than the inner world. Fear and anxiety keep us in beta state most of the time. You're less likely to trust, have faith, or act intuitively in this state.

Gamma waves (32-80 Hz) These waves connect us with the Superconscious Mind. This is where the brain can synch up with the super consciousness theorized by Carl Jung. In gamma synchronicity, we are better able to perceive higher realm activity and may experience the true nature of the unified field (law of one). This unified experience typically doesn't last very long but gamma waves allow us to catch (through feeling) glimpses. Whales and dolphins also operative within Gamma wave frequencies. Gamma appears to relate to simultaneously processing information from different brain areas: memory, learning abilities, integrated thoughts, and information-rich task processing. Gamma waves are associated with astral projection and remote viewing as well as the outer and higher dimensional layers of the aura. The Gamma synchronicity pattern is associated with transcendence, love, compassion, mystical union, and spiritual ecstasy. It has been scientifically shown that Gamma waves enhance the mystical experience, which can be described as follows:

Gamma Waves and The Mystical Experience:

* Experience of pure awareness
* Feelings of universal love
* A sense of complete awe
* Experience of unity with Source
* Awareness of divine truth
* Experiences that defy description
* Loss of sense of time and space

When you're controlled by the hormones of stress, you produce incoherent brainwave patterns. When you begin to connect to Source, brainwave patterns synchronize into resonance. You are able to trust, love, imagine, create, and connect. Through meditation, yoga, Tai Chi, Qi Gong, breathwork, connection with nature, and other mindfulness practices, our brain waves become more coherent, organized, ordered, and stable, which allows them to achieve higher and higher levels of consciousness.

Next-Level Sleep

As lucid dreaming, remote viewing, and astral projection become even more desirable for those on the conscious path, there is good reason for us to seek a better understanding of their advantages. Next-level healing will focus on the mind and in the particular brainwave frequencies mentioned above. There is already quite a bit of science and research available, and this will only continue to grow. If you're seeking to be ahead of the curve where health and healing is concerned, gently seek out credible resources, scientific studies, and teachers in the fields of quantum medicine, consciousness, and quantum sleep. (Many of my teachers have referred to The Munroe Institute over the years, as they have both in-person and online trainings and research available.) Sleep will continue to gain incredible momentum in the consciousness world as astral projection and lucid dreaming become everyday language. For some, technology will be intriguing to help enhance these states while others will prefer using meditation and prayer. Plant medicine is also available for those who desire to connect with the astral world. What is important is that you stay true to you and listen to your inner guidance for what path feels true and authentic for your soul. Many souls are on the planet today to learn how to access the astral realm without the use of plant medicines. Trust your inner guide.

The Matrix

A habit creates a routine, which in turn creates a program. This creates the autopilot life where free will has gone missing. Through our repetitive thoughts and feelings, we have created our own prison. By the time we're 35, 95% of who we are is a memorized set of behaviors, emotions, habits, beliefs, and perceptions that function like a computer program. This is a subconscious mind-program that runs our entire life and keeps us repeating the same patterns over and over unless we become conscious enough to escape. The miraculous news is that we can escape this matrix by first becoming aware we are in one. As self-awareness develops with greater strength, we become integrated, aware, and awake. The six spiritual practices of Auric Living outlined in chapter 1 are designed to facilitate this mind-awakening. It is important to understand that as one begins to break free from the matrix of their very existence, the world takes on new meaning, new relationships, and often a new career. This can be a deeply vulnerable time which is one of the reasons I am so committed to creating an Auric Living community. So much love and support are needed for so many right now. Trust in the higher order of things and create a community of like-minded individuals who love you unconditionally exactly as you are.

The Pineal Gland

The pineal gland is the cosmic portal of the body and the gateway to the cosmos. The pineal gland receives information directly from the soul and subtle bodies, and is a physical manifestation of the third eye. Just like an eye, the pineal gland has rods and cones and is a hidden source of divine wisdom and vision. Most ancient sacred texts contain hidden elements referencing the inner eye, including the Christian Bible: "The eye is the lamp of the body. So, if your eye is healthy, your whole body will be full of light,'" Matthew 6:22. There is much debate as to whether or not there is a hidden reference in this verse to the pineal gland. The third eye tunnel (third ventricle of the brain) is known in ancient Vedic texts as "The Cave of Brahma" where one is in resonance with The One. Mystical wisdom lies hidden within all ancient texts, and when you begin to find associations and similarities, life on the physical plane really starts to animate!

The pineal gland is a pea-sized gland located in the middle of the brain. It is part of the old reptilian brain (our dinosaur brain). It controls such things as melatonin production, circadian rhythms, and consciousness; it is also the master regulator of time. Far beyond regulating sleep, the pineal gland is the wonder of the body and the portal into cosmic and spiritual realms. It is often referred to as the body's light meter and our spiritual third eye. The pineal gland is also our means of connecting with higher realms and Source energy; as we awaken the third eye and its associated pineal gland, we are able to truly discover the higher senses worthy of our beings, including psychic abilities, clairvoyance, lucid dreaming, astral projection, telepathy, remote viewing, and intimate connection with Source (or whatever term you prefer for the origin of ultimate Truth, power, and love). The pineal gland also keeps our bodies closely attuned to nature. It is the source point where the cosmos meets the brain—one of the great crystal portals within the body. It is the source of spiritual experience, creativity, insight, intuition, inner strength, ultimate bliss, and even eternal life. Not only is the pineal gland activated by light, but it is also responsible for activating light in the form of life force energy throughout the body.

As we raise our consciousness through meditation and prayer, we begin to experience our sleep state as vividly as our waking one.

We develop abilities within our sleep to awaken in the dream and move between realities.

When our pineal gland is healthy and vibrant, we feel showered with spiritual energy, creativity, and inspiration, so be mindful of all of the toxins in your home, air, water, and food. Many foreign substances to the body, such as fluoride, pesticides, chemical cleaners, mold, fungus, and certain ingredients in beauty products can cause calcification of the pineal gland and hinder its function. As we ascend in awareness and consciousness, engaging in activities that decalcify and awaken the pineal gland will take greater and greater priority. Taking time out of your day to decalcify your pineal gland will be so much more important than loading up your Day-Timer. Why not start today? Meditation, prayer, sun gazing, dance, rhythm, crystal healing, fasting, darkness, and herbs are all helpful activities for decalcifying the pineal gland. The production of DMT (the God molecule) by the pineal gland is also enhanced as we work to decalcify the pineal gland. Diet is also important when it comes to pineal gland health, and this will be discussed in a later chapter.

Building Mental Muscles

Now that we have a better understanding of the mind and how thinking creates our reality, let's start training the mind and learning how to consciously think. Mental fitness requires a daily workout and a devotion to the divine mind. Although it is possible to achieve high performance mental fitness by way of one technique, several of these modalities used in conjunction with one another will yield better results. Transforming your mind into an Auric Mind requires a variety of practices done with consistency, including mantra, meditation, prayer, breathwork, visualization, creative expression, and sound techniques.

The following are daily practices and activities that enhance mental muscles by synching them up to cosmic creativity and divine mind—that is, highest-realm thought:

1. Illuminated Thinking

This practice may seem simple, but it's not easy. We have lived with an untrained monkey mind for most of our lives. As previously mentioned, from early childhood, we are trained not to think but to obey, repeat, and fit in. Training the mind to animate illuminated thinking takes time, patience, and great compassion. It doesn't happen overnight. The monkey mind wants to wander, indulge, and find distractions while the illuminated mind wants to soar, create, and conduct a symphony. From the moment you wake up to the moment you fall asleep, the goal is to take careful notice of your thoughts. When one isn't aligned with the destination you seek, cancel it out and build a new one. Every morning, practice intentionally directing your thoughts to perfectly align with the outcomes you seek for the day. This can be as simple as saying "cancel, cancel" to yourself when a negative or unwanted thought passes through your experience. In the beginning, you will notice how difficult this is as the untrained monkey mind is a wild one. With time and practice, however, you will begin to develop this new skill. The best times to practice this are when you wake up in the morning and just before you go to bed. You will get to a place and space where every thought is intentionally crafted to align with highest vibrational living for yourself. Directing positive thought just before bed, is a perfect way to train your subconscious mind. This is a magical time to speak only high realm words to yourself and think out your highest vision.

2. Mantra

A mantra is a powerful spiritual tool that can be used repeatedly to silence the mind. Mantras have the ability to transform consciousness. In Vedic teachings, a mantra liberates one who meditates on its significance. Mantra is traditionally a word, sound, or statement in Hinduism and Buddhism used to enhance concentration while in meditation. We are tapping into superconscious energies and, without labels or judgements, using mantra as a simple tool for calibrating the mind back to center.

When thought or spoken, a mantra induces vibrational qualities in the air and ether, producing a certain effect. It is the vibrational sequence of energy behind the word that holds interconnectivity rather than the word itself. The vibrational sequence created through mantra creates a ripple effect throughout the air and ether and travels multidimensionally.

According to the great spiritual teacher Eknath Easwaran, "The mantra is a short, powerful spiritual formula for the highest power that we can conceive of, whether we call it God, or the ultimate reality, of the Self within." Mantras have, indeed, appeared in almost every spiritual tradition in some form and can be successfully used throughout the day to bring mental clarity, inner peace, and spiritual connection. The mantra is the living symbol of the profoundest reality that the human being can conceive of, and the highest power that we can respond to and love. When we repeat the mantra in our mind, we are reminding ourselves of the supreme reality living in our hearts.

As we practice repeating our mantra throughout the day, it will sink deeper and deeper into our consciousness, strengthen our will, and heal old conflicts and divisions. Gandhi said that "The Mantra becomes one's staff of life and carries one through every ordeal." I was always curious what Mantra Gandhi used. After time searching, I finally found out that his mantra was "Rama, Rama, Rama," a mantra tied to allowing one's mind to be absorbed into transcendental consciousness of the divine mind of the Hindu god Rama.

Using your Mantra:

1. Select a mantra that feels intuitively right. Trust yourself and commit to not changing your mantra for the duration of this book.
2. Repeat your mantra silently in your mind throughout the day (as often as possible).

3. Speak your mantra out loud throughout the day when it intuitively feels right.
4. As you walk, work, drive, wait, and workout, repeat your mantra.
5. Use your mantra when you feel angry, upset, afraid, jealous, frustrated, or nervous.
6. Prioritize your mantra throughout your day until it becomes as natural as breathing.
7. Write your mantra.
8. Fall asleep to your mantra.

It can, of course, be helpful in the beginning to say your mantra out loud, but this is not necessary. A mantra's vibrational energy extends beyond any word or sentence—it is a power of its own.

You may already have a mantra that you use, or perhaps you are like me and deeply curious about different mantras practiced around the world. I also invite you to research and explore other mantras from your own spiritual traditions and choose one that intuitively feel right to you. Speaking the word three times creates loving and supportive spiritual force. There are many rooted in sacred spiritual texts, but here are a few, should any feel right to you:

* Rama
* Divine
* Light
* Joy
* Peace
* Grace
* Sun
* Amen
* Love
* Breathe
* Ava Maria
* Om
* Jesus

* God
* So Hum
* Lam
* Vam
* Ram
* Yam
* Ham
* Om Namah Shivaya

Finding a sacred word that resonates with you from a spiritual tradition you respect will help you focus the mind on a single point. A simple practice I have found helpful to still the mind is using the mantra *Om* on the inhale and *God* on the exhale during my meditation practice. Names of saints and archangels can also be helpful for this practice. Using primordial sounds (seed sounds) as mantras during meditation is also blissful. We also will discuss using seed sounds such as *Om, Vam* and *Ram* for energy center activation in an upcoming chapter.

AURIC ACTION

Take time today to choose a personal mantra. You may receive clear, intuitive guidance on what mantra is best for you. It should feel absolutely right. If you practice yoga, your teacher can help guide you by offering some of their favorite mantras. My teacher gave me a book of mantras, and after speaking them out loud, I instinctively knew which one was for me. While working through this book, I encourage you to keep the same mantra throughout. Whenever your mind wanders throughout the day or while in stillness, silence, or meditation, repeat your mantra. Saying your mantra out loud throughout the day is helpful but saying it silently in your mind throughout your day is also important. As you work to order and recalibrate the mind, say your mantra as often as possible each day.

3. Meditation

There are two types of meditation: active and receptive. Both are important for developing mental muscles. It is also important to understand that both active and receptive meditation techniques are important for building an Auric Mind.

Receptive meditation is stillness meditation. The goal is to quiet the mind and focus on the void between the thought. Mantra is often used to train the mind to prepare for the state of stillness desired in receptive meditation. Active meditation is a common practice today and is a form of meditation in which imagery, color, and symbols are encouraged through the creative and imaginative process. The mind becomes active and projects a stream of imagery upon the screen of the mind. Guided meditation, visualization techniques, and healing meditations are often active in nature. In active meditation, relaxation is encouraged as well as creative and focused thought. Visualization is a powerful active meditation technique. Both active and receptive meditation are very important practices for a fully integrated and ordered mind. When you only practice receptive meditation, life in the physical world can lack color and inspiration as you neglect to develop the powerful manifesting powers lying dormant within. On the other hand, if only active meditation is prioritized, it can be difficult to maintain simplicity, peace, and order in life. For this reason, it is important to practice both forms.

Prior to making Auric Living a daily way of life, we distract the mind as a coping mechanism for dealing with the monkey mind. These distractions include multitasking, keeping busy, living superficially, leading with ego, overstuffing our days and our bodies, and overstimulating our senses. We do anything and everything to avoid the present moment. As we begin to see the world and ourselves from higher perspectives, we become beautifully aware that quieting the mind is the only true resolve for the monkey mind. This transition from distracting the mind to quieting the mind can only take place by centering and grounding all of our awareness and energy in the present moment. Only then can we become the master of our physical senses. Prior to this, they rule and wander us with tornado forces until, one day, we finally surrender in exhaustion. We either surrender to substance (this includes a buffet of physical, emotional, mental, and energetic substances), or surrender to soul. To create symphonic harmony in daily life, set an intention each morning to consciously and lovingly command the Auric Mind to lead throughout the day over the monkey mind. I have added a few meditations to auricliving.com to support this practice.

4. Visualization

I never really realized the absolute importance of visualization when it comes to our physical reality until I stopped my visualization practice. In my thirties, visualization was a daily practice for me. I would sit quietly to calm my mind and my body in preparation for visualization practice. I would plug into an in inspiring and powerful song, close my eyes, and get to work designing my highest vibrational reality. In the beginning, I would visualize material things and abundance. My practice then progressed to visualizing my partner (now my husband), my family, my first book, my business, my health, and my highest vibrational day. When I let my busy mom life eat up my visualization time, life began to lose order, calmness, and clarity. It was as if I got coiled up in chaos. Much of this is surely due to my new motherhood phase of life, but I believe with my whole heart that losing my visualization practice was a major factor as well.

I can absolutely confirm that visualization is the most powerful manifestation technique. This practice must become a daily practice for all who seek to experience highest vibrational reality, and it is of the highest importance that parents teach this technique to their children. The invisible world is far more powerful than the visible one. The physical world is much lower in vibration and holds much more density that higher worlds. Our manifested reality exists first as energy and is created in the energetic realm before being called into reality. This means that everything we see and experience has an energetic blueprint that eventually drops into physical reality. The trouble with our conditioning is that we are trained to spend all of our time chasing and doing, and none of our time on visualization. We must swap this equation and consciously choose to spend much more of our time on visualization with the remaining effort on aligned action. If we're not visually clear on where we're going, what a heartbreaking reality to spend an entire lifetime feeling scattered, chaotic, and busy. Visualization must absolutely become a regular practice in schools!

Through visualization, you discover that you are a creative being. The very process of creation is where happiness lies. The higher self is in charge of this process, so a big part of powerful visualization is in the letting go. Visualization is highly underrated and unused. We forget that 90% of the work that goes into manifesting a highly worthy vision happens in the energetic realm. The remaining 10% of the work is done on the physical plane. The more focus and energy you give to fueling your vision, the faster it will manifest. Remember that we are now experiencing quantum leaps on a more regular basis, so what may have taken you 10 years to do or build before can now happen overnight. Visualization is creating an internal reality which is then attracted to you externally.

To begin a visualization practice, try these four steps:

1. Relax. Be seated or lying down.
2. Practice your breathwork.
3. Concentrate on accessing a deeper level of consciousness.
4. Create an experience within yourself of whatever it is that you want. This can be a feeling, an experience, or a state. See this as happening right now in your life.

5. Prayer

Prayer is a powerful Auric Mind-developer and heart-opener. Little by little, prayer opens the very flower petals of your heart. As we connect to Source, we also connect to the divine mind. As previously mentioned, prayer is when we speak to God or Divine Source Energy. It is a magnificent path towards enlightening the mind.

Prayer will play a predominant role in most of our lives over the next few years, regardless of spiritual or religious beliefs. Prayer is prayer. It is an intimate experience between you and the divine and the feeling is the secret. You know when you are entering prayer and you can stay as long as you'd like.

6. Focused Thought

Many spiritual teachers train on variety of practices that develop focused and clear thought. One of these exercises was not well welcomed by my monkey mind in the beginning. This exercise consists of taking an uninteresting object that does not bring forth any stimulation or activation for your creative mind, such as a pencil, paperclip, or spoon. For about five minutes, you describe the object in your mind, out loud, or on paper. The goal is to think of as many focused thoughts that describe the object without getting hooked or distracted by your monkey mind. Describe the object in color, texture, shape, use, geometry, weight, etc. for as long as you possibly can. Although this exercise may seem extremely boring (as it did to me in the beginning), I realized that this was exactly what I needed to reorder my mind. When done daily, this exercise will sharpen the mind to mastery. Try this exercise daily for one week and notice improvements in clarity, focus, and mental power.

7. Breathwork

As we have already discussed in detail, breathwork is a powerful practice for training the monkey mind. Breathwork also circulates lifeforce throughout the brain and body and trains us on how to still the mind. Breathwork is the ultimate tool for the mental, physical, and emotional body. It isn't necessary to perform the same breathwork technique each day; what is important is that some kind of breathwork becomes a daily practice today.

8. Affirmations

Affirmations are powerful tools for developing an Auric Mind. Affirmations are power statements that train the mind to focus on a particular vibrational state that has an end goal of activating an emotional response. It is always best to select a present tense affirmation, which is why I AM affirmations are so very powerful. We are training the mind to already experience the desired state. In the beginning, it may be difficult to activate an emotional response using the selected affirmation as we may not have yet experienced this state in our physical reality. This is why repetition is so very important. With time and practice, an emotional response will eventually activate, and the expressing of the affirmation will be felt as a true, present experience. For example, you might repeat, "I am an expression of highest vibrational light throughout my body." It can be helpful to find an affirmation written by a teacher or guide in the beginning. With time, however, writing your own affirmations give a particular vibrational signature that the mind can better resonate with.

9. Sound Science

Many research and healing institutes are reconnecting with the ancient knowledge that sound is a miraculous healer. Sound is the most powerful healing modality. When tuned correctly, sound waves create a super-healing state. Techniques such a vibroacoustic therapy, which uses low frequency sound vibration and music to train and order the mind, are gaining great momentum. Binaural beats are also methods of brain wave entrainment supporting states of higher consciousness and expansion. Binaural beats are when two tones with slightly different frequencies are listened to at the same time using headphones. This creates resonance and cohesion between the left and right hemispheres of the brain. Gamma wave entrainment is also research being conducted at The Munroe Institute to support the expansion of consciousness.

Participating in a group sound bath is also a deeply healing and expansive experience and a beautiful way to end the waking day. Chanting seed sounds (such as *Lam, Vam, Ram, Yam, Ham* and *Om*) are also highly effective methods of synchronizing the body and brain. Synching our brains to natural sound rhythms such as ocean waves or trees blowing in the wind are simple ways to experience consciousness expansion through sound. We are first baptized in vibration and sound in the womb. Our journey along this life path is to come back to spiritual home and cosmic center. Sound is the most powerful tool on earth for this. Consider filling your home with sounds of nature, fresh air, singing bowls, wind chimes, and beautiful music, as well as mystical moments of silence. My favorite wind chimes are Koshi wind chimes, which are crafted from bamboo to represent the four elements (earth, air, fire, water) and play intricate chords when moved.

It is also very important to be aware of the specific frequencies of the music you listen to, as many frequencies actually limit consciousness expansion and brain harmony. Much of the popular music today has been recorded at frequencies that cause higher states of anxiety, stress, and disorder in life. Filling a home with classical music, sounds of nature, sacred music, or meditative sounds enhances and expands our consciousness.

10. Spiritual Sleep

Sleep rituals for developing the Auric Mind are deeply transformative. It is important to use your own intuitive guidance to prepare a sacred practice before going to bed each night. Here are some valuable rituals that can activate the Auric Mind through sleep. With time, this may lead to mystical experiences, astral travel, divine wisdom downloads, and more. In many cases, getting answers to questions in sleep becomes a more regular practice. It is also important to understand that many people today are being initiated into higher spiritual realms and will be gaining high clairvoyance abilities. In order to hold this light, sleep rituals are of the upmost priority as one prepares for Astral Body travel during sleep.

- *Shower or ritual bath before bed:* Along with cleansing the physical body, a ritual bath or shower before bed also rinses the psychic energy that may have collected throughout the day. For empaths and sensitives (which is almost everyone today),

this ritual is an absolute necessity. A ritual bath before bed is also important for detoxification in today's world, which is why I personally prefer a bath over a shower before bed. It is, of course a personal choice. Adding detoxifying elements such as salts, essential oils, herbs, flowers, clays, and detoxifiers to bathwater is on a daily basis is an excellent idea.
- *Auric beauty rituals:* Body brushing, aura brushing, holistic oral healthcare, and natural beauty care are all ways for preparing the body for sleep. Applying herbal tinctures, oils, and healing creams to the body before bed is also encouraged as long as they are naturally derived. Natural creams and serums containing rose oil and lavender oil is a particular favorite for body and face nurturing before bed. More in a future chapter!
- *Herbal tea:* mindfully sipping a delicious and healing tea before bed is a gentle signal to the body and digestive system that the body is preparing for rest. Always be mindful of the herbs you choose before bed, though, and avoid anything energizing; lavender, chamomile, magnolia bark, passion flower, valerian root, and lemon balm are some great options before bed. Anima Mundi's Lucid Dream tea is also a great way to prepare for mystical sleep.
- *Empty stomach:* When the body has to digest food during sleep, all of the restorative power of sleep is lost. Sleeping on an empty stomach allows the body to fully surrender to deeply restorative, restful, and healing sleep. Try to avoid eating at least three hours before bed. Juicing is a better option if your body requires fuel close to bedtime.
- *Sway the subconscious:* We have the ability to lovingly influence and program the subconscious before bed. The gift of doing this practice each night is that, as you sleep, your subconscious will work to create and manifest this experience. When doing this exercise, be clear, confident, and certain of the directive you seek to give. It is also important to provide this directive to the subconscious with compassionate confidence in a way that is pure of heart but certain of mind.

- *Embracing nature and rhythm:* It is important to create beautiful order and rhythm in your body and bedroom in preparation for spiritual sleep. Clothing should be loose and made of natural fibers. Wearing constrictive underwear with elastic is also not recommended. *Au naturel* is always best. Bedding and mattresses should be made from natural and organic materials whenever possible.
- *Gentle breathing practice:* a gentle breathing exercise before bed is a wonderful way to slow down the body, detoxify the waste and stale energy from the day, and prepare the body for deep cosmic sleep. I prefer to have a practice of inhaling through the nose and exhaling through the mouth before bed (such as in belly breathing or auric breathing). What is important is that you are kind and gentle to your body as you prepare for sleep.
- *Meditation and prayer:* A gentle meditation or prayer in preparation for sleep is also a beautiful rhythm to have each day. In our present times, prayer is incredibly important and should be a top priority.
- *Journaling:* Having a journal by your bedside is not only a wonderful way to contemplate the day but can also be valuable for any creative writing or activities that remain swirling throughout the body before bed. I often get a full download of a book idea in the evening and having an opportunity to transcribe it to paper helps my body wind down well. Having a journal at your bedside is also helpful to write out any insights, offerings, or solutions received in dreams. We often think we will remember insights from our dreams, but if we don't write them down right away, they are usually lost.
- *Heart opening:* Welcoming the energies of grace, gratitude, and divinity into the heart and body before bed is a beautiful and expansive practice. This can be done by placing one or both hands on the heart and giving thanks to all the lessons and beauty that the day brought into your experience. It is also a beautiful practice to lay your hands on any other

areas of the body that you intuitively feel could use some love, nurturing and grace.

Preparing for sleep is one of the beautiful and sacred rhythmic practices of life. The sleep ritual practices should be gentle, calming, mindful as well as yin in nature.

The Creative Process

We tune into super-consciousness to get continuous downloads of inspiration. With strong self-esteem and will, we can then train our thinking mind to accept this inspiration with an intention to act. The thoughts are then manifested into our physical reality through the body. Once the creative manifestation completes, the energy returns to the creative cycle for future birthing to take place. This is why we often have a slight spiritual depression or emotional low after we achieve or manifest a goal, project, or vision. This can be a common feeling as this creative energy returns to Source and to the cosmic creative cycle.

It is also important to understand that the mind is to be used as a creative tool. When we train the mind, we have unlimited cosmic potential within. This creative mind power works within certain divine principles (such as love, joy, goodness, patience, etc.) and universal laws (as well as sub-laws), which could be an entire book on their own. For the purpose of this book, we will focus on the law of cause and effect. Creative energy is always available to us and is there for us to play with (and work with). A well-trained mind is able to continuously work with creative energy by downloading it, ordering it and transforming it into physical form (through manifestation). It takes an open heart and an ordered mind to reap the full creative potential each and every one of us have and hold.

The Law of Cause and Effect

The law of cause and effect creates absolute order in the continuum of existence. Karma is one element of the law of cause and effect. It is helpful to understand this law from a perspective of order, intelligence, and love. Often, when we think of Karma, we think of either good or bad actions. As an expansive perspective, the great law of cause and effect is one that creates divine order and reminds us of the importance of purity of heart. Every happening has a cause, and every cause has an effect. Your guardian angel has this law as its very nature. This law is not rooted in judgement but in order. The law of cause and effect is also a continuum, which is why karma expressed in this lifetime may have its cause in a past lifetime. Many of us are also starting to experience instant karma as timelines converge and time speeds up. My husband and I have both had experiences of instant karma that has kept us on a truthful path. The law of cause and effect is the most wise and loving teacher keeping you on the path of truth, integrity, and love. When we deviate from this path, we experience the disharmony between our existence and our soul in our physical reality. We may see this deviation as a misfortune or as bad luck when actually, this deviation is expressed in perfect proportion to the lesson we need to learn. It is true that we all carry karma from many previous lifetimes, but it is also true that we are gifted with free will and reason, which are sacred tools for navigating karma and creatively birthing the most beautiful human experience for ourselves. The objective, then, is to purify our bodies, minds, and hearts as we become masters of thought and aligned action. This is a karma clearing time in our evolutionary history. Our work is to surrender to higher divinity, live with grace and kindness, open our hearts, and order our minds. It is difficult to put into words the magnitude and significance of this sacred time in human history. You may not understand it but you likely feel it.

Today is the day to become the miraculous master of the mind. Through meditation, breathwork, mantra, prayer and mind techniques outlined in this chapter, the very foundation of your life can be reordered into one of beauty, peace, and personal power. Living in true integrity requires one to master the mind.

Chapter 4: Auric Heart

> *"In the region of the heart there takes place a union of the cosmos with the earthly realm."*
>
> —Rudolf Steiner

Love is like a sacred glue that holds matter into form. The auric heart (or illuminated heart) is a spiritually activated heart that is infused with grace and beaming with light. The auric heart has an immense capacity to manifest into matter and form with the highest order of beauty and grace. It also holds the power and possibility for total and absolute body harmony and wellbeing. True physical healing happens through the heart. As discussed in the last chapter, within the Auric Mind lies the portal to the cosmos—the auric heart is the activation switch. The cosmic power lying within the heart is beyond your wildest dreams and far exceeds what the mind can comprehend.

It isn't by chance that so many people today are surrendering to the superficial and trivial world. There are others who are hearing the spiritual call but have fallen prey to the luring powers of the five senses. For many of us, there is a period in life where we hear the call of the soul, but we aren't quite ready to answer, as this would require a drastic cleanse. Answering the call would also demand a deep and honest conversations with ourselves about our virtues and values and how well integrated we truly are in our lives. For many of us, we hear the call, but we aren't actively listening. We can still tune out the call enough to go on with our daily lives and the superficial life blueprint that someone ages ago constructed for us. It's as if our five senses have hypnotized us and trapped us into a game that we no longer wish to play but can't seem to escape. This is one of the reasons that bodies are breaking down at quantum speeds all over the place. As a collective, out-of-integrity living is resulting in an out-of-integrity body. Our bodies are now commanding us out of the grid game and into the soul sanctuary. The body does patiently wait for us to listen to the call of the soul, but eventually steps in and makes the choice for us. This is true body intelligence. The soul and the body communicate with glorious grace, and when the soul takes charge, the body must comply. In the short term, the physical surrender may be viewed as negative in one's life (especially if physical dis-ease manifests), but there is divine order in everything.

Regardless of our readiness, we are enfolding into the heart. Many of us are spontaneously weeping with spiritual grace without having a clue as to why. We're beautifully bawling all over the place! It's a little messy but extremely healing! The very essence of "How can I serve?" is illuminating within us glorious gateways to the angelic realm. When we illuminate the heart, we can only feel fulfillment through service. This is the path of the mystic and one where divine guidance is clear and absolutely non-negotiable. We don't always like what we hear, as it may shake up our present reality (relationships, homes, cities, jobs, etc.), but we know that we must act. We are now coming to a full understanding that to be guided by divine grace, we must surrender to selfish hoarding and hustle. Once we surrender to personal gain, we will be guided towards our true divine will, which is always rooted in service. This is a tricky one to navigate as our egos love getting and gaining. It is in the subtle and quiet conversations we have with ourselves that we will come to feel and experience when we have spiritually shifted. To intimately commune with the angelic realm, we must surrender to service.

In order to experience synchronicity, intuition, healing, and peace, one must be in resonance with heart magic. The auric heart has the power to transform chaos into rhythm. When we awaken to the auric heart, our heart holds within it the absolute power of the sun, and our entire body glows. It is the sun within each and every one of us. Not only is the heart the most miraculous and mysterious physical organ in the body, it is the portal to the soul. The human heart is the greatest organ of spiritual perception within the body. Our work at this very moment in cosmic time is to establish an intimate spiritual relationship with the heart. This work leads us on a mystical, spiritual quest as we navigate the mansions of the soul and develop the divine qualities of the heart. In the Vedic tradition, the heart chakra is described as a twelve-petal lotus. Each petal represents one of the high qualities of the heart. It is said that we incarnate with six of these petals being developed while our work during incarnation is to develop the remaining six.

> **AURIC ACTION**
>
> Consider the high qualities of the heart in your own life at this very moment and identify which virtues are the virtues that now command deeper contemplation, understanding and development. Which virtues have you been guided to develop right now based on life patterns and experiences? The universe always leaves clues.

The auric heart has awakened to higher living. The materialism and superficialness that once suffocated the soul is now aurically absent. It's not that we don't enjoy the perks of the physical realm, but we aren't as attached to them as we once were. We are complete with or without them. For many years, without knowing it, we have been preparing for this very awakening. And now we find ourselves in the first phase of the dark night of the soul: the dark night of the senses. The 16th century Spanish mystic St. John of the Cross writes about this experience in detail in his book *The Dark Night of the Soul*. It's as if the planet is going through a dark night of the soul right now—a spiritual cleansing. Many of us are experiencing this on the personal level, but we are also part of a collective dark night from which the world is only just emerging. During this first phase of the dark night of the senses, we are being cleansed and purified from the superficial and the dense. The heaviness that has been carried by the heart is starting to lessen. Although this phase of the dark night does not fully lighten the heart, it starts the process. There are three common things that one experiences when entering the dark night of the senses:

1. You can't seem to animate your life like you once could. You feel somewhat dried up and lifeless. You can still function, and things physically appear the same, but *something* is different.

2. Although you feel somewhat lost, confused, and out of order, you don't have an interest in going back to your old ways or the old you. *Something* is pulling you forward.
3. You are being called by some higher force to deepen a practice of meditation and/or prayer and are beginning to crave and feel very comfortable with quiet, still, and alone time.

If you are aware that you are in the dark night of the senses, know that you are not alone. Millions of people around the world have been initiated into this spiritual stage right now. This is a spiritual rite of passage and indicative that you are approaching the very castle gate that is housing your soul.

Our work at this moment in cosmic time is to establish an intimate spiritual relationship with the heart as a symbolic castle housing the soul. We have been trained to perceive the heart as the most important organ for physical life but not to perceive the heart as the most sacred organ for spiritual perception and communication. There is a superficialness to how we are trained as children and adults when it comes to the physical body. Much of this is because of a lack of knowledge, but even more so, it is due to a lack of curiosity. Why isn't our educational system deeply curious? We should be questioning everything we are teaching right now, and in a deep state of contemplation, asking our hearts if what we are teaching is valid and true. We are trained to keep up with the continuum rather than to animate creative curiosity. We have not been trained at all on the cosmic mysteries hiding within the heart. There is a superficial and limited approach to teaching when it comes to the physical organs of the body and how they dance together. When I was a medical student, I was heartbroken to witness the lack of depth and holistic integration when it came to human anatomy and physiology. It is, of course, important to understand structure and function when it comes to medicine, but we haven't really evolved our thinking or our consciousness when it comes to medical school. Yes, there are exceptions, but they are rare. The heart is the organ of high perception- the spiritual symphony.

What if for each organ, we were taught the great spiritual secrets hiding within each one of them as well as how they relate to our emotional, mental, spiritual, and physical bodies? The liver, for example, contains all of the forces of the entire earth within it. The heart is surely the most sacred organ to contemplate. We are all primary students when it comes to the infinite workings of the heart.

As we swap priorities in our daily lives to prioritizing our inner landscape over our external one, everything about ourselves and our lives change. This doesn't mean that our outside world loses love and attention in our hearts, but it no longer leads to the emotional drama, exhaustion, and conflict that it used to. In order to reorder our lives with spiritual grandeur, we must learn to return to the heart many times throughout the day until it becomes a natural and regular rhythm. This is a multi-lifetime journey and requires a very committed spiritual practice.

As we progress and evolve through many lifetimes, we learn and grow. Although it may not be the goal or endpoint in this lifetime, the objective on the continuum is to attain spiritual mastery. This is the result of a fully open, activated, and animated heart. This spiritual mastery includes the following characteristics:

1. Truth
2. Wisdom
3. Boundlessness/Limitlessness
4. Goodness
5. Immeasurability/Infinite capacity
6. Beauty
7. Peace
8. Blessing/Grace
9. Integrity

The Auric Heart is an ever-expanding portal to the soul and to God. Everything in your life flows when you are in resonance in your heart. This doesn't mean that there won't be trials, but they don't emotionally drain and exhaust you as they once did. Your trials no longer burn out your etheric body (more on this shortly). As taught by St Teresa of Avila, another 16th-century Spanish mystic, in her book *The Interior Castle*, the interior castle of the heart is where the soul resides. She writes about the seven stages of spiritual maturation that one goes through when seeking complete unity (marriage) with God. The seven mansions she describes also provide insight into the different stages of prayer on one's ascension journey. At the very core of the interior castle is the principal chamber where the soul and God experience perfect union. The first mansion can be considered the entry point to the soul as one begins a practice of prayer and steps into the castle. It is interesting to contemplate possible correlations between the seven mansion of the soul and the seven chakras, which we will discuss later. Both describe an intimate and sacred maturation process as one reunites with God.

Meditation and prayer may be complementary practices for some, while others prefer to have them as individual practices. Many sacred books differentiate between the two by the subtle nature of the practice. I believe both to be sacred and spiritual practices that develop divine communication. This is one of personal choice, and when it comes to seeking union with the divine, there is no wrong path. What is important is that spiritual practices are integrated into daily rhythm with great care and priority. Both require discipline, patience, commitment, and consistency. I invite you to explore the differences or similarities you are drawn to in both practices. Many, like Dr. Wayne Dwyer, associate prayer with speaking to God and meditation as God speaking to you. In my own life, I have meditation and prayer as individual practices. I do, however, expect that at a certain stage of spiritual maturation, that there will be a merging of the two. At advanced stages in both practices, graces simply download into your being and are experienced as pure ecstasy and bliss. In St. Teresa of Avila's teachings, this starts to occur in the sixth mansion. This advanced stage of spiritual bliss is also described in many ancient meditation teachings.

One of my early childhood memories that still plays out vividly in my mind is going over to the house of my Grade One teacher, who was also a Catholic nun. There was something sacred in the air of her home. She brought me to a part of her house that was set up as her prayer room. It was dark, calm, quiet, and very peaceful. She had set up a small altar with candles, crosses, and other spiritual symbols. We had a moment of prayer together before wrapping up my visit. The experience was short and sweet, but I remember it vividly to this day.

Along with growing up going to Catholic school, I also grew up with a grandmother who prayed the Rosary every day. I always felt the energy of grace and love when I was around her. I didn't have language to describe it at the time, but now I understand it to be grace. Although she passed away when I was a teenager, I can feel her energy near me to this day. My father also held this very special virtue of grace. There was not one moment in time where he swayed from truth, integrity, goodness, and wisdom. We definitely had some interesting discussions in our home where religion was concerned. My parents went to different churches, of different branches of Christianity, which gave me perspective and insight. As kids, we enjoyed rotating between the two churches and, ultimately, preferred my mom's church when it came to overall experience. What was beautiful about both was the incredible sense of community, support, and respect. There was a feeling of family, which is one of the most beautiful aspects of any church or spiritual organization. I am forever grateful to my mom for empowering me to find my own path and seek out my own spiritual truth. She developed in me a curiosity for spiritual exploration and sent me on my own quest for truth (likely without knowing it!). I was also gifted with an ability to discern from an early age what felt light and right. I have always had an ability to feel denser, darker energy signatures, which I think has kept me on a cleaner path. I sense and feel invisible warnings quite easily and am able to filter through spiritual information quickly. This skill can always be improved and strengthened, but I am grateful to my mom for sparking it within me.

I was blessed to learn from such an integrous family. Although I somewhat dissociated from identifying with one particular religion as I grew up, I developed a keen interest for sacred texts of all kinds. I bought myself a pretty pink Bible while also studying the *Tao Te Ching*, the *Upanishads*, the *Bhagavad Gita*, *The Interior Castle*, *The Dark Night of the Soul*, the *Yoga Sutras*, and many others. I studied Joseph Campbell, Daskalos, Madame Blavatsky, Rudolph Steiner, esoteric teachings, Christian teachings, Taoist teachings, Yoga Sutras, Mystery Schools, Vedic teachings, and Buddhist works. What fascinated me was not only the brilliant light that emanated from these books but also the correlation and connections between these texts. Finding similarities and connections between them thrilled me. Many people have shared their stories of healing by simply reading sacred texts. The vibrational frequencies of these works have a power beyond our awareness. My rhythm is to contemplate the links and connections between the teachings and find my own way to express and strengthen this wisdom in my daily life.

It is important to find a balance between studying and practice. Becoming addicted or attached to studying can often hinder the process of transforming knowledge into wisdom within the body. It is very important to balance between learning, processing, and doing. For this reason, I always take breaks between periods of study. These breaks allow me to consciously and mindfully apply my recent season of learning and mental knowledge. This is how one develops wisdom—through the application of knowledge. If all of the knowledge we learn stays in the head, it is unable to transform into wisdom. We need to move the knowledge throughout the body and out into the world for true wisdom to develop.

I also believe that we have hit a nodal point in our evolutionary timeline where rigidity, control, and boundaries around spiritual learning must dissolve. Spiritual intimacy is now the calling of the heart. Once we begin to see the soul as a symbolic castle and ourselves as saints in training, a portal opens for us. We transform from the inside out, and everything about us changes (including the physical body). We expand in all directions and embrace our very God and master within. We must now activate our own inner teacher and embark on our own powerful quest for truth. We must all become spiritual students and learn from a variety of spiritual sources until we experience union. The guru approach to attaining spiritual wisdom is not as relevant nor is it appropriate today. We are all masters today just waiting to be activated. We must empower ourselves to seek truth through purification, in a way that feels right and true. Each and every one of us must feel free to wander, to explore, and to learn from all traditions and spiritual texts. Spiritual knowledge should be shared with generosity and kindness as well as with an understanding the we must develop great discernment. We must develop the spiritual muscles to know what feels light and what feels dark. We must learn to let our higher senses guide us along the journey and signal us when something is right for us and when it's wrong. We must develop discernment for truth. There are many teachers who may seek to hide knowledge or expect a lifelong commitment prior to sharing knowledge. This guru approach to spiritual learning is no longer truth for the world we live in today. We must be free to express, create, and learn in a way that feels intuitive, loving, and true for us. It is, however, our work to develop the discernment to filter light from dark and truth from untruth. This takes patience and practice (and often a few little sidetracks along the journey).

It is also important to note that there may be a period (or several) on the spiritual path where one doesn't hear God. It's as if divine communication shuts off. This, too, is frequently written about by mystics as a common experience during spiritual maturation. Here is an illustration of the stages of spiritual maturation through prayer that can also be compared with the seven chakras (discussed in chapter 5).

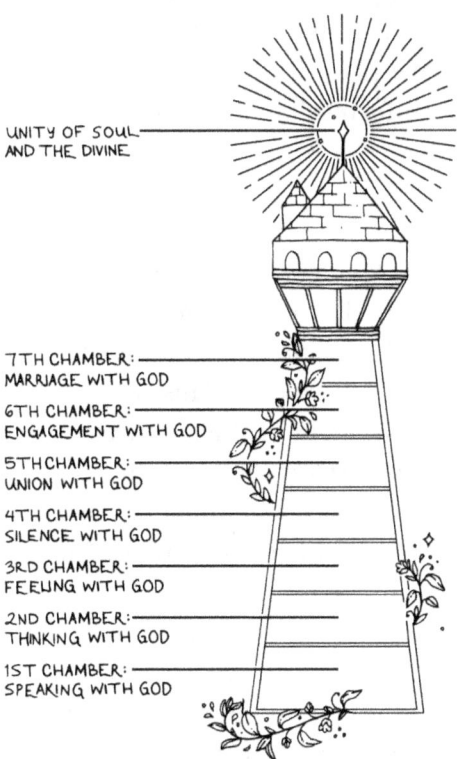

1st chamber: Vocal Prayer - This is the beginning level of prayer when one begins to pray or speak to God. This can also be in the form of a mantra, chant, poem, or song. This is where the soul begins the journey to illumination.

2nd chamber: Mental Prayer (meditation and contemplation) - This stage of prayer develops discernment of thoughts, motivations, and intentions. The chamber begins to reorder the mind and illuminate conflicts within the soul in a kind of mental makeover. This is a deeply cleansing stage of prayer.

3rd chamber: Affective Prayer (prayer of the heart and feeling) - Surrendering to fears and reason is the practice in this mansion, and the practitioner illuminates feeling God within the heart. Subtle shifts in beliefs, thoughts, and personality begin to take place in the mansion. Although subtle in nature, these shifts result in a reordering of life as you know it.

4th chamber: Prayer of Quiet (silence in your soul) - In this chamber, cosmic faculties and perceptions begin to awaken and appear. High clairvoyance may become a regular and daily thing. In this chamber, intuition is heightened, and divine guidance is channeled. This is also where we experience the first dark night of the soul (the dark night of the senses). This is where God detaches you from material things and the senses. We feel something is not working, and we can't seem to animate life the way we used to. It's as if we are dried up and stale. This is the beginning of the mystical life.

5th chamber: Prayer of Full Union - The three faculties of understanding, will, and imagination are united and attached to God in this mansion. Here, you begin to fully live in cosmic time and are not bound by the shackles of human conditioning. Your active life and prayer life are now one. This is where unity between your spiritual and physical daily life happens. In this chamber, your soul is truly free and is now in the driver's seat of your life.

6th chamber: Spiritual Engagement and Union (bliss and ecstasy) - The three faculties (understanding, will, and imagination) are united with God as well as the senses. You move inward in this mansion and begin to embody the mystical experience without expecting it. The soul may start to experience intellectual visions as the mystical experience heightens. This mansion also brings the second dark night: the dark night of the spirit. Faith, hope, and charity/love are developed during this second stage of the dark night.

7ʰ chamber: Spiritual Marriage - This is the stage of transformational union where your spiritual life becomes completely one with God. This stage is where one lives in heaven at all times on earth and becomes consumed by the divine, by God. This is the most sacred and interior chamber of the soul.

A prayer of surrender is a powerful prayer for opening and animating the heart. In today's cosmic age, devotional prayer is becoming more spiritual in nature rather than associated with a specific religion. Little by little, as we spiritually surrender, we let the divine move us in directions that serve our highest good. This includes moving us to the people who make up our soul family, careers that animate our highest gifts, and locations that act as spiritual portals for our souls. It takes time, patience, and practice to get to a place where we fully surrender and trust in divine relocation but when we get there, it is the deepest internal freedom there is. We are expanding beyond time and space, and as we transform into bodies of light, what is most important is that we have a spiritual focal point—a spiritual center. Prayer, meditation, and other spiritual techniques are powerful heart openers and activators. As the heart activates and animates, all other energy centers within the body are harmonized. This is experienced in daily life as a constant state of peace, joy, patience, and integrity. We therefore use heart opening exercises such as prayer and meditation not only for spiritual maturation but to calibrate and harmonize the entire body and all layers of the aura. Meditation and prayer are two of the most powerful ways to harmonize and heal the body. Accessing heart intelligence is also achieved through meditation and prayer.

Learning how to access the heart's intelligence is the key to everything. Learning this will move you from separation to connection and from depleted to beaming with life force energy. Every time the heart beats, it produces current flow and an electro-magnetic field. In fact, the heart is the largest rhythmic source of electrical energy in the body. This electromagnetic field created by the heart is detectable up to three feet away from the body and likely even further than that. The heart is the true energetic engine of the body and connects us with the earth and with the cosmos. This heart field carried by each of us is our electromagnetic signature. This signature carries an enormous amount of information about us including our emotional state. This is one of the reasons you can feel the energy in a room when you enter a meeting or an event—you are feeling all of the heart signatures. Our nervous systems are exquisitely tuned to the magnetic fields of other people. For sensitives, this is experienced at a heightened level on a daily basis. The energetic synchronization between heart signatures of individuals creates social coherence as well. This is demonstrated when you meet someone and instantly like them. It's as if you've known each other for years. This is also why many sensitives can feel trauma, grief, and sadness in others.

From a physical perspective, the heart is an information processing center in the body and has a complex nervous system called the heart-brain. This system intricately links the neuron pathways in the heart to the neurological organ in your skull. This is one of the physiological reasons as to why your heart is always speaking to you. Appreciation, courage, care, love, kindness, patience, and compassion are the true heart/love language. Together, they create the heart "voice," which we refer to as intuition—the voice of our soul. When we learn to connect and communicate using heart language, we experience heart resonance. The quality of the neural signals being sent to the brain when using heart language is of much higher frequency. When we speak love to ourselves and others, we emit high light from the heart and body. Our heart signature is of the highest order and quality.

The heart also has its own independent nervous system. The heart sends signals to the brain. Messaging is sent from the heart to the amygdala (emotional processing center) and to the thalamus (which helps coordinate clarity of thought and decision making) before making its way back to the heart. Heart and brain are in constant communication *with the heart doing most of the talking.* That's right—the heart is an electrical organ producing the strongest level of rhythmic bioelectricity. This energy then goes to every cell in your body. There are more than 40,000 sensory neurons in the heart, and learning to use it as the master perception organ in the body is greatly enhanced through spiritual fasting. "Heart first, brain second" is a good rule of thumb. Our experiences in the world are directed and filtered through the heart *before* being sent to the brain for further processing. There is a continuous neural conversation going on between the heart and the brain.

It is also possible for the heart to override the brain, which is a significant move where healing is concerned. True healing is done through the power of the heart because it acts as a portal for divine light, which is the most powerful and transformational form of energy. This form of energy is also intense, which is why preparing the body to hold and receive it is important. Prayer, meditation, and spiritual fasting are examples of preparatory practices. Keeping stable and grounded throughout the day is also key so that we are able to hold such high-order light without losing our abilities to well manage and thrive in the physical realm. It is no longer common nor practical for most people to exit their current life and seek spiritual shelter in the mountains or a monastery. We are being groomed and trained to be monks *outside* of the monastery today, which is no easy task! We must now learn to keep center, channel light, hold light and illuminate the heart all while keeping jobs, managing households, raising children, caregiving, etc. If only heart intelligence was as much of a priority as mind intelligence. The shift is happening! Thinking is not superior to feeling even if we have been conditioned to "think" this way.

The heartbeat is a reflection and total sum of all of the frequencies in the body in a state of quantum coherence. It also produces an electromagnetic power 60x greater in amplitude than that of the brain. It is therefore the heart that has the true healing power to rejuvenate your vital, emotional, and mental body. The heart has the power to heal the physical body by harmonizing and revitalizing the layers of the aura. This is why some people experience instantaneous or miraculous healing—it's the work of the heart.

When we are in a state of heart coherence, we experience higher levels of consciousness and harmony within our external reality. Coherence is the cooperative alignment between heart, mind, and emotions. Everything is synched up, tuned up, and in harmony. When coherence is present, our nervous system functions optimally and in a state of balance. When in coherence, we also experience higher levels of healing, inspiration, energy, emotional balance, stability, intuition, and mental clarity. Heart coherence also supports the development of the high heart qualities discussed earlier in this chapter. HeartMath Institute has developed a method for measuring heart coherence by way of heart rate variability analysis. When we are experiencing states of compassion, gratitude, appreciation, and kindness, high heart cohesion is present. This results in the brain synching well with the heart resulting in a balanced and optimally functioning nervous system. Our wiring is right!

The Four Virtues

As taught by Lao Tzu, the virtues of Taoism are beautiful commandments of the heart. The way of the heart is the way of the Tao. These four simple virtues are beautiful ways to ensure that heart activated living is daily and divine:

1) *Reverence for all life.* When we see the beauty and divinity in all of life, we communicate with all of nature on a deeper level. We are more aware of nature spirits, we hear trees, and we communicate with animals. We see ourselves in all of life. When squishing a bug becomes traumatic for you, you are on this angelic path.
2) *Natural sincerity.* This virtue is felt and understood when kindness, authenticity, and integrity rule your day. This is very different from inauthentic kindness. When we are conditioned to develop "fake kindness," we may smile on the outside but there is an incongruency inside. Natural sincerity takes time and practice as it requires one to hold grace and kindness near as we speak our truth. *Gentleness.* This

virtue is one of the master keys to heart-centered living. One who is filled with gentleness embodies kindness, compassion, and grace. Strength and gentleness go hand in hand. One who harmonizes life by way of gentleness understands when to ease the gas pedal. Gentleness is the buffer for hustle or over-action. Gentleness towards oneself is the primary practice, because if we are not gentle towards ourselves, we are not gentle towards the world.

4) *Supportiveness.* Supportiveness is a condition of the mind. When our thoughts are supportive towards our own ascension as well as the planet's, we harmonize with the divine. We are typically just a few thoughts away from a loving, supportive, and magical mind. When our thoughts are supportive in all directions, we transform our reality and the world in a quantum second.

Heart Harmonics Breathing

Meditative beathing techniques can support heart cohesion by way of breathing in heart-centered qualities such as gratitude, appreciation, love, and compassion. This activates heart qualities and helps to restore mental clarity, balance, and peace during periods of stress and anxiety. I have created The Heart Harmonics Breathing Technique that you are welcome to use as you develop your own practice for strengthening heart coherence. It is also helpful to use this technique before important meetings, higher stress situation, and transitions. With this technique, you can activate the higher centers of the brain and begin to perceive your day and your reality differently and with much more compassion and care. (The Heart Harmonics Breathing Technique is available at auricliving.com as well as on Insight Timer.)

Synchronicity

Consider synchronicity to be living life by the cosmic clock rather than the earth-time clock. The difference between the two clocks is that the cosmic clock is tuned to flow, grace, heart, and joy while the earth-time clock is tuned to productivity, control, rigidity, and structure. There is place and space for both, but dancing between cosmic and earth clocks is a truly beautiful art. Intuitively reading when it's "time" to put your earth-time clock to bed and wake up to the cosmic clock is a pivotal point in life. I woke up to the cosmic clock about 20 years ago and have not owned a watch or clock since. Trusting in the cosmic clock takes time and practice but eventually becomes a way of life. It's scary for many to let go of the power the earth-time clock has over their lives because they haven't yet fully developed the faculties of trust and faith. Again, there is a place for the earth-time clock; it's highly beneficial when setting daily rhythms and functioning in the physical world, as well as maintaining health and wellness. But when an unhealthy attachment to the earth clock is developed, our lives become constricted and small.

What we want to strive for in life is a rhythmic state of wellbeing and order in the physical world while experiencing frequent instances of synchronistic activity. When things happen beyond reason at just the right time (without planning, scheduling, or effort), you have synched up your being with the cosmic clock. It is a very mysterious subject but worthy of study. Carl Jung, in his book *Synchronicity*, writes about the meaningful and chance grouping of two or more events. When coincidences pile up in this way, it is termed "synchronicity." The better you become at reading cosmic time, the more synchronicity you experience in daily life. Activating the heart and enhancing heart cohesion are powerful synchronicity accelerators.

Manifestation

The secret to manifestation is through feeling. We are often trained to create vision boards, focus on them, and make miracles happen in our lives. The trouble with this method is that it doesn't emphasize the fact that that not only does the process of manifestation require strong will, it also requires an open and activated heart. As beginners, we often try to manifest with our head. This process might work for a while and even create a little momentum in the right direction, which is great. It's not that the head-focused method to manifestation is wrong, but it only has so much power. If you have been caught in a cycle of vision board creation without seeing much coming to fruition, it's likely because the time has come for deep heart-activation in your life.

Along our spiritual path, it is important to practice the art of manifestation initially through self-will. As one matures spiritually, divine will tends to take the lead and the co-creative process with the Divine is absolute and true. In early stages of spiritual development, personally focused intentions and visions (such as a job, home, travel, car, career, abundance, etc.) tend to be a starting point for practicing the art of manifestation. This is an example of learning to use self-will for grounding a vision or dream.

For a period of time in our lives (typically mid-teens to our mid-30's), we tend to be more focused on personal will and personal gain. We know what we want, and we want it now. As we move through the chakras in the next chapter, you will better understand that the energy center associated with personal will is housed in the solar plexus. This also means that if we didn't develop self-belief, self-esteem, and inner fire when we were young, manifesting can feel like an impossible task. Without strong self-esteem and a fire within that moves us to act, the ability to manifest what we truly desire in our lives can feel impossible. It's as if we cannot seem to animate what we really want in our life or we aren't really sure what we want at all. This is why supporting children through creative play, positive reinforcement, and intuitive processing is so deeply important. It is imperative that they are encouraged to develop self-will through a variety of ways and that they are encouraged and supported along their personal power path.

As we mature along our path, our visions and dreams also tend to mature. We become more focused on service to others rather than stuff for ourselves. This is a sign that you have begun the process of maturing to a higher type of will: divine will. This is where true co-creation happens. When we practice the art of manifestation from the higher of the two (divine will), we are in constant communication with our soul through the heart. We are less focused on personal gain and more focused on great service, love for others, and leaving a legacy. When we mature on our spiritual path and unlock divine will, if it isn't spiritually true (centered on love), it simply will not manifest. Temporary gains may pop into our existence, but they will only ever be temporary. At this level of spiritual maturation, if it isn't fully aligned with universal law and truth, it simply won't animate—no matter how beautiful your vision board! This is why it is important when we are young to practice the art of manifestation using the power of self-will (the inner solar plexus fire) but to learn some detachment from the things we bring into the physical realm through this practice. If we understand this is a sacred art and that it is lovely to develop but eventually it must be used for greater good, human good and planetary good.

It becomes difficult as adults to strengthen the art of manifestation if self-will is not well developed as a child. It's never too late, though, so if you recognize that your personal power, self-esteem, and inner fire are all in need of development, begin today.

If you're reading this book, there is a strong likelihood that your spiritual maturation process has ascended to that of divine will. It's not that you won't use the fire in your belly or past methods of manifestation that worked so well, but that the intention behind what it is you seek to manifest is of higher spiritual order and truth. This also means that your greater purpose, higher gifts, and spiritual forces are being revealed to you. For you, the art of manifestation has now taken on a higher spiritual order and the skills and powers you developed and practice by way of self-will manifestation are ready to fly! As higher order abilities activate within your body, it is important both to understand and prepare for divine manifestation to take place in your life. This truly is a co-creative process where it will often seem as if grace is making miracles happen in your life.

Here are some simple suggestions as you graduate to new heights of spiritual power and unlock divine will:

1) *Prepare for an infusion of spiritual light.* This phase of divine will activation can seem like a never-ending period of

limbo that has left you confused, impatient, emotional, and frustrated. It's as if the skills you were so good at before simply don't animate anymore. This phase can feel like a never-ending marathon. You're even too exhausted to strive for material things and wishes. This is exactly the point. This phase is supporting your surrender. You are learning to tame the senses and awaken to your soul. What used to bring you happiness before seems so very trivial and superficial now.

Here, you are patiently awaiting spiritual directive on what your purpose is, where to turn, and what to do. Patience is the name of this game. During this time, it is vital for you to continue to study, ground, lead, create, and function in daily life as best you can without forcing or exerting yourself. You must learn how to stay the course, but not leak all of your energy. Practice prayer and meditation as well as a solid daily rhythm for sleep, self-care, and health is essential. Your soul is starting to take charge of your life, which means a period of grief, confusion, and pause is likely. This is a transition period where you may also experience body reorder, which can appear as hair loss, inflammation, vision changes, autoimmune symptoms, etc.

2) *Increase stillness.* Decrease chaos. As you awaken to your spiritual path and higher call, the need for stillness and void becomes imperative. You cannot hear the voice of your soul with great clarity in the midst of chaos. Practicing stillness through prayer, meditation, and a quiet walk or swim must now be top priorities as your soul demands more moments alone.

3) *Purify the body.* Taking a spiritual approach to nourishing and cleansing the body will greatly facilitate the activation of your soul life. Ancient Essene texts included the symbolic significance of purifying the body through diet, fasting a prayer. This practice will be discussed further in the Auric Nutrition chapter.

4) *Activate the heart.* Heart activation can be done in many ways. The secret is practice, patience, and persistence. Meditation, prayer, nature, children, music, and swimming are just a few examples. Activities that promote present moment awareness and heart centering illuminate the virtues of the heart and transform your being into a beam of the highest frequency of light.

Trauma

We cannot discuss heart activation without touching on trauma. We have reached a major healing point in cosmic history. Not only must our planet now integrate and heal, but it is time for each and every individual living on our planet to return to wholeness as well. This is critical in the evolutionary process of humanity and our world. When we experience significant trauma, we disconnect from our soul. We do this in an almost instantaneous and automated way as a means of survival and protection. Our reaction to significant trauma is to shut ourselves off from all outside sources and channels, which also includes the higher realm ones. As a response to trauma, we create a fortress around our physical and energy bodies. We shelter up and bunker down physically, energetically, and spiritually. It is as if we enter a holding tank where survival and security become the only focal points. We then remain in this guarded fortress for as long as necessary until one day, we hear a quiet knock at the door of our interior castle. No matter how hard we try, we simply cannot outrun trauma healing forever. We can do our best to try (by making our lives as busy, addicted, and chaotic as possible), but eventually the divine will sneak in a little pull on a heartstring or a subtle whisper that cannot be ignored. Whether the trauma is from this lifetime or a previous one, we have all landed on a nodal point in time where healing is happening whether we like it or not.

Trauma is an internal response to one or several emotionally straining events in life. We have all been born into a pre-traumatized field, which means that the traumas of our parents, ancestors, and society all leave a signature and imprint. We are all swimming in a sea of trauma, much of which is lying in the very depths of our subconscious. Whether big or small, trauma has the capacity to impact the brain, body, and entire nervous system, because it leaves an imprint and signature within our physical body and the brain stores the memory of it. Many people who experience an intense trauma or a series of traumatic events hold emotional heaviness in their fat and lymphatic tissues and often experience chronic puffiness, inflammation, and/or bloating. Healing trauma through the heart will begin to release the energetic and physical blockages. Self-love, compassion, and forgiveness are transformative states for facilitating this release. When the heart is awakened, trauma heals and the body illuminates. Loving oneself and one's body will facilitate the body's natural return to center, in terms of shape, proportion, flow, and function.

Trauma is, fundamentally, a disconnection from self to some degree. In response to trauma, we find a way to detach whether through withdrawal, outbursts, risky behaviors, or other coping mechanisms. According to Dr Daniel Siegel, M.D, it isn't as important what happened to you, but rather how you make sense of what happens to you. What is important is the process of coming to clarity in your own heart, head, and gut as well as learning to regulate yourself. It is often a pattern of behavior to project pain from trauma onto a safe and non-threatening person in our life. They are rarely the cause of the trauma but become the target for projected pain.

The stronger the emotional reaction to a traumatic experience, the more one focuses on the cause. This creates long term memory as one begins to think within the boundaries of this experience and continue to recall the event. There is a cyclical looping repetition that happen—a pattern that will emerge in one's life. The storyline and the characters will change, but the same pattern will play out. I was once taught that we often freeze in spiritual maturation at the age that a significant trauma takes place. From then on in our lives, we are simply replaying the very same trauma in different forms indefinitely until we come to conscious awareness and begin to heal. Prior to healing trauma, we get caught in a cycle of fight, flight, or freeze to survive. Survival and stress become dominant in emotional life. Trauma conditions the body to remain in a chronic state of fear.

The way that trauma manifests into physical symptoms and later dis-ease has been well documented by many medical pioneers and healers. Trauma effects how our brains develop, how we handle stress, how we interact with people, how much empathy and insight we have, and how much compassion we are able to show others. In children, highly traumatized brains actually look differently than the brains of children who have not absorbed as much direct trauma. It is important to remember that children don't get traumatized simply because they get hurt. They get traumatized because they are *left alone* with their hurt. They are not given the love, support, and help that they need to allow their bodies and minds to process the harm done to them. Trauma isn't only about the event that happened, but the imprints left in the body and the residue left in the nervous system. As children, when the quality of love and care we receive is conditional or based on certain approved behaviors, we experience trauma.

Many children exposed to trauma develop nervous systems that stay in a state of stress response, which lays the foundation for how their nervous system responds to stress or resilience as they grow into adulthood. Supporting their nervous systems is therefore deeply important. Many children can have large stretches of time without showing any symptoms of trauma. This is why in some cases during the teenage or early adult years, an individual can all of a sudden fall apart or experience energetic and emotional breakdown. It is often the case that there is a time lag between the trauma and the symptomology. Being exposed to major trauma early in life could be just what the soul needed to activate divine will earlier than most and get right to destiny's path at an early age. When we become too constrained by our tribal community (although often loving and nourishing in so many aspects), we often worry so much about what others think or about fitting in that our true divine will gets significantly delayed until we muster up the courage to graduate beyond the tribe. This tribal community may consist of immediate family, extended family, religious community, cultural community, social community, professional community, etc. This, of course, does not mean physically leaving the extended family unit, but is more of a symbolic act of courageous independence. For some however, this will mean creating at least a temporary distancing from the tribe. The gifts and blessings received from our very own tribe should be cherished, but along our spiritual maturation process, there comes a time when we must find our own feet and shine our highest light. As many of my clients and friends and friends can attest, sometimes the tribe means well but doesn't know how to handle (or positively support) members who ascend too high, aspire too grandly, or embark on divine will's path sooner than they were prepared to facilitate.

Regardless of the level of trauma, the rapid social change and breakdown in our world over the past few years has resulted in some level of trauma for everyone. I believe that those who work in the professional therapy industry must have a degree of spiritual science integrated in their work; we simply cannot heal trauma without spiritual strength. When we recognize that the time has come to integrate and heal trauma, we bring the unconscious to the surface for processing and union. When our level of self-awareness blossoms where trauma is concerned, we take full and complete responsibility for our lives, regardless of details. We de-activate our victimhood and withdraw from the unconscious pattern of projecting (and sometimes puking) our unhealed fragments on other people. When we develop heightened personal power through the act of healing our trauma, we relinquish projecting and blaming. We lovingly put our victim to bed, and although they may wake up every once and a while, we no longer let them lead in our lives. We have fully graduated from victimhood.

Unfortunately, the traditional approach to integrating and healing trauma is not as effective today, as we are in a new cosmic age. A deeper understanding on the workings of the soul as well as the mind is desperately needed. This is why I always recommend seeking out therapists and practitioners who are trained in spiritual science and have a degree of spiritual development in their own lives as well.

Here are a few modalities that support trauma healing:

* Spiritual psychology
* Trauma healing specialist
* Sound therapy/Sound baths
* Subconscious restructuring
* Cognitive behavioral therapy
* Music and sound therapy
* Somatic therapy
* EMDR therapy
* Equine therapy
* Art therapy
* Cranial Sacral therapy
* Vogel crystal healing (as well as traditional crystal healing)
* Colon hydrotherapy
* Yoga
* Qigong/Tai Chi
* Meditation
* Prayer
* Body Work
* Journaling
* Reiki
* Swimming in the ocean
* Coherence techniques
* Nature walks/Gardening/Farming
* Earthing
* Flower essences/Herbs
* Psilocybin
* Ceremonial plants
* Sacred geometry

Note that when working with psilocybin and medicinal plants, it is recommended to have both medical and spiritual supervision. Not only is it important to have healers and therapists that are of the highest integrity and the right fit for you, but it is also critical to develop discernment yourself. This is one of the downfalls of the networking craze, as we are trained to just go with a referral, but this doesn't build our own discernment muscles. Asking for referrals can be helpful but remember that your heart holds the power to magnetically draw in exactly what and who you need—all on your own. I have found that the people I attract using my own energetic signature tend to be the best fits. If you are going to ask around for referrals, do your research, get a few different ones, and tune in to intuitive messages. Make sure the person you are asking for a referral is someone you deeply trust and is of highest integrity. When it comes to my own healing process, I am intuitively drawn towards yoga, meditation, walking, bodywork, prayer, and time in nature. It is very important to work with your own intuitive powers when choosing healing modalities. If something doesn't feel right and true to you, trust that. There has always been a strong knowing within my body not to consume alcohol, psychedelics, or psilocybin. I don't always understand my guidance, but I always trust it. I have always been more drawn to yoga, crystals, cleansing, colon hydrotherapy, spiritual fasting, meditation, nature, and body work for healing. Mild fasting is also a spiritual practice for me. This often includes a half to full day fast consuming only water, herbal teas and green juice (I include my auric green juice recipe in the Auric Nutrition chapter).

Building a sacred relationship with the physical body is an important process in trauma healing. This is also deeply challenging for many and requires great patience, commitment, and self-love. Baby step by baby step, every inch of the body must be nurtured, loved, and appreciated as the healing process reintegrates the whole with the soul. This can be supported by ritual baths, body work, mirror work, therapy, dance, music, cognitive behavioral therapy, tantra, yoga, breathwork, spiritual psychology, sensuality coaching, and pleasure workshops as just a few examples.

For women especially, unhealed trauma can exit in bursts during menstruation. Timing is, of course, individual but often for a few days before and after a woman's period begins, little trauma bubbles can surface out of the body as emotional outbursts, voicing anger and frustration, and emotional eating. As we embrace our bodies and beings, we begin to love and roll with the seasons and cycles that make up the healing path. We gain perspective and wisdom where our wounds are concerned and develop deep spiritual gratitude for our menstrual cycle as sacred rhythm for trauma healing. During your next period, observe your feeling fluctuations and consider how they each might symbolically represent little bursts of trauma rising up and out—a multi-layer monthly cleanse.

Resilience

Resilience refers to how easily we can return to our original function following a stressful or traumatic event. For smaller scale stressors, taking a hot bath or having a good cry may be all that is needed to heal and bounce back. For other situations, this process can be much more involved and may take days, weeks, or even years. The capacity to prepare for, recover from, and adapt in the face of stress, challenge, or adversity can vary greatly from individual to individual. We are all energy bodies, and we all have different energy signatures. We expend and renew energy at different rates, and we must explore and develop curiosity about how our unique inner battery operates. As a sensitive, helping myself recover from stressful situations takes more care, attention, and nurturing than it might for other people—especially over the past few years, given all of the stress and trauma in the world. My energy signature is primarily (if not dominantly) yin, which can easily leave me overcompensating in personality through yang activities. This can result in a yang hyperdrive and excessive doing, if I'm not conscious and careful. My home is filled with tuning forks, crystals, healing equipment, color therapy, and images and sounds of the sea. I am consciously aware of what resilience means to me and how to function at my most resilient resonance, so I equip my space and myself accordingly.

The four dimensions of resilience include:

1. Spiritual (commitment to values, tolerance of others' values)
2. Physical (endurance and strength)
3. Mental (mental clarity, attention span, ability to focus)
4. Emotional (outlook and self-regulation)

Coherence is experienced when all dimensions are nurtured and cared for.

Self-Regulation

As children, we have two fundamental needs: attachment and authenticity. The foundation for a healthy nervous system is laid through secure attachment interactions as infants and children with an attuned, nurturing, and consistently available parent or caregiver. Over time, this nurturing and healthy environment allows for the development of self-regulation skills as the child grows. As a society, we limit and even deter authenticity and attachment from a very young age. This is deeply traumatic. I had the most beautiful discussion with one of my son's teachers yesterday. She shared with me that it is her most profound work to make every child feel comfortable and safe being exactly who they authentically are. My heart melted! She wanted to make sure my son feels completely comfortable and free to express *all* of his emotions, including anger and sadness. It is our work as individuals, as well as a collective society, to understand this simple truth: *Our work is to heal our way back to authenticity and to the heart.*

Our nervous system has an optimal level of firing and wiring. When a child's caretaking and emotional needs are unmet, physiological dysregulation is created within the nervous system. This can result in physical and emotional responses such as emotional outbursts, rage, anxiety, difficulty concentrating, difficulty relaxing, disconnection, dissociation, and emotional numbing. This can also impact a child's resilience to trauma later in life.

If a child is taught or conditioned to believe it is necessary to suppress gut feelings and authentic emotional responses, that child will disconnect from their anger and store it in the body. Over time, it may physically manifest in a variety of ways including depression, physical illness, and/or mental illness. This is why it is so very important to encourage children to stay true and connected to their authentic self. As adults, it is important to help guide children through behaviors and feelings without projecting our own expectations for how they should behave.

When it comes to addiction of any kind, the first issue is not "Why the addiction?" but "Why the pain?" Addiction is a normal response to trauma. A hurting individual seeks addiction to complete themselves. Addiction is the primary problem, but it is ultimately a response to unresolved trauma. Underneath the trauma is a healthy individual that has never found healthy expression. When it comes to technology and gaming addictions today, it is important to better understand the emotional bodies of children and why they are so prone to technology addiction when introduced too young.

Breathwork and meditation are beautiful tools for self-regulation as they can be taught at any age and work wonders on the nervous system. Regardless of our history, we can retrain and rewire the nervous system to find calm and center, regardless of what is happening in the physical realm. Having a sacred song that is easily accessible in times of need, is also a powerful tool for self-regulation. *Meditation* by Jules Massenet is that song for me. As soon as I hear the beginnings of that song, I find my center and my sacred place.

To embody Auric Living, I encourage you to seek the beauty in the simple. When it comes to self-regulation, what activities helps you find center? A bath, a song, a breath, a tree-hug? All that matters is that you find deep connection with a few activities that help you self-regulate back to sacred center.

Emotional Radiance

Emotions are a flow of energy that add texture and tone to our lives. They can also create challenges. In his book *Power vs. Force*, Dr. David Hawkins proposes the concept of energetic frequencies associated with different emotional states, as well as the attitude that corresponds with the emotion. This way of thinking has been very helpful for me to recognize and replace an attitude that is vibrationally higher in times of emotional and nervous distress. Guilt, for example, is actually a productive shift up the vibrational scale from shame in terms of connecting to my heart and elevating my vibration in the right direction. It may not be joy or peace, but it is a baby step in the right direction.

It is my belief that being exposed to chronic fear by most of our institutions from childhood has deeply traumatized us as a collective, which is why an understanding of trauma is so critical in the world today. In order to heal ourselves, we must create high cohesion with our own hearts, which will support the healing of those around us as they, too, create high cohesion with their hearts. Fear has been projected on all of us and on our children from school systems, medical systems, government systems, and corporate systems. All of these systems, consciously or not, use fear to dominate, gain power, and attempt to keep our vibrational states at a high-enough level to function, but not a high enough level to transform our lives into cosmic expressions of complete cohesion, joy, and well-being. It is our work right now to do all we can to release this fear and resistance from our bodies in order to create cosmic space for a new reality—for ourselves, our children, and the world.

As many experts have asserted, fear, grief, guilt, and shame are among the lowest of the low on the vibrational scale. The frequencies emitted by these states not only hinder energetic flow throughout the body but cut off cosmic channels for intuition, creativity, imagination, and wellbeing. According to Dr. Hawkins, different states emit different energy frequencies that he measured on a scale that runs up to 1000. Fear emits an energetic frequency of 100 on the energetic frequency scale while enlightenment ranges from 700-1000. At the very bottom of the energetic frequency scale sits shame. Shame emits an energetic frequency of 20, which is why it creates such density and resistance in the body. Here is a summary of the emotional radiance scale from the highest frequency to lowest:

1) Peace/Joy/Love
2) Happiness
3) Acceptance
4) Willingness
5) Courage
6) Pride
7) Blame
8) Anger
9) Jealousy
10) Fear
11) Grief
12) Guilt
13) Shame

I use this scale often as a positivity tool to support my progress. As an example, if I had a day of feeling deep guilt over a variety of things, and transform my state of guilt to one of grief, I have actually made great progress. The energetic signature within the body emitted by grief actually creates less density and resistance than guilt. This is very helpful to support healing as we navigate the emotional body and daily life.

Focusing on how you want to *feel* rather than how you want to be or what you want to do is a great way to transform into the most radiant Light Body inside and out.

Fear

Have you ever noticed that certain people can be the most happy and friendly people on the planet—as long as you don't ruffle their fear-feathers? As long as you don't bring up certain topics or express certain opinions that trigger their specific fears, then all is well. For some individuals, certain fears are absolute trigger points that activate unexplored and unhealed trauma. As an example, for someone who has a great deal of fear around not having enough money, the very conversation that something may cost them more than originally expected may turn into an energetic and emotional tornado. Fear and unhealed trauma go hand-in-hand, yet no one really speaks of it. They are almost always the elephants in the room. It used to be that small talk and smiles did the job of cloaking the fear and trauma in a situation. Today, however, we are all energetically naked, and it's time to truly heal. No clothing, plastic surgery, makeup, or accessories will feel quite enough anymore. Less is now more as we navigate ourselves back to wholeness and integrity. Spending much of my year in Costa Rica was deeply healing for this very reason. Everyone around me was very aware and open about their healing path. No one wore makeup or fancy clothing or pretended to be totally put together. It was about being raw, honest, authentic, true, and awesomely authentic. The only items on the daily do list included yoga, healing, peace, health, nourishment, kindness, and connection.

You may have become frail with fear. Nothing voids the body more of vital lifeforce than fear. It can age the body in an instant and wreak havoc on the organs. You simply cannot get to higher states of consciousness until you learn to dance with fear. For most people, at some level, fear is in charge of daily life. Some have managed to tame it, while others tense up at the mere scent of it. The fact is, we cannot truly heal until destructive fear (such as self-doubt, abusive situations, and phobias) has been released from the body, and we can learn to have a new relationship with positive fear (such as the avoidance instincts that keep us alive). Fear will suck the lifeforce from your body and leave you feeling confused, victimized, and void of connection with Source. Not only can you not thrive in a chronic state of fear, you can't even function. When fear is chronically circulating the body and mind, you live in a world of fight, flight, or freeze at every moment, and you are imprisoned in low vibrational jail.

In *Outwitting the Devil*, Napoleon Hill explains how fear moves in and occupies the unused space of the human brain. It then sows the seeds of negative thought so it can control space and spread throughout the body like a virus. Hill believed that fear controls 98% of the population and takes up roughly half the space of every atom. That really hit home for me. I have always known that I incarnated in this lifetime carrying fear from a monumentally traumatic experience in another lifetime. From my earliest memory, I have carried large amounts of fear in my body. I knew that this fear was not my own but was likely a combination of cellular fear I brought in from a past life and the fear I was inviting into my experience from others as an intuitive and a sensitive. The totality of this was a personality that was very composed, kind, and successful on the exterior, but a big bundle of nerves and a volcano of emotion on the inside. Of course, I hid this anxious entanglement very well from others by using distance and separation to contain it. I figured if I could keep it under wraps, I could contain the extensive amount of resistance within the body that I felt on a daily basis. For years, I couldn't figure out how all of this fear had accumulated in my tissues. I had a lovely childhood and had been blessed with beautiful experiences—so why all the fear? After undergoing some bodywork for trauma-healing, my practitioner detected that my psoas had as much chronic tension as victims of childhood abuse. What was going on?

What I just recently unraveled through heart-centered attunement was that the fear that had invaded my body was a result of massive amounts of collective, unconscious fear. As an intuitive empath and sensitive, I lacked the tools and skills to protect my body from harmful energies swirling around the planet. One of my teachers explained that this situation that is common to sensitives and light-workers and is commonly referred to as "hitchhiker syndrome." It was if I were carrying a hitchhiker on my back that continuously filled my body and being with fear; it wasn't coming from me, but it was certainly coming along beside me and impacting my journey. In my case it was subtle, a sort of continuous flow of understated fear over decades. It was hardly noticeable until I started to experience disharmony in my body after having children.

Although having breech babies and three c-sections in less than four years didn't help the situation, I now realize it was divine unfolding in my healing journey. When you have a body that is filled with fear—even if you are a highly functional fear-carrier like I was—eventually that body loses its luminescence and vital force. For me, this happened during my second pregnancy. I had reached a breakpoint where the universe was delivering all sorts of human experiences that brought this fear raging to the surface—as if the universe was throwing multiple fear-balls at me and counting how many I could catch until I no longer had the energy to keep going.

It is my experience that when we birth our babies, we birth with them some of the lesser appealing energies, such as fear or stored trauma, that exist within us. What doctors call postpartum depression I believe is actually a letting go, and it is a natural part of our healing process so we can come to wholeness as we raise the child. It sounds great, but in reality, we are now oozing unpleasant energy while caring for a newborn. Welcome to conscious parenting!

Here I was with a one-year-old and a newborn, healing from surgery, and being profoundly aware that something major had happened in my energy body. I was experiencing intense amounts of fear in my mind without experiencing them in the physical realm. These included the fear of not being financially able to take care of my family, the fear of losing complete security, the fear of my home falling apart (the ceiling did begin leaking at one point, so that one may have actually manifested!), the fear of thriving in my business, as well as a major hit to my self-esteem. Thriving in my business unleashed fear within my mind and body that I would be less available for my family and would carry mountains on mom-guilt. I once flew across the country for a speaking engagement just to get a phone call that one of my little guys was in the emergency room. Within minutes, I rescheduled my flight home and cancelled my speaking gig. Everything ended up fine, but this experience was just one example of my nervous system being chronically wired to fear. I have deep compassion for any new mother (or any mother) who is living through a season of significant fear. It is a complete out of body and out of mind experience. At this time, I was aware that I had an unusually significant fear of losing security (which I have always carried), but I wasn't yet conscious enough in my journey to know how to expand beyond this experience. It took another baby, a few more moves, and many more experiences to bring me to a place of true understanding and compassion.

In my heart, I have the highest state of love for myself and my journey. It is likely that this resistance within my body that I am labelling as "fear" is indeed from a major past-life event coupled with incarnating as a highly sensitive person who easily takes in fear from her surroundings. But I uncovered a deeper secret: Our entire society runs on fear. And what's more, our children are being showered with it chronically. When you sit with this reality, it hits you like a ton of bricks.

From the time I was a young child, I was showered with fear. I was afraid to get a bad mark, to speak up, to not fit in, to not be liked, to get in trouble, to speak my truth, to get pregnant, to not make a sports team, to not perform well, to not get a job, to not get into the right university, to not be perfect, and so, so many more. I am not alone in this. Consider your own experience as a child and how much fear you were exposed to. Psychologists tend to break down human fear into six distinct types:

1. The fear of poverty or loss of security
2. The fear of criticism
3. The fear of poor or loss of health
4. The fear of loss of love/someone leaving you
5. The fear of old age
6. The fear of death

(Some would argue that the fear of public speaking or public embarrassment should be on that list, too, but such a fear is ultimately rooted in the consequences of it, such as loss of income or friends.)

Within those six main types, however, are countless other fears, many of which you probably experienced as a child. These may have included but are not limited to:

- Fear of a parent
- Fear of a teacher or instructor
- Fear of failing
- Fear of not being good enough
- Fear of not fitting in
- Fear of a classmate (or a group of classmates)
- Fear of not being smart enough
- Fear of illness
- Fear of not making friends
- Fear of meeting new people
- Fear of starting a new class or course
- Fear of the new school year
- Fear of being late
- Fear of forgetting to do something
- Fear of being abandoned
- Fear of losing a game or competition
- Fear of not getting into a school or program
- Fear of not making the team
- Fear of not being liked
- Fear of not being loved for who you authentically are
- Fear of loss
- Fear of not having enough money
- Fear of losing money
- Fear of being who you truly are
- Fear of not being good enough
- Fear of not being relatable
- Fear of not getting good grades
- Fear of failing a class
- Fear of not getting into university or college
- Fear of not getting a good job (or any job at all)

- Fear of not "making it"
- Fear of the unknown

At this very moment, our work is to integrate and release harmfully high levels of fear from the Auric Body. The antidote to fear is faith. This integration and release activation is done through the heart. We must have a practice to deepen faith and trust in our divine nature—our God within. As we work daily to deepen our trust in divine and cosmic intelligence, the fear we have been carrying throughout our lives loses its grip and releases, pouring from our body. As we partner this personal practice of growing faith and trust with bodywork, miracles occur. Bodywork, yoga, breathwork, prayer, Tai Chi, meditation, cranial sacral therapy, and neuromuscular massage, all support the release of this fear from where it is stored in the body, be it the jaw, the hips, the psoas, the glutes, the ankles, the fascia, etc. This is why the imprint of fear on the body, beginning in childhood, has such a profound impact on the rest of our lives and on our ascension path, and why it is so essential that we do the work required to heal from it.

Fear is implanted in the body before birth and grows in size with age. As adults, we carry additional worries about our homes, our security, our health, our jobs, and our mortality. When we become parents, we not only have our previous fears to deal with, but we also carry all the new fears about keeping our little ones safe, protected, sheltered, healthy, and well. It's no wonder today that our beautiful mothers are grieving and hurting like never before. They feel all the increasing pressure and fear without much hope for relief or resolution.

On a global scale, there is a complete lack of luminous light and heart-centered leaders who are spiritually evolved enough to make highest-order decisions for the greater good. It's not that there aren't incredibly luminous people, organizations, and experiences all over the world today, but they tend not to be the ones in the upper echelons of power. We need more light-workers and heart-centered leaders to rise to public roles. Over a decade ago, I was recruited to run for office, and I remember telling my parents after that meeting that I would never do anything of the sort. That encounter ended up leading to a dinner party at the Canadian Prime Minister's house where I spent most of the night hoping no one could read my aura or my mind because I felt so wildly out of place! That dinner opened my eyes to how completely different I saw the world and how heart- and soul-centered leadership was, in some way, my destiny. Even though I didn't enter politics, I made a decision that day to pursue the highest expression of myself I possibly could and committed to the path of spiritual leadership no matter what. It took me some time to detach from my preconceived ideas about what that path would look like rather than allowing the universe to direct me where I needed to go, but I eventually got there. It also required me to totally surrender to what other people thought of me. I had to be ok with disappointing people, not being liked and not fitting in. As difficult as this process was (and still is), it was actually extremely therapeutic and healing for someone who lived the majority of her life as a people pleaser. Learning to detach from the opinions of others is one of the unavoidable lessons on the spiritual path.

I recently found out that one of the most beautiful light-workers I know is running for office, and it made my heart sing. Lightworkers in politics are paving a new path for world-healing to take place. This is something we should actively encourage and manifest in an effort to help move our world towards healing and wholeness.

Releasing Resistance with Heart Surrender

Every day, I have made it a practice to scan my entire body for energetic blocks that I refer to as resistance. As body awareness strengthens, it becomes extremely easy to feel even the slightest block or resistance in the body. You develop a heightened ability to feel exactly where it is. Strong resistance often develops in the ankles, knees, lower back, upper back, chest, hips, belly, throat, jaw, and head, but it can develop along all meridians of the body and throughout any and all major and minor chakra centers.

Fear (along with shame and guilt) takes up residence in the body with a particular weight and density that can feel like a heap of bricks is sitting in your hips and belly. With time, carrying fear or any other low vibrational energy in the body can feel like you have heavy bricks in your solar plexus. Although we all store and carry weight differently, energetic weight tends to accumulate in similar areas throughout the body or where blockages or weaknesses lie. I have had countless clients who have beautiful nutritional practices but carry excess energetic waste that has manifested over time, as physical weight. Very commonly, this is stored in the abdomen around the solar plexus but can accumulate anywhere throughout the first through third chakras. Aside from hormonal differences and individual body chemistry, there are energetic reasons as well why women (in particular) tend to have areas that hold more resistance in the form of energetic waste and weight.

Many of us go through life stuck on an emotional loop. Through the eyes of the heart, we can begin to understand that emotions are not just reactions and that we can actually choose what emotional state we would like to experience. We don't have to be victims of our emotions.

Some emotions renew us, and some deplete us. Your body knows the difference. Every time you make an emotional shift (e.g., from anger to joy or from fear to love), approximately 1,400 biochemical changes take place inside you immediately, especially hormonally, and affect your body for hours. Depleting emotions release excessive amounts of hormones such as cortisol and adrenaline into the bloodstream. This excessive release acidifies the body. Renewing emotions produce regenerative hormones such as DHEA and oxytocin. This supports body-repair, renewal, and healing. By activating the power of the heart, we can effectively move from depleting to renewing emotions.

As a species, humans' energy bodies have undergone some major shifts recently. This means that the things you used to do to feel light and lively may not give you the same results now that they did a few years ago. You can blame it on age or hormones, but I tend to see hidden messages in these realities. When energy shifts within and around our body, it can be a signal that it is time to ascend to higher levels of light with new modalities and practices for our minds, emotions, and bodies. Perhaps the workout regime that kept you so fit a few years ago is actually harming and degenerating your vital body today. Perhaps a more yin lifestyle with less fire energy would serve your body best in transformative healing. Rather than adding fire to the fire by doing high intensity hot yoga, perhaps it is cosmic time to substitute for a more gentle and restorative practice. I will speak more on this in Chapter 6 (Auric Health), but these changes might be temporary or they may, in fact, be your new normal. This is why it is so important to be in total resonance with your body—so you can listen and know.

As you seek to release resistance stored in the body, consider the following questions:

1. *What resistance do you feel you are carrying in your body right now?* Some examples include fear, guilt, grief, anger, rage, frustration, sadness, despair, hopelessness, or shame.
2. *Where do you feel you predominantly store this resistance within your body?* Some examples are legs, throat, heart, lungs, abdomen, intestinal tract, reproductive organs, hips, knees, feet, or elbows.
3. *With your eyes closed and your hand on your heart, ask yourself if you are ready to release this resistance from the body.* If the answer is yes, speak out loud "I am ready to release all resistance from my body."

As authors and pioneer energy workers Esther and Jerry Hicks would say: "Ask and it is given." Although you may not feel instant change, the process of release and surrender is activated through that simple action. You have already started a journey towards cellular, body, and auric integration and harmony. Over the next few days, months, and maybe even years, you will be taken on a journey of high coherence. Now that you have begun, you work is to align and communicate with your heart as often as possible throughout the day and use other techniques throughout this book that feel right to you, as well as your own intuitive messages and guidance.

Heart Centered Ascension

"The longest journey you will ever make in your life is the one from your head to your heart"

-Sioux Saying

The first path of ascension taught throughout history is the bottom-up approach to spiritual awakening. Many ancient texts (such as the Vedas) explore and teach on the activation of the spiritual energy lying dormant at the base of the spine (*kundalini*). This path of spiritual ascension focuses on awakening kundalini energy and moving it up the spine until it activates the pineal gland in the brain (the portal to the cosmos). Kundalini is often confused with Prana, but Prana is the basic lifeforce energy in the body while Kundalini is a much more subtle form. Prana is always active in the human body while Kundalini rest dormant at the base of the spine unless activated. When kundalini is activated, there is a very distinct energetic charge that is often referred to as Kundalini awakening.

A second spiritual ascension path is taught in many traditions, including Christian mysticism, where God's grace enters your crown and travels down and throughout the body illuminating the light-body. This top-down ascension path is often illustrated in guided meditations as the sensation of feeling and seeing the light of the sun above your head entering your crown and travelling down throughout your entire body. When light is travelling down your body starting from your crown, this is an illustration of the top-down path for spiritual ascension.

The third path of ascension focuses on the heart. In this path, the heart is at the very center of spiritual activation. It is a center-out approach. This is the activation of the fire in the heart that then expands out from its center to activate the entire body as well as the world around. In this approach, the focus is to activate the heart chakra first, which then balances and harmonizes all other energy centers of the body.

I believe all three paths to be beautiful and true, and not one path works for everyone. It is highly likely that all three are valuable and hold truth at different spiritual stages in life. It is possible that they each hold great power but are more relevant during different cosmic ages. Many traditions also recommend using these paths in combination. Chinese medicine, for example, uses the top-down and bottom-up approach to energy flow where internal alchemy is concerned. It will be up to the individual to explore, examine, and educate while intuitively connecting with the master within. For the cosmic age we have recently entered, there is great relevance today to the third path of spiritual ascension—awakening through the heart. Based on where we are today on the cosmic continuum, heart-centered ascension and activation is the key to healing, awakening, and high clairvoyance. I encourage you to study all three paths as well as integrated practices from each method to feel and explore your own evolutionary soul path.

Intuition

It is important to understand that unless your childhood included a highly expressive and artistic daily rhythm, it is likely that connection with intuition has been severed. We are designed to be deeply intuitive on a moment-by-moment basis. We are guided beyond physical comprehension at every single moment. The trouble begins early in life where we begin to prioritize the outside world, society, and our five senses above our *internal* vibes. This is one of the greatest reasons for the current state of chaos in our lives. We are given directives throughout the day, direct from our soul and Source, but we are conditioned to ignore the guidance. We have our very own built-in therapist who is patiently waiting for her one and only client. When the intuitive wire is cut, our being falls out of resonance with Source and soul.

Surrender to the heart

The art of true surrender is one of the most difficult things to do. We all understand it in theory, but practice is another story. It is an entirely new thing to experience full surrender in every cell of your body. This experience is one that requires spiritual support and what some call "the power of grace." Think of a time when you knew in your heart you should forgive someone, but your head just couldn't let it go. You tried and tried to shake the wrongdoing, yet you still felt the need to cling to the betrayal or event, even if it cost you months or years of energetic hemorrhage, health decline, and rapid aging. The energetic fortress we have built around us is a powerful one. When we feel threated or harmed in any way, the fortress is activated—often by an inflamed ego.

Heart Harmony

As we build awareness, there is a desire within us to create harmony between our heart, brain, and emotions. We all seek to build high heart cohesion. This work should be taught to children and flood the educational system. I am committed to making sure my children understand this work so that they can support their own bodies and beings as well as support others during their lifetime. Many souls are incarnating right now that are evolved at an extremely high level. Perhaps you are a parent to one of these evolved ones. I joke to my husband that on top of the mom-guilt I already carry, now I have to digest the fact that at least one (if not more) of my children is a more evolved soul than I am! Our job is to support their journeys on earth with the tools and techniques that we wish we had much earlier in our lives.

The most efficient and effective ways to activate heart harmony is to immerse yourself in nature every day. To the greatest extent possible, set up your home as if it were a garden. Infuse your home with natural smells, shapes, sunlight, moonlight, hydration, simplicity, colors, and beauty that you find in nature. Remove all clutter and chaos that will constrict the heart and confuse the mind. (More on this in a future chapter.) Breathwork and meditation and/or prayer are the complimentary practices that, when practiced daily, will create the most intimate relationship with your heart.

Exercises and suggestions for creating high heart cohesion include:

* Meditation
* Prayer
* Music
* Baths
* Intimacy
* Time with loved ones
* Art
* Herbals
* Hugs
* Spiritually centered therapy
* Sound healing
* Flower essence medicine
* Homeopathy
* Yin and restorative yoga
* Chakra healing
* Tai Chi
* Qigong
* Reiki
* Laughter
* Crystals
* Journaling
* Bodywork

Death

Our soul does not fear death. Our soul does not grieve the death of others. Our soul has a cosmic understanding that our soul-family travels together and will be united again. When we understand the truth of the cosmic continuum of all things, our relationships with loved ones do not change after death. Ego love is seasonal; soul-love is eternal.

Your Spiritual Council

It can be difficult to navigate the twists and turns that come with incarnating in human form. This spiritual council facilitates the union of individual mind with divine mind. A practice that can be very healing and beneficial is to form a spiritual council for yourself. This purpose of your spiritual council is to create a board of directors of sorts that is made up of highly evolved beings, ascended masters, saints, and any soul-family member who now dwells in higher dimensions. As an example, you may wish to include your guardian angel, a parent who has passed, a favorite family member, an archangel, a great mystic or saint. Call a meeting with your spiritual council anytime you feel spiritual guidance is needed or helpful. It is also a lovely practice to call in your spiritual council before bed should a higher realm conversation or discussion be in order.

Auric Ascension

As spiritual initiation draws near for many, we begin to focus much more on our internal landscape than our external one. We become more engaged with our inner universe as well as how it dances with the outer one. We have many portals within the body that help us gain access to cosmic wisdom that can then be used to infuse art, beauty, and rhythm into our daily life. Two powerful portals that lie within the body include the pineal gland and the heart chakra.

When we use yoga, meditation, prayer, and other spiritual practices, we use them as tools to move our awareness up to the pineal gland. Many beings right now are preparing for spiritual initiation or have recently been initiated into the higher dimensions of cosmic wisdom. When one is initiated, they are invited into the divine temple of absolute knowledge. This is also often referred to as having access to the Akashic records. For anyone on a spiritual path, everything up to this point has been spiritual fitness. We have been working out our spiritual muscles in order to be able to handle higher frequencies of light in our lives while staying grounded and balanced in daily living. When ascension happens too quickly, it is difficult for the mind and body to handle such high frequency light and can result in body and/or mental breakdown. A slow and steady pace may not always please the ego, but it is a perfect path for the soul.

As we move to and through the quantum field and fourth dimensional space, we are gaining a better understanding of how very mysterious and infinite our reality really is. As our spiritual quest gets juicier, we open our minds and hearts to the possibility that much of what we believe to be true is not. We are connected with everything in every dimension. This means that the likelihood we are intergalactic in nature and genetic make-up is high. Are we a genetic cocktail of many different cosmic species? It is a very high probability. For this reason, we are now evolving our spiritual questions and moving beyond Ancestry DNA. We are now seeking even deeper truths including our very planetary origins. I do believe the ancient continents of Atlantis and Lemuria to have existed, as do many highly evolved philosophers, channelers, and scientists. I also believe that at this moment in time, we are being drawn to a more technology inspired lifestyle or a naturally inspired one. This might be linked to a stronger cellular resonance towards technology and artificial intelligence for those with stronger genetic ties to Atlantis. Those more intuitively drawn to nature, flower essences, limited technology, minimalism, and human connection could be tuning into their Lemuria intuitive vibes.

There is so much scientific evidence proving our history goes back far beyond ancient Egypt and even Sumer. Our history stretches hundreds of thousands of years into the past—a fact that does not seem to be taught in any of our history classes in school.

My journey is similar to many others who have also had the veil of disinformation and limited vision lifted during this incarnation. For me, the process was a kind of thinning that happened gradually over many decades. For my husband, the veil was ripped off like a bandage when he was young. Regardless of when and how this process occurs for you, the ascension path takes commitment, courage, integrity, and spiritual resilience.

Over the past few years, my spiritual journey has challenged my spiritual resilience in many ways. Although I have been preparing for this shift in human thinking most of my life, like any strength-building activity, physical world experiences that strengthen our souls are never easy. Maybe you've felt this, too. Pulling back the curtain to reveal our immense spiritual potential can be exhausting and enlightening at the same time. For me, these past few years have been an experience of healing grief—both personal and collective. I have gained a deeper spiritual understanding of the collective trauma children are exposed to when their authentic nature is supressed and healthy attachments are under-developed. The detrimental impact chronic fear has on the body (especially for children) has been a particular focus for me. Most bodies are riddled with fear, which results in dis-order not only in the body but in life. Because fear is so conditioned, chronic, and common, it creeps along unnoticed as most people are unaware of which chef is actually in the kitchen—Chef Fear.

As parents, we have a sacred responsibility to help our children heal, and an essential part of this process is healing ourselves first. Our children will often play out the disintegrated pieces of ourselves leading to a little extra triggering on our end. The parent that isn't being triggered by the child's behavior is likely integrated and healed for that particular life lesson. The parent who is watching their child play out the very wound in their being, however, is particularly emotionally charged. What a divine play we find ourselves in. As we strengthen spiritual sight, we slowly begin to heal with grace and gentleness.

The first thing we have to understand is the "innocent child" archetype that exists in all of us. For some people, profound trauma such as a near-death experience or the death of a parent tragically crushes that innocence early in life. For others, the innocence is preserved well into adulthood; that was the case with me. The death of my innocent child archetype began at 35 with a series of experiences including several traumatic conflicts, a miscarriage, the death of my father, and finally culminating in the massive planetary and humanity shift in 2020. As I became aware of the layered grief I was storing in my body—the death of my innocent child archetype was taking place. This symbolic death gave me a reason to fully grieve. Not only was I grieving personally but the world around me was grieving a symbolic death of "old ways" and "normal life." It felt as though my personal experience was fully playing out at the planetary level, which was quite a trip. The whole experience was beyond language. Please know that if you are also experiencing layers of both physical and spiritual grief right now, this experience can be a lonely one. You may be surrounded by people, but this intimate experience of symbolic death and mourning (which may or may not also include grieving the physical death of a loved one) must be processed alone. Stillness must be created where it is just you and the divine. Entering the interior castle now begins. As lonely as this stage in spiritual maturation can feel, know that you are never alone. The angelic realm is holding you very tightly and will likely share a sign or a signal from time to time to remind you that you are deeply held and loved.

Grieving is healing, so allow yourself to experience it fully. This will better equip you for helping your children (if you are a parent) as well as others in your life who look to you for guidance and support. We must all gain a deep understanding in our bodies that we indeed incarnated into this lifetime and timeline with specific contracts and tasks to fulfill. We are here to experience, learn, and grow.

Our work is to not only heal ourselves but to do the very cosmic work of healing multiple generations and timelines of experiences. Lucky us!

Free will and the power of choice are tools of ascension, and when our bodies are imprisoned by fear, our decisions are as well. Throughout our lives, we are faced with many experiences and choices that impact the ascension process; there really are no neutral choices. The law of cause and effect, or karma, plays out in some way based upon what we choose. Free will is a tremendous power, and in today's reality, choices have consequences that seem to be playing out faster than ever before. As timelines are merging and the illusion of time speeds up, we are all experiencing what is often referred to as "instant karma" or quicker impact from the choices we make. Over the past few years, choices have become heavier and more impactful, and the fallout more significant. We must make a commitment to purposeful choices, such as:

* To keep our bodies pure and clean
* To steer clear of drama, gossip, and superficial chaos
* To always be kind and compassionate towards ourselves and others
* To practice mindful movement (such as yoga, tai chi, dance, etc.)
* To meditate daily (This one took me until my forties to commit to!)
* To study spiritual science
* To have a daily spiritual practice
* To be mindful of words and language
* To be deeply authentic and integrous
* To create beauty and order in life
* To hydrate the body
* To always lead with love

The universe always leaves clues as to what it desires from you, and your body does as well. You will gain so much insight and wisdom from your body as to whether you are on your best spiritual track. Making spiritually wise choices each day (these are typically ones that benefit you in the long term rather than the short term, but sometimes it's actually both!), equips you with the cosmic muscles to ascend with grace and purity. As you strengthen your spiritual muscles through beautiful choices, you will notice, with time, your physical world as well as your body, dramatically transform. For some it can seem instantaneous; for others this transformation may occur over several years.

It is important to be mindful of the "limbo lull" along the ascension journey. This phase frequently manifests as confusion, dullness, frustration, and an inability to animate amazingness in life. For many of my clients, this is frustrating as they used to be so good at manifesting visions and vitality. Now, all they seem to be able to manifest are less-than-favorable physical body funks, such as:

* Numbness and tingling without any medical explanation
* Memory Fog
* Brain fog
* Joint pain
* Inflammation
* Digestive Issues
* Sadness/Depression/Anxiety
* Vertigo
* Seeing colors/Auras
* Astral Projection
* Lucid Dreams
* Hearing or feeling thoughts of others (detailed and strong)
* Significant increase in empathy, compassion, sensitivity
* Heightened sensitivity to chemicals, foods, environmental factors, EMFs (Electric and Magnetic Fields)
* Dizziness
* Trouble sleeping
* Blurred vision
* Skin rashes or itching

* Vaginal discomfort/pain/itching during intercourse
* Food sensitivities
* Auto-immune symptoms
* Hair loss
* Having trouble making decisions
* Feeling stuck or in limbo
* Feeling unclear and unsure

The physical body, and especially the immune system, must be guarded and nurtured throughout life with great care and sacredness. Doing so will greatly enhance the ability to self-heal and rebound from life's curveballs. As you open, expand, and ascend, you must protect your immune system like a child, because the immune system is, in many ways, the gateway between the physical body and higher self.

According to Rudolf Steiner, the end of the dark age (known in Hinduism as the Kali Yuga) happened at a nodal year in time: 1899. Since this date, we have entered an ascended cosmic time in which we are beginning to experience unity with the cosmos. This new age will also bring with it a new clairvoyant phase. Many of us will begin to experience high clairvoyance. Unlike traditional clairvoyance, where higher dimensional truth and wisdom were pulled down into the third dimension, this new clairvoyance brings with it an ability to ascend into higher dimensions of consciousness to see, hear, and feel cosmic truths. We will develop abilities to ascend into the higher realms gaining unlimited access to Akashic records, divine truth, and cosmic wisdom. This is rapidly taking place at quantum speeds, so don't be surprised if your new clairvoyance has recently kicked in. Kriya yoga is an example of a practice that supports this new clairvoyance awakening.

Working with the Archangel systems is a helpful and important daily practice that serves the ascension and high clairvoyance process. Archangels are expressions of total wisdom, total power, and total love. Archangels do not have a subconscious but, rather, have absolute self-awareness. Total attunement is required to access the Archangel order, which is why a daily spiritual practice is so important today. Through meditation, prayer, and other spiritual practices, we can tune into the total wisdom, power, and love of the Archangel order. They work to keep the planets in balance in space as well as with the sun (Archangel home base). Archangels communicate through color and sound. When our heart is attuned to the frequency of the Archangels, we can shape symbols and images, and put into matter the perfect order that these angelic beings are able to deliver. We each have a guardian Archangel who accompanies us through all of our incarnations. This guardian archangel is always within us and is sometimes referred to as our "twin soul." In addition to our guardian Archangel, here are a few of the Archangels always available and accessible to you:

Archangel Michael: The great god and the Archangel of fire and light; the Archangel of protection, cleansing, and clearing; forces of movement and of the sun.

Archangel Rafael: The god of sun vibration and controller of electromagnetic forces and lifeforce; healing and health restoration throughout the entire Auric Body (including healing from addiction); forces of healing.

Archangel Gabriel: Ruler of water and liquids and the steward of the physical kingdom; the divine messenger; forces of nourishment and of the moon. Gabriel can be called upon for the protection of children and through pregnancy and parenting and to help with authentic expression and loving communication.

Archangel Uriel: Coordinator of all work within the physical body; holds the law of harmony and order; forces of thought. Uriel can be called upon for loving doses of creative inspiration and to illuminate the mind.

Archangel Chamuel: Worker of peace and light within the material body; healer of chronic worry and anxiety. Chamuel can be called upon when seeking deep inner peace or peace within a relationship.

Archangel Ariel: The angel of earth and water; healing angel of nature. Call upon Archangel Ariel to protect Mother Earth and all of her creatures.

Archangel Metatron: the angel of presence; guide of "indigo children" (children who are more sensitive and attuned to the spiritual world and often exhibit high perception abilities) and all who commit to the spiritual path. Metatron can be called upon to help you warp time and breakthrough limits of human conditioning by heightening and developing high clairvoyance. Metatron also helps to clear lower vibrations from your auric field.

Archangel Sandalphon: the angel of music and prayer; giver of clarity and vision. Call on Sandalphon for discernment when seeking highest spiritual choices and truth or to bring a desire to full expression and manifestation.

Chapter 5: The Auric Body

"The sun is the seed of this solar system from which all manifestations of ideas in the entire system extend, and to which they return. All things in the solar system come from the sun and return to it."
—Walter Russell

The Auric Body is a Light Body that radiates light from the inside out. As self-actualization develops, one can consciously engage in practices and rituals each day that illuminate the physical body and expand the aura. With practice, it is possible to extend and expand the Light Body. As we reorder the body, the emotions, and the mind back to a state of wholeness and integrity, we expand our aura and light signature. As we realign our posture and being with the heavens above and earth below, a radically higher frequency can be felt by the self and by others. The body is an expression of the mind. When you impress an idea upon your subconscious mind, it alters the vibrational structure of your body. The Auric Body is the continuum of vital lifeforce that spans all layers of the aura as well as the physical body. It is the continuum of energy that flows between the physical and energetic body. If we do not fully embody the Auric Body, we will never find beauty and happiness in the world—no matter how beautiful our home or city is. It may be comforting to come to the realization right now that we are all in the etheric body shop. We are all upleveling and recalibrating our physical and energy bodies, the results of which will be felt on the physical plane. Physical, mental, and emotional tune-ups are happening right now at warp speeds, which is why self-compassion, patience, and incredible self-love are all of highest order of importance at this very moment.

The single most sacred principle of illuminating the Auric Body is to fully love and embrace every aspect, dimension, and inch of YOU. This seems so simple, but it is the very principle that keeps most people away from the most glorious and illuminated Auric Body. This chapter will review and reflect on many aspects of the physical and subtle bodies, but they are ultimately meaningless unless we first choose to hold ourselves sacred within our heart. This is the very foundation of for Auric Living.

'Those whose vital spirit is scattered outwardly and whose intellectual ruminations ramble inwardly cannot govern their bodies. When what the spirit employs is distant, then what it loses is nearby. So know the world without going out the door, know the weather without looking out the window; the further out it goes, the less knowledge is. This means that when pure sincerity emerges from within, spiritual energy moves in heaven'.

—*Lao Tzu*

True happiness comes from being connected to the higher self, to Spirit (to Source), and to Mother Earth, and you can only accomplish this through integrated and harmonious living. We are all connected. The law of correspondence teaches "as above, so below." (You're going to hear me say that a lot.) In other words, we are micro-expressions of an infinite macro, and it's time to recognize that everything is energy first, matter second. What we experience in the physical realm originates in the energetic realm. This must also apply to the human body. If we truly want to heal, we not only care for the physical body, but we must also deeply nurture the energy body. We must remember that our energy body holds the blueprint for the physical body, so without healing the energy body, the physical body simply cannot heal. More and more integrative health care providers and healers are beginning to teach that the energy signature of a person is the primary focus for true healing. Yes, treating the body is important, but the true practice is to re-establish the continuum of vital lifeforce flowing throughout all layers of the Auric Body. We must learn to see our physical body and energy body as a continuum of *prana*—the Auric Body.

When we experience dis-ease or disharmony at the physical level, this is not the root cause of the experience, just the final manifestation of it. Everything is energy first, which means that the manifestation of disharmony in the physical body was an energetic one before it showed up physically. We must explore our bodies and beings as harmonious units of light that have infinite potential and power to heal. We must take a multidimensional approach to healing by understanding the link between the physical body and the aura, as well as how both communicate via channels of light throughout the body and energy centers (which I often refer to as portals).

Light is the foundation of all matter–a collection of etheric vibrations spreading out from a center. For earthlings, this most important source light is the sun. Information travels on rays of light (from the sun and throughout our entire body. Einstein explained that matter can be understood as light energy condensed with a slow enough vibration to see and interact with. Tibetan Buddhism and Daoism beliefs include the existence of a body of light known as the "Rainbow Body" that surrounds the physical body in highly ascended spiritual masters who have experiences of higher consciousness. Sacred teachings associate this Rainbow Body with the "Great Perfection" or "Great Completion" (also called *Dzogchen*), as the body functions optimally from a very high state of consciousness and harmony. The reference to the rainbow, comes from the color associations of the elemental makeup: white as space, red as fire, green as wind (air), yellow as earth and blue as water. A rainbow is the cosmic manifestation of divinity. Those who attain the Rainbow Body have the ability to perceive the essence of everything as pure light in motion. One of the reasons a regular meditation practice is so powerful is because it can reverse or lighten the manifestation process from dense physical matter back to pure light. The objective is to remain in physical form yet transmit the brightest light. If we want to fully express and experience ourselves as Light Bodies, silence and stillness must become a regular practice—not only for our own healing and awakening but also for that of the planet.

To better understand the light that we seek to radiate from our beings, it is helpful to understand psychic light. Aside from the physical light we see, there is also psychic light. This is the divine light that lies within each atom, each cell, and all of existence. All of our emotions are birthed and develop from this psychic light. The brighter our own psychic light, the brighter our absolute experience in this world. (We will discuss this auric brilliance as we learn about the layers of the aura.) When we shine bright with psychic light, we truly become Light Bodies. We require less external motivation, less food, less activity, and less of everything to feel complete in physical form. We are in a state of aura expansion and heightened spiritual influence in the physical world. When our psychic light shines bright, all we require to feel happy and complete is optimal breath, simple food, and simple living. This is the happiness we all crave. This doesn't mean that we don't enjoy and show gratitude for the frills and festivities of life, but they do not define us nor do we need them to feel complete. We practice compassionate detachment. Does this then mean that we are not attached to our families, our children and our precious friends? In a sense, yes—but probably not in the way you are thinking. Compassionate detachment from this perspective means we love simply and purely, not to gain something or to expect something but simply to shine our love. When expectation sets in, chaos in some form always follows. When we expect our children, friends, and family to behave or react in certain ways after we do a good deed, we have detached from compassionate detachment! Living every day with an open heart that doesn't expect anything in return may take many lifetimes to achieve, but starting the journey today is a cosmic choice!

The personal transformation journey from one of physical density, energetic heaviness, and inner resistance to one of Light

Body living takes commitment. This is an evolutionary process as we ascend to higher states of light and consciousness as a collective. Becoming a Light Body is a state of being grounded and present in physical form yet embodying and illuminating pure divine light. This is a state where the Auric Body is beautifully ordered, aligned and expansive. In this state, the physical body experiences harmonic health while the aura beams so bright that an entire city is spiritually shifted. A Light Body individual holds and radiates superlight. This is a very self-aware soul! This individual is perfectly attuned with nature and with the entire universe. A superlight soul seeks nothing in return for his or her action and experiences continuous harmony and happiness.

I hope the teachings in this book will support the highest expression of your very own Rainbow Body as a full and authentic expression of the sun. The Auric Body is that very expression of highest order, light, love, and radiant health. Your shimmering body of light is ready to fully shine and resonate with its own very special tone that harmonizes with the cadence of life. When you unlock your Auric Body, your light and sound will fully align with the cosmos above, and the earth below.

As we know from quantum physics, even light is caged by the force of gravity to the point that intense gravity can shape and bend light. In humans, these light fields are related to the electromagnetic signature of the body, or as a person's aura. These biofields, which are present throughout the body but also surrounding it, can be felt, measured, and photographed. Those with high clairvoyance abilities can often see the colors, shapes and textures that make up a person's aura. There is a stream of light travelling in subtle physical structures throughout and around the body. In other words, *we truly are Light Bodies.*

According to Walter Russell, author of *The Universal One,* "Everything in nature is a moving extension from a still point of the one light." This is a particularly powerful statement for understanding the heart of Auric Living, because I have always believed we come from and return to the sun. Who hasn't experienced moments of tremendous beauty and wonder when witnessing a sunbeam break through the clouds? In my own life, when loved ones have passed away or I've felt particularly low, I've felt the sun come out of nowhere and beam its cosmic rays directly onto my face. I felt calm and warm, knowing that the sun is far more than just a heating and lighting machine for our solar system. There is something primal in our connection to the sun as a source of light and life.

In a subsequent book, *The Secret of Light*, Russell wrote, "the underlying law of creation is rhythmic balanced interchange in all transactions in nature. It is the one principle upon which the continuity of the universe depends." Russell explains that we are all on a journey towards cosmic oneness and that we cannot deviate from the fixed orbit that will eventually take us to our divine destination. Oneness of the light is divided on the physical plane into an equal and opposite two, according to Russell, in order to experience independence and physical expression. All interchange between the two separates must be equal in their giving so that balance is always maintained or achievable by a rebalancing. The yin/yang balance is illustrated perfectly here. Our work is then to set natural rhythm, regain cosmic harmony, and find unity within ourselves and the world around us.

When I speak of your Auric Body, I am referring to the harmonious continuum of light between your physical body and the numerous layers of the subtle body that make up energy body. Although the subtle bodies are mostly disregarded in medical schools today, they have played a significant role throughout history. My medical school anatomy class had zero mention of the aura, yet ancient texts from around the world understood the slight but powerful significance of the subtle bodies that surround the physical body in terms of physical body wellbeing, as well as the devastating physical effects that can result when subtle bodies are damaged and disrupted.

Auric Living includes looking at our bodies and beings as multidimensional illuminated crystal grids that have powers beyond our wildest imagination. If we consider the main chakra centers of the body to be portals, imagine how our abilities and gifts will grow as we learn to work with them. No longer can we perceive our beings as physical bodies alone; they are light beings of the highest order, capable of magical expression. All we need to do is find harmony inwardly so we can cosmically create outwardly—shouldn't be so hard, right?

We must consciously choose which experience to bring into our reality from an infinite number of possible experiences, but... how does one choose? How does the selection process work at each moment for whatever reality we actually experience?

The answer lies in our Auric Body. We have been trained to believe that only what we see is what is true. Our physical bodies have therefore been given center stage and have been groomed to look good, fit in, and take in all sorts of emotional and energetic baggage without filtration. We have been conditioned to consume and fill all aspects of life, including our physical bodies. As we stuff our bodies, we are filled with grief and heaviness rather than the lightness and completeness we so desperately seek. The practice of Auric Living inspires us to shift our focus from physical body obsession to Auric Body awareness. Auric Body awareness unlocks a level of compassion that deeply transforms all dimensions of life.

One of the great illusions is that we are predominantly physical matter rather than cosmic energy. The flow of all things works in this direction as well: energy first, matter second. If not, what is it that makes this big bundle of chemistry think and feel? Where do feelings come from? Where does inspiration come from? How much energetic potential do we really have? As we awaken as a collective, we are now transforming knowledge to wisdom where cosmic truth is concerned and truly embracing the fact that we are spiritual beings having a temporary physical experience.

What is most important to understand is that energy should flow harmoniously and healthily throughout the body. We should also have an intuitive ability to release lower vibrational energy that doesn't serve our greatest good, just as we do physical waste. Unfortunately, we are not trained as children how to create our light shields and our boundaries, or how to protect our portals.

Without knowing it, we welcome all kinds of negative energies that take up residence in our bodies and eventually manifest into physical waste and even physical weight as well.

Your Auric Body is the unity between all dimensions and aspects of you—physical and non-physical alike. You cannot heal by treating the physical body alone, but neither can you ignore the physical body while working with the subtle bodies that make up your aura.

There is also integration and cohesion with the planetary and cosmic bodies, which we will touch on throughout the book, but this chapter will predominantly focus on your personal field of love and light. Just know that as you strengthen, further integrate, and build cohesion throughout your own Auric Body, you will shine brightly as a unified field that connects with all life—the planetary field as well as cosmic fields.

As with so many things, the very center of health, healing, and Auric Living is the heart. The heart is the center of your universe, and all healing happens through it. When we experience disease or, more accurately, *dis-ease*, we are observing late physical manifestations of earlier conflicts and misalignments. Often, these earlier occurrences are mental and emotional in nature. Everything is an energetic experience. If you lower your frequency, you lower function and performance of your body as well. Although we may feel certain specific areas of discomfort, injury, or dis-ease, our *entire* physical body must be nurtured as we heal. We must also remember that attending to the physical body without also caring for the aura will not result in true healing.

As Dr. Edward Bach, the esteemed 20th century doctor, bacteriologist, and homeopathic practitioner, wrote: "Disease will never be cured or eradicated by present materialistic methods, for the simple reason that disease is, in its origin, not material." Disease, at its very root, is a conflict between soul and mind, and therefore must be healed through spiritual and mental efforts.

Samuel Hahnemann, the founder of modern homeopathic medicine as a branch of study, understood the true nature of our divinity. He studied mental attitudes and sought to find herbs and natural remedies that would not only heal the body but also the mind. He stands as part of a long line of enlightened healers throughout history who understood that disease originates in a plane above the physical. The gift that disease brings is greater awareness, an opportunity to surrender, and more compassion towards the human condition.

The Crystal Body

Consider the body to be a living and breathing crystal emporium! From the iron crystals in our blood (as confirmed by Dr. Harvey Bigelsen, MD in *Holographic Blood*) to the mysterious crystal properties of the pineal gland that respond to light, we truly are living crystal grids. Bones have the ability to convert vibrational energy (such as sound or light) into electromagnetic energy. Crystals can absorb, amplify, store, and transmit vibrational energies. Our bones alone give us a glimpse into the miraculous ability our body has at absorbing and transmitting energy from the earth, from food, and even from the cosmos. Each cell communicates to one another by way of electromagnetic conversation emitted from the nucleus of each cell. Cells speak crystal! Every cell in your body responds to the energies of love, light, and sound. It is as if we are living, breathing and animated crystal structures.

Quartz crystals, in particular, are playing significant roles today in human healing. Vogel crystals are specifically cut quartz crystals that transmit subtle energy to and from human beings. In many of his readings, Edgar Cayce cited how beneficial quartz crystal healing work was on human healing.

Torus Tuning

Energy flow throughout the body creates a pattern known as the torus. The torus is the primary pattern of energetic flow that shows up throughout our world from the smallest cell up through the farthest reaches of the cosmos. Swirls of energy form a particular repeated pattern that curves out and then back in. The torus is *holonomic,* which means that every tiny piece of the torus contains the information of the whole. The torus is also the most stable energy field; once set into motion, it is mostly self-generative and can sustain itself for an indefinite period of time. The torus can be found around the sun, planets, the earth, the heart, and our bodies, and is the most stable energetic pattern. Meditation, breathwork, and simplicity in life significantly promote the torus fields within and around the body. When torus flow is unobstructed, we are in healthy and harmonious flow in our lives. When life becomes disordered, chaotic, and out of integrity, torus flow is hindered, and we feel it with every cell of our being. I have found sound baths as well as tuning fork sessions to be very helpful when torus flow is suffering.

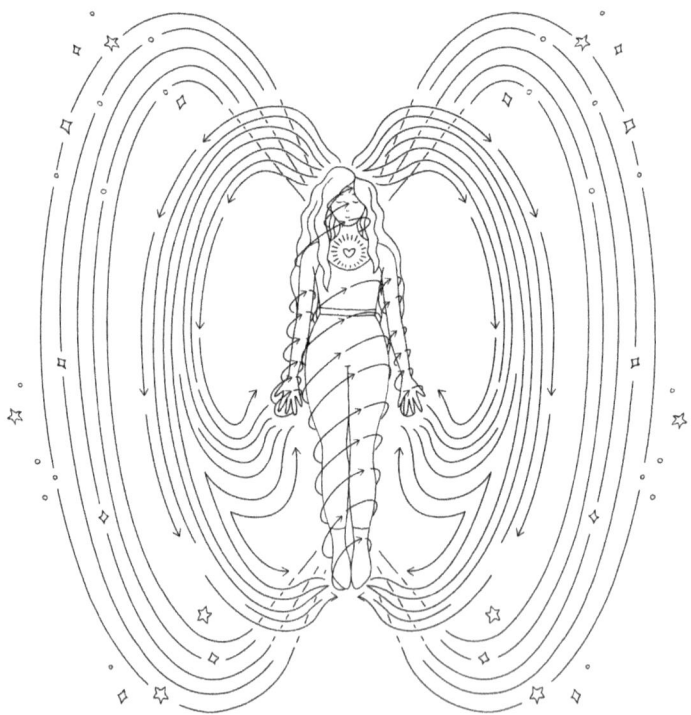

Cellular Coherence

Quartz crystals seem to play a particular role in cellular coherence and harmony within the body. All rhythms in your body are coordinated. In this way, Auric Living is rooted in having deep appreciated for all of the precious rhythms of life.

According to Mae-Wan Ho, PhD, when you are in coherence with yourself, you are producing a brilliant, unified field within all 78 trillion cells of your body. This coherence is controlled and maintained by the heart through cell-to-cell communication via electromagnetic energy exchange. Torus-tuning facilitates this energetic exchange and communication that results in cellular coherence. When we understand the symphony being played throughout our bodies at each moment, we will have the most graceful and sacred gratitude for what our body truly is and does.

The Immune System

Many mystics and spiritual teachers believe the immune system is the physical component of the body that links the individual being to the higher self. The theory is that when spiritual connection to Source is weakened, so is the immune system; when the connection is stronger, so is the immune system. For this reason, enhancing the body's natural immune response system is at the very foundation of Auric Living, because of its deeper spiritual significance and its role in linking us to the higher self.

The Endocrine Glands

The endocrine gland system is the true companion of the body. This system is at the very heart of Auric Health and is the focal point for healing and reharmonizing the body. A thriving endocrine system goes hand in hand with illuminated living. When functioning optimally, the body is fluid and flowing, and it functions with highest order. According to some health professionals, more than 75% of all dis-ease can be attributed to an under-performing endocrine gland system. This is where hydration, herbs, and Auric Nutrition comes in! Our endocrine glands impact almost every area of health because they produce hormones that are vital for normal bodily functions. When one gland's function is out of balance, all the others are impacted as well. Each gland is also beautifully connected with an associated chakra, which we will discuss below.

Consider your endocrine system as series of spiritual centers located throughout the body and vital for optimal function of the organs by which they reside. The endocrine glands play significant gatekeeper roles when it comes to the chakra system. The endocrine glands include the pituitary, pineal, hypothalamus, thalamus, thyroid, parathyroid, thymus, adrenals, pancreas, testes, and ovaries. The thymus gland is responsible for weaving the heart's love with the throat's creative expression. It is also the gland regulating a thriving immune system and producing white blood cells when healing is required. The hypothalamus is believed to be the captain of the ship and the master switchboard as it has both endocrine and neural functions. It controls everything in your body acting as both a gland and a nerve. The pituitary is a master controller itself, as it is responsible for producing hormones that regulate many of the other endocrine glands. The pituitary is the true thought receiver and switches between activation mode (will) and receiving mode. For Auric Health, it is important for the pituitary and pineal glands to work in harmony with each other. When this occurs, higher-self actualization and communication takes place. Along with being the portal to the cosmos, the pineal gland is also referred to by many mystics as being the key to eternal youth. While most of the endocrine glands are either paired or consist of chambers, the pineal is the only true singular gland within the endocrine system. This is mystically significant as it is the gland associated with the connection to the One—the I Am.

Fascia

Fascia is a thin casing of connective tissue that surrounds and holds in place organs, tissues, and structures; imagine it like the thin, white, external membrane of an orange—except that it surrounds every organ, blood vessel, bone, nerve fiber, and muscle in our body and contains nerves that make it almost as sensitive as skin. Consider fascia the divine matrix within the body where energy and consciousness flow freely—almost like a living, breathing web of consciousness that carries and stores information from both the physical and spiritual realm throughout the body. The fascia is your consciousness grid network—it is an organ in itself. When fear, tension, stress, and trauma hit the body, much of this energy is stored in the fascia. The more the fascia stores this emotional trauma, the less mobile and flexible it becomes. Physical, mental, and emotional stress all impact the flex and flow of this divine network. It is therefore very true that "our issues are stored in our tissues," and most within the fascia. One of the reasons I am such an advocate for fascial body work that there is a great deal we can do to support the body by regaining flow and mobility in our fascia.

Psoas

One of the most significant areas of the body for holding tension, stress, and trauma is the psoas. These powerful muscles are responsible for flexing our hip joint, flexing our torso, and stabilizing our spine. They are also our deepest core muscles. They have a role in breathing as well as embodying our survival instincts. Consider them to be our fight or flight muscles. The psoas muscles (there are two) are also referred to as "The Muscles of the Soul." They hold traumatic experiences at the cellular level, which is why gentle hip openers, yoga, and other forms of body work are helpful for releasing trauma. Considering a yoga therapist and/or bodywork expert is a brilliant way to begin or deepen a healing journey.

Organs

Every organ in the body is a key player in our soul symphony. When fueled with lifeforce energy, a sound mind, and healthy emotions, they make symphonic vibration. It is true that diet plays a key role in organ wellbeing, but let's not underestimate the roles mental and emotional health play on this synergetic system as well. When one organ is hindered or harmed, all organs suffer. We must gently awaken our organs as a whole and nurture them as a harmonious system of lifeforce and light.

Here is some insight as to where emotional waste may linger within the body:

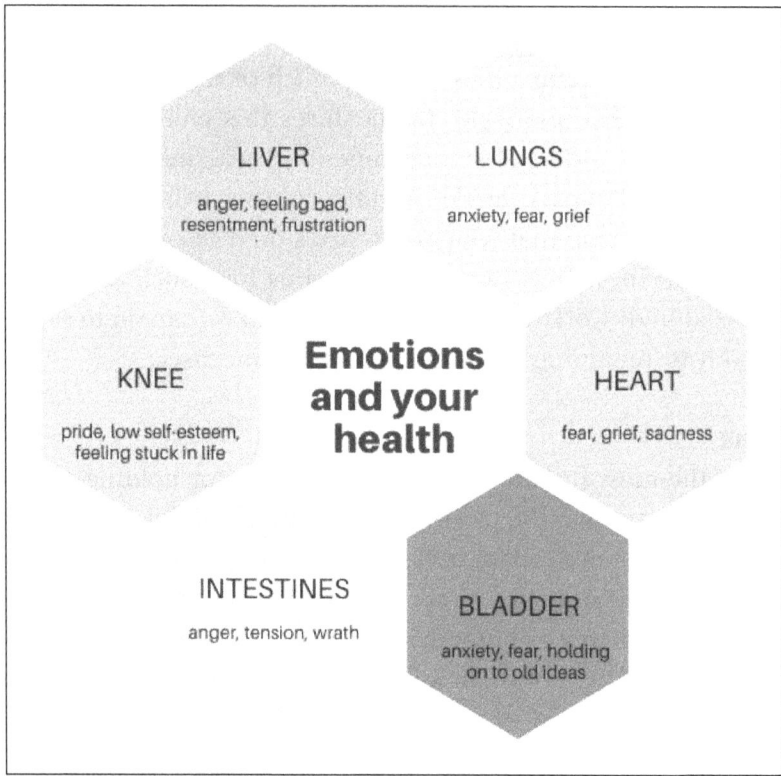

As we progress through this chapter, it is important to grasp that everything is connecting in the quantum field. There is, of course, a cosmic dance between all of this and a unified field, but for our intellectual minds to make sense of universal truth, there is great value in understanding associations and relationships between individual aspects such as meridians, chakras, the aura, and dimensions of consciousness should be taught at an early age so that we aren't introduce to it for the first time as adults.

The Vagus Nerve

Beyond the physical realm, the vagus nerve plays a powerful role in the discovery of life purpose and spiritual ascension. Vagus nerve health impacts integrity of mind, body, and soul. The vagus nerve is the longest cranial nerve in the body and spans from brain to base of the spine. It is the mystical and physical mind-body connector. In kriya yoga, this nerve plays a central role in kundalini awakening as a bioelectric communication channel for this mystical energy runs up the spine. It therefore plays a prominent role in both physical and spiritual health. When the vagus nerve has optimal function, you will feel peace and security because the vagus promotes relaxation. It is also the mystical master of the parasympathetic nervous system and impacts almost every organ of the body.

The vagus nerve controls all involuntary body processes such a breathing, speech, swallowing, heartbeat, blood pressure, bladder function, orgasm, fertility, hearing, taste, circulation, and digestion. A thriving vagus nerve connects us with creativity, inspiration, cognitive function, and clear decision-making. A hindered vagus nerve can result in chronic states of fear as well as fight, flight, or freeze and can keep us living from primal instincts instead of Auric Living. Conditions that negatively impact the vagus nerve include poor nutrition, stress, exhaustion, anger, shallow breathing, poor sleep, and lack of exercise. Conditions that support optimal vagus nerve function include breathwork, meditation, Auric Nutrition, yoga, laughing, hugs, healthy relationships, movement, stretching, relaxation, classical music, and sunshine.

The 12 Anchor Points of the Physical Body

The physical body is a physical manifestation of the forces of the 12 constellations of the zodiac as well as the spiritual forces that occupy these cosmic areas. In Chinese medicine, these anchor points are related to meridian channels within the body, to which there are 12 primary ones. Meridians are channels in the body by which life-force energy travels throughout our physical being. Meridians are the energetic rivers to the larger energy portals/chakras.

The 12 anchor points of the physical body are as follows in relation to each constellation:

1. Pisces illuminates the forces that form the feet
2. Aquarius illuminates the forces that form the ankles and calves
3. Capricorn illuminates the forces that form the knees
4. Sagittarius illuminates the forces that form the thighs
5. Scorpio illuminates the forces that form the genitals and reproductive system
6. Libra illuminates the forces that form the hips and hara region of the lower belly
7. Virgo illuminates the forces that form the solar plexus and stomach region
8. Leo illuminates the forces that form the heart and chest
9. Cancer illuminates the forces that form the ribs
10. Gemini illuminates the forces that form the shoulders and arms
11. Taurus illuminates the forces that form the throat
12. Aries illuminates the forces that form the head

It can be helpful to contemplate your particular astrological sign to identify a primary area of the body that would regularly benefit from love, attention and energy healing. I am a Virgo, and the solar plexus is also the region of excess energy storage for me. Virgos have a tendency to be hypersensitive and empathetic, which directly correlates with excess energy storage in the solar plexus region. On another healing note, your birthstone color is also a cosmic indicator as to which chakra and associated color is of great significance in your own healing journey.

The Chakras

Within the body, there are portals of light. These key energy centers are responsible for receiving and processing energy similar to a transformer. As with auras, there are many chakras throughout the body (the Vedas acknowledge the existence of 114), but we will focus on the main seven. Each chakra takes source energy in from the unified quantum field. Chakras then act as portals and transform this energy into useful information for the human body to make use of. To add to the deliciousness, each chakra also corresponds to a particular level of the auric field as well as a particular dimension of consciousness. In Vedic tradition, of the 114 chakras, two exist outside of the body, and only 108 are able to be worked with through the self-actualization process. The Vedic tradition also holds that of the 108 chakras, 54 of these chakras are energetically female and 54 are energetically male. (This is the foundation of Sanskrit having 54 letters, each with a male and female expression.)

Many of the great teachers throughout history agree on key principles associated with each chakra but differ slightly in detail. I believe the best way to find your own harmony with your chakras is to understand the key concepts and principles for each while learning to feel the movement of life force throughout your own body. Avoid getting too caught up in technical definitions and wording, which can differ from person to person, and you will have a much more intuitive experience with your own body and chakra system.

It is interesting to understand the relationship between our bodies and each chakra and also between the chakras themselves. The first three chakras (root, sacral, solar plexus) are primarily involved with how we relate to our physical world. The higher chakras (throat, third eye, crown) are still relevant to the physical realm but are more spiritual in design and function. We must also understand that although we can play a role in understanding each chakra and how it might be under- or over-performing, it is very important to understand that our body works as a harmonious unit. When there is a hypo- or hyper-state in one chakra, there is a ripple effect that impacts all other chakras. When a body is in overall harmony and balance, an imbalance in one chakra can usually be brought back in alignment with ease and simplicity. The trouble lies when a body is void of lifeforce and filled with conflict and trauma. It takes greater love and care to repair the imbalances. Although we will go through the chakras as individual aspects, remember that they are in association and dynamic synergy with one another, so a change in one affects them all.

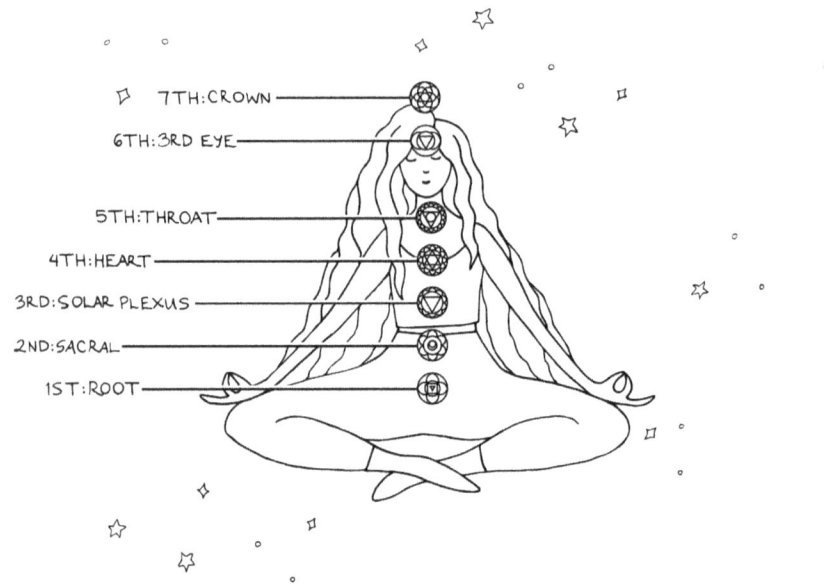

1st Chakra (Root Chakra). Your first chakra is located at the end of the spinal column and is associated with the color red. This is the seat of lifeforce (*Kundalini*). This chakra is associated with instinct, groundedness, stability, safety, security, and a sense of belonging. The first chakra is associated with the reproductive glands (testes in men, ovaries in women). Your root chakra is responsible for your association with nature, your family, your culture, and your ancestry. If you feel you are stuck, ungrounded, or unable to let things go, these can all be feedback that you need to tune the first chakra. Affirmations to support first chakra wellbeing include I AM SAFE, I AM LOVED, I AM SUPPORTED, I AM SECURE, I AM GROUNDED.

2nd Chakra (Sacral Chakra). Your second chakra is located in your sacral area and is strongly associated with the adrenal glands. This chakra is associated with the color orange. This chakra is associated with movement, sensuality, sexuality, fluidity, abundance, and creativity. Frustration, disappointment, guilt, and shame can be strong signaling that second chakra-healing is needed. This is also your center of pleasure and power. Affirmations to support your second chakra wellness include I AM CREATIVE, I AM INSPIRED, I AM EXPRESSIVE.

3rd Chakra (Solar Plexus Chakra). Your third chakra is located in the upper abdomen, below the rib cage, and is your source of self-esteem. It is also associated with the color yellow and regulates personal will, fears, gut feelings, inner fire, and personal transformation. This center is also associated with the digestion of food, water, and emotional energy. The third chakra is associated with the pancreas, which regulates metabolism. Powerlessness, low motivation, low self-esteem, and/or anger, are all third chakra related. Affirmations to support your third chakra include I AM EMPOWERED, I AM COURAGEOUS, I AM FULLY IN MY POWER.

4th Chakra (Heart Chakra). The fourth chakra is the center of compassion and love. It is associated with the thoracic cage, including the heart, lungs, and chest. It is also associated with the color green. The thymus gland, which regulates the immune system, is associated with this chakra. Sadness, grief, loss, depression, being a people-pleaser, and over accommodating others are all associated with the heart chakra. Affirmations to support your fourth chakra include I AM PEACE, I AM LOVE, I AM KIND, I AM COMPASSION.

5th Chakra (Throat Chakra). The fifth chakra is located in the throat and associated with self-expression, communication, and leadership. It is associated with the color blue and is also the center of divine will (which is of a much higher order than the will of the personality). The thyroid is the associated gland and regulates body temperature and metabolism. Not expressing oneself, not feeling authentic in life, feeling not heard, and not finding purpose in life are all associated with the throat chakra. Affirmations to support your fifth chakra include I EXPRESS MY FEELINGS, I AM FULLY SELF-EXPRESSED, I AM CREATIVE, I SPEAK MY TRUTH, I AM HERE WITH GREAT PURPOSE.

6th Chakra (Third Eye Chakra). The sixth chakra is associated with awareness, mental clarity, intuition, and insight. This is commonly referred to as the "third eye." The associated gland is the pineal gland, which regulates biological cycles, including sleep. The sixth chakra is associated with the color indigo. When we finally see things with great clarity and awareness, we have opened and unlocked the 6th chakra portal. Worrying about the future or focusing too much on the past can bring the sixth chakra out of tune. Affirmations to support your sixth chakra include I AM GUIDED, I AM ATTUNED, I AM CLEAR.

7th Chakra (Crown Chakra). The crown chakra is associated with the full unfolding of human potential as well as our spiritual center. It regulates consciousness, spirituality, and imagination. The color associated with the seventh chakra is violet. The crown chakra is associated with the pituitary gland, which produces hormones and governs many other glands. Affirmations to support your seventh chakra include I AM CONNECTED, I AM DIVINE, I AM LIGHT.

8th Chakra (Star Chakra). The eighth chakra is also known as the Soul Star and is located about one-to-three feet above the head, in the auric field. It lies above the crown chakra and is associated with the color white. This chakra interweaves you with the cosmos and is your gateway to the entire universe. The eighth Chakra is also associated with our soul-purpose. Affirmations to support your eighth chakra include I AM COSMIC, I AM MULTIDIMENSIONAL, I AM UNCONDITIONAL LOVE.

Each chakra is associated with a different layer of the aura. This is why the Auric Body is so mysterious in its magnificence. If you're trained in ancient knowledge, mystery school teachings, or ancestral wisdom, you will likely be familiar with the layers of the aura. If you aren't blessed with ancient wisdom access at the moment, this information may just activate galactic coding in you and leave you wanting more.

Typically, addictions and trauma result when we have not fully developed healthy lower dimensional chakras (1-3) as these chakras are responsible for how we conduct ourselves in the physical world. If we are limited in nurturing, love, and security we received as an infant or child, we will seek to fill this void later in life through artificial and unsuccessful means such as food, work, substance, sex, power, etc.

Healing in the 3rd dimension alone require much time, effort, and energy. It can be a full-time job! We are now able to travel through the 4th dimension where emotional healing and trauma integration can take place with greater support. For those who aspire to enter the 5th dimension, spontaneous healing can happen here as we communicate with our higher self through the heart portal. For those who travel to 5th dimension consciousness, healing happens spontaneously and with so much grace. Time and effort are really not required in this realm of consciousness.

The Aura

Surrounding your physical body are energetic and mystical layers, or sheaths, that are described in some traditions as beings of their own with a specific care that lies within each layer. The physical body is the densest of all the layers of an individual. As you move outwards from the physical body, each layer becomes lighter in density and increasing in 'Light Body' composition. Your aura consists of many energetic layers. There isn't one agreed-upon number of layers to the aura but many advanced healers and channelers believe the number could be infinite and expand out in the universe forever. What is important to understand is that each layer of the aura corresponds to a specific energy center (chakra) in the body as well as a specific dimension of consciousness.

When we are born, with each seven-year cycle of life (approximately), we are developing and strengthening a particular layer of the Auric Body beginning from the physical body at birth and then moving outward to the auric layers for development and strengthening.

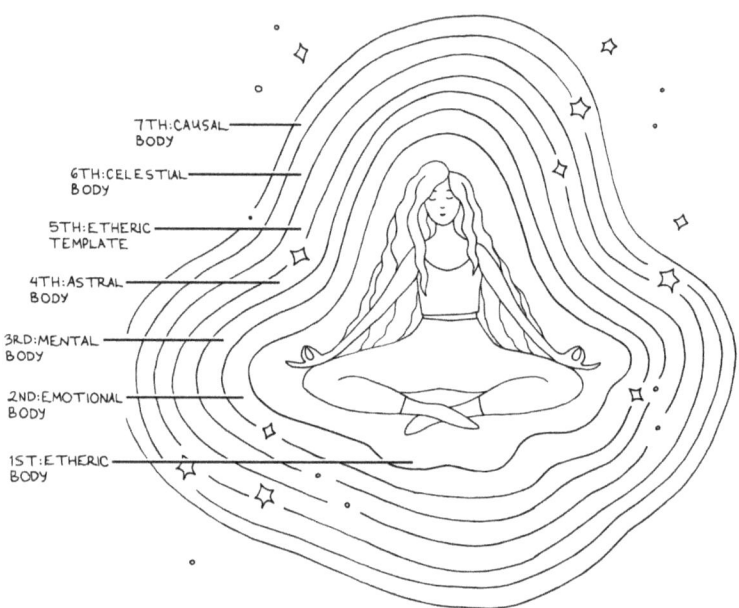

For grounding and simplification, we will focus on the first four layers of the aura:

1) **The Etheric Body** (Vital Body): The etheric body is what animates your physical body. It is the lifeforce body. This is the layer of the aura that many breathing techniques such as pranayama work with. The etheric body is a dimensional field of awareness containing structural models for life. It holds the blueprints that create and sustain the physical body. The etheric body is the lowest energy level of the aura and is the most primitive, direct, and dynamic form of lifeforce/chi/prana/ether/orgone. This is the level of your aura closest to your physical body and is responsible for regulating organ and metabolic function as well as respiration,

which is why breathing techniques have such a powerful impact on the vital level. The etheric level is responsible for our overall feeling of wellbeing and lifeforce energy. This field must be coherent in order for you to open fully to the next field, which is the emotional body. This is also the body of time and memory, which means that rhythms (such as the circadian rhythm) are stored here.

After death, over a three-day period, this etheric body breaks up and forms a symbolic tableau for your soul to experience a life review before merging again with the cosmos. Creating rhythm and order in your day is fundamental for vital body health. When daily rhythm (sleeping, eating, self-care, spiritual practices) is lost, the etheric becomes depleted and energetically dehydrated. Most humans today are suffering from etheric body dehydration. Divine beauty, rhythm, and order in life are keys to rehydrating this auric layer. Breathwork practices can impact this layer of the aura to physically alter the carbon makeup of the physical body. This is often why those who practice regular breathwork have such radiant and glowing physical bodies. The vital body is the body we typically burnout as we attempt to hold all the energetic stress and chaos within our day. Eventually we fully deplete it, burning it completely out, which then forces us to graduate to mystical and spiritual practices for daily living.

2) **The Emotional Body:** The emotional body is responsible for the emotional areas of our subconscious. This level of our aura is responsible for feelings, emotions, and desires—it gives our life tone and meaning. When we synch into the rhythm of life and feel harmony, our emotional body is healthy. Our nightly dreaming also takes place on this level, as do astral projection and deep contemplation during the day. We often experience energy deficiency and depletion when our emotional bodies are unwell. For this field to be coherent, the first field (the vital body) must also be coherent.

3) **The Mental Body**: The mental body is an expression of our rational thoughts and consciousness of self—this is where the individual personality is stored. We spend most of our everyday life in our mental body, as it is responsible for our sense of "I" and individuation, and also has a fully developed concept of time. I find it very helpful to remember that our mental body layer is a glorious fragment of the One divine mind. When I view my mental body like a child of that greater divine mind, I keep my thoughts as sacred, loving, and positive as I am able in the moment.

4) **The Astral Body**. This layer of the aura bridges the physical realm with the spiritual one. Higher spiritual information is stored here. This is where we are all connected as one through what many call "the divine matrix," and guardian angels or spirit guides may be energetically linked at this level, too, as well as holding an association with astral projection. While you sleep, your Astral Body works to restore order and harmony to your daily life. During the day, the Astral Body has the responsibility of receiving and transmitting sensations. The challenge with how we live today is that with such a high degree of chaos and imbalance, the Astral Body is not able to perform its restorative, rhythmic, and cosmic work during sleep. This leaves the subsequent lower layers of the aura (emotional, mental, vital) unable to optimally function. As a result of this, the physical body also lacks high order vitality, radiance, and lifeforce and is why a daily spiritual practice is of such pressing importance.

We are all somewhat in the dark when it comes to the true mysteries hidden in the auric field. Many ancient texts hold the keys to these mysteries, but we are all students in mystery school. We listen, we learn, and we use our own higher senses to assimilate what possibilities exist. If we are all multidimensional, who really knows the infinite possibilities that exist for us and how expansive our auras really are? Many highly enlightened spiritual practitioners have recently begun studying a possible plasma body as a layer contained within our auric field. Theories on plasma and its role in understanding creation, the cosmos, and the auric field is going to lead to some fascinating findings in the coming years!

Coherence (which we will discuss further in future chapters) must also be present in each layer of the aura. When the heart brings the first and second layer into a single coherency, the third field (the mental body) can then mesh with the electromagnetic field of the earth. The greater our own internal coherence, the more we are open to the coherence of the planet and of the cosmos. In this way, we can see that the heart is the true center of harmony and coherence both for our own health and healing, but also for the planet. The heart is also our gateway into cosmic unity.

Rudolf Steiner, a philosopher and social reformer in the late 19th and early 20th centuries, explained that the human etheric body lives in sacred union with the physical body until the stage in childhood where baby teeth fall out. He believed that this change in teeth symbolizes the birth of the etheric body. Puberty symbolizes the birth of the Astral Body. Although under-valued and under-played in today's social system, these times in a child's development are quantumly significant. These milestones in a child's spiritual development should be celebrated and held sacred. Steiner also writes that etheric body itself is a universe on its own; our etheric body has with it a sort of eternal blueprint of the cosmos.

The Seven Anchor Points of the Etheric Body

The etheric body is the body of vital life energy/prana/chi/ki/lifeforce. "As above, so below" is a perfect phrase to describe the very planetary influence on our own vital life source. The higher planetary forces from the seven classical planets illuminate here in seven specific regions—the chakras—within the human body. Our etheric body also connects us to the greater cosmic rhythms that play out through time. The planetary forces flow in through both the front and the back of the body at each chakra location. It is common for my clients to explain to me that it is as if they have lost energetic connection with the back of the body. This is a gentle reminder to always embrace and love the entire backside of your body. Even though you don't look at it often, give it love, attention, and movement. Embrace the beautiful nature of your entire backside!

The Three Anchor Points of the Astral Body

The sun, the moon, and the earth all project their powerful forces to form the Astral Body. These three forces anchor themselves at specific locations in the physical body as well. In Chinese medicine, these three anchor points are referred to as the upper Dan Tian (head), the middle Dan Tian (heart), and the lower Dan Tian (just below the navel). These are powerful spiritual reference points pertaining to the astral layer of the aura. These three centers can also be viewed as the three powerful forces of thinking (head), feeling (heart) and willing (abdomen). These three centers are energetic anchor points that link the forces of the sun, moon, and earth to specific points in the human auric field. The moon forces are reflective, the sun forces radiate heat and light, and the earth forces produce metabolic energies for food and emotions. This is why emotional health and gut health are so very closely tied.

The One "I AM" anchor point

The I AM anchor point is a perfect fractal or slice of the divine itself. This anchor point is the I AM that so many spiritual teachers such as Neville Goddard speak about in their teachings. This anchor point is said to be located deep in the cosmic cave or third eye tunnel that runs from the root of the nose to the back of the skull. This is where the spirit anchors during incarnation and why the pineal gland is referred to as the seat of the soul.

Aura Expansion

As with all of life, rhythm is key. Although it is beautiful to focus on ways to expand the aura and illuminate the world around us, there are seasons for everything. In winter months, we may feel the need to withdraw. We want to shine brightly but taking a season to retreat and rest is just as important. The emotional radiance scale we discussed earlier is also a helpful tool when it comes to aura expansion.

Here is a simple summary of how different emotions impact your aura:

Foods that hydrate, like fruits and vegetables, as well as herbs, are gorgeous aura expanders. Times of rest and retreat are also very important in the long term for keeping an aura healthy and radiant. One of the most beautiful aura expanders is authenticity. The more you embrace and honor your true divine nature, the more your aura illuminates. As you spiritually mature in your life from a frequency of self-will *(How can I serve myself?)* to one divine will *(How can I serve others?)*, the aura will naturally intensify and strengthen.

Dimensions of Consciousness

Healing becomes much less complicated and mysterious if we better understand the different dimensions of consciousness. There are many levels of consciousness (more than 12, in fact) as well as many sublevels, but we will cover the fundamentals. Consciousness is a complex and cosmic study. Mystery schools, galactic studies, and ancient civilization teachings (such as the Maya and Sumerians) all interpret information in a different way, but there is much common ground. We all have the ability to travel along an axis that spans the cosmos. One end of the axis anchors in the center of the earth (earth heart) while the other end of the axis anchors into the center of the milky way (cosmic gateway). The higher up the axis we travel, the lighter we become. We also increase in vibration and in consciousness as we travel upwards (ascend). We also have an ability to travel down as needed, too. We may have travelled in consciousness up into the 4th dimension but now need to firmly ground ourselves for integration purposes by planting into the 2nd dimension more firmly and accessing mineral/plant consciousness. Our journey in this lifetime is to find our way travelling in both directions while eventually travelling back to Source. We are all going home, but we have the free will to navigate our individual journey up and down the axis. Sometimes we may need a little more grounding and earthing while at other times we may need a little more angelic support and nature spirit nurturing. As we travel up and down the dimensions, we are all trekking up the mountain back to God. Be aware that the more you study, the more models you will find for the dimensions of consciousness. This is a simple starting point for the first eight levels of consciousness.

1st Dimension- Mineral Kingdom (Iron Core Crystal). This is the kingdom where Akashic records are stored. Each planet/star/galaxy has Akashic records stored in their mineral iron crystal core. As this core spins, it communicates and shares with all other spinning planetary cores. This is how Akashic record storage and sharing takes place. In order to tune into planetary intelligence, one must be well grounded to the earth. Some spiritual teachers believe that at the very center of the earth is an iron crystal core surrounded by hematite crystal, which forms a protective crystal grid that surrounds the very crystal castle where the earth's soul resides. As you tune into the iron core center of the earth, you also tune into and activate the healing powers of the iron crystals in the blood. When we are in beta frequencies in our brains, we are vibrating with the frequency of the center of the earth—with earth intelligence. This is when you get hunches and guidance on a continuous basis on where to be when, weather patterns, what home to buy, how to set up your home, etc.

2nd Dimension: Elemental Realm (The space between the center of the earth and its surface). Creation happens in the 2nd dimension before it manifests in the 3rd dimension (where our consciousness resides). This summarizes that we arise from the very elemental realm. This is why grounding and earthing is crucial for Auric Health. We must keep connected with plants and minerals continuously, in order to thrive. According to astrophysicist and author Thomas Gold, author of *The Deep Hot Biosphere*, creation in the 3rd dimension comes from the 2nd. As we learn to tune into the frequencies of the 2nd dimension, we tap into the master healer within. The very chemistry of our body originates from this dimension, which is why flower essences, herbs, crystals, and homeopathics are so effective in rebalancing wellbeing. The higher frequencies of the second dimension can be use with great effectiveness to attune the body.

Barbara Hand Clow, author of *The Alchemy of Nine Dimensions*, shares that the 2nd dimension is always in manifesting mode in this dimension. You always have access to this dimension and can make use of it for healing and harmonizing through Vogel crystals, herbs and herbal teas, homeopathy, gardening, nature walks, sun gazing, salt Baths, earthing, swimming, and dancing. Barbara shares that throughout history, religious institutions consciously cut us off from the wisdom and beauty of the 2nd dimension to increase our dependance on institution. She argues that if you are fully connected and tuned into this dimension, you will have no need for pharmaceuticals or modern-day physicians. It is our work to be curious enough to discover the hidden truths (which are now more easily accessible) when it comes to harmonic health.

3rd Dimension: Animal Kingdom (Surface of the Earth). This is our current physical reality on earth. This is also the dimension of linear time. As I said previously, we manifest in the 3rd dimension, but our origins lie in the 2nd dimension. As we ascend and pass through higher dimensions, we must not forget to stay well rooted in the 3rd in order to maintain individual as well as collective integrity. As we spiritually ascend, it is important to continue to learn and to develop skills for three-dimensional thriving. We won't fare well in the higher dimensions if we are plugged into and prioritizing the lower ones. The reason so much of our current reality seems absolutely bizarre right now is because the 3rd dimension as we know it is undergoing breakdown. What is most important is that we remain as centered, calm, and grounded, as we possibly can right now. A new and much higher consciousness realm is awaiting us- but we must keep stable and as courageous as possible as we witness the dissembling of 3rd dimension illusion. Those we are beginning to see through the illusion are now passing through higher dimensions (4th and 5th) while remaining in three-dimensional physical reality themselves. This is no easy task! Self compassion and self nurturing are absolutely imperative right now. Ask your guides and angels for support and draw upon the mystical wisdom of the 1st and 2nd dimensions every day in every way!

4th Dimension: Astral Plane or Astral Body of the earth. This is the dimension of the quantum field and is the layer surrounding the earth. In the 4th dimension, reality follows thought. This dimension holds codes that support emotional healing and integration, which means it is the plane where we have an opportunity to sort through and heal trauma. Myths, archetypes, and collective consciousness also exist in this dimension. Here, you can warp time, astral project, telepathically connect, and *feel* your way through life. This is the feeling dimension, and it is complex to navigate. Trauma, fear, confusion, and paranoia can easily hook us in this dimension and keep us stuck on our lives, which is why mastery of the 3rd dimension is so very critical.

There are many sub-levels of consciousness circulating in each dimension, including lower vibrational dark and destructive energies all the way up to ascended masters, angels, and Archangels. We can pick up and tune into energies and messaging from celestial beings coming in from higher dimensions in this realm. You can also pick up astral hitchhikers in this dimension (energetic parasites and entities). For years, I knew I had picked up an astral hitchhiker, and when I finally understood how this dimension works, I commanded the thing to get off my back. It worked!

The fourth dimension is where we can clear duality, play with nature spirits, get good at the game of life, clear trauma, and strengthen mental power. It is where we break out of the invisible prison we have been conditioned to inhabit. This dimension is a stormy one to navigate and can take multiple lifetimes to navigate, but we are now ready to conquer things here. We are healing, integrating, and waking up. We are becoming spiritually strong!

5th Dimension: The Causal Plane. This is thee dimension of love, light and unconditional love—where we awaken the heart. This is the dimension of our higher self. We are experiencing more of the 5th dimension right now as we become more spiritual mature and awakened. In the 5th dimension, reality is thought. The more we connect and synchronize with heart harmonics, the more we connect with the cosmos. In this dimension, we connect in the unified field and experience cosmic heart, so processing trauma is instantaneous and effortless. When you hear people talking about being more "5D," what they are really experiencing is an opening of the heart and a gradual evolution towards unconditional love. I do believe some souls here on earth are nearing a state of unconditional love, and I believe more and more souls will incarnate and successfully achieve this state. Perhaps you're parenting one now!

6th Dimension: The Spirit Realm.—The 6th dimension is the invisible dimension of form. As the heart opens, forms take shape, and the link between sacred geometry and divine order is apparent.

The 6th dimension is mysteriously magnificent. In sacred texts, there are many references to sound being the precursor to form. Ancient sites, temples, pathways, and labyrinths were created with 6th dimensional purpose. This is why light, sound, and sacred geometry are the true healing modalities. Color and sound exist in blueprint form in this dimension. According to astrophysicist and author of *The Discovery of Dynamics,* physicist Julian Barbour, PhD suggested that forms exist in an invisible dimension. We can bring these forms into the 3rd dimension from the 6th dimension using yoga through the various geometrical forms into which it moves our bodies. This is likely the reason certain movement exercises such as dance, yoga, and tai chi impact our spiritual self more than other forms of exercise. It's because they act on and open the heart through form.

7th Dimension: Source/The Unified Field. Seventh Heaven. The 7th Dimension hold the highways of light. This is the dimension of the ascended masters, God-conscious beings, and the angelic realm. Sound healing, meditation, prayer, and cranial sacral therapy are great modalities for accessing this dimension. This dimension is beyond all form and is everywhere. It is the God source, the light of all lights.

8th Dimension: Divine Mind and Divine Light. This dimension is the divine level of the sun. Entering the mind of the sun to contact divine intelligence is possible and written about across cultures. This is the dimension of the infinite. The sun directs our intentions, which opens up so many discussions about why we have been conditioned to be afraid of the sun, block the sun, and significantly limit exposure to the sun. Sun gazing and sun worshipping are regular ancient practices with extraordinary benefits to both the energetic and physical level. I am not suggesting you toss out sunscreen and overexpose yourself to UV rays, but our family significantly limits the use of sunscreen and embraces sun gazing and healthy sun exposure as healing rituals. We also limit the use of sunscreen on our children and intuitively use it just when they will be overexposed to the sun.

We have entered an age where we are now able to evolve into the 5th dimension while staying in our own physical bodies. Indigo children and crystal children were born being able to do this, but for their parents, this journey is just beginning.

We are most directly influenced by both the 2nd and 4th dimensions, which is why we must have daily practices and rituals to keep our bodies grounded and connected in 2nd dimension while keeping our hearts expansive and opening by way of 4th- and 5th-dimensional healing. It is not uncommon for highly evolved individuals (such as daily meditators or spiritual masters) to struggle with maintaining order and excellence in the physical dimension (financially, for example). They may struggle staying grounded, fully manifesting creative projects, managing money, and interacting with society in general. In ancient times, spiritual students were able to train in monasteries, forests and temples and didn't have to manage other affairs of life. Today, we have the added complexity of growing careers, raising children, nurturing relationships, and managing the home. We are all monks out of the monastery today to some capacity.

In terms of healing, we must understand that as we enter and pass through the 4th dimension, a new skillset is required for which we have not been trained. It is more important than ever to deeply connect to the earth, create beauty and order in our physical world, and pursue the study of spiritual science. We must also pray.

Chapter 6: Auric Health

"Disease of the body itself is nothing but the result of the disharmony between soul and mind. Remove the disharmony, and we regain harmony between soul and mind, and the body is once more perfect in all its parts."

– Dr. Edward Bach

Auric Health is absolute and harmonious flow of vital lifeforce—the state of being when there is an integrous continuum of lifeforce energy throughout the body. Although this continuum spans all layers of the aura as well as physical body (the Auric Body), it is experienced as pure integrity and harmony on the physical plane. We have entered a new cosmic time in which the integrity of our auric field has everything to do with the state of our physical health. To achieve Auric Health, integration and integrity must be at the very foundation of daily life.

To make matters even more pressing, if the soul is not free to express, evolve, and ascend, health troubles can manifest with quantum speed at this cosmic time. The cosmos are encouraging us all to reconnect with the order of the soul and steer our bodies back to truth, integrity, and wholeness. The law of cause and effect is in full expression right now; we sow what we reap and experience quicker karmic delivery. Simply put, to experience true peace and joy within, we must reintegrate the aura back to a state of integrity, wholeness, and balance. Auric Health results when we prioritize our spiritual life with as much care as we do our physical life. This does not always equate to a 50/50 split in linear time but is more of an intuitive and cosmic time split. This means that you don't have to spend half of your day on spiritual practices (although I often do!), but you will intuitively learn to let the soul guide when more spiritual time is necessary. Having time allocated in the morning and evening for spiritual practice is a great start. If your life has been filling with emotional distress and chaos, it is likely perfect time to get started. When these are in balance, mental health, physical health, and emotional health are expressed in our lives. In the *Wen-tzu,* Lao Tzu writes:

> Spiritual light is attainment of the inward. When people attain the inward, their internal organs are calm, their thoughts are even, their eyes and ears are clear, and their sinews and bones are strong. They are masterful but not contentious, firm and strong yet never exhausted. They are not too excessive in anything, nor are they inadequate in anything.

All dis-ease is a lack of lifeforce and often a lack of rhythm. When rhythm is lost, so is health. This is why it is essential that, for the restoration of Auric Health, daily rhythm is also restored. Rhythm can be restored by selected sacred times throughout the day to stay consistent on the cosmic clock for such things as eating, bathing, sleeping, tidying, healing, etc. Illness is also caused by an exhausted and excessively active Astral Body. Consider illness to be Astral Body burnout. When our daily life is excessively busy and overactive, and our sleep is not restorative, we break. Waking life is actually quite destructive to the physical body, which is why restorative sleep and meditation is so important.

Another interesting perspective on illness is from the 20th century Christian mystic, Daskalos. Daskalos writes that "illness, be it physical or psychic, arises within a personality when an uneasy subconscious psycho-noetical climate fosters an environment that will nurture and proliferate a destructive energy." When soul and mind do not travel in harmony, there is dis-ease. Dr Edward Bach taught that disease is, in essence, the result of conflict between the soul and the mind. Allan Watts taught that a feeling of tightness and constriction in the body is the physical manifestation of the psychological image we have of ourselves. Edgar Cayce, the most documented clairvoyant of the 20th century, believed dis-ease arises for two reasons: spinal misalignments and endocrine gland disfunction.

This chapter focuses on your sacred health. At the very core of Auric Health is heart harmonics and mind musculature. We are well trained to memorize and repeat in school, but we're not well trained on how to develop critical thinking skills—on how to truly think. For this reason, our mind is not trained to keep us healthy, nor does it know how to think when we fall out of alignment with Auric Health. Our minds might be academically brilliant, but true mind power is a skill not taught in schools. In order to be in resonance with nature, with yourself, and with the higher realms of consciousness, you must have an intimate and sacred relationship with the heart *and* mind. If you have gotten out of harmony with health in some way, heart-opening and mind-training is often even more powerful than treating the physical body. The heart is the most powerful portal in your body and when open and unlocked, it draws in all of the cosmic consciousness and pure prana that your body requires to get back into resonance. The healthy mind is the manifestation power center of highest order wellbeing. Together, the heart and mind lovingly collaborate to not only create Auric Health but to also bring one back to Auric Health when a sway from center has occurred.

There are hundreds, if not thousands, of healing modalities. For the purposes of this book, the modalities that will be of particular significance over the next decade and beyond will be discussed. As we enter the quantum era where your master healer within takes charge, the most important thing to remember throughout this chapter is that your intuition knows best. Gone are the days of giving all of your power away to others where your body and healing are concerned. Take many moments throughout the day to practice meditation and heart-harmony breathing in order to keep your lifeforce flowing and bioelectric system beaming. Your body knows best, and for this reason, you must play the primary role in your own healing by enhancing the connection between you and your heart. Your heart is at the very center of your healing. As you still the mind and create calm resonance in your nervous system, you will begin to receive more frequent and clear messages from your heart. You will be provided answers to questions and given highest-order choices to make in your life that will support not only your healing, but the full expression of your Auric Body.

Many ancient spiritual systems taught that the solar plexus was the at the root of all healing. As the planet evolves in consciousness (right alongside with us), we are now ascending through a new age and a new dimension. Through these higher dimensions (4th and 5th dimensions), the mind and heart are the power centers of harmonious health. By enhancing our own field of self-actualization, our ability to make use of inner sight (insight) is highly enhanced. As self-actualization develops, the true secret to healing is uncovered: opening the heart and stilling the mind. These processes synch us back up with divine mind and unconditional love—unity with all that is well.

As we discussed in Chapter 4, heart-activated ascension that focuses on illuminating the heart first is a powerful healing technique for this nodal point in cosmic time. Here is the order of energetic flow with heart-activated ascension (that is, the 5th dimension):

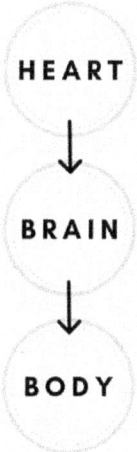

HEART

↓

BRAIN

↓

BODY

Don't be fooled, the heart is the orchestra conductor of life. You may think the mind is in control, but in 5th-dimension consciousness, the heart is the portal through which divine intelligence enters. All of the feelings, hunches, intuitive vibes, higher perceptions, and cosmic gifts enter through the heart portal. Mind is absolutely the great manifestation machine, but in 5th-dimensional consciousness, the heart is the conductor. In the 5th dimension, it becomes necessary to *feel* our way through life in harmonious relationship with mind. Many empaths, indigos, and sensitives are already at this stage. They are doing their very best to navigate their way through this higher dimension of consciousness while at the same time functioning in a world that rewards intellect, certifications, and a well-conditioned mind. This is no easy task, there are very few easily accessible tools for us to make us of. Hence, the very reason for this book!

During these times, we are witnessing the breakdown of systems that are not rooted in a foundation of truth. We are watching many systems undergo significant turmoil, including educational, medical, political, financial, etc. What we sometimes fail to remember is that our physical bodies are also systems that are not able to thrive in current conditions during this lifetime. Our bodies are hungry for truth, purity, and harmony, but we are feeding them with products and ideas that are fake, dysfunctional, and impure. We must take control of our own physical experience today and begin to return our bodies to a state of absolute integrity.

We have not been educated with purity and truth in mind when it comes to the conditions that optimize radiant health. We are told that we should eat according to government food pyramids, that medicating is normal, and that we should expect to experience certain body disfunctions at certain ages—"It's all a part of the aging process," we are told. We are now living on a planet where our bodies simply cannot function in such a lie. Our bodies are designed to thrive, repair, and heal with mysterious magnificence. It's time to return to nature and to simplicity—-to return back to our center. If we were taught truth as children when it came to the human body and human health, why would pharmaceuticals, autoimmune disorders, chronic disease, and mental unrest be so prevalent in society? Why would it be so very rare to meet someone who was beaming with radiant health? If absolute truth was taught where health was concerned, wouldn't everyone have such powerful auras that they could light up a room? There are simple truths that are never taught and never even mentioned when it comes to the physical body. Your body is actually a physical manifestation of an infinitely expansive quantum field. You are energy first, physical second.

Disharmony within our bodies takes place at many energy levels beyond the physical, which is why harmonizing the Auric Body is essential. An Auric Body approach to healing requires us to take a unified and multidimensional approach to our whole being. This will result in true integration between all layers—true quantum healing. If you hear the whisper of your soul telling you it is the right time to heal and integrate, know that you have all the power within you already to accomplish just that. Mind and soul-force can absolutely control everything in your physical body by way of the spine and nervous system.

The Auric Body, as a whole, integrates and harmonizes all frequencies of energy for the purposes of health and healing. My biggest wake-up call was when I realized that healing the physical body cannot be done without bringing the entire Auric Body back into resonance (which means all layers of the aura). The very blueprint of the body is contained within the aura, so to alter the physical body, we must repair the aura and the flow of vital life energy back to the physical body. This doesn't mean that you ignore the physical body on the healing path, but that you must place more attention on the layer of the aura that is most out of resonance. For me, the mental body and emotional body became top priorities for healing in my 40s. I was mindfully aware that daily practices to keep my physical body strong were important, but I began to apply healing practices to the mental and emotional body as well. This was a fascinating journey that introduced me to neural therapy, sun gazing, sound therapy, rife therapy, flower essences, homeopathy, light therapy, so much more! It is important always to remember not to *force* the physical body to heal but to invite the energy bodies to harmonize with the physical body. We often put so much pressure on the physical body to heal that we overtrain, over-focus and obsess with far too much force. Will and power have their roles in creating the discipline needed for health, but too much yang and not enough yin will only exacerbate disharmony. Without mindfulness and self-awareness, we become obsessed with healers, appointments, and techniques, and we exhaust ourselves running from appointment to appointment. What if surrender and a rest are the current keys to healing?

Processes for Auric Health

There are five processes that must be functioning well for Auric Health to occur. This includes the processing of energy, emotions, and food.

1) *Intake:* The intake process is a loving reminder that we are what we physically eat but also what we energetically eat. It is not only important to hold ourselves to the highest level of divinity and begin to align our eating with purity and grace, but also to energetically only take in that which serves our highest order and good. Eating heavy dehydrated foods is just as relevant as eating heavy dehydrated feelings. Mindfulness is key with intake. Eating when one is angry, anxious, standing, or overstimulated will contract the body and the aura from the very start. Eating in these states prevents digestion from happening and leads to energetic toxicity and acidification of the cells and deeply harmful to the Auric Body. There are many spiritual texts that promote prioritizing vegetables that grow above ground as well as tree-fruits in the diet. Some of my favorite nutritional texts describe that the higher off the ground it grows, the healthier it is. Melons are an exception, as they are also incredibly hydrating and put a smile on the digestive tract. As we will see in the

next chapter, spiritual nutrition practices highly harmonize the Auric Body.

2) *Process:* The processing of our food and energies is such a significant action. It not only accounts for the digestion of physical food matter but also of emotions and energies. This process is greatly enhanced when we set rhythm and ritual in our lives. It is a beautiful practice to bless our food and our body. This process begins with chewing our food, enhancing energy awareness, and feeling our feelings—we actually don't want to eat our feelings, we want to process them. This means that we have to build enough self-awareness and actualization to process them at a healthy rate. The processing of food, energies, and emotions are all very important for Auric Health. When we take in unhealthy energies, eat our feelings, and shove down food, the belly bloats in despair. The belly is not only our center of microbiome magic but also the center of self. Building strength in this area at the physical level will also support the ability to better process energy and emotions. A strong physical core does indeed support emotional and energetic processing skills. Herbs (teas and tinctures), probiotics, and enzymes can also be helpful here. Castor oil packs on the belly and over the liver are brilliant for both the processing and elimination phase of physical and energetic waste. A simple principle to follow is just not taking in so much (energetically, emotionally, and physically). We are evolving into Light Body beings, which means we don't need density weighing us down.

3) *Circulate:* The continuum of vital lifeforce throughout all layers of the aura, as well as the exchange with and within the physical body, must be harmonious. This includes optimal circulation of blood, lymph, and electricity/lifeforce. We are electrical beings, and movement of this soulful electromagnetism is life itself. Nutritionals, herbals, microcurrent treatments, chi machine treatments, rebounding, movement, yoga, dance, fitness, swimming, lymphatic massage, essential oils, and sound baths are all wonderous and work well for this process. When the endocrine

glands are backed up and blocked, not only is energy flow through the chakras diminished but lymphatic back up happens. This can lead to all sorts of trouble including inflammation, fluid buildup, and an overall sense of sadness. Shaking out the body by jumping, rebounding, or chi machine charging is helpful to do daily.

4) *Discharge:* The clearing and cleansing of waste matter is vastly underpromoted today. Consuming, stuffing, and feeding always get center stage. When you unplug from what is unhealthy and get into the gap (the space between thoughts and things), you realize that less is absolutely more—in the body, in the home, and in life. In a very literal and physical sense, regular and healthy waste elimination is absolutely necessary. Prioritizing poop is one of the biggest keys to health. Colon hydrotherapy is a wonderful way to promote healthy waste discharge—but always remember that being naturally regular is the name of the game. This means eating living and hydrated foods, keeping the body hydrated, the microbiome healthy and building a strong and flexible core. It is also important to ensure that we feed our bodies a dose of healthy oils to keep the digestive track sliding smoothly. When it comes to the emotional and etheric body, we must implement regular practices for clearing energies and emotions that don't serve our highest good. Human cells must also be well primed to both take in nutrition (both physical and energetic) and also excrete waste matter and toxins. There are a number of simple but powerful ways to enhance healthy discharge, including drinking hot water with lemon in the morning, green juicing, taking a spoonful of cod liver oil or plant based organic oils, and breathwork.

5) Rest: Rest rules—especially today. We are all rest-deprived and running on empty. The physical body is exhausted and dehydrated because the etheric energy body is exhausted and dehydrated. We have been trained and conditioned from childhood to hustle our way to happiness, but the happiness never comes. Rest can be deeply uncomfortable for those addicted

to busy which is why sharing your restful intentions with those close to you, can infuse a layer of support. The adrenal glands are exhausted, the endocrine glands are taking a nap, and the entire body is desperate for restorative rest. For now, it is vital to prioritize yin-dominant activities to counterbalance all of the years of excessive yang dominance. Astrology, yin yoga, meditation, restorative yoga, kriya yoga, nature walks, breathwork, music, art, moon bathing, crystal healing, prayer, creative writing, reading, play and lots of rest is helpful. 'Tis the season of joyful yin!

Rhythm and Resonance

Rhythm and resonance are master keys for Auric Health. When rhythm and resonance is lost, so is Auric Health. A disordered life results in disordered health. A disordered mind is at the root of disordered health.

Releasing negative energy

Clearing and releasing lower and heavier energies from the body is a necessary daily practice. When one learns to sense these heavier energies lurking in the body, it is quick and simple to clear them. When you feel like you have an energetic hitchhiker on your back, a brick in your stomach, or an energetic entity circling your aura, a quick clearing is a beautiful thing. You will feel a physical lightness and soul-freedom almost instantly. There are a variety of ways to clear the physical and subtle bodies; select one or a few that feel most aligned with your soul. It is also important to avoid feeling the forceful need to incorporate too many or all practices all at once. Gentleness and kindness towards oneself are now, more than ever, deeply important. Here is a selection to choose from:

1) *Sacred Sound:* Ancient sound instruments were used not only for healing but to communicate with the divine. Frequencies of sound are keys to Auric Living. The ancient musical scale was said to be comprised of six pure notal notes. Harmonizing

your life with Solfeggio Frequencies, which align with the Gregorian Monks in their chanting, creates body harmonics. Our modern musical scale is out of synch with the Solfeggio frequencies, which are the original sacred healing codes. Their currents of vibration are being powerfully activated right now across the planet. These frequency forces are at play right now and are being felt across the globe. This may account for the drastic number of sensitives and empaths undergoing significant physical change and transformation. These codes are awakening and activating consciousness and spiritual, emotional, mental, and physical healing beyond our conscious comprehension. (More on this shortly.)

2) *Breathwork:* Bee Breath and Lion's Breath are particularly beneficial when it comes to energy clearing. The humming sound in Bee Breath as well as both the power and mouth movements of Lion's Breath make these two techniques incredible etheric dischargers. Tummo breathing is also a powerful technique for clearing energy and cleansing the physical body.

3) *Meditation:* Active meditation can be helpful for discharging unwanted energies by way of visualizing the etheric body that surrounds the physical body. Imagining a golden shield or a blue shield surrounding the body during meditation is a simple exercise for protection and clearing.

4) *Energy Clearing Bath:* Water is a conductor of electromagnetic energy. If you are using tap or city water for your clearing bath, add a little fresh lemon juice to cleanse the water. Submerging your body underwater is the quickest and surest ways to discharge heavier energies. For sensitives, a daily bath is a helpful practice. Adding salts, baking soda, clays, charcoal, essential oils, or flower essences will further support energetic discharge. Just a few drops of essential oils or flower essences can have a powerful effect as the water distributes their vibrational qualities harmoniously throughout the entire body. For example, a few drops of Bleeding Heart flower essence supports both trauma and grief processing, as it is a beautiful heart chakra

balancer and thymus gland stimulator. If you aren't able to have a bath at the time of heightened awareness, run water down the inside of your arms from a sink (inner-arm shower).

5) *Downward Dog Discharge:* Making a triangle with your body by planting your hands and feet on the ground with your bum up to the sky is not only a master yoga move but a brilliant way to discharge waste energy from the body. Not only does this pose discharge waste energy, but it also refills the body with the very healing currents of Mother Earth. This is a great pose to do anytime you feel the need to release some energetic steam or when you need a charge up. And remember—barefoot is always best!

6) *Crying:* A good cry is the most beautiful and healing way to quickly cleanse and clear the body. You may not always be able to practice this due to the setting or company (like your boss), but it absolutely heals. There is nothing better than an authentic cry-cleanse.

7) *Massage:* Massage and body work are extremely important for releasing tension and resistance lurking in the tissues of the body. As the body is worked and maneuvered, trapped energy is also released from the Auric Body. Massage is one of the most effective ways to give yourself an energy cleanse as well as a body reset.

8) *Hug a tree/Hold a plant:* Trees are truly our ancient ones. They speak to us and are always available to support our healing. For children, it is often intuitive to go hug a tree with no particular reason at all. This is wise, soul-rooted wisdom. I had a year of deep distress as I navigated my way through fear-dominance, and a daily tree hug honestly got me through it.

9) *Colon Hydrotherapy* (or even a good poop): Colon hydrotherapy is not only a method to support body cleansing, but it also cleanses the emotions and energies that get clogged in the colon along with physical waste. It is not a surprise that when you are not eliminating well, you feel emotionally dis-eased, anxious, and off.

10) *Yawning:* Yawning is a simple discharge that can be done anywhere and on a moment's notice. When time is limited, this is a perfect discharge.
11) *Vibrational absorption:* A beautiful way to infuse the vibration of the sun into your etheric body is to lie down and place either a fruit or flower on the sternum (directly against the skin). Using a ripe organic orange or grapefruit is particularly beneficial. Close your eyes and become sensitive to and aware of the vibration of the fruit. Visualize yourself taking in the vibrational qualities of the sun directly from this fruit into your etheric body.
12) *Fasting:* For sensitives and empaths, the Auric Body can reach a state of being overloaded with the energies of other people. When this happens, regardless of how healthy or light one eats, the body always feels heavy and full. A simple practice can be a half- or full day fast to see how it feels. This gives the body the space and rest it needs to not have to work as much digesting food so that it can better process energies and emotions as well discharge those that are not our own.
13) *Vogel Crystal/Crystal Clearing:* The very specific cut of a Vogel quartz crystal gives it an extremely powerful healing ability. You can get Vogel crystals with a variety of number of sides, and each one has unique healing properties. For example, the eight-sided Vogel crystal is powerful for spiritual activation as well as healing trauma, while the four-sided crystal is said to enhance meditation practice.
14) *Aura Brushing:* Aura brushing is a beautiful process that supports the clearing of lower vibrational energies as well as other people's energies from your auric field. It is a beautiful compliment to skin brushing. You can simply use your hands, or you can use a crystal (such as a clear quartz crystal). Teaching children the aura brushing technique is lovely as well. Either with your hands or a crystal, imagine brushing your entire body yet a few inches from your skin. As you work your away around your body, brush the energies off your body and away from

you. Some energy healers offer aura brushing as a treatment. You can also pull unwanted energy from inside your body and toss it away from you (especially solar plexus area) using your fingers and hands (again a few inches away from the body). Intuitively feel around your body where there is heaviness in your auric field and brush that stale energy aside.

15) *Sweating:* A good sweat is a marvelous way to release not only the toxins from within your body but energies, too. Try an active visualization technique in your sauna or sweat session where you visualize all of the dense and unwanted energy pouring out of your body.

16) *Cold Plunging:* Not only does cold plunging enhance brain, nerve, and immune function, but it has a miraculous impact on the mental and emotional body. Making cold plunging a ritual is a powerful daily practice for healing trauma as well as the physical body.

17) Smudging: Clearing your auric field can also be done through smudging. Sweetgrass, palo santo, sage, and cedar are options. Create a combination that feels right to you and let yourself be intuitively guided. Let the smoke from the sticks travel throughout and around your auric field. It is ideal to do this practice outdoors or near an open door or window. There are also specific incenses, such as Bharat Darshan, that are particularly good for a good aura clearing practice.

Did you know that wrist watches create tiny energy disruptions in the etheric body that then transfer to the physical body? If you must wear a watch, be sure to give your body breaks from the energetic wrist weight on weekends and evenings. Energetically speaking, a better option than wearing a watch is to carry one in a purse or bag.

The physical body is made up of the food and water we consume and what we take in from our physical environment. Likewise, the vital (or etheric) body is made up of the energies we consume and take in. It is crucial today to understand that we must care for and nurture our vital body with the same love and care we do our physical body. We must learn to listen to it, feel it, and lighten it on a daily basis. For sensitives and empaths, the etheric body can easily become heavy, overloaded, and weakened.

Auric Body Health and Healing

True healing is multidimensional. We are conditioned to put almost all of our focus on the physical body when it comes to healing, but this keeps us from true healing and often leaves us frustrated and defeated as we navigate our way back to harmonious center. Dr Dietrich Klinghardt, MD, was the first physician that I ever encountered who was educating students on the importance of true holistic healing that embraces all layers of the aura, including the physical body, energy body, mental body, intuitive body, and spirit body.

When we lack harmony in our bodies, finding ways to heal can be a full-time job. Healing has layers and realms. Spiritual healing is at the very top of the power hierarchy although most are not tapped into it. It's easier to focus on the superficial layers of physical healing but not so easy to reorder one's life to prioritize the inner spiritual castle. It's easier to keep the chaotic, dysfunctional life rather than to make the difficult yet highest-order spiritual choices that could lead to quantum-speed healing. The surface mind (or "conditioned mind") has trouble letting go of well-groomed beliefs when it comes to health—even if they are untrue. I knew that my vital body was in need of love and care. I just didn't have the language or information to express it clearly. This is what new medicine must look like. Ignore all the modalities and complexities for now, and simply seek to understand how treating layers of the aura while gently and lovingly treating the physical body. It is a much more harmonious and correct approach to healing.

When we take a multidimensional (6th realm) approach to the healing journey, we can consider each level of the Auric Body to be its very own realm. This illustrates the quantum nature of our being and reminds us that we really are living a multidimensional existence. Each layer of the body is, in fact, occupying different dimensions of consciousness. Here are several healing modalities as well as the corresponding layer of the aura on which they work. (Note that many modalities influence more than one layer of the aura as well as the physical body.)

1) *1st Realm: Physical Body Healing:* In the first realm, we must nurture and care for the physical body. Hydrating the body with nutritious and living foods (Mother Earth foods), moving the body daily, and grounding to the very earth beneath our feet is key. This is also the realm of biochemistry, anatomy, and structure/function relationships within the body. Although the 1st realm must be well managed to witness the fruits of healing, true healing actually takes place in the higher realms. This is why we must reintegrate and reorder the invisible layers of ourselves before experiencing a return to physical whole.

    Modalities: nutrition, fitness, yoga, dance, earthing, osteopathy, chiropractic work, supplements, medicine, naturopathy, massage, body work, herbs, physical therapy, sauna, cold plunge, ice bath, sun gazing, aromatherapy, colon hydrotherapy, juicing, cryotherapy, hyperbaric treatment, chi machine, rebounding, foot masks, salt chambers, sea salt baths, detoxification, anti-parasitics, ozone therapy, fasting

2) *2nd Realm: Etheric Body Healing:* In this second realm, the first layer of the aura that surrounds the physical body is housed. This is the realm that holds the blueprint for the physical body and is the energetic and vital life source for the physical body. In this realm, practices and modalities that work directly with prana/lifeforce/chi is priority. This is the realm of electromagnetic forces encapsulating and flowing through the human body. The process for manifestation is always energy first, matter second, which means we must

work to heal the energy body before reaping the healing benefits at the physical level. Breathwork and microcurrent therapy are some of the most effective healing modalities acting in the 2nd realm.

Modalities: acupuncture, breathwork, dance, yoga, tai chi and qigong, music, laughing, art, meditation, Rife therapy, microcurrent medicine, etheric healing, Vogel crystal healing, neural therapy, bodywork, cranial sacral therapy, reiki, homeopathy, flower essences, sound baths, herbs, anthroposophy, energy medicine, aura brushing, salt baths, earthing, grief work, gardening, tuning fork sessions, forest bathing

3) *3rd Realm: Emotional Body Healing*: In the third realm, healing trauma (large or small) becomes the gateway to true health. You can eat all the superfoods and do all the yoga you wish, but if the emotional body is unwell and experiencing disharmony, you won't experience much resilience at the physical level. The aura glow we all seek can only happen when we integrate and heal trauma. During this cosmic time, we are not only healing our own trauma but collective trauma as well as ancestral trauma. This is some of the most challenging and intense work in all of human history—and you wonder why adrenal fatigue is running rampant?

Modalities: trauma healing, heart centered healing, emotion code, grief therapy, crying, herbs, flower essences, microcurrent therapy, EFT, music therapy, art therapy, dance, movement, swimming, nature walks, gardening, forest bathing, earthing, EMDR, and yoga. Flower essence therapy is particularly helpful for supporting the emotional body.

4) *4th Realm: Mental Body Healing:* In the fourth realm, we explore the quantum field of mind. This is also the realm of the third eye's cosmic cave. The wellbeing of the pineal gland is key in this realm, and quantum healing is experienced with much higher possibility when one focuses on

mental body health. Illuminated thinking (intention-based thinking) and daily meditation is the most miraculous place to start. Just a few minutes a day will do wonders for healing in this realm.

Modalities: meditation, spiritual psychology, Jungian therapy, psychotherapy, neurolinguistic programming, mental field therapy, EMDR, EFT, plant medicine, herbs, affirmations, neurobiology, TFT, brain wave therapy. Note that whenever researching or considering psilocybin and or plant medicine, it is wise and suggested to consult a healthcare or professional healer who is deeply experienced working with these substances. I personally prefer to use meditation, prayer and yoga to support 4th realm healing, but I do know many people who have found plant medicine to be supportive.

5) *5th Realm: Astral Body Healing:* In the fifth realm, the infinite matrix is explored. This is the realm of great mystery and higher perception as well as the realm of the Akashic field. This is where we explore the mysteriousness of mathematics, symbols, archetypes, dreams, the sixth sense, and so much more. The mysterious golden ratio and the Fibonacci sequence dwell in this realm. Mystery school wisdom is also helpful here.

Modalities: family constellation, sound therapy, light therapy, color therapy, hypnotherapy, past life regression, shamanism, Jungian therapy, radionics, crystal therapy, healers, lucid dreaming (IRT), PEMF therapy, dream analysis, sacred geometry, visualization, active meditation, light and sound healing, Akashic record sessions, psychic healing

6) *6th Realm: Higher Spiritual Body Healing:* This is the realm of highest-order divinity— where God dwells. This is the realm of miracles and spontaneous healings, the absolute and most powerful realm of healing, but time, patience, and discipline to access. Many spiritual masters spend a lifetime working to access this realm, but it is always available to those who commit to the journey.

Modalities: prayer, meditation, chanting, spiritual practices, spiritual healers, mysticism, angel healing, acts of devotion, music

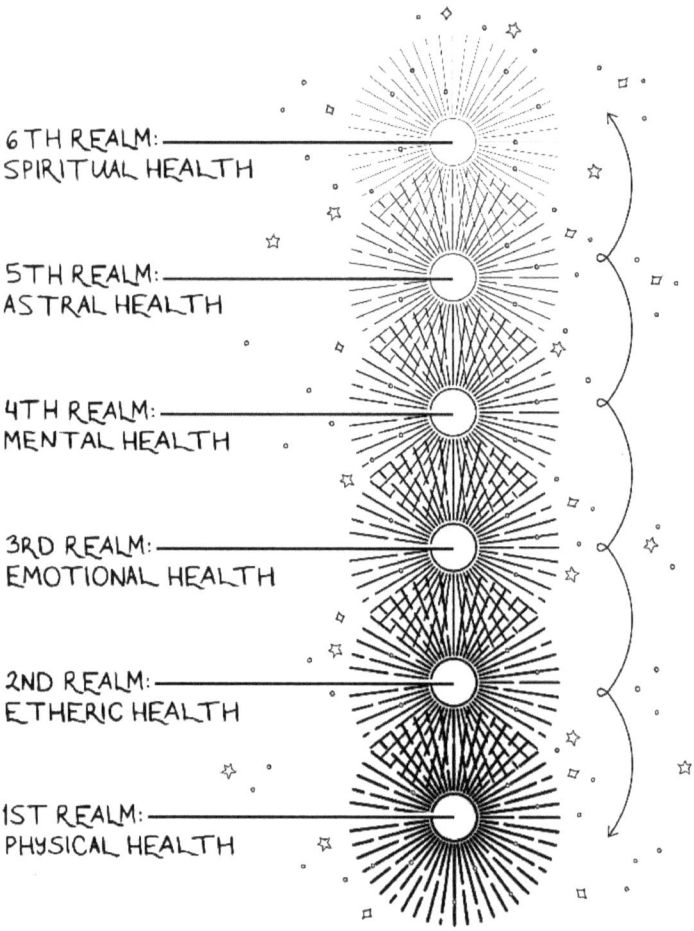

6TH REALM: SPIRITUAL HEALTH

5TH REALM: ASTRAL HEALTH

4TH REALM: MENTAL HEALTH

3RD REALM: EMOTIONAL HEALTH

2ND REALM: ETHERIC HEALTH

1ST REALM: PHYSICAL HEALTH

Begin to build a relationship with these realms and how they relate to the physical body. Each realm is of a higher order of light, with the physical body as the lowest, yet because it is the one we see, we often place all of our attention on it at the expense of the other realms. In terms of healing, however, the invisible realms are the more powerful and significant. Don't be surprised if the conversation around healing takes a galactic gallop over the next few years. Ancestry tracing will shift from earthly DNA tracking to galactic-origin sourcing. When we only question our history, behaviors, and traumas at the earth level, we are often left with even more confusion, questions, and mysteries. When we leave out the cosmic and spiritual dimensions of healing, we get stuck in stuck-ness. Seeking answers in the 3rd dimension alone simply doesn't work; this is just one of the reasons so many of us are feeling drawn to spiritual healers today. I do believe that academically trained healers can offer goodness, but very few of them witness true healing. This is because the gaps stemming from spiritual and galactic aspects are completely missing from almost all degrees and certifications. How can one help another heal and integrate if *all* dimensions of life are not explored—including soul connection and cosmic consciousness? If communication is cut off from our soul, is a trained therapist really going to be able to help us heal? This is where spiritual psychology comes in. This field of psychology is just in its infancy, but it is developing. Spiritual psychology is extremely important, but unfortunately, because it is so new, it can only get you so far, and you will need to look to other modes of healing, as well.

Trauma healing is going to take a truthful turn over the next few years and decades as it expands into spiritual and galactic realms. We are learning to understand more deeply that life and the incarnation cycle is a mystery to most. Even if we're lucky enough to have been passed down knowledge from mystery schools, we are still left with even greater mysteries. As we explore our lineages and the genetic coding with regard to health, healing and trauma, we find ourselves having a more cosmic conversation. What if the past 15-20 generations of our lineage are only a tiny window into a galactic lineage that spans hundreds of thousands of years? It is highly unlikely that a child will be taken seriously if they coming to school talking about their Lyran and Lumerian heritage to explain why they are so highly intuitive, empathic, and sensitive. Suggesting you may just be a starseed to your teacher likely won't help you score a Harvard-worthy letter of recommendation. But why don't we explore these galactic mysteries a little more with children, even if just for the sake of storytelling and mythology?

Quantum healing will also begin to take shape over the next few years and decades. My kids and I love watching the film *Dr. Strange* for the mystery school introductory information it contains. When my children tell me that they wish they had the powers held by Dr. Strange, I teach them that they do and are just getting started on tapping into them full force. In today's reality, we must tune into a new set of superpowers (though they are ancient in origin) to effectively navigate the quantum realm.

More and more evidence is coming to light that confirms that much of the science we were taught as children is outdated and untrue. Much of the *real* science available takes decades, if not lifetimes, to reach our children in the school systems—if it ever does at all. We must change this and awaken to the fact that much of what we learn in school is of no spiritual or scientific significance at all. What I mean by this is that it really doesn't expand our auras or answer the meaningful questions in this life.

We can now feel the acceleration of time that the ancients talked about. Even those who haven't yet tuned into the 4th dimension can feel a heightened strangeness in reality as well as a slipping of time. Dimensions are dancing together as time accelerates.

This is where I get *really* real with you. For most of my life, I have felt comfortable and well cared for here on earth, while at the same time feeling misplaced to some degree. I was well trained and equipped to be highly functional and socially sweet, but the 3rd dimension has always felt a little superficial and strange to me. I believe that many people feel the same way I do—like our souls are starving, and we don't truly know our story. We aren't even taught to question our reality or infuse more depth and meaning into our days. We're trained to be robots when we're designed to be cosmic creators. Is it any wonder why we stuff our face and our life with meaningless clutter and chaos? We are trained from childhood not only to tune out intuition but to work against it.

In my early forties, I started to receive very subtle information through my system that seemed to answer the bigger mysteries in my life. Although I cannot prove any of it, I believe it to be true. I may be an intuitive empath, but I am also a trained scientist who spent some time at medical school, and my strength is balancing head and heart in a very grounded way that allows me to play in multiple dimensions at the same time. Through these small revelations, I began to intuit that I was a starseed. According to Dr Norma Milanovich, author of *The Light Shall Set You Free*, starseeds are here on earth to fully awaken and hold the light for the world until humanity's consciousness is raised to a point high enough to stabilize and harmonize the world. Starseeds understand oneness and that all is and can be transmuted with light. Starseeds can't get away with living inauthentically and untruthfully as they are here to anchor oneness and purity. They must practice a daily lifestyle that is in complete congruency with the law of one. They are karmically bound to higher truths and values and are here to open the cosmic heart (both for themselves and for humanity). According to Dr Norma's work, starseeds have a spiritual contract to leave a legacy on earth, which is why they are so deeply committed to better understanding the spiritual realm and connect with the higher self. Even if they try to kick back and settle into three-dimensional living and enjoy the good life, their karmic and cosmic responsibility haunts them. They cannot hide or deviate from the yearning within them to leave a great legacy. This was the same burning I felt within my bones.

Returning to the physical plane in this reality, this book is a result of my own healing, which is still in process. As I mentioned earlier, body degeneration and misalignment can be caused by many things, and one of the biggest triggers for me was having three C-sections within a relatively short period of time. Surgery can lead to individuals developing what seems to be non-related physical symptoms and dis-ease after the procedure. In many cases, this is labelled as an autoimmune disorder, but according to

Dr. Harvey Bigelsen, M.D, who studied this phenomenon, most autoimmune patients had undergone some form of surgery within just a few years of their diagnosis. I fit this pattern. Within a few years of giving birth to my third child, my optimal state of health began to crumble. I experienced swelling of both of my knees and an inability to do yoga or run. On many days even, a walk was a challenge. My vaginal walls were giving me tremendous pain, which I later recognized was womb-grief. My skin would itch at night, and I even developed a rash on my stomach that would come and go even when my diet was extremely limited. I broke down in tears several times in despair. I desperately wanted to experience the radiant health I had enjoyed before children, and I couldn't figure out what was happening. My diet was filled with green juice and vegetables; I stayed away from gluten, sugar, meat, and all the other inflammatory foods. I was eating exactly what I was told I should be, but nothing changed. If I couldn't enjoy the activities that made my heart sing such as yoga, walking, and activities with my family, how was I supposed to *live life*?

This experience started me on what became an addiction to healers and healing modalities. Like most of us all-or-nothing, *yang* gals, I refused to be a victim and was going to use my default response to an uncomfortable situation: action! I booked appointments, researched healing modalities, and loaded up on as many as I could in search of perfect health.

Yet all this time, my heart was already quietly giving me all of the answers. My vital body was depleted. It was time to commit seriously to meditation and simplicity, and stillness was the gateway to my soul and my life purpose. I had heard my heart whispering this for years, but I just couldn't get my legs to slow down and stop moving. Isn't it interesting how divine the unfolding of our lives can be? I wasn't listening to my heart telling me to slow down, so my body literally made it so that I couldn't run, move, or even walk away from the divine message. As humans, we often need a big energetic hit to awaken us. I truly believe that if it wasn't for experiencing such profound body messaging, I would still be unconsciously running my life away (both literally and symbolically). After much introspection, analysis, and listening, I realized that I had been depleting my body for most of my life. I was a busybody who couldn't sit still, and my nervous system was always hyperactive. My outer composure was calm and stable, but my inner landscape was highly frazzled. I had lost coherence and resonance, and I had unplugged from the cadence of life. Having three C-sections in a row was simply the final cut to my vital body.

This was a personal experience that showed me how very intricately our auras connect with our physical body. I understood from my heart-speak that the rebalance and realignment to resilience was not rooted in the physical body alone, and I was given guidance on some physical body modalities that would be helpful in the short-term, but I intuited that my bigger focus should be on my vital body and emotional body. My guidance also led me to unplug significantly from technology, reorder my life, toss my strict daily schedule, reprioritize my life, and keep daily living as ultra-simple as possible.

I won't lie—it was challenging to make this shift at first. Even going into a city for a few hours was exhausting; I had to follow a trip like that with an hour walk in nature, a bath, and no other obligations for the rest of the day. I actually dedicated about a year to low-pressure, low-obligation professional pursuits, but I felt guilty and somewhat shameful for having no big project, no direction, and what seemed like no purpose. My ego was speaking loud and clear that unplugging and making my health a fulltime job was not important or significant enough. I had enough training and heart-power to quiet the ego, but there were certainly many times where it flared up and took over my being for a day or two. I have so much compassion for anyone who is at this crossroads in their life right now—blessed with the personality and will to achieve dramatic goals, to have impact and create significance... but also blessed with the divine will to be still, heal, and be. This is the bridge and transition in one's life from that all-important distinction we discussed at the beginning of the book: the shift from *human doing* to *human being*. This transition is happening to so many of us right now at quantum speeds, but very few are actually talking about it.

If you are on this bridge right now, I know it takes creativity, courage, patience, and love, but it is time to awaken your Auric Body. I am standing with you with all heart and energy. This requires *un*truth to be broken down and released from your life. This is what I call "The Untruth Cleanse." Untruth in your life is as real as physical waste matter stuck in the body. It has to get out, be released, and cleansed from your body and your life. Energetically speaking, every choice you have made in your life is stored in your body. Over time and with all sorts of experiences, there comes a moment when it is time to regenerate, renew, and rebirth. The difference right now on the planet is that this is happening as a collective, as well as at an individual level, which is why your experience is likely so heightened and feels so strange or surreal. It's a cosmic rebirth, but you are feeling it on the physical level.

Personally, I had a big realization that much of my grief leaving my body during this time was womb-grief rising to the conscious mind. I was experiencing and releasing the grief my body was holding from those three traumatic C-sections and from a miscarriage. That's a hefty load of emotional heaviness that I shelved at the time so that I could function well as a mom. Womb-grief is not often discussed but should be recognized and talked about. It should be given priority across healthcare systems so that women don't spend years wondering why they are experiencing such emotional distress and how they can heal.

The reason I am sharing all of this is because, from an allopathic perspective, I was labeled as someone with early onset autoimmune and arthritis in my knees. I even had one physician say, "Why wouldn't you just sign up right now for knee surgery? Just get it done." The problem was that, in my heart, I knew what I was dealing with was not a true physical experience. I was feeling it at the physical level, but it was sourced in higher realms. True healing was not going to happen through surgery, medication, and more appointments; healing was going to happen by tapping into my master healer within. My heart-communication told me clearly that I was already fully healed and in high coherence in many other dimensions of life; I just had to link to them and plug into these realms to experience this possibility in my current physical reality. I was also given the following directives:

1. Follow a fruit, green juice, and vegetable-based diet. Eat your water and drink your food. (Food ingested should be living and have high water content to hydrate the body.)
2. Drink high quality and organic loose herbal tea three-to-four times per day.
3. Study and experience herbalism, flower essences, and homeopathy.
4. Measure, charge and calibrate the aura using tuning forks and/or microcurrent instruments
5. Meditate twice daily. (Start with 10-15 minutes and work up to an hour.)
6. Forgive everything and everyone.
7. Walk daily.
8. Have a daily detox bath to cleanse the physical body and etheric body.
9. Rekindle a sacred relationship with the sun.
10. Surround and infuse every aspect of life with nature.
11. Create beautiful rhythm for days, cycles, and seasons.
12. Begin daily conversations with guardian angel, with archangels, with God, and with higher-realm beings.
13. Start a self-guided yoga practice. (I was used to being guided by a teacher but found what I actually needed was a self-practice.)
14. Release everything from your schedule with the exception of study, writing for healing, and taking on a few clients.
15. Let go of everything that doesn't feel completely in harmony with your heart.
16. Practice breathwork daily, even if it's just for a few minutes.
17. Work with a Vogel crystal.

18. Get regular bodywork.
19. Live near the ocean (or visit it frequently).
20. Reorder the home for highest vibrational living.
21. Prioritize sleep and rest.
22. Have regular colon hydrotherapy sessions.
23. Shift all aspects of existence from self-will (serving self) to divine will (serving others).
24. Clear all that no longer serves.
25. Several times a day, place a hand on the heart and say, "I love you."
26. Seek truth, integrity, and wholeness in every moment of every day.
27. Purify the body through detoxification.
28. Clear the mind, train the mind, order the mind.
29. Create art in any form that feels beautifully joyful.
30. Practice spiritual fasting with mindfulness (and avoid extremes).

These directives are meant to activate curiosity and inspiration and do not need to be acted upon in any order or with any urgency. These were simply what worked for me during that time. Sit with them, settle with them, and see if any of them spark a smile or an intuitive tap in your own life.

Electromagnetic Fields

Life is an electrical energy field, and your body is an electromagnetic producer. The primary producer of this charge is the heart. The electrical activity of the heart is ten times that of the brain. The heart also produces almost one thousand times the magnetic force-field than that of the brain. This is why emotions are so very powerful when it comes to health and healing. Even very low charges can significantly impact the electromagnetic charges found in the auric field.

Lower frequency forms are constructive and healing to the body, while high forms are destructive in nature. Microcurrent therapy, rife therapy, radionics, and electromagnetic therapy are examples of health-enhancing modalities using low frequency electromagnetics. Higher "dirty" forms that are produced from plugged in appliances, household items, cell towers, etc. can have detrimental impacts on health. Cell phones, smart meters, electrical lines, cell towers, etc., are just a few of the big "dirties." This is a touchy topic for me, as a vast majority of schools today have a cell tower either right on property or very nearby. I have declined enrolling my children in some fabulous schools because of a nearby tower. There are numerous studies showing the detrimental impacts on health from cell towers—especially 5G. Dr. Magda Havas, PhD, is a fabulous resource for much of this scientific information.

I am definitely the proverbial canary in the coal mine when it comes to EMFs, and my aura is an antenna to these negative fields. I can also feel mold in a home as soon as I open the front door. Although frustrating at times, this sensitivity has become a blessing when it comes to home purchases. Many individuals like me are highly sensitive with regard to exposure to environmental toxins like mold, toxins, preservatives, gluten, caffeine, dairy, several foods, energy vampires, even lunar cycles. Nausea, tinnitus, dizziness, redness, rashes, headaches, ear pain, anxiety, migraines, pressure, and body weakness are among the symptoms that sensitives report. For me, this hypersensitivity resulted in significant changes in lifestyle as well as relocation. You cannot always change where you live, however, and if you can't, you can strengthen the aura as well as the physical body instead. It is also highly effective to do active meditation daily to protect the body and the auric field from any negative forces (including EMFs). Visualize your body being surrounded by a golden shield that protects you from all harmful and chaotic electrical forces. Many health advocates today are also protecting their homes through a variety of techniques including crystals and faraday cages, which will be discussed further in our "Auric Home" chapter.

Radiation and dehydration are two of the health harmers when it comes to EMFs. EMF's hinder blood flow, lymphatic distribution, and healthy oxygenation at the cellular level. Zeolite, glutathione, nascent iodine, homeopathics, ozone therapy, and activated charcoal tablets can be helpful at combating these issues. Placing shungite crystals throughout the home, having a regular sauna practice, and practicing colon hydrotherapy are all also a powerful method of cleansing the Auric Body of EMFs. Our family has an EMF reader that we travel with to monitor best options when it comes to living, sleeping, and relaxing choices. It is helpful to take an EMF reading round the home, especially in the bedrooms. We will discuss more EMF protection gear for you and your home in Chapter 7.

The journey home to health and healing is already perfectly designed and blueprinted in the higher realms of consciousness. As the heart portal fully awakens individually and as a collective, this lost information is making its way back into our physical reality at a quantum speed. We are already developing higher states of awareness and insight into the power of our master healer within. No longer can humans haphazardly run to medical specialists to fix us or heal us; we have now unfolded and ascended to the divine knowledge that we are own very own master healer. This does not mean that healers, practitioners, and medical doctors will become unnecessary. Quite the contrary. The difference is that we will begin to develop our higher and more attuned senses to see with our inner eyes what is troubling us as well as possible areas and sources where disharmony exist. This will allow us to have more conscious conversations with our healers and practitioners; it will make conscious, heart-centered communication possible. Our relationship with healers will radically transform. We will begin to develop more meaningful, compassionate, and awakened relationships with our healers that will cut the energetic ego cord between many of these relationships in order to create space for much richer ones. Many of us will be developing higher abilities that make it easier to see, hear, and feel not only subtle bodies but full blueprints along with heart communication on how to regain high coherence. Many will awaken to cosmic abilities that were dormant before but are now in full expression. More and more individuals will awaken to healing abilities both for themselves and also for others.

Auric Living

You may not see it, but you radiate with a luminous force capability of creating perfect health. Yes, you. Lifeforce Illuminated health is a possibility for each and every one of us at any moment in time. It in embedded in all of us in the quantum self. As you gain new perspectives through knowledge of quantum medicine, the more you will attune yourself to higher states of order, harmony, and well-being in your physical experience. As you develop your quantum mind, you will no longer accept choosing thoughts or attitudes that are not attuned to your greatest vision of possibility.

We need a new biology and a new foundation for integrative medicine. Today, we are witnessing conflict and separation between allopathic and alternative healing systems. As we observe separation within ourselves and within most systems, there is light and space being created for a much more harmonious and conscious systems.

When we seek to be well through allopathic medicine alone, we are often only addressing the physical layer of the Auric Body. There are, of course, exceptions and wonderful practitioners who are well versed in the energetic and spiritual aspects of healing in addition to the physical one. But as a general rule, pharmaceuticals and the current pharmaceutically dominated industry focuses only on the physical body and entraps us into a regime that does not align with healing. There is a reason why physicians are only given a tiny window of time to spend with you.

When you encounter *true* healers who understand whole-being health, you never forget. I will always hold deep gratitude in my heart for all medical healers and practitioners who support us in times of trauma and distress. After suffering a miscarriage at four months, I was blessed with the kindest physician who gave me almost an entire day to process and grieve before making any choices. She had a full room of patients to attend to, but never did I feel rushed or that I was an inconvenience. She gave me time to sit with my grief and even supported me by staying at the hospital far beyond her shift to provide me with the time and care to process everything. She even approved two ultrasounds just to reassure me of what had just happened, as I was in complete disbelief. It was what my heart needed to help me come to terms with this sudden loss. As much as the surgery was not what I had planned for that day, she did almost a double shift to be sure she was the one to perform it. She made sure I was well supported and left a forever-imprint on my heart. I will forever be grateful for Dr. Jane Baillie for being the most heart-centered and compassionate physician I could have hoped for in that difficult moment.

We are in a new time on earth today—a completely new spiritual era. We are being rewired and recalibrated in terms of frequency as the planet awakens at quantum speed. This is one of the reasons almost every system in the world is breaking down simultaneously. It's like we are watching a movie as everything false or fabricated crumbles before our very eyes. This is divinely planned and divinely timed. No longer can we tolerate living a life that falls below highest-vibrational spiritual truth. False living will no longer be tolerated by the higher realms. We must now muster up the courage to activate high coherence, fearless action, and deeply authentic living.

The great news is that all of this is part of a larger ascension process. Each and every one of us is waking up to stronger inner voices, more powerful intuitive messages, and an overall intolerance for choices and behaviors that are not in the best interest of our highest self, humanity, or Mother Earth. When we do slip up and make choices that fuel the ego rather than the soul, we can more quickly and efficiently navigate ourselves back to center. This is because we are synching in to the pure and harmonic resonance of the cosmos *right now*. Our bodies, our minds, and the world around us are experiencing a complete rewiring at speeds we cannot even comprehend. Our healing system today must quickly shift to a cosmic one that addresses the needs of the entire Auric Body rather than the physical body alone. This means that healing modalities today must not only support body attunement but also harmonize the layers of the aura.

Ancient healing wisdom is resurfacing and thriving globally today. These modalities will only continue to animate across the globe. These modalities include:

* The full power and potential of quartz crystals in healing
* The role of the sun in healing as well as modalities such as flower essence therapy to capture the healing energies of the sun
* Homeopathy and its role in subtle body healing
* Sound and light therapies for subtle body coherence
* Plant medicine as aura medicine
* Frequency medicine to support and heal the Auric Body
* Higher-sensory healing potential both for self-healing and with healers
* Free energy and healing
* Plant medicine for subtle body healing (and their role in healing trauma)
* Hydrogen and its role in healing
* The role silver and gold play in healing
* Crystal and Color Therapy
* Plasma and healing

Homeopathy

Homeopathy is the medicine of the vital body/etheric body. Consciousness matters in homeopathy; it is based on individualization and information. The practitioner is seeking to find resonance with the client through investigation and information. Information is what structures consciousness. Samuel Hahnemann, the father of homeopathy, describes vital force as a spirit-like energy that sustains and maintains life. As mentioned in earlier chapters, this vital force radiates around us like a luminous sphere, maintaining the body in a balanced state of health, and, according to quantum physics, is an entire universe of its own. Homeopathy is therefore vital body medicine. This vital energy body is a universe of information about the body, the organs, how it is functioning, and all details about its state. According to Hahnemann, illness is a block between the soul and the body. Classical homeopathy works by way of one specific remedy being recommended to a patient by a trained homeopath. Modern homeopathic modalities often recommend a combination of remedies. It is important to work with higher guidance and intuition to determine which modality is the best fit for you. It is always important to consult with a well-trained homeopath to ensure you have appropriate remedies for your individual needs. Classical homeopathy requires an in-depth intake with a well-trained homeopath to help match individual needs with the best remedy.

There are also some common remedies for everyday indications that are listed below. These are just a few to get you started. We will also discuss homeopathic staples for your home and for first aid in our Auric Home chapter.

Remedy	Indications
Phosphorus	Vomiting, bleeding gums, hair loss in clumps, multiple fears, catches colds easily
Sulfur	Constipation, diarrhea, anal itching, hard stools, allergies, shortness of breath, vaginal burning, forgetfulness, hemorrhoids
Pulsatilla	Indigestion, heartburn
Carbo Vegetabilis	Indigestion, gas, chills, bloating
Galphimia Glauca	Hives, cold sores, skin allergies
Nux Vomica	Daytime runny nose with evening stuffiness, constipation, vomiting, nausea, hangovers, overeating, stress, anxiety, backpain, digestive troubles, anger
Arnica	Head injury, burns, joint pain, wound healing, muscle aches, inflammation from insect bites, pain and inflammation reduction, shock and trauma from injury, bruising
Ignatia	Chronic cough, acute grief, anxiety, depression, grieving the death of a loved one
Belladonna	Sunburn, high fever, sunstroke, boils, fevers with high temperatures, migraine
Glonoine	Throbbing headache
Chamomilla	Teething, colic, irritability in infants, fevers, PMS
Kalium Bichromicum	Sinusitis, thick nasal discharge, croupy cough, hoarse voice
Calendula	Burns, cold sores, cuts, wounds, hemorrhoids, fever, menstrual cramps

Aconite	High onset fever, eye injury, sudden sore throat, sudden headache
Magnesia Phosphorica	Cramps and menstrual cramps, calf cramps, sciatica, swelling, insomnia
Rhus Tox	Strains, sprains, rusty gate syndrome, backaches, arthritis, sciatica, body aches associated with the flu
Borax	Helpful for sensitives that have with the sensation of downward motion (like in an elevator or plane descent), canker sores, air sickness felt on descent
Arsenica Album	Anxiety, tension from depression or loneliness
Gelsemium	Headache, chills, fever, exhaustion, anxiety before a special or big event, jetlag
Pulsattila	Symptoms from cold and flu (especially fluxing between feeling chills and hot)
Cocculus Indicus	Sea sickness, motion sickness, vomiting, dizziness, muscle weakness, vertigo
Coffea Cruda	Mental hyperactivity, sleeplessness from worry, migraines, tooth pain triggered by hot drinks

Flower Essences

Flower essences are liquid consciousness. Flower essence is one of the most sacred and powerful methods for infusing the highest-order vibrational qualities of the sun into our Auric Body. Flowers are the very essence and highest vibration of lifeforce in a plant. In ancient Lemuria, flower essences were used to shape and mold the human form. In ancient Atlantis, they were used as a system of medicine. The biomagnetic signature of the flower essence itself gives it great healing force and power at the subtle body level. The very healing powers of the sun are vibrationally contained within each flower essence at different frequencies. Although these remedies do harmonize the physical body, they primarily work on the ethereal levels such as the mental and emotional body. There are, of course, many other flower essences available as well as combinations that can be purchased. What is of the highest importance is how the flower essences are extracted and made. This is an art form. Working with an experienced flower essence therapist is helpful when it comes to selections. One book that has been a precious guide in my home is *The Encyclopedia of Bach Flower Therapy* by Mechthild Scheffer. Another book that has been helpful along my journey is *Flower Essences and Vibrational Healing by Gurudas* (channeled through Kevin Ryerson and Jon Fox).

Here are a few essences that may resonate with you:

Daisy Flower (Bellis Perennis): Daisy flower is a wonderful remedy for spiritualizing the intellect. When your thoughts are scattered, daisy flower is helpful. Daisy aligns the entire Auric Body and focuses on harmonizing all of your bodies, which leads to emotional, mental, and spiritual balance.

Rock Rose: Rock Rose is helpful in situations of sudden trauma, accident, or panic. This is a great remedy in an emergency situation. Rock Rose flower essence helps to strengthen the will, develop courage, and is a supportive essence in times of intense stress.

Aspen: Aspen is very helpful when fears seem to come out of nowhere. When there is a state of overwhelming worry or terror (including night terrors), aspen is a good choice. This essence also supports overall feelings of security and safety because it helps soothe feelings of unsettlement and brings forth peace of mind.

Red Chestnut: This is the flower essence for chronic worry. Red Chestnut promotes peace of mind and harmony in the mind. This essence supports a loving peace of mind and helps us care for others without an unhealthy and excessive dose of worry. This would be a wonderful choice for what Dr Robert Morse calls "detached compassion."

Honeysuckle: Honeysuckle is a helpful remedy when we are grieving or homesick. It is also a wonderful remedy for situations when we are too attached to things—including the past. Honeysuckle promotes the letting go and surrender.

Wild Rose: Wild Rose is a strong heart chakra opener and a beautiful choice for supporting trauma healing. This essential oil uplifts the spirits and speaks directly to the soul. Wild Rose also brings the astral and mental bodies into harmony and has the ability to enhance telepathy.

Bleeding Heart: Bleeding Heart supports the heart chakra and, in particular, heart and thymus gland health by promoting healthy circulatory function and blood pressure. Bleeding Heart is also beneficial for supporting muscle tissue. It supports both the physical heart but also the etheric and emotional bodies associated with this region.

Calendula: Calendula flower essence supports healthy relationships and self-expression. It supports deep listening as well as speaking our authentic truth. This is the essence for communication and connection.

Morning Glory: Morning glory is a wonderful essence for the entire nervous system. Just as its name implies, it helps you get up in the morning. It is also a wonderful essence to help cut ties with addictions and supports mental clarity and well-being. This is a wonderful essence for vitality, endurance, and stamina.

Chamomile: Chamomile enhances the entire nervous system as well as supporting respiratory, skin, kidney, and mental health. Chamomile also stimulates the pineal gland. It is also a wonderful flower essence for children.

Lilac: Lilac promotes mental clarity and acts on the etheric, mental, and spiritual bodies. Lilac also promotes spinal column health. It can also activate kundalini energy and is helpful when one is too attached to people or things as well as when we need more emotional and mental flexibility.

Passionflower: Passionflower opens the heart and throat chakras and also supports access to higher levels of consciousness. Passionflower helps support a healthy pituitary gland, regulates sleep, and promotes balance and harmony within the body.

Crab Apple: This remedy is a master cleanser and supports mental, physical, and emotional cleansing. When we're feeling too obsessive, self-conscious, or energetically heavy, crab apple is a perfect choice.

Centaury: This remedy is very helpful for empaths, sensitives, and starseeds. This essence supports gentle and kind hearts to build healthy boundaries and speak their truth. This is also a great remedy for individuals who are being pressured or bullied as well as for people-pleasers.

Lotus: Lotus acts on the energies between sky and earth and is a powerful crown chakra harmonizer. Lotus is like an equivalent to the philosopher's stone in flower form—a master healer flower essence. Lotus is also wonderful as a booster for other flower essence remedies. Lotus supports healing and peace on all levels of the Auric Body. It is also a wonderful flower essence for emotional healing.

Herbals

Plants hold a specific spiritual signature, which make them powerful forces when it comes to Auric Health. Every plant has specific vibrational qualities that set specific tonal patterns within the body. Herbs truly do make music in and on the body. Plants lock in the healing and spiritual properties of the sun and then transfer them to the Auric Body upon use. I highly recommend booking a consultation with a certified herbalist. They can best guide you in a safe and healing direction when it comes to herbs. Herbs come in a variety of formats including teas, tinctures, balms, and supplements. I suggest looking into an ethically- and mindfully sourced herbalists near you. There is also growing intrigue in the field of Astroherbalism, that studies the relationships and union between cosmos and plants.

Here are a few wondrous herbs that support physical and subtle body illumination:

Gotu Kola: This is the herb of longevity. This herb has been used to support skin health, mental health, lymphatic flow, joint health, and circulation, as well to reduce swelling. It is also used to reduce appearance of stretch marks and to help with insomnia as well as general body detoxification.

Oregon Grape: Oregon Grape promotes detoxification, bowel, and digestive health as well as clearing heat from the body for those who tend to have an excess of "fire" energy. This is also a wonderful herb for the lymphatic system.

Ashwagandha: This herb has a long history of being used to reduce anxiety and stress. It is also a wonderful herb for immune system support as well as for lymphatic flow and detoxification.

Shatavari: Shatavari is a hormone-balancing herb that can help regulate vaginal pH levels. It also reduces vaginal dryness and is an overall vaginal anti-inflammatory. It nourishes female reproductive organs and increases libido. This herb also helps with night sweats and hot flashes.

Moringa: Moringa is one of the best natural multivitamin and mineral supports. It is a superfood that includes all 18 amino acids. It is a good source of folic acid and has a multitude of benefits and actions including reducing swelling and water retention, hair and skin radiance, and promoting digestive health.

Hawthorn Berry: Hawthorn Berry is a wonderful overall antioxidant. It is helps promote healthy blood- and lymphatic flow and has been used to treat skin conditions such as boils and skin sores as well as hair loss and anxiety.

Cleavers: Cleavers are often used as a diuretic as they reduce swelling and water retention and are often the herb of choice for swollen glands and fluid build-up. Cleavers support healthy lymphatic flow, detoxification, and healthy kidney and bladder function as well as treating psoriasis and skin conditions.

Blue Vervain: This herb can increase milk production in mothers as well as calm the nervous system and harmonize mood swings. Blue Vervain also supports healthy digestive function, lymphatic flow, and a thriving immune system. It can also be used as an aid for depression, pain management, and stomach disorders.

Licorice Root: Licorice root has been used for weight management, stomach ulcers, and digestive issues. It is also used for reducing symptoms of menopause. The herb has also been used in cases of low blood sugar (bringing levels back into balance and harmony) as well as to treat acid reflux, heartburn, and indigestion.

Goldenseal: Goldenseal supports immune function and has been used to treat hay fever. It is also used for respiratory infections, skin disorders, sinus infections, and painful periods.

Wormwood: This herb is helpful for promoting healthy digestion and can eliminate intestinal parasites. It has also been used to treat insomnia, anemia, and indigestion. It is also showing much promise for cellular repair, healing, and regeneration. Wormwood is also often used for soothing the symptoms of Crohn's disease.

Siberian Ginseng (Eleuthero): This herb is used to enhance energy, immunity, memory, libido, mental clarity, bone health, and restorative sleep.

Dandelion Root: Dandelion Root works as a digestive aid, detoxification aid, and kidney function. This herb helps to regulate blood sugar and cholesterol as it promotes liver health.

Milk Thistle: This herb supports liver health and detoxification. Milk thistle also promotes bone and skin health and is often used to reduce insulin resistance and cholesterol, as they tend to spill out back into the body when the liver becomes clogged.

Calendula: Calendula is a beautiful herb for healthy hair, skin, glands, and immunity strength. It can be helpful for wound healing, rashes, scars, and varicose veins. It is helpful for mastitis, cold sores, hemorrhoids, ovarian cysts, and mild fevers.

Astragalus: One of the most powerful immune-strengthening herbs on the planet, this herb has been used to treat allergies, inflammation, viruses, and lung infections. Astragalus is also helpful for promoting liver health and may be helpful in treating hepatitis.

Olive Leaf: This powerful herb helps boost immunity and fight free radicals. It supports cardiovascular health and brain function. Olive Leaf has been used to lower blood pressure and insulin resistance and as a natural remedy for candida.

Marshmallow Root: Marshmallow root is regularly used in stomach teas to help heal gut lining and for digestive health. This herb also promotes skin health, heart health, and immune system health. It can be helpful for colds, bronchitis, and respiratory conditions.

Red Clover: Red Clover is often used in the treatment of skin conditions and to detoxify the body. This herb promotes lymphatic and circulatory health. Red clover is also often used in menopause and for respiratory congestion.

Galangal: This anti-inflammatory herb is often used in the treatment of osteoarthritis and rheumatoid arthritis. It is also used to support mental wellbeing, digestive health, and in the treatment of ulcers. It is helpful to treat nausea and motion sickness as well as supporting healthy blood and lymphatic circulation.

Burdock Root: This herb has been used to support lymphatic flow and function as well as to support blood health. Burdock root is a natural diuretic and works to lower blood sugar as well as inflammation throughout the body. Burdock root also supports spleen health and is a beneficial herb for protection and healing.

Mullein Leaf: Mullein Leaf is another incredible herb for promoting lymphatic flow and detoxification. It also soothes skin, cold sores, and hemorrhoids. This herb is also helpful for promoting healthy joints.

Butcher's Broom: This is a popular choice for promoting cardiovascular health as well as bladder and bowel health. Butcher's Broom also enhances circulation of blood and lymph throughout the body and has been known to act as a diuretic and blood vessel supporter. Herbalists use this herb for clients who suffer from restless leg syndrome, ankle swelling, hemorrhoids, dark circles under the eyes and inflammation.

Rhodiola: This herb supports energy and relieves stress and anxiety. It is also helpful for supporting adrenal function, brain health, and immune system resilience. Rhodiola has also been used to support those suffering from chronic fatigue and depression.

Triphala: Triphala is actually the combination of three fruits: haritaki, bibhitaki, and amalaka. This gem has been used for centuries for healthy weight management, hair growth, constipation, colon health, skin health, and for treating arthritis. It is also used to maintain healthy blood pressure.

Here are a few herbal practices that greatly enhance and activate Auric Living:

1. Replace many, if not most, cups of coffee with herbal tea (although coffee in moderation does have health benefits).
2. Have a cup of herbal tea each morning and night to start and end the day.
3. Replacing current beauty care, health care, home care, first aid care, and skin care with herbal blends
4. Consider booking a consult with a certified or master herbalist.
5. Develop an auric relationship with herbs and study their subtle body goodness. As you develop a relationship with plants and herbs, you may begin to feel, see, and even speak to their auras.
6. Make use of herbs to cleanse your home, aura, and body.
7. Incorporate a few herbal tinctures into your daily life (with the guidance of a trained herbalist).
8. Start an herb garden. (One of my favorite books for learning more about herbs is *The Lost Book of Herbal Remedies* by Nicole Apelian.)

Crystals

Crystals are living consciousness, and the time is right to develop a sacred relationship with them. In his book *Flower Essences and Vibrational Healing*, Gurudas (channeled through Kevin Ryerson and Jon Fox) describes that in the beginning of creation, all creatures on earth were to be created as crystalline and quartz-like in structure; instead, due to other forces, life here on earth became carbon based. Perhaps this is why quartz crystal resonance with the human body is so very powerful. Ordering individual and family life around the balancing properties of crystals can be very beneficial. Many people (including myself) believe that crystals have already achieved their highest level of consciousness, which makes them powerful conduits of high-order charge. They have the capacity to hold and to transfer charge—first as electricity, then as light, and finally as thought. Crystals hold a great deal of mystical information and are powerful tools for a healing and ascension journey. Consider creating crystal grids in rooms throughout your home, especially where you practice movement, pray, or meditate. It is also wise to fill your home with crystals to support Auric Body balancing day and night. I believe our bodies are aware that our original make-up was intended to be crystalline in structure, and that there is a divine pull to head in that direction. Take a peek at Dr Harvey Bigelsen's book *Holographic Blood* to inspire you further.

Crystals are tools for us to develop higher-realm communication. They support our development and ascension when it comes to consciousness, manifestation, healing, energy work, and communication. We all hold a natural ability to communicate with crystals—we simply need to practice. For any crystal you have in your home, consider yourself to be the guardian of that crystal. Take the time each day to feel, move, and communicate with the crystal. As you practice this regularly, you will develop an ability to feel the charge of the crystal and feel when the crystal needs a clearing, a charge, or a new location in your home. Working with crystals is an intuitive practice, which is why I believe there is no one way or right way to work with crystals. Crystals are there to support your journey as you unlock and unleash your master healer within. They work to harmonize and calibrate your Auric Body. Quartz crystals, in particular, vibrate the aura at such fast rates that they have the ability to dispel and shake away lower vibrational and/or darker energies that are no longer welcomed into one's reality field. This is why quartz crystals are magnificent aids and facilitators for soul healing work.

Many meditation teachers guide students in creating a crystal shield around the body. During visualization techniques, it is helpful to focus on the thymus gland (located in the center of your chest behind the sternum and between the lungs). Visualize the thymus producing crystal-like frequencies that travel through the physical and subtle bodies for healing. It is also helpful to wear quartz crystals and even keep one in your car and pocket as well as one on your bedside table (and on your children's).

Crystals deserve a full book of their own but here is our Auric Living must-have crystal list:

Clear Quartz: Clear quartz is the universal healer and master energy amplifier. You really can't have or get enough of this crystal if true Auric Health is your objective.

Rose Quartz: This is the crystal that illuminates the heart. When we listen to our soul, all we hear is unconditional love. Rose Quartz speaks this very language.

Fluorite: Fluorite is not only beautiful to look at but also promotes spiritual and clairvoyant development as well as protects the aura from all unwanted energies. It enhances self-esteem, enhances communication, relieves anxiety and stress, and the body's bioelectrical system, too. This is one powerful gem!

Citrine: This one is a master stone for abundance and for moving creative energy to and through the physical realm. If you are always flowing with great ideas but can't seem to manifest them into money, this stone is for you. This stone is a beautiful choice and a staple in any crystal collection. Citrine also supports mental clarity and strong self-esteem.

Hematite: Consider Hematite to be the cloaking shield stone. Hematite is a master protector and creating an occasional or frequent hematite shield around your body is very helpful for nurturing the Auric Body. Hematite is an iron oxide crystal and communicates well with the iron crystals of human blood. This is one of the reasons it makes a perfect protection companion. The following diagram can assist you with creating a Hematite shield around your body (in a lying position). This grid can be used for grounding, healing, protection, and rejuvenation. Grounding and protection are two beautiful benefits of working with this shiny crystal. Using the diagram below as a guide, place hematite stones on the main cosmic axis of the body as well as around the body. Place hematite stones in both hands and directly under both feet. Above the head, a pyrite crystal can be used.

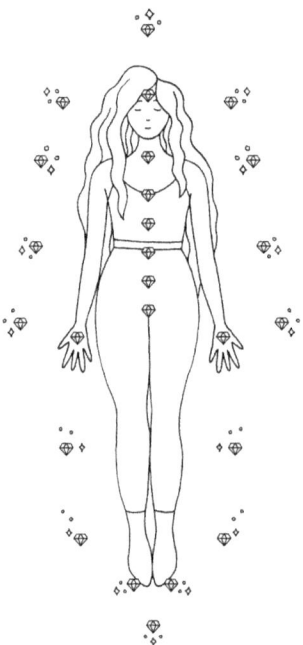

Pyrite: Pyrite is also known as fool's gold and it a pure gem when it comes to infusing creative energy into one's life. Pyrite is also a wondrous protective stone which is why it is also included in the crystal grid for the body (illustrated above). Pyrite enhances purity and cleansing as well as protection.

Amethyst: This is the stone of divine manifestation and of peace. It is wonderful for a meditation practice or to fill a room with an overall sense of calm and beauty. This stone also works through the heart chakra to promote mental, spiritual, emotional, and physical health.

Aquamarine: This stone is an emotional balancer and mental stabilizer. Aquamarine helps to release anxiety, stress, fear, and feelings of anger or hate. This stone helps to harmonize the 5th chakra and bring divine will and clear communication to your reality.

Azurite: This gorgeous gem is a wonderful aid for clearing the mind, soul, and karma. It also helps to enhance self-esteem, clairvoyance, and the courage to pursue you true purpose and path. Use this stone to balance the mind and bring waves of love into your life, as Azurite is one of the celestial stones that brings great divine energy into your life. This gem is the complete package when it comes to cleansing and harmonizing all layers of the Auric Body.

Celestite/Celestine: This is the stone of angels. If you're seeking your true path and highest purpose, Celestite is the gem for you. Celestite also facilitates communication with higher realm beings. As one of the most beautiful gems, Celestite is a true physical manifestation of the heavenly realm in mineral form. This gem supports deep inner peace, spirit world connection, and intuition enhancement. Celestite is also a powerful Auric Body cleanser. It purifies and cleanses the physical body with angelic grace.

Jade: Jade is the stone of abundance, luck, prosperity, and love. This is a powerful gem in Chinese medicine. This is a true metaphysical master as it works its magic in both awake and dream states. This stone works to calm and support the entire body as well as harmonizes the 2nd and 4th chakra.

Lapis Lazuli: This one is not only fun to say but is simply a beauty. This gem is known as the wisdom stone and was one of the highest order stones in ancient Egypt. This stone activates inner peace and helps to relieve insomnia and depression. This gem also works on the 5th chakra to support thyroid health as well as your true and authentic voice. This stone is a great choice for developing self-awareness, higher consciousness, and higher realm abilities.

Malachite: This is the healer stone and has a wondrous ability to absorb all forms of negative energy from the Auric Body. This stone is an important one to cleanse often. This can be done using moonlight and sunlight, but using water to cleanse this stone can wear away at its surface. Malachite is a supportive and healing stone for arthritis, bone repair, tissue healing, menstrual cramps, joint pain, body aches, and liver health. This gem is also a very powerful detoxifier. Malachite is a guardian of the heart and helpful for healing trauma. Because of the strong yin energy of Malachite, it has earned the name of "the Midwife's Stone."

Selenite: Selenite is known as the goddess stone and is named after the Greek goddess of the moon. This is one of the only crystals that doesn't have to be cleansed. This stone brings peace, protection, harmony, and soul healing. This is a highly spiritual stone and is a fabulous companion for any meditation practice.

Shungite: One of the oldest minerals from the earth, this stone is a super gem. Not only does this stone help remind you to always balance technology with nature but it is also a cosmic superconductor; Shungite has higher conductivity than gold. It can remove harmful energies and also recharges the entire Auric Body. This stone is a powerful body detoxifier and may also protect the body from radiation. It is beneficial to place Shungite near electronics, routers, computers, and anywhere that EMFs are strong.

Sunstone: This stone is a joy gem. It helps to bring joy to life and enhances mood. On days when a smile is needed, Sunstone is a perfect choice because it is said to harness the power of the sun. This gem positively harmonizes the 3rd chakra.

Seraphinite: This gem is named after the highest order of angels, the Seraphim. This is the stone of angel wings and spiritual flight. This stone supports the rising of Kundalini and harmonizes all chakras. This stone can also activate communication with angels and higher realm beings. It is a heart chakra activator and promotes unconditional love.

Black Tourmaline: This is the most powerful protection stone. Using this stone will support boundaries around your Auric Body and protect you from energy vampires and lifeforce leaches. This stone is particularly connected with the 1st chakra supporting grounding, security, and protection. Black Tourmaline is a shield against EMFs, increases metabolism, and is helpful for optimizing circulation, lymphatic flow, and organ function.

Cell Salts/Tissue Salts

Cells salts (also known as tissue salts) were developed by German homeopath Dr Wilhelm Schuessler. Dr Schuessler concluded through his research that when mineral salts are not balanced within the body, disease developed. This makes sense when you review the levels of consciousness from earlier in the chapter. These salts can be used in combination with homeopathy as well as on their own. Cells salts are a form of homeopathic mineral therapy that work to restore balance and harmony both to the physical body and etheric body. Cell salts are homeopathic microdoses of the body's 12 essential minerals, making them easy and natural for the cell to take in as they are in micromineral form. Often, they are combined to offer an array of cell salt offerings. Tissue salts are a beautiful way to connect with first and second dimensions of Mother Earth, because the earth's core and crust naturally contain the mineral salts that are also vital for human health and metabolic function. They are also very helpful for harmonizing the etheric, mental, and spiritual body. There is a salt for every zodiac sign, which mystically blends the field of astrology with tissue salts (as well as with herbs and flowers). I believe cell salts will continue to rise in popularity across the globe over coming years and decades.

Here are the 12 Primary Tissue Salts:

1. *Calcium Fluoride*: strengthens tooth enamel and bones; helps with hemorrhoids and hernia
2. *Calcium Phosphate*: supports healthy cells and digestion and helps to heal bone fractures
3. *Calcium Sulphate*: purifies blood, supports infection healing, promotes healthy and glowing skin; helpful for the prevention of colds and sore throats
4. *Ferrum Phosphate:* anti-inflammatory, accelerates healing, helps reduce fever
5. *Potassium Chloride:* supports recovery from cold and flu, reduces mucous congestion and enhances blood purification and relieves digestive issues.
6. *Potassium Phosphate:* supports brain function as well as emotional wellbeing and mood; helpful for headaches, nervousness, fatigue, anxiety, and depression
7. *Potassium Sulphate:* a wonderful cell salt for the skin; helps with skin inflammation, acne, dandruff, eczema, dry patches, and to balance and regulate the moisture and oil content of the skin
8. *Magnesium Phosphate:* an incredible cell salt for relieving migraines, muscle cramps, and muscle spasms; one of the key cell salts for heart health and pain relief
9. *Sodium Chloride:* balancing body fluids and reducing fluid retention as well as eczema and digestive issues; can restore a lost sense of taste and smell as well as relieve allergies, constipation, and migraines
10. *Sodium Phosphate:* a wonderful antacid; helps to relieve heartburn, joint inflammation, and rheumatoid conditions
11. *Sodium Sulphate:* excellent for the liver and digestive system; offers relief for upset stomach, diarrhea, and flu symptoms
12. *Silica:* nourishing for hair, skin, and nails because it improves collagen production in the body; a must for a glowing aura!

Essential Oils

Essential oils carry with them the highest-realm vibrations from the sun and support luminous Auric Bodies. They can be diluted in carrier oils (for use on the skin) or diffused to enhance the very vibration of your entire home. They can also be added to organic soaps and cleaning products to create your very own signature scent. Rosemary and Mint as examples are two of my favorite oils to add to my organic unscented shampoo or castile soap. My home is loaded with essential oils for making cleaners and soaps as well as to add to dryer balls. I use them for oral care both to make mouthwash and for applying a few drops on my gums each morning and night. An essential oil diffuser is always going in my home, and I spritz my linens often throughout the day. My children get to select which scents to spray on their pillows each night. There are many popular essential oils that are commonly used, but for the purposes of this book, I'd like to include a few unique ones that you might consider adding to your collection:

Forest Amber: This is one of my favorites. Forest Amber calms the mind and nervous system, protects the heart, and increases libido.

Lilac: Some of the benefits of Lilac include boosting the immune system, reducing anxiety, and supporting skin health. The sweet smell of Lilac will bring instant joy to your heart.

Cacao: Cacao is also a wonderful skin illuminator and also enhances collagen production. It is helpful for healing wounds and skin conditions in addition to being a well-known aphrodisiac. Cacao is also wonderful for joint, brain, and heart health.

Bergamot: Bergamot is helpful as a pain- and stress reliever. It also has fabulous antibacterial properties and is very healing for the skin.

Vanilla: Vanilla is another one of my favorite oils. It is a natural antioxidant and also a powerful aphrodisiac. Vanilla is also beneficial for skin and hair and for supporting the healing of scars.

Clove bud: This gem is fabulous as an antimicrobial and pain reliever, especially for toothaches. Clove essential oil works well for relieving muscle aches, too.

Grapefruit: Grapefruit supports healthy skin and metabolism and is a fabulous mood enhancer. I like to call this oil the "happy essential."

Honeysuckle: This magician soothes headaches and alleviates pain. It is also deeply nurturing for skin and hair. With its great antibacterial properties.

Calendula: Calendula is an anti-inflammatory and antioxidant. It is deeply soothing to the skin and helps alleviate rashes and redness. It is also antimicrobial and deeply hydrating. It is even helpful as a scalp treatment, wound healer, sun protector and has anti-aging properties. This one is a mom-must!

Cardamom: Cardamom also has wonderful antibacterial properties and promotes healthy skin. Cardamom is helpful for insect bites, toothaches, and healthy gums. Cardamom also has anti-nausea and anti-inflammatory properties. This oil can also be applied topically to the chest to reduce congestion from a cold and to the belly to promote healthy digestion and metabolism.

Cinnamon Bark: This essential oil enhances mood and relaxation and calms the nervous system. It is also a beautiful air purifier and supports deep and healthy breathing.

Chamomile: This essential oil is helpful for wound healing, anxiety relief, and emotional peace. Its anti-inflammatory properties make it a perfect choice for alleviating skin conditions.

Helichrysum: This oil is pure rejuvenation and illumination as a beauty oil. Helichrysum oil promotes cellular health, cell repair, and cell regeneration. This oil inhibits microbial growth and is a great choice for wounds, cuts, and scars. It is also helpful for acne.

Sweet Orange: A supportive choice for insomnia, anxiety, mental wellbeing, and mood, this oil also has antibacterial and anti-inflammatory properties.

Frankincense: This oil is an ancient healer. Use it to promote cellular health, skin health, relaxation, mental clarity, and so much more. Frankincense has astringent properties and is helpful for promoting oral health. This oil also helps in scar healing and is a powerful breathwork promoter.

Geranium: Geranium is beneficial for soothing anxiety, depression, and pain. This oil is an excellent anti-inflammatory and is helpful for supporting deep and restorative sleep.

Jasmine: Jasmine is a definite mood and libido enhancer. It also helps alleviate insomnia, stress, anger, depression, and anxiety. Jasmine also supports scar healing and a healthy and balanced menstrual cycle.

Myrrh: This essential oil is antibacterial and antiparasitic. It supports oral health, skin health, and reduces pain and swelling. Myrrh also fights fungal infections and supports a healthy nervous system and circulatory system.

Magnolia: Magnolia essential oil calms the nervous system and promotes a healthy emotional body. This oil promotes an overall feeling of peace and relaxation.

Myrtle: This gift of an oil helps to combat bad odor. It also supports healthy nerves and prevents infection. Myrtle relaxes the entire body and is also a powerful aphrodisiac. (In fact, it was even associated with Aphrodite, the Greek Goddess of Love.)

Palo Santo: This cleansing oil purifies the air and the mind and translates to "holy wood." This oil is great in a diffuser to energetically cleanse the air of lower vibrational vibes. This is a beautifully grounding and calming oil that reduces stress and positively supports a meditation practice.

Peppermint: Peppermint is a must for every essential oil collection because of its versatility. It promotes healthy digestion, breathing, mental wellbeing, and emotional health. It is a wonderful oil to reduce stress and anxiety as well as to promote hair growth and repel insects.

Rockrose: Rockrose (or Cistus) is the wound-healer essential oil. It is beneficial for treating eczema and psoriasis as well as for treating wounds and skin conditions. Rockrose supports lymphatic draining, a healthy lymphatic system, and healthy and glowing skin.

Rosemary: Rosemary is another must-have in any essential oil collection. This gem enhances hair growth, supports brain function, repels insects, and reduces stress. I often combine this essential oil with peppermint in my dryer balls and for room and linen sprays. Rosemary also reduces join inflammation and enhances circulation.

Rosewood: This essential oil acts as a natural deodorant, aphrodisiac, antimicrobial, antibacterial, and analgesic. Rosewood is helpful for relieving pain, stress, inflammation, and bad odor. It is also a natural insect repellant and mood-booster.

Sea Buckthorn: Sea Buckthorn oil can be used without a carrier oil for wounds and cuts. It is one of the most powerful skin health enhancers and natural dark spot corrector for skin. It is also a natural antifungal and antibacterial and is a wonderful companion to an oral health regime.

Sandalwood: Sandalwood is a powerful aid in meditation and for calming the mind and body. This oil also has anti-inflammatory properties and is both a skin and mood enhancer. It is a natural disinfectant and astringent. This oil is not only a memory booster but also a great way to reduce stress, tension, anxiety, and fear.

Tulsi (Holy Basil): Tulsi is a master promoter of spiritual and physical wellbeing. This oil is helpful for treating acne and small wounds and for healthy skin in general. It also functions as an aura protector and can be used as an auric shield. This oil is a body, mind, and spirit purifier and cleanser.

Vetiver: Vetiver is another oil that promotes restful sleep and body-calming. It is used to reduce stress, anxiety, and fear. This oil works on all chakra levels and is a master mind-harmonizer. This is also a healing oil for the skin for treating acne, scars, and skin conditions as it is a natural skin cell illuminator.

Ylang Ylang: Ylang Ylang is another natural aphrodisiac and skin illuminator. This oil is also beneficial for rheumatism, gout, and acne as well as to support skin and hair health. It is a natural insect repellant and a beautiful heart activator.

Mastic: Mastic is used for bacterial and fungal infections and to relieve muscle aches. Traditionally, Mastic was used as a lymphatic and circulatory health promoter. This oil is often used in the treatment of spider and varicose veins as well as a pain reliever.

Zdravetz: This essential oil is a psyche clarifier and wonderful for the entire Auric Body. This is the essential oil of luck and wellbeing. Add a few drops of this oil to a bath for soothing the skin, mind, and body.

Most companies who manufacture essential oils have their own version of the "Guard from Thieves" blend, which is my absolute favorite oil for daily use. This blend is a combination of clove bud, lemon or orange, cinnamon bark, eucalyptus, and rosemary essential oils.

Each version varies slightly so you can feel free to add your own style to the blend. I often add a few drops of vanilla.

> ## *AURIC ACTION*
>
> Here is a recipe for a homemade "Guard from Thieves" blend:
> 25 drops: Clove bud essential oil
> 20 drops: Lemon or Orange essential oil
> 12 drops: Cinnamon Bark essential oil
> 8 drops: Eucalyptus essential oil
> 6 drops: Rosemary essential oil
> (I also add a few drops of vanilla)

Auric Health is a deeply personal, spiritual, and intuitive journey. The prescriptive I offer here is just a small selection of offerings as a starting point in your own healing journey. It is important to note that for supporting the chakra system, there are hundreds of minor chakras throughout the body, and sounds and colors that support each chakra vary greatly across traditions. For the purposes of this book, a suggested sound and frequency may be useful as a starting point for you, but healing is always a personal process. Your body has its own unique biosignature, and self-discovery and self-mastery are deeply sacred and deeply personal. In particular, frequencies for each chakra vary from person to person. Sound healers and sound experts are wonderfully supportive for Auric Health. Consider a tuning fork session or sound bath to feel the different areas of the body that light up at different frequencies of sound. As we get more intimate with our own chakras, we will see that the chakra system is a multi-universe. The following guide acts as a starting and centering point for you to begin this journey towards self-actualization.

1ˢᵗ Chakra Healing: Survival, Security, Roots, Trust, Nourishment, Family, Health
Crystals: Jade, Black Tourmaline, Malachite, Garnet, Hematite, Black Obsidian, Red Jasper, Bloodstone, Carnelian, Smoky Quartz, Black Onyx, Shungite.
Essential Oils: Ylang, Ylang, Rosewood, Vetiver, Frankincense, Amber, Cacao, Patchouli, Cedarwood, Sandalwood, Palo Santo
Flower Essences: Rock Rose, Chery Plum, Mimulus, Red Chestnut, Ginseng, Lotus, Chicory, Centaury, Honeysuckle, Blue Jade, Douglas Fir, Aspen
Herbs: Ashwaganda, Ginger, Dandelion, Sage
Cell Salts: Calcium Fluoride, Calcium Sulphate, Calcium Phosphate, Potassium Chloride
Sound: LAM/Do/Middle C
Frequency (Hz): 174, 285, 396

2ⁿᵈ Chakra Healing: Movement, Pleasure, Intimacy, Money, Desire
Crystals: Orange Calcite, Citrine, Carnelian, Tigers Eye, Sunstone, Amber, Aragonite, Goldstone, Jade
Essential Oils: Rosewood, Sandalwood, Tarragon, Juniper, Olive, Tangerine, Wild Orange, Grapefruit, Ylang Ylang, Cinnamon, Saffron, Calendula, Gardenia
Flower Essences: Willow, Wild Rose, Calla Lily, Hibiscus, Orchid, Pomegranate, Snapdragon, Trillium, Zinnia, Gardenia
Herbs: Damiana, Hibiscus, Gardenia, Black Cohosh, Nettle, Rasberry Leaf, Moringa Leaf, Marshmallow Root, Red Clover, Cinnamon, Cardamom, Calendula, Fennel, Licorice Root
Cell Salts: Sodium Phosphate, Potassium Chloride
Sound: VAM/Re/D
Frequency (Hz): 417

3ʳᵈ Chakra Healing: Self-Esteem, Will Power, Personal Responsibility
Crystals: Citrine, Amber, Yellow Jasper, Lemon Quartz, Sunstone, Agate, Yellow Topaz, Tourmaline

Essential Oils: Rosewood, Sandalwood, Tarragon, Juniper, Lemon, Rosemary, Bergamot, Lavender, Cardamom
Flower Essences: Willow, Wild Rose, Cerato, Red Chestnut, Borage, Cherry Blossom, Lilac, Pansy, Sunflower
Herbs: Chamomile, Milk Thistle, Ginger, Tumeric, Marshmallow Root, Mint, Lemon Balm, Fennel, Slippery Elm, Rosemary, Golden Rod, Licorice, Galangal, Lemongrass, Sage, Basil
Cell Salts: Calcium Phosphate, Sodium Phosphate, Sodium Sulphate, Potassium Sulphate
Sound: RAM/Mi/E
Frequency (Hz): 528

4th Chakra Healing: Love, Relationships, Harmony, Devotion, Self-Love
Crystals: Emerald, Gold, Green Tourmaline, Malachite, Scarab, Rose Quartz, Green Aventurine, Rhodonite, Green Jade, Rhodochrosite, Chrysoprase
Essential Oils: Rosewood, Sandalwood, Tarragon, Juniper, Rose, Lavender, Lilac, Honeysuckle, Cacao, Bergamot, Amber, Peppermint, Cardamom, Myrtle
Flower Essences: Willow, Wild Rose, Bleeding Heart, Sage, Borage, Heather, Impatiens, Pine, Sweet Chestnut, Star of Bethlehem, Passion Flower, Lotus, Ylang Ylang
Herbs: Hawthorn Berry, Rose, Lavender, Jasmine, Peppermint, Holy Basil, Nettle, Red Clover
Cell Salts: Magnesium Phosphate, Potassium Chloride
Sound: YAM/Fa/F
Frequency (Hz): 639

5th Chakra Healing: Communication, Creativity, Listening
Crystals: Aquamarine, Labradorite, Blue Quartz, Lapis Lazuli, Sapphire, Amazonite, Sodalite, Blue Lace Agate, Blue Kyanite, Celestite, Blue Chalcedony, Chrysocolla, Larimar
Essential Oils: Rosewood, Sandalwood, Tarragon, Juniper, Basil, Bergamot, Peppermint, Amber, Chamomile, Vanilla

Flower Essences: Willow, Wild Rose, Cosmos, Iris, Morning Glory
Herbs: Slippery Elm, Licorice Root, Cinnamon, Fennel, Orange Peel, Bayberry, Red Clover, Blue Vervain, Peppermint, Sage
Cell Salts: Potassium Chloride, Calcium Sulphate, Magnesium Phosphate
Sound: HAM/Sol/G
Frequency (Hz): 741

6th Chakra Healing: Intuition, Insight, Visualization, Imagination, Dreams, Vision
Crystals: Amethyst, Gold, Cat's Eye Tourmaline, Azurite, Blue Kyanite, Clear Quartz, Purple Fluorite, Charoite, Celestite, Lapis Lazuli.
Essential Oils: Clary Sage, Chamomile, Rosemary, Lavender, Sage, Sandalwood, Neroli, Frankincense, Rose, Lilac, Geranium, Vetiver
Flower Essences: Chamomile, Lotus, Dandelion, Forget-Me-Not, Plumeria, Passion Flower, Lilac, Wild Rose
Herbs: Passion Flower, Chamomile, American Ginseng, Gingko Biloba, Gotu Kola, Kava Kava, Blue Lotus, Ashwaganda, Siberian Ginseng, Eyebright, Slippery Elm, Jasmine, Mint
Cell Salts: Potassium Phosphate, Ferrum Phosphate
Sound: OM/La/A
Frequency (Hz): 852

7th Chakra Healing: Compassion, Total Acceptance, Self-Actualization, Higher Consciousness, Divine Connection, Clarity, Presence
Crystals: Selenite, Clear Quartz, Lepidolite, Sugilite, White Agate, Fluorite, Lapis Lazuli, Charoite, White Diamond, Calcite, Moonstone, Celestite
Essential Oils: Jasmine, Vanilla, Lavender, Neroli, Frankincense, Sandalwood, Palo Santo, Lotus, Tulsi, Vetiver
Flower Essences: Lotus, Passion Flower, Orchid, Lily of the Valley, Silversword, Cosmos
Herbs: Lavender, Gotu Kola, Valerian, Tulsi, Gingo Biloba, Calendula

Cell Salts: Potassium Phosphate, Silica
Sound: OM or silence/Ti/B
Frequency (Hz): 963

Detoxification

As previously mentioned, healing and detox baths are a regular practice for Auric Living. Dead sea salts or Himalayan salts are ideal for this kind of detoxification.

Auric Bath (For physical and energetic detoxification): It is helpful to begin an Auric Bath with a body blessing. I have included one at the end of this chapter. Setting tone and rhythm for detoxification is highly encouraged as it becomes a way of life. For highly sensitive and empathetic souls, an Auric Bath should become a daily ritual. It is important to use heart and intuitive energy to customize your own Auric Bath but here are a few suggested ingredients:

* Flower essences
* Essential oils
* Herbs
* Wild flowers
* Bentonite clay
* Blue clay
* Montmorillonite Clay
* Activated charcoal powder/tablets
* Organic body oils
* All-natural baking soda
* Healing salts (Epsom, Himalayan, Dead Sea)
* Glutathione
* Zeolite
* Shungite crystals (powerful for drawing out toxins)
* Quartz crystals

Detoxification from heavy metals, radiation, fungus, and parasites can all be supported by regular Auric Baths.

Activated Coconut Charcoal: Coconut charcoal tablets can be helpful for helping to eliminate toxins from the body. Taken orally, the positive charges of the toxins and waste matter bind to the negative charge of the porous activated charcoal. The charcoal therefore acts as a binder for these unwanted toxins and supports detoxification and elimination.

Superfoods: Many superfoods such as moringa offer the physical body vibrations of higher health and attunement. The *Auric Living* superfood list is compiled with specific criteria including enhancing lymphatic flow, optimizing the immune system, illuminating skin, alkalizing the body, hydrating the skin, and reducing inflammation as well as eliminating unwanted bugs in the body. In our next chapter together, Auric Nutrition, we will profess great love to 22 top superfoods!

Castor Oil: The ancient uses for castor oil are grand! Not only is castor oil helpful for removing toxins but it acts as an antimicrobial, anti-inflammatory, joint health promoter, skin illuminator, immune system booster, circulation enhancer, and lymphatic system activator. Rubbing castor oil directly on the skin and hair can be a good regular beauty practice, but when it comes to a good therapeutic treatment, castor oil packs are pure magic for Auric Living. I recently partnered with a company that creates user-friendly castor oil packs and self-care kits to make using castor oil convenient and simple. They are available at AuricLiving.com.

Oils: Healthy oils are deeply healing and very beneficial when it comes to detoxification. Not only are healthy oils important for the maintenance and repair of cell wall structures, but they keep the microbiome healthy as well as the colon. They aid in the hydration process and keep everything moving. A daily swig of wild Norwegian cod liver oil, organic hemp oil, or organic MCT oil are just a few options. I have included a few favorites at AuricLiving.com.

Juicing: Juicing is a powerful way to pull toxins from the body and hydrate the cells with live alkaline goodness. It is tough for harmful and toxic critters to thrive when the body is hydrated, alkaline, and clean. Green juice has been a staple for me for the past 25 years. I have even traveled with a juicer or searched out the nearest juice bar before a trip. Often, local juice bars will even agree to fill your hotel room mini fridge prior to your arrival should you ask.

Ozone Therapy: Ozone therapy is making waves in naturopathic medicine and is backed by over 6,000 scientific studies that point to its effectiveness as an anti-viral, anti-bacterial, anti-fungal, and/or anti-inflammatory treatment. Ozone is a powerful oxidative therapy that has been shown to leave healthy cells unharmed but oxidizes unhealthy cells such as viruses, bacteria, fungi, and other unwanted cells. Ozone therapy has also been shown to inhibit fungal cell growth. Ozone therapy is currently used for Intravenous ozone, joint ozone injections, and vaginal and rectal ozone treatments are all gaining traction in the naturopathic and integrative medicine fields.

Colon Hydrotherapy: Colon hydrotherapy is a powerful practice for supporting the body when it comes to waste, toxins, and density. The value of this practice is much deeper than the physical matter it eliminates. For sensitives and empaths in particular, emotional waste can also build up in the colon tissue. Over time, this heavier energetic matter manifests into physical waste, which can leave the body feeling heavy, dense, and dull. Often, my clients share their experience of weight gain even when eating very well and with frequent exercise. Feeling light in the body happens when we are light in the mind and the heart. When we detoxify our cells, it is helpful to use colon hydrotherapy to promote and facilitate the removal of this released waste matter. Gravity-fed colon hydrotherapy services are best. When I am not able to find a colon hydrotherapy clinic during travel, I bring my travel unit with me. It fits into luggage and is easy to set up in a hotel room.

Chlorine Dioxide: There is much debate and controversy around chlorine dioxide, so I suggest you do your own research. Chlorine dioxide has been used as a water purifier and in the treatment of malaria around the world. Its role as a potentially powerful support for the treatment of disease, bacteria, and parasites is growing in influence. Given that our physical bodies are mostly made up of water, chlorine dioxide is thought to act as a powerful anti-parasitic. At low concentrations, it is safe, effective, and inexpensive to produce. It may also be supportive in treating malaria. Dr Karl Schustereder believes that chlorine dioxide does indeed have a place in medicine and healing. He explains, "Chlorine dioxide has a profound impact on human beings and it has to do with the body's electrostatics." Zoltan Noszticzius, PhD, is pioneering significant scientific research in the effectiveness of chlorine dioxide for wound healing and health promotion. In a paper published in 2013, *Chlorine Dioxide is a Size-Selective Anti-Microbial Agent,* his research concluded that within safe concentrations, chlorine dioxide eliminates fungi, bacteria, and viruses but does not do any harm to healthy cells. Quantitative data now supports this use and availability worldwide for disease management, wound healing and as an antiparasitic, and antibacterial agent. Dr. Schustereder has often shared that remote villages around the world that don't have easy access to medical treatment nor the financial resources, could greatly benefit from chlorine dioxide for medical uses. If your access to medical attention is limited, you may want to have chlorine dioxide on your list of essentials. It's definitely worth further research.

Anti-Parasitics: There are some who claim many of the more serious illnesses today are parasitic in nature. While this is not the consensus of all healers, the list of medical professionals who are considering this theory is growing quickly. Parasite cleanses are becoming one of the top reasons for visits to the local naturopath. I studied parasitology for a semester during an exchange at the University of South Pacific in Fiji, which was the perfect location for training in this topic. It is highly likely that anti-parasitics are going to lead the way in naturopathic as well as conventional medicine over the next few decades. It is my belief that anti-parasitics will become a common staple for the first-aid kit. (They are already in mine!) Here are a few actions to explore when it comes to parasite prevention and detoxification:

1. Parasite cleanse (consider a naturopathic parasite cleanse)
2. Microcurrent therapies (often have specific frequencies for eliminating parasites)
3. Fasting
4. Colon hydrotherapy
5. Juicing
6. Herbal protocols such as olive leaf (Herbals are powerful but they take time, so patience is important.)
7. Ozone therapy

Microcurrent Therapy: The body, mind, and heart are deeply connected to the earth. We must ground into 1st and 2nd dimensional consciousness to experience harmonious health. The frequencies of the earth (such as the Schumann Resonance) are essential for health and for healing. The rise of electrosmog and time spent indoors has limited to our exposure to natural frequencies from the sun and Mother Earth while introducing artificial man-made frequencies that harm our health. The earth magnetic frequencies are the same as the body and brain. The earth has a magnetic field made up of two components:

1) Geomagnetic Frequencies (0-3 Hz). The heart links up to these frequencies.
2) Schumann Frequencies (7-50 Hz). The brain links up to these frequencies.

The tissues and cells of the body resonate with both of these frequencies (0-50 Hz), but we simply are not getting enough of them today. Not only have we become disconnected from the earth, but we are also bombarded 24/7 with unhealthy man-made frequencies. Bryant Meyers, author of *PEMF: The 5th Element of Health* suggests supplementing with what he calls "vitamin P." PEMF stands for Pulsed Electromagnetic Field Therapy, which can help supplement your body, mind, and heart, and bring you back into resonance. PEMF therapy assists the body in healing itself by helping to recharge cellular voltage. Healthy cells always have a strong cellular voltage. High cellular voltage is key to health. PEMF also induces current flow (nerve, lymphatic, and meridian). PEMF opens flow and increases charge of the body. This helps increase energy and release toxicity. One of the first books I read on this topic was *The Body Electric* by Robert Becker, and it continues to be one of my favorites.

Mystics and Spiritual Teachers: A major step for me in my own journey was finding the spiritual teachers who resonated the most with me. Daskalos, Rudolf Steiner, Theresa of Avila, St. Francis of Assisi, Paramahansa Yogananda, Patangali, Rumi, Hafiz, Lao Tzu and many other mystics have been influential mentors on my journey. As you study more of their work as well as ancient sacred texts, you will come to realize that much of the wisdom has a common thread. Many spiritual teachers are praised for their wisdom but criticized for their methods. It is always beneficial to develop intuition and discernment as you study and research to filter and focus on what resonates with your own soul. Ultimately, though, when you get quiet with yourself in meditation and prayer, you come to realize that the master healer is within, silently waiting to be activated by opening the portal of the heart. Mystical detoxification is one of the most powerful methods of cleansing and healing yet demands the most discipline and commitment.

Visualization: Daskalos taught that visualization is the key to healing. Not only did he believe that visualization is a master skill when it comes to maintaining body resonance, but he believed that visualization is needed once a person passes away and crosses over to the astral realm because everything in the astral realm is created by visualization. In his teachings, Daskalos suggests surrounding yourself with the color light blue in your visualization practice. Your birthstone color can also give you a good cosmic clue into the color that will be of great significance for your healing and visualization practice. Blue is very near and dear to my heart, so this teaching connected strongly with me. Not only is it the color of my birthstone but it is the color associated with divine will and the throat chakra. Blue opens you up to self-realization and to your high purpose on this planet, both of which are highest-order priorities. The color blue exalts us upwards towards spiritual heights and is the spirit ray. Blue helps you to awaken and activate your 5th chakra and unlock (or unblock) divine will.

Neural Therapy:

I first learned about neural therapy when I read about how surgery can significantly hinder the bioelectrical flow throughout the body. We often focus on healing at the point of entry or wound when recovering from surgery, but we neglect to put attention on the inner reintegration of the bioelectrical system. If our bioelectrics are off, we are off. Neural therapy works to treat disturbances in the body's electrical system often due to surgical scarring. It works to restore homeostatis and optimal function to the ANS (Autonomic Nervous System). Neural therapy has become one of the most popular healing modalities in Germany. As we discussed at some length above, Dr. Harvey Bigelsen, M.D shared in an interview that he theorized based on his own clinical statistics that many of his patients who underwent surgery ended up with an autoimmune diagnosis within a year or two afterward, and I saw this play out in my own life.

Some of the uses of neural therapy include restoring gut health, improving organ function, relieving lymphatic congestion, and reducing joint and muscle pain and/or inflammation.

Sacred Sleep

We have already discussed sleep in previous chapters, but I am going to mention it again here as well as in a future chapter. This is because it is absolutely imperative that sleep be held sacred. Sleep disorders are growing at exponential rates which is also leading to etheric body breakdown and dehydration. A lack of sleep not only depletes the vital body but leaves our cells depleted, dehydrated and impaired in terms of structure and function. I invite you to use a few or several of the suggestions throughout this book to reset and rebirth the most magical preparation practice each night for sacred sleep. Simplify your bedroom, remove electronics, cleanse the air, add aromatherapy and/or incense, create a mindfulness mood and go *au naturel* in the bedroom! It is also encouraged to test your bedroom for EMF levels so that you know how healing (or non-healing) it is. I have found taking a ritual bath before bed to be deeply healing and sleep enhancing. Asking your angels to support you with a healing and restorative night's sleep is also a beautiful practice.

Color Therapy

The Divine speaks in terms of color and tone. As divine white light enters full manifestation in the physical realm, colors of the spectrum come into existence in the form of the human aura. This color spectrum unfolding is directly proportional to the spiritual maturation and actualization that occurs. When one seeks protection again fear, visualize being surrounded by a shield of pure white light. Color therapy (along with many other topics in this book) could be a book on its own but here is a quick summary of what structures/systems each color controls and maintains as well as astrological influences for each color:

Green (the moon): supports the glandular system. The color green enhances lymphatic flow, reduces stress and supports a calming feeling throughout the body. Green is the color associated with nature and all of life and enhances lifeforce and connection with our soul. Just as time in nature does, the color green soothes the nervous system and also helps with headaches, anxiety, and tension. (Just as a side note, I have also read that pink is very soothing to the nervous system. I have a pink light in my sauna at home and found this to be true for myself.)

Orange (the sun): supports the heart and sympathetic nervous system. The color orange also elicits happiness and supports healthy digestion. Orange supports the activation of pleasure, creativity, optimism, and healthy emotional expression.

Yellow (Venus): skin and kidneys. The color yellow is considered the mind color. Yellow promotes and stimulates mental clarity and order. Yellow activates and animates true wisdom and supports one in life by seeing the higher order of all things and the divine nature of all things. Yellow also promotes healthy colon health and can be helpful for constipation

Red (Mars): muscular system, left cerebral brain hemisphere. The color red energizes the body, supports the reduction of inflammation, supports healthy blood circulation and optimizes the blood. Red stimulates life force, security, grounding, vitality, and endurance.

Purple (Jupiter): circulatory system. Purple is the color associated with spiritual actualization and highest spiritual order. This color is deeply supportive for spiritual maturation and to gain insights during life's challenges. Purple also stimulates intuition and wisdom. Purple helps to soothe the stomach, spleen, and kidneys.

Indigo (Saturn): skeletal structure. The color indigo is the color of introspection and supports a daily life that is aligned with the law of one. For starseeds, living the law of one every day is a must. Indigo supports the activation of inner strength, clairvoyance, calmness, and intuition.

Blue (Uranus): ductless glands and portal activation within the bod are surrounded by the color blue. The color blue is associated with creative expression, protection, divine will and is supportive for reducing inflammation and skin conditions. Blue is helpful in times of acute pain, fevers, headaches or in times of excess menstruation.

Lavender (Neptune): electrical currents throughout the body, nervous system are supported by the color lavender. This color is ideal for supporting and promoting healing, purity, detoxification, and inner peace. Lavender is also the color associated with grace.

One of the pioneers of modern chromotherapy was Dr. Edwin D. Babbitt, MD. In his book *Principles of Light and Color,* Babbitt discusses fascinating correlations between colors and minerals, as well as how colors represent the various expressions of cosmic forces: "Light is the greatest truth-teller in the outward universe, flashing forth by means of its reflections the forms and colors of all nature."

Color light therapy devices are now widely available and inexpensive. Having one at home is ideal for aligning with Auric Living.

Sound Healing

> "Life is music, complete with overtones."
> —Michael Hayes, author of *The Hermetic Code of DNA*

The entire world is structured in octaves. The twelve zodiac constellations act as a sounding board for the symphony played by the planets as they circle the sun. The relationship between cosmic pattern and musical science has been profoundly researched by philosophers, scientists, and spiritual greats throughout history. Music is therefore based on the rhythmic principles of the universe. My husband and I (both trained musically) have agreed that we feel major tones in music associate more with the sun, while minor tones in music associate more with the moon.

In her book *Healing and Regeneration through Color,* Corinne Heline writes that "Music emerged with the very first breath of divine creation. This music, being the first of the arts, shall also be the last, the alpha and the omega, the highest and the most important of them all." Our world has prioritized the faculties of sight (yang) over those of sound (yin), which isn't surprising when we contemplate the excess of yang dominance in society today. We are on the verge of harmonizing this imbalance, which will be greatly facilitated by the symphonic conductor of sound. The very first sense organ to develop in the womb is the inner ear, and it is also the last sense to go when we die. The auditory nerve directly connects to every organ in the human body. The ears are also more accurate in perception that the eyes. Sound is the method to most directly connect with Source. One of the most contemplated and referenced versus of the Bible is John 1:1 "In the beginning was the Word, and the Word was with God, and the Word was God." In almost every tradition, sound is at the very source of creation. In Vedic tradition, the ancient sound of *Om* (Aum) is the very seat of the soul and enables one to not only directly connect to source but also to create from Source.

The ancients understood the secrets of sound far better than our world does today. Nikola Tesla was one of the great researchers of the mystical properties of sound about a century ago, and while we may be behind in unravelling the mysteries, we are certainly committed to the path. Sound healing is mystically exploding with quantum speed, and it is becoming more and more accessible to anyone and everyone. Just yesterday in my town there were more than six sound bath ceremonies happening on the same evening. Sound not only reharmonizes the body with Source but unlocks higher perceptions powers lying dormant in the DNA. The pyramid structures found across the globe were closely associated with sound and were specifically designed to be power centers for energy enhancement. Sound and sacred geometry also go hand in hand, as the very projection of sound into matter creates a pattern. All ancient civilizations understood this. Matter is vibration and sound is the key to the higher realms. Sound has everything to do with the manifestation of form and all physical matter. The blueprints of all form are sacredly stored in the realm of sound before we are every visibly aware of them. As we develop insight and higher perception, however, we will begin to see form in our mind's eye prior to it ever manifesting.

There are many sound healing modalities include sound beds, drum/rhythm circle, sound mats, binaural beats, tuning fork therapy, sound journey, music therapy, vibrational sound therapy, vibroacoustic therapy, sound baths, gong bath, chanting, Tibetan bowls, humming, and kirtan. In our home, singing bowls, wind chimes, tuning forks and classical music are everyday delights. I encourage you to find the modality that feels right to you. Sounds of nature are always ideal when it comes to healing which is why the sound of running water, birds singing, and leaves blowing is a healing art in itself. Singing bowls and chanting are also up there on the priority list when it comes to sound healing. There is much technology available when it comes to sound healing. It is important once again, as with any other topic we discuss in this book, that you use your own discernment when it comes to your own healing journey. Some sound technologies available today may not feel light and bright to you—trust that.

As we discussed previously, the six original notes known as the Solfeggio frequencies were the original notes chanted in meditation as spiritual blessings by Gregorian Monks. These six ancient and original frequencies have been long associated with highest order spiritual, physical, mental, and emotional health. (Consider these six notes to be the Auric Living 6-pack!) The six frequencies are 396 Hz, 417 Hz, 528 Hz, 639 Hz, 741 Hz, and 852 Hz. There are, of course, several other healing frequencies, but these are believed to be the original six. There is much information to suggest that our modern understanding of pitch is different from these six frequencies. Even the modern piano is tuned in a way that is slightly off from the original Solfeggio scale, which cuts us off from the highest-order healing force. As a classically trained pianist, I invite you to listen to your own body as you contemplate this theory. Highest-order sound contains the blueprint of form. This means that you can absolutely reorder the body and physical wellbeing through sound. The Solfeggio frequencies are mathematical codes containing great mystical wisdom.

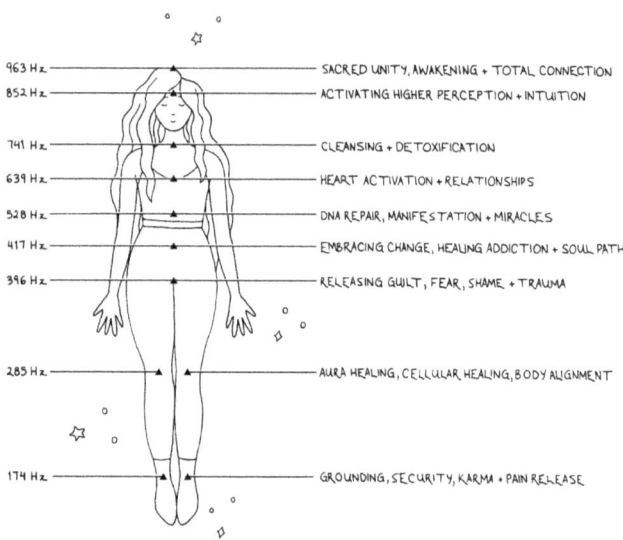

What is important to remember is that there is not one set of right or wrong choices, as these key codes are a part of the greater cosmic mystery. The following frequencies act as guidelines and starting points into discovering the much deeper wisdom lying dormant within your very divinity. You are a master healer and are absolutely being activated at this very moment. There are many different experts on this topic all with different suggestions for which frequencies are best. For the purposes of this book, I am giving a general guideline to start you on your journey. There are of course many other frequencies that have wondrous impacts on the body- as you learn more and experiment, you may just find your own sweet spot set of frequencies!

174 Hz: Release pain and past karma with this noetic note. This frequency also relaxes the muscles throughout the body and supports surrender.

285 Hz: This frequency is used to support healing of cells, tissues, and organs. Balancing the root chakra is also a benefit of this frequency. If you're seeking enhanced feelings of safety, security, and grounding, this frequency is a wonderful choice.

(The following six items are all original Solfeggio frequencies.)
396 Hz: This is the liberation frequency—a wonderful frequency to release guilt and fear.

417 Hz: This is helpful for realigning with your true soul path and releasing negativity as well past trauma that may be lingering in the body. This powerful frequency can be used to energetically lighten the body at any time by helping you facilitate change by letting go of the past.

528 Hz: Enhanced creativity, inner peace, and DNA repair are benefits of this fabulous frequency. Initiate transformation and miracles with the "me" note from the basic scales you may have learned as a child.

639 Hz: This frequency is good for cell communication, harmony in relationships, and communication with the divine.

741 Hz: This is the cleansing and detoxification frequency. Use this frequency to release the body from toxins, parasites, viruses, harmful bacteria, and EMFs. This is the master frequency for awakening the third eye, higher perception, and intuitive powers.

852 Hz: Spiritual connection, high-order wellbeing, and enhanced intuition are activated with this frequency. This frequency aids in the activation of the pineal gland and resonates throughout the cave of Brahma. This is a golden key code for cosmic insight.

963 Hz: Though not an original Solfeggio frequency, this is the spiritual world connector and the unity note. This is the frequency for crown chakra activation and total unity with highest order and self.

Auric Body Blessing

Blessing our body day and night is a sacred practice for Auric Living. This practice is heart activating and multidimensional. Here is an offering and blessing option for you as well as for those readers who are parents.

I AM PURE LIGHT
I FEEL PURE LIGHT
I EXPRESS PURE LIGHT
MY BODY IS AN EXPRESSION OF PURE LIGHT

MY BODY IS LIGHT
MY BODY FEELS LIGHT
MY BODY MOVES LIGHT
MY BODY IS AN EXPRESSION OF PURE LIGHT

I AM CREATIVE LIGHT
I AM DIVINE LIGHT
I SHINE LOVE AND LIGHT
MY BODY IS AN EXPRESSION OF PURE LIGHT

I GIVE THANKS TO THE SUN AND STARS
I GIVE THANKS TO MOTHER EARTH
I GIVE THANKS TO MY BODY
I GIVE THANKS TO THE ONE

I AM COSMIC LIGHT IN FULL EXPRESSION
I AM DEEPLY GRATEFUL

-AURIC LIVING BLESSING

Auric Living

Auric Body Blessing for Kids

I THANK THE STARS
I THANK THE SUN
FOR MY AURIC BODY
AN EXPRESSION OF ONE

AND ON THIS DAY
AS I PLAY
I HAVE THANKS IN MY HEART
AS IT SHOWS ME THE WAY

IN MY HEART
I AM FILLED WITH LOVE
FOR MY AURIC BODY
A GIFT FROM ABOVE

—AURIC LIVING BLESSING

Chapter 7: Auric Nutrition

Auric Nutrition is the sacred practice of spiritually, energetically, and physically nourishing the body. Food is physical, mental, emotional, and spiritual medicine. Auric Nutrition is the healing practice of spiritual nutrition. We are often guided to start practicing nutrition at a soul-level at a certain spiritual nodal point in our lives—typically happens when we are somewhat disenchanted with the external world and inspired to explore the caves within. It is as if a switch has turned on in our lives so that we still function and appreciate the external world, but we no longer leak energy and emotions into it. We become interested not only in mastering our own energy but becoming beings of light. This simply cannot happen unless we travel within and let go of the obsessive attachments we have to the outer senses. Little by little, as we begin to tame our physical senses, we will start to crave simplicity, nature, and *true* soul food. We become less enchanted with stuffing our feelings and more drawn to cleansing and emptying our vessel. We want to feel light, free, and radiant. We reach a point in our lives where the only thing that can move us past a plateau is to empty our lives of all that no longer resonates, and this often includes many foods.

Eventually, spiritual fasting may become a necessary practice to hold the light and stay on path with the soul. We are light beings in physical form that are sourced from the sun, which is why, as we sit down to eat a heavy meal today, our body switch feels off. We simply cannot eat like we used to even a few years ago. To practice Auric Nutrition, the hydration factor and aliveness of the food is what takes precedent. If it infuses the cells with live prana from the sun and showers the cells with hydration—it is food worthy of the soul. The prevalence of food sensitivities and intolerances are simply the body's way of revealing that it is time to uplevel nutrition intake to a higher level of purity: sunshine sourcing. This means that body nourishment should prioritize the transference of the sun's lifeforce energy into the body, which can be done through the consumption of farm fresh organic fruits, vegetables, nuts, seeds, plants, flowers, and herbs.

With Auric Nutrition, one commits to a mindful, patient, and soulful experience when it comes to nourishing the body and purifying the cells. This initiation also invites a commitment to releasing states of rushing, standing, multitasking, frustration, anger, stress, and anxiety when it comes to body nourishment. This practice is also one that welcomes you to feel the vibration of the food, energy, and environment before, during, and after body nourishment. As you practice Auric Nutrition more and more, you will come to a place where you can feel the vibration of almost everything you select, prepare, and choose to welcome into the body. You will be able to feel the quality and energetics of most foods including if they are filled with chemicals, genetic modifications, or radiation. You will be able to feel the vibrational differences between frozen, canned, fresh, and cooked foods. Auric Nutrition also highly encourages a microwave-free home.

The primary objective for Auric Nutrition is the hydration, purification, and spiritual activation of cells. When this occurs, continuous and efficient detoxification happens naturally throughout the entire body at the cellular level. Auric Nutrition also enhances optimal lymphatic flow, which means your lymphatic and endocrine system are running radiantly. *The true purpose of Auric Nutrition is to attune every cell in our body with divine truth.*

Auric Nutrition is a spiritual journey into your very soul as you discover and investigate what is most true for you. This journey is a lifetime's work and evolves with time, which is why how you eat today may not be written in stone, even if it is a life-filled choice right now. Be open and flexible enough to be guided by your soul when it comes to body nourishment. As you collect more clues over time, you will come to feel deep peace in your heart as everything about your relationship with food over your lifetime thus far finally makes sense. You connect all of the divine dots and begin to surrender to the cosmic order of all things, including food. What is most important to understand is that as you spiritually evolve, so does your way of eating. As your frequency changes, the impact of things that enter the body also changes. Nourishing the body becomes more of a resonance practice as you find the foods and superfoods that most resonate with your new frequency.

As you move away from foods that don't resonate with your body, instead of looking at it as a food intolerance, consider it to be a momentary frequency dis-resonance. This "intolerance" may be permanent, or it may only be temporary; you really can't say with 100% certainty except that you periodically check in with your body and re-evaluate your food choices. Although food intolerance tests can be helpful in some cases, what I have found to be true for most of my clients is that they already intuitively know which foods are not a vibrational match with their Auric Bodies long before they ever get tested. I also find that when we rely on or give too much power to these types of food tests, we lose connection with our high healer within. The intention of Auric Living is to honor tools, practices, and techniques that support your healing journey, but to remember that the true master is the great healer within. Aura scanning, tuning forks, muscle testing, and meditation can be magnificent tools when it comes to aligning body nourishment with healing and higher-self living. Simply getting quiet and closing your eyes with a certain food or supplement in your hand can also be a very effective practice. All you have to do is close your eyes and start to connect with the food or nutritional item. Ask your higher self if this item is of highest order for you and your Auric Body? As you ask this question, how does your body feel? What do you feel throughout your solar plexus? Do you feel a happy, joyful *yes* or a dense and dull *no*?

One of the challenges with many nutrition programs today is that the entire Auric Body (physical and auric layers alike) is not nurtured as a whole. When the physical body is treated or counselled on its own, there is very little power when it comes to radical healing and vibrance. Your body and soul are perfect and divine in nature. When they are in synch, you will want nothing more than to eat only the purest of foods and make only highest vibrational food choices. In my own life, I use off-course eating and nutrition habits as indicators that one of the energetic layers of my aura needs attention (usually my emotional body). The physical body alone is a perfect biochemistry factory, and it's pretty simple to understand how to eat well for optimal function—so why don't we? As we are taught to discard rhythm and simplicity, we invite chaos, anxiousness, and hustle instead. We forget to practice the art of living (and of eating) on a minute-by-minute basis in our lives. Just the other day I had the pleasure of watching a group from a Buddhist retreat enjoy a mindfulness walk beside me as I was on my way home from my power walk. This was just the medicine I needed! I found myself slowing down, gazing at every tree, and calming my nervous system through my breath.

From a personal perspective, food has been my teacher and my tool for achieving present moment awareness. After all, how we feed ourselves is a reflection of how we love, nurture, and care for ourselves. Throughout my life, achieving and action were almost always prioritized over rest and recovery. It isn't a shock, then, to conclude that my relationship with food and eating would be a path for healing. Food is a vehicle for expressing self-love, self-compassion, and self-care. My conditioned nature is to eat standing up, rush my eating, and binge on acidic foods. My authentic nature, however, is, to mindfully eat while seated, to bless my food, and to enjoy the emptiness as well as the nourishment I take in. Consuming green juice, herbs, herbal and green teas, as well as short, regular spiritual fasts is how I feel most authentic and filled with integrity. Edgar Cayce taught to never eat when angry, stressed, or anxious because the entire vibrational quotient of the experience will be off. Prior to eating, take a moment to breathe, find center, and sway into an attitude of gratitude. As an intuitive empath, it often happens that my energy system loses ground. It's as if my nervous system and chakra system spin so quickly that they start sending my body into a tailspin. For my Light Body, this amount of voltage might be completely doable, but for my physical body, I require tremendous effort to ground all of that energy. It wasn't until my mid-thirties that I really understood that a good portion of the energetic load I was feeling was the emotional energy of others that I took in. I had trouble sorting through what was mine and what was not. At the end of the day, my nervous bundle of energetic sparklers often had trouble finding ground. That is where food comes in. For anyone who experiences frequent bursts of nervous energy, energy overload, or anxiety, taking a moment to meditate, breath, and/or pray before eating is deeply healing.

For sensitives and empaths, energy is more easily ungrounded, which can lead to more chronic states of nervousness, anxiety, and overwhelm. The body often runs to food as an energetic response to this need for grounding and balance, even though it is more of an energy-calibration situation than a food or nutritional need. The energy body is seeking nurturing and rest. Food helps us feel connected, grounded, and secure. On days when my energy system experienced energy overload, carbs and sugar were there to comfort and ground me. I am certainly not alone in this. The miraculous part of this multi-decade experience was that what was once a confining cycle (feel nervous, eat sugar and carbs, feel shame, commit to a detox) blossomed into what is now my life's work. After trying for decades to get out of the anxious eating cycle on my own, I finally surrendered to soul. I stopped being hard on myself and trying to resist so much. I surrendered to the soul and let the heart (and my guardian angel) guide me towards a brighter light. This led me to juicing, detoxification, spiritual fasting, and prayer.

Unlike many spiritual teachings, we have not incarnated only to leave the body. We are here to experience and appreciate the physical while gaining spiritual wisdom and strength. When we leave the body, the body dies. While alive, we want to practice staying in the body. Food just happens to be one way to keep grounded and enjoy the fruits of the planet we call home. Food is a tool for experiencing nurturing, love, pleasure, and connection. When we don't feel deeply nurtured from our mothers as children, later in life there is a tendency to overcompensate by seeking emotional nurturing through food. We want Mother Earth to make up for the void we feel, when it is the very journey to self-nurturing that is the answer. For me, my body naturally sought out food at the very signal of my energy going astray. For a long time (decades, actually), sugar and carbs were my grounders, my slow-downers, and my nerve neutralizers. It took spiritual maturity (along with some adrenal fatigue and exhaustion), for me to gain appreciation for the role that carbs and sugar had in my life. I came to appreciate the frequent fill-in role they played until I finally learned to better nurture myself. There was my *ah-ha* moment. There was no shame in this. My temporary reality was a perfectly designed cycle for that moment and was in resonance with where I was then. It served me at that stage in my life and at that particular frequency. Today, I choose soul food rather than physical food in moments of nervous distress. Often, what a frazzled nervous system needs is not a food moment, it's a barefoot one. Prayer, meditation, breathwork, baths, yoga and earthing are all great practices in times when energy become ungrounded and chaotic. Channeling light is one thing, holding light is a whole other ballgame. When we struggle with holding light, our food choices and eating habits can become a struggle as well. This is why learning how to hold light is so very crucial when practicing Auric Nutrition.

We, as a species, are moving towards using light and free energy principles for fuel, although we are not quite there yet. You may have noticed your body is needing less food—fewer snacks, smaller meals, and more time away from food so that lifeforce energy can be used for ascension rather than digestion. Our bodies are already intuiting and acting upon what needs to be done.

As mentioned in previous chapters, the chakra system carries as one of its functions to transduce or transform subtle cosmic energy into the body. Chakras are often referred to as wheels, portals, even energy transformers that work to harmonize our body, mind, and Auric Selves. Because mind and body are not separate, we must regain an understanding that they work as a whole. When we are out of balance, we may get our physical bodies in shape (at least temporarily), but without working out the mind and transforming our thoughts, we usually don't truly integrate long term.

Auric Nutrition has everything to do with energy. As we age, there is a draining of energy from our bodies. As children, we are not adequately taught the spiritual principles of energy management and how hold energy within our bodies and also to refuel and draw energy into our bodies. Because of this, we have a major imbalance in the energy being sucked out of us vs the energy we take in, due to factors like unhealthy eating habits, trauma, imbalance, disharmony, stress, rushing, living in the past, living in the future, and always wanting *more*. We have a massive lack of energy in our bodies. We are completely dehydrated from lifeforce. Not only do we not take in enough clean water, but we, for the most part, live off of food that is dead and impure. How does one go about feeling deliciously radiant when lifeforce energy is only leaking out and not flowing in?

In your own life, how much lifeforce energy has leaked out of your body even before 11 AM? Rushing, stressing, working, doing, hustling—all of these activities lead to a body that lacks energy, which is the main cause of all illness in the body. There are many factors that attribute to this, including how we live, how we fuel the body, how much trauma we have experienced, and how stressful (energy-hemorrhaging) our life is.

The philosophy of Auric Nutrition is to seek harmony in life so that the infusion of lifeforce energy into your body is a graceful, continuous flow on a daily basis. There will always be energy leaving the body, but the focus will be on the infusion of energy and how to more quickly plug the leaks in your life. Instead of spiritual nutrition being about food fixing, it is about energetic and lifeforce recovery as a whole.

Auric Nutrition: The Fundamentals

Auric Nutrition is the study and practice of attuning the physical body with highest truth and state of integrity. Consider it to be the prana-flow practice of nutrition. It is a spiritual journey into the soul by way of sacred exploration and expansion. My training in biomedical toxicology, clinical nutrition, detoxification, spiritual science, yoga, energy medicine, quantum healing, and esoteric studies have all supported the creation of this work. There is no single perfect answer when it comes to individual nutrition needs. This is truly a spiritual practice. As we get quiet and into the gap, we will hear the tiniest voice sharing an offering. This offering is infused with divine wisdom where nourishing the body is concerned. How one eats and nourishes the body is a sacred and personal practice. It is all right to gain inspiration and wisdom from teachers you trust, but all wrong to fill our lives with labels, limitations, and rigidity. How we eat today may not be how the soul wishes to eat tomorrow. As we evolve and ascend, we may be guided to tweak our food and adjust how we nourish the body. A practitioner of Auric Nutrition is always open to spiritual messaging and has developed the will (ability to act) well enough to quickly implement new wisdom. When we shift our way of nourishing the body away from calories, rigidity, hustle, and regime, we let go of these confinements and pressures. We lovingly invite in sacred, intuitive, and fluid practices that feel good to the body and aligned with the soul. As we do this, our bodies will surrender to divine intervention and let themselves be carried by much higher frequencies of light. We have reached a point in human evolution where spiritual forces are blowing in and carrying our bodies to new heights. What is most important to clearly understand today is that we are all evolving souls whose needs may vary day to day, season to season, and cycle to cycle. Being a label-hoarder with a hit list of things we must tag onto our souls will only lead to more density, despair, and dis-ease. I'm not saying that gluten free, dairy free, sugar free, meat free, grain free, etc., is good or bad, it's just that it's no longer necessary when the soul is in charge of food and nutrition. Although there may be foods that one stays away from or doesn't permit into the body temple, adding a label or tag to their soul just doesn't feel right or worthy. It becomes much more aligned to simply *be*. This doesn't mean that a food allergy or need to avoid gluten will be ignored, it simply means that a big sign or label is not fixed on the soul. Labels only fix our lives into narrow lanes and tiny boxes. Who knows what tomorrow may bring—perhaps a healing?

Cosmic Influences on Nutrition

The key to practicing Auric Nutrition is an open heart. When our hearts are open and activated, continuous intuition is also activated. We become true conduits of light and receive key pieces of information relevant to next steps in daily life, including nutrition. Auric Nutrition truly is an intuitive and spiritual practice. The practice takes into account specific pieces of insight that may be relevant to soul group, ancient wisdom, ancestral lineage, blood type, intuition, organ communication, and divine will. At any time, key pieces of wisdom such as this may enter your field of perception to support higher living. These gems of grace are not always necessary but may drop into your aura from time to time to help guide and support an auric upgrade. It isn't that these cosmic nuggets are absolutely needed to practice Auric Nutrition, but they can be helpful along your journey. Consider them to be complementary to muscle testing. They are insights that clearly guide you towards highest vibrational choices in life, including how to eat.

To enhance the clarity and frequency of these divine downloads, prayer and meditation is helpful. When our intention is focused on food and nutrition, we begin to receive finely tuned pieces of spiritual wisdom on a more regular basis. What is best for you is deeply personal and should not follow trends and fads. As you tune into divine wisdom and deep intuition, you will receive the highest vibrational choice where your personal nutrition practice is concerned. Whether you should eat meat, take supplements, detox, fast, cleanse, juice, rest, or even increase nutrition intake will all be delivered to you at exactly the right time—if you create the space.

I want to add a loving reminder that we will often get higher insights and wisdom, but we're not yet quite ready to apply the nuggets. That's perfectly okay! Be sure to show grace to your former self. All in divine time. For years, I have been guided to do spiritual fasts. It took me over a decade to get on board with this guidance. It is completely okay if you aren't yet ready to commit to the insights that reside in your heart. Hearing them and loving them until you are ready to listen is perfectly perfect.

When a soul incarnates and births in the third dimension, the chakras usually develop in an ascending fashion; we spiritually mature from our lower root chakra all the way up to the higher chakras above our head. There are many factors that influence how our chakras develop as well as how harmoniously we are able to keep them functioning with pranic power. These factors include genetic coding, karma, past life integration, our lineage, the spiritual lessons we came here to learn, our birth experience, our experience in early infancy, our childhood, etc. Diving too much into your history or becoming obsessed with figuring out why certain things are the way they are in your life can not only be exhausting but move you off course from destiny. There may be a few pieces of information from your past that become helpful when integrating trauma, but at the end of the day, healing, and radiant wellbeing happen in the now. Spiritual nutrition goes hand in hand with trauma healing. You cannot have one without the other.

Breathwork, prayer and meditation are keys to keeping channels of cosmic communication healthy and happening. Cosmic clues like insights, reminders, images, voices, feelings, messages, or nudges, support highest self expression (including body nourishment). These intuitive insights offer vision for the bigger picture of how your Auric Body is impacted by food and nourishment. For some, these pieces of information can explain why all of a sudden, entire food groups no longer resonate with the body. These cosmic clues are also evidence that nutrition is deeply personal and deeply unique. One method of eating (as healthy as it may be) is not right for everyone.

Auric Nutrition is both beautifully mysterious yet so intuitively simple at the same time. Our mental and emotional bodies have powerful pulls on the fundamentally simple practice of healthy eating. This is why Auric Nutrition is really the practice of returning to the soul. Having access to even some of the information below will help guide you along your spiritual nutrition journey. Eventually, we will enter a stage of life where outside information or validation is no longer required. This becomes our reality as we spiritually mature and as our breathwork, meditation, and prayer practice advance. This is an ever-evolving path, which means that your nutritional needs will vary and change as you ascend and evolve. Although food sensitivity testing can be helpful in some cases, it is not ideal for everyone nor is it an all-in-one solution. When we explore the relationship between our bodies and food only through surface metrics, we miss the real lesson. Each layer of the aura is speaking to us in different ways, and the end result is how the body reveals each expression. We must take into consideration highest divinity, spiritual, emotional, mental, etheric, and physical insights, not just intolerance tests. The physical symptoms are just the final expression, not the cause. What is most important to remember is that Auric Nutrition is a lifelong class. It is one that requires deep self-love, patience, kindness, contemplation, surrender and healing.

Factors that contribute to our Auric Nutrition needs and expression include:

1. Blood type
2. Rhesus (Rh) factor
3. Intuitive guidance or downloads
4. Medical intuition reading information
5. Astrological chart (such as a Vedic astrology reading)
6. Soul group insights (Atlantean/Lemurian/Essene as examples)
7. Ancestral lineage
8. Medical information

9. Birth country and address
10. Birthdate
11. Akashic reading
12. Energy/Quantum information (chakra health)
13. Aura reading/Photography/Scan
14. Archetypal chart
15. Emotional wellbeing and resilience
16. Trauma exposure
17. Mental wellbeing
18. Live blood analysis
19. Nurturing quotient (How well you were nurtured as a child)
20. Chakra and auric strength

How are these pieces of information helpful? The key thing to remember is that the universe leaves clues. Ask for guidance and help, and you will receive it. For example, if you are guided or instructed to revisit your blood type and its possible influence of diet, do it! If you have just noticed an aura photography session being offered, perhaps this is divinely timed for you. Maybe you bought a book years ago on healing trauma, and it seems to be calling you now. Perhaps you are being called to book an aura scanning session to learn more about your very own aura and chakra health. Go where the guidance takes you.

For an expansive number of people around the planet today, eating practices have lightened significantly. For more and more earthlings, sitting down to eat three hearty meals each day is no longer a vibrational match to the soul. For the more cosmically attuned individuals who are being activated right now, it is very likely that eating the way we ate even last year is feeling absolutely outdated and out of alignment. Even if one replaces traditional foods with more holistic options, it is the density (physical and energetic heaviness) and energetic signature of the food that is no longer a match. If we clog our light channels with too much food, we simply cannot receive or transmit. As Mahatma Gandhi said: "The light of the world will illuminate within you when you fast and purify yourself." Although spiritual fasting may not be a priority at the moment, it will likely enter the field of consciousness soon. For today, what becomes of highest order as one cosmically connects and attunes to the soul is the hydration factor, sunlight quotient (or lifeforce quotient), and aliveness of the food that enters the body.

The Practice

The energy of eating is the focus of Auric Nutrition. We have forgotten to hold the practice of eating sacred. Our busy lives have harmed our sacred relationship with food. Setting tone, rhythm, and intention when it comes to nourishing our bodies must be re-established. One of the most beautiful practices to introduce into each meal is as follows:

1) *Create Beauty.* Make your mealtime environment beautiful. Set the tone with beauty, order, and love.
2) *Feel your food.* Take a few moments to close your eyes and feel the vibrational signature of what you are about to eat. How does it feel? Does it make you smile or make you sad? Does it align with highest vibrational nourishment or as a lower vibrational trauma or stress response? How is the food speaking to you? Do you see any light, colours, sound, or symbols? How is this food going to benefit your body, mind, and soul?
3) *Bless your food.* Finding a blessing that speaks to your heart, or even creating your own, is a beautiful practice to show thanks and gratitude to the food you are about to eat. There are many beautiful mealtime blessings across all spiritual traditions as well as in a number of books rooted in Waldorf education, such as *A Child's Seasonal Treasures* by Betty Jones.

   An Auric Living food blessing I composed specially for this book, and which is especially great for kids, reads like this:

Auric Living

STARS ABOVE
EARTH BELOW
SUN ABOVE
SEEDS BELOW
WITH AN OPEN HEART
AND COSMIC LOVE
I SHINE MY THANKS
TO ALL
-AURIC LIVING BLESSING

"All" in this blessing includes all of the people in the physical realm who have helped grow, nurture, and distribute this food. It also includes the self for making high vibrational choices as an I AM of divinity and vital lifeforce and the elementals (fairies and nature spirits) as well as angels, archangels, and divine forces that support highest vibration body and wellbeing.

4) *Sit and Surrender.* With love and grace, mindfully eat and drink your food while seated. Eating while standing up is harmful to the body and to the soul. Another suggestion is to eat your water and drink your food. This is a loving reminder to eat high water-content foods as much as possible and incorporate juicing into your daily life. Making hydration the priority when it comes to eating is a beautiful practice and will revolutionize your health.

Transforming density into a Light Body is the practice of Auric Nutrition. Increasing alkalinity in the body is one of the best ways to this. You can increase alkalinity by using the following:

1. Breathing/Breathwork (We alkalinize the body when we breath. This is the most critical activity and most powerful method for reducing acidity of the body and bringing us back to alkaline.)
2. Spiritual practice
3. Rhythm
4. Nourishment/Food
5. Herbs
6. Aura healers
7. Trauma healing
8. Simplicity
9. Colon hydrotherapy

Conditioning

The conditioned mind has been trained since birth to function in the opposite direction of truth, harmony, and order. We are conditioned from infancy to fit a mold, suppress authenticity, and shut off intuition. We are told that sunlight is bad, consuming is good, and feeling uninspired, unmotivated, and unwell is normal. As infants, developing the mind has been given much higher priority than connecting with the earth and properly grounding our feet. As infants and children, we aren't really taught to develop a sacred relationship with our feet and our connection to the earth. This work should be at the very foundation of our development rather than rushing, pressing, and pressuring the mind to get ahead. Have you ever wondered why baby checkup appointments never honor or discuss the proper rooting and grounding of the feet? Let's begin promoting feet-favoring today! Regardless of age, take a moment to honor and give thanks to your feet. Standing tall and barefoot today, notice how much of your food is well planted on the ground and if there is a balanced and harmonious distribution of weight throughout the entire foot and between both feet. At a yoga workshop I attended, we spent an entire hour standing in mountain pose observing how rooted and grounded to the earth we are. It was life changing. Why is this important? Because the lack of sacred importance we give to the feet and to grounding as infants has much to do with how well we nurture the body as adults. We should be sacredly developing from the feet up, but we are conditioned to detour the entire body and head straight for the mind as quickly as possible. We are then pressured by both the medical system and educational system to stay on track and on point. It's no wonder we are not only disconnected from the earth but from our beautiful bodies.

If that weren't devastating enough, we are taught that more is better and that our "job" in this lifetime is to achieve, chase and hustle. Our conditioned mind is programmed and trained from infancy to speed up, chase more and be more. If we lag behind in any capacity at the pediatric office or at school, we are traced, tracked, and timed until we accelerate. Our walking, talking, teething, reading, writing, eating, interacting, and so on is all monitored to ensure we don't stand out, expand out, or vibrate out of constructed social norms. When one of my children got his first "X" at the doctor's office for being slightly behind schedule with walking and toilet training, there was an energy of shame projected onto my aura even if it was unintentional and unconscious.

For those curious as to why lower vibrational or unwanted habits form around food, patterning around food and nutrition is unavoidable. From before birth, we have been patterned and programmed in a multitude of ways that all influence what and how we eat. Our nervous system, emotional, mental, and developmental wellbeing all impact how we nourish and nurture ourselves. Exposure to trauma (which we all have) also significantly influences our ability to nourish and nurture the body. In other words, using food to feed the soul is deeply imprinted within the body and mind. The soul's desire is to be free, so in a society that supports conditioning, limiting, and confining, the soul gets stuck. It is not surprising that confining of the soul leads to trying to feed and stuff it. The trouble is that not only does this not work but it also weighs down the body both physically and spiritually. We eventually get caught in a cycle of stuck where nothing seems to work. This is when Auric Nutrition, as a practice, sets sail.

Rhythm

One of the surest ways to lose our path when it comes to highest vibrational nourishment in life is a lack of rhythm. When it comes to rhythm, consider the multitude of areas in daily life where rhythm is on or off. This includes how you move, eat, sleep, wake, work, connect, breath, speak, rest, and live. The cosmos and the planet have such beautiful rhythms, and our bodies are yearning to synch up to them. When it comes to nourishing the body, rhythm is deeply important. Rhythm creates a cadence in life and a symphony in the soul. Rhythms in the minute, hour, day, week, month, season, and year are all significant. Consider the following as gems of inspiration for infusing more rhythm into your nutritional life.

1. Have a rhythm ritual when you wake up. This may include starting your day with room temperature or warm water with lemon or simply performing breathwork, prayer, and/or meditation. Stuffing the body as soon as we wake up is a practice of the dulled and conditioned mind and prevents the soul from speaking to the body. Creating gentle, healthy rhythm in the morning for saying hello and thank you to the body is key. The conditioned mind may have difficulty kicking old, unhealthy patterns that silence the soul, especially in the morning. This is why it is best to start some new rituals in the morning that enhance peace, order, and spiritual beauty. This may include a prayer or meditation session, breathwork, a swim, a bath, or even a walk. Just observe how powerful our conditioning wants to stuff the body and silence the soul.
2. Create a rhythm in your day around food. Sitting down when eating, slowing down the chewing and eating process, blessing food, energetically connecting with food, and touching food are all significant ways to enhance rhythm. Eating on a similar schedule each day is helpful for body harmony and optimal wellbeing. It is also important to give your body a break from digesting and processing food. Eating

throughout the day doesn't give the body the spaciousness it needs to restore, regenerate, and heal. Eventually, longer periods of spiritual fasting may feel intuitively right. In the beginning of an Auric Nutrition journey, 3- to 4-hour increments without eating throughout the day is helpful for body beauty. This may seem obvious, but for those (like me) who have a tightly wired or energetically coiled nervous system, snacking all day long can become more of a nervous thing than a hunger thing. For those who resonate with this, it requires commitment and determination to take an all-day snack break, but eventually we learn to replace this snacking habit with meditation, a bath, breathwork, walking, and prayer.

3. Eat in season. Dance with the seasons in terms of eating and nourishing the body. Explore the temperature, colour, vibration, scent, and feel of food in different seasons. Explore your own nature and emotional radiance in different seasons. Consider the impact of strength and duration of sunlight throughout different seasons. Consider creating variety in color throughout the seasons when it comes to nourishing the body as well as keeping food choices as in-season, fresh, and close to their natural state as possible. For colder climates, drinking warm broths throughout colder months as well as including more soups and steamed foods can greatly support the physical and energy body.

4. Have a rhythm ritual as you prepare for sleep. The winding down of the physical and energy body before bed is vital for regenerative and spiritual sleep. Do your best to avoid eating right before bed. Give your body an hour or two before bed a break from digestive and processing work. After dinner, consider sipping herbal tea to sooth and enhance the body as well as prepare it for sacred sleep.

When we think of rhythm, we don't often think of food and nutritional rhythm. It doesn't have to be complicated, but putting a little extra rhythmic love into when, what, and how you eat will go a long way and will animate your food with much more soul power. Exploring how your own cycles and rhythms impact cravings, emotions, and food choices is wondrous. The rise and fall of energy systems and centers throughout the circle of life is deeply beneficial for spiritual nutrition practices. The circadian rhythm includes the body's natural rhythmic cycle throughout a 24-hour period. Waking up the body to natural light and in a way that gently breaks the fast that took place during sleep hours is best. A little water with lemon or some soothing herbal tea is an ideal way to break this sleep-cycle fast. Seed cycling can also be a helpful way to nourish the body in a rhythmic way in harmony with infradian rhythm (one that lasts longer than the 24-hour circadian rhythm). Seed cycling is a practice of rotating different edible seeds within the diet at different phases of one's menstrual cycle. For example, including pumpkin seeds during the follicular phase and hemp and chia seeds during the menstrual phase. There are also several other healing foods that are helpful to include during each phase of the menstrual cycle. This practice promotes deep nurturing and healing and is a rhythmic practice that is helpful for hormonal balance, grounding, and vital body rejuvenation. When we move through the phases of our menstrual cycle with rhythm, love and grace, our bodies harmonize into happy.

Nurturing

Our ability to nurture ourselves has a lot to do not only with how well we were nurtured as children but also how we were nurtured in previous lifetimes. Everything is a circle and cycle. It is wise to ask how well are we currently caring for ourselves? Do we carry fragments of grief in our bodies over not feeling emotionally or physically nurtured as a child? How does this hidden grief impact how well we nurture ourselves and our bodies today? Consider the possible impact between feeling a lack of emotional nurturing as a child and feeling shame and unworthiness as an adult. The two go hand in hand and have much to do with Auric Nutrition. How we eat is how we live. If self-nurturing and self-love don't feel natural right now, consider today to be the very first day of a self-love life. At any moment, we can consciously commit to nurturing ourselves like the divine and radiant being that we truly are. A body and being that is well nurtured and cared for begins to illuminate from within. The eyes gain new shine and every cell within the body illuminates. Regardless of how well you were nurtured as a child, you are one thought away from nurturing yourself anew. Starting right this very moment, commit to a completely new way of nurturing yourself—one that is sacred. Moment to moment throughout the day, speak to your body and being as you would a beloved child. Shower yourself with words of love, blessing, kindness, patience, care, and present-moment awareness. Rushing is the surest way to negate nurturing, so keep rushing to a minimum in your life. When you lose your nurturing way, take a moment to hug a tree, go barefoot, say a prayer, or simply place your hand on your heart.

Archetypes

We don't often think about it, but our archetypes and cosmically set patterns have much to do with how we eat. For example, if you carry the warrior archetype (like my son does), there may be an innate and intuitive pull towards eating meat. Often, body type can leave some clues around what archetypes we hold. I have one son who was born with physical strength, musculature, and a personality to match. For years I fed him mostly fruits, vegetables, nuts, and seeds. At the age of about 5 or 6, he took a bite of meat and as I watched the expression on his face change, I knew his body was happy. He carries the warrior archetype, and his body resonates with occasionally eating consciously raised and prepared meat. My youngest son, on the other hand is like me; he has never craved meat in his diet and is happy living off of hemp, seaweed, honey, nuts, seeds, vegetables, and fruit. His body is perfectly content and in harmony without the need to eat meat, and one of his archetypes is the artist—so this totally tracks. I believe this area of study weaving archetypes and food will become more prevalent moving forward (especially for parents). The physical structure and chemistry of our body both influence how our body responds to food. This response also evolves and changes throughout our lives as some archetypes activate and others go dormant. Some archetypes only activate later in life, which may be why you are suddenly called to start consuming something that previously held no resonance for you. This may also result in an intuitive call to initiate a spiritual fast or a juice cleanse. Take a moment to investigate your own archetypal patterns and which ones more heavily influence your daily life.

Here is a diagram that lays out Carl Jung's twelve archetypes as well as some key insights into not only how they influence daily living but what qualities are most important to each. It is also helpful to consider how archetypes may impact food choices, eating patterns, and body nourishment practices. Where the innocent child may be more prone to use food as a tool for grounding and security, the outlaw may become more inspired to spiritual fast, and the magician may have what it takes to thrive in the kitchen as a culinary chef or recipe creator.

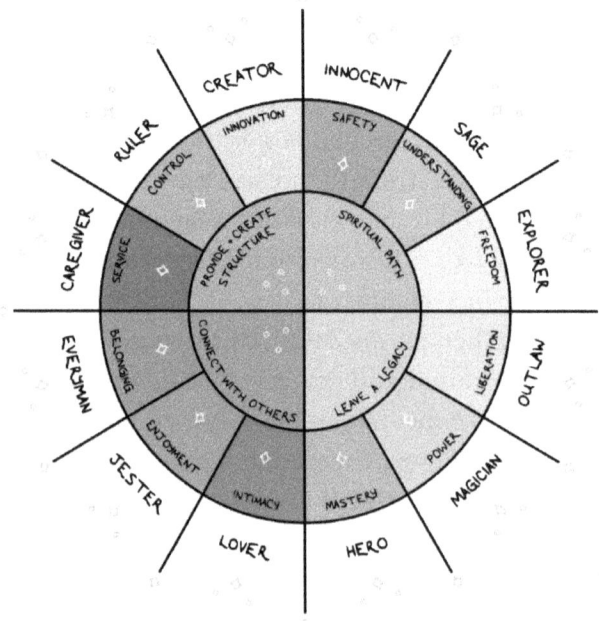

Prayer

As the world accelerates in speed and chaos, prayer will be the preferred and prioritized communication channel. Invoking prayer can be very helpful on our spiritual nutrition journey back to whole, center, and truth. We must always remember to ask for guidance, support, and grace as we navigate through our own stormy waters before the calm. Angels (including archangels and our guardian angel) and elementals can all play a supportive role on your spiritual nutrition path. They are always by your side and available to support you if just remember to ask. Remember to be intentional with prayers and create as much clarity and focus as you can.

Food and Healing

When the body isn't busy ingesting, absorbing, digesting, and eliminating, it can heal. This is why occasional spiritual fasts and juice fasts are helpful on the healing path. When we are healing, we don't need as much food. Our bodies actually prefer to spend less time on physical food and more time on soul food. Often, we stuff our bodies in an attempt to stuff our feelings. What we forget to also understand is that we have been conditioned and programmed to supress, ignore, and hide authenticity. This is a foundational factor associated with stuffing the body as a collective. We think overfeeding and stuffing ourselves will make us feel better, until one day we finally connect the soul destiny dots and have a huge wake up call. What our bodies are craving is a little quiet, void, and nothingness. Is your body telling you to give it a rest? Get ready for spiritual fasting to take on new momentum in upcoming years. We don't only cover up our bodies, faces, and lives in an attempt to look just a little "better," but the food cover-up is a way for us to blockade our auras. We create emotional, energetic, and physical fortresses around our bodies as a means of protection. This is why healers often add a little excess density to their bodies. Their bodies respond to the intense energies being drawn into the aura by creating a heftier physical shield as protection, as well as to guard against response to heavy metal toxicity, chemical toxicity, EMF toxicity, and emotional toxicity. For empaths and sensitives especially, excess weight is often the body's way of protecting the auric fields from the darker and more toxic energies of others. For this reason, energetic weight is more of a meaningful discussion than physical weight. If there is excess energy being carried by the auric field, it will eventually manifest into excess physical weight carried by the body.

Another point to consider is spiritual ascension. Sometimes, when we are either too attached or too focused on spiritual ascension or exiting our bodies, food is helpful to ground us back to earth. We are meant to experience both the ground and the stars while in physical form. We want to take in light but also be able to hold it. This means we have to be in our bodies and feel the ground as we spiritually learn and grow. Empaths can also seek out food as a means of grounding in times of taking on way too many energies from others. Eating our feelings isn't always a bad thing; it's about coming to a loving place with ourselves where we surrender to ourselves. As much as I stive to eat as clean as possible, sometimes eating my feeling is just the order of the day. It is important to enjoy the food we eat and build a healthy and loving relationship with body nourishment.

A great place to start when it comes to supporting body healing is to feel some emptiness when waking up in the morning and before bed at night. Experience the discomfort and mind-chatter that goes on when we don't stuff our bodies like clockwork. It's uncomfortable and yet so very revealing.

Fear, Worry, Guilt, and Shame

Heavy energetic states, including fear, worry, guilt, and shame, are nutritional nomads that can set up camp in our Auric Bodies and throw us off course. These heavy energetic states can cause us to lose touch and connection with the body. In these states, it's as if we don't even reside in the body but dwell off in the ether somewhere, obsessing over ourselves. When chronic, these states cause tears and discords in the higher layers of the body (mental, emotional, and etheric) only to result in physical body distress. We may choose to emotionally eat or emotionally starve our bodies in these states, as they can leave us feeling deeply in despair. They are not in resonance with your highest self and are not worthy of your divinity.

Auric Water

One of my great passions is water. I am often asked what type of water is best for drinking, and I usually respond that all water that touches the body should be considered and appreciated, not just the water you drink. There is no shortage of water treatment companies and products, but let's remember that we do not want to be drinking dead water. The more we purify, filter, and expose our water to UV light, the less alive and sacred it becomes. It is also important to be mindful that reverse osmosis water is not the healthiest option when it comes to drinking, but it may be the only option for some who need to filter their water. I do test my water, but I also taste, feel, and connect with my water. I have developed an ability to feel the vibrational qualities of the water as well as how clean, pure, and toxin-free it is. This is something that everyone can develop with practice and a heart that focuses on the intention of speaking to water. The more we speak and connect with water, the more messages we will get. Our bodies are mostly water, and the water within us speaks to water everywhere on the planet. All waters are connected, which is why I believe natural spring water with gentle filtering is best. Sometimes we don't need to overdo it in terms of filtering. Having your water tested is a good idea but be mindful not to get swayed into buying the super works of filtering if your water doesn't need it. If you can vortex your water (structure and charge it the way nature intended) or you have access to naturally vortexed water, this is ideal. Structured water is a way of lovingly supporting water to be in its highest vibrational form (which can exhibit sacred geometry patterning when frozen). Water takes its most geometrical sacred form when we love, appreciate and care for it. When in this form, it is also in its most healing state. It is possible to get your hands on glass structured water bottles (we have some at AuricLiving.com), as well as structure your own water by talking to your water, loving it, and attaching loving affirmations to your water jugs and containers. Here are a few suggestions to amp up the charge and order of the water in your home:

* Consider glass containers for storage and travel containers.
* Earthen clay water dispensers and containers are great.
* Build a relationship and connect with your water daily.
* Say a daily blessing to your water.
* Structure your water through communication, blessings, and affirmations.
* Natural spring water in glass bottles is best.
* Avoid plastic water bottles.
* Carbon filtering is simple, inexpensive, and effective.
* Crystal-charge your water. Placing clear quartz in your water for a few hours and enjoy drinking the crystal-power-packed water goodness. Simply remove the crystal when you feel the water is ready to work its magic. Be sure, of course, not to use small pieces, and stick with a solid unfragmented piece. I do know people who use crushed quartz to charge their water, so please make sure if you are using this method that you have a very good system for filtering the quartz.
* Thank your water before drinking it.
* Appreciate your water with every shower and bath.
* Essential oils, flower essences, and herbs can also be used to structure drinking water or bath water.
* Add a little chlorophyl and fresh mint to your water.
* Adding fresh organic lemon to your water is always a great cosmic choice.
* Give your glass of drinking water a few moments in pure sunlight to structure and charge.
* Drink room-temperature water.

Ultimately, just do your best. Reverse osmosis water is not the highest-vibrational water, but sometimes it is the only option available. Distilled water can be a good option at the beginning and end of a fast as well as when detoxifying, but spring water is a better choice for regular drinking water choices. Testing for uranium in drinking water is also suggested in many parts of the world. Artesian wells are ideal options for working with high vibrational sources as well as water from high in the mountains and naturally filtered ecosystems. Even if we can't all get our hands on water from artesian wells or mountain springs, we can set the intention.

Oxygen

Auric Nutrition begins with breath. In Vedic traditions, it is said that about 90% of energy used by the body is from the oxygen taken in by the skin and lungs. We may be able to live without water for a few days, but we certainly cannot live without oxygen for more than a few minutes. Oxygen is truly our most precious nutrient, which is why breathwork is essential for not only oxygenating the body with spiritual strength but also for ensuring that at every moment, every cell in the body is being showered with vital lifeforce. When practicing breathwork, visualize not only the lifeforce energy entering your lungs and your skin as rays of sunlight. Most of the oxygen we take in goes to the brain, which can also be helpful in active meditation as we visualize light and lifeforce showering down the body, starting from the crown.

Another form of oxygen uptake is in the form of food. High oxygen intake supports Auric Health and Healing. If we consider oxygen to be like illuminated orbs travelling throughout our bodies, seeking out vibrantly charged (negatively charged) electrons is its passion. Electron movement to the oxygen pole is the natural and high-order process. Optimal levels of oxygen are therefore essential for keeping this process highly functional. High prana power foods are those that maintain the lifeforce energies granted by the sun, like fruits, vegetables, herbs, flowers, nuts, mushrooms, and seeds. These foods provide a glimpse of what it is like to consume pure sunlight. The sunlight is literally stored in these foods and transferred to our bodies upon eating. It is the vibration of pure sunlight that our bodies seek. We are truly beings of light. In terms of our Light Bodies, it's less about the food content and more about the light content.

A decrease in oxygen in the body can be caused by a variety of factors including poor diet, a highly acidic diet, fear, stress, toxins, coffee, carbonated drinks (even carbonated water), pharmaceuticals, environmental toxins, trauma, viruses, parasites, and infections.

Ozone therapy, daily breathwork, hyperbaric oxygen therapy, hydrogen peroxide therapy, and juicing are among the holistic practices offered today. Essential minerals and nutrients are also crucial for the entire carrier system that circulates oxygen rich blood throughout the body. These include iron, zinc, vitamin B12, vitamin D3, calcium, and copper.

Acidity

Nobel prize-winning physiologist Otta Warburg once said, "The cause of disease can be simply described as excessive acidity in the body." Body acidity is not blood acidity. Acidification of the body is what leads to chronic inflammation and deterioration. When the body becomes too acidic on a regular basis, the body compensates itself by pulling calcium from the bones and other tissues. It uses its own mineral stores to alkalinize. A diseased body is highly acidic while a harmonious healthy body is slightly alkaline. Acidosis is the build up of acids throughout the body and accounts not only for the acceleration of the aging process but for many chronic diseases as well. The lymphatic system is our body's system for working and eliminating acids.

Ionization leads to pH factors in the body. pH is simply the potential for hydrogen (hydrogen being the universal atom.) A diet that is highly acidic often leads to dehydration, stagnation, and corrosion in the body. Acids do not hydrate the body; instead, they steal your electrolytes. When the body becomes too acidic, corrosion accelerates. Too much acidity (including proteins) also switches on nature's way of compensating for by way of stealing calcium from elsewhere in the body. In many cases, the energetically weaker systems of the body are targeted first (heart, kidneys, bones, liver, etc.). This is why alkaline-dominant foods are helpful. When speaking about alkaline foods, it is actually the alkalinity of the ash of the food that is important—what is left over after the food has been burned up by the digestive process. Foods that leave an alkaline ash are ideal. Lemons, for example, are acidic fruits but leave an alkaline ash. Although early corrosion in the body may not be detectable, eventually, trouble in the joints as well as lymphatic stagnation occur. For this reason, joint issues and slow lymphatic flow (swelling) can be used as indicators of acidosis. Acidosis in the body can be caused by ingesting too much acidic food or drink, cellular waste, ill thinking, parasites, fear, pharmaceuticals, trauma, emotional distress, and irregular and sub-optimal breathing. Empaths and sensitives are also at higher risk of acidosis as they invite the thoughts, feelings and frequencies of others into their field. This is why strengthening and protecting one's aura is so very important for radiant health.

pH matters in every process of the body. When your pH factors are off, not only is food absorption impacted but the entire metabolic process. The key to radiant health is homeostasis in the body. Eating alkaline is a significant step in keeping pH levels throughout the body in homeostasis. Breathwork as well as body hydration further enhances this homeostasis. It is important to remember that everything is always in a state of flux and change, which means achieving some perfect stopping point is simply not going to happen. A body in a state of homeostasis, however (with a slightly alkaline nature), is not only able to maintain radiant health, but is also able to quickly pivot back into the driver's seat after a short and temporary sway from healthy center.

Always remember that optimized breathing is the first and best way to alkalize the body. Eating a diet that is dominantly alkaline is next. The following list is useful tool for making alkaline food choices. (Remember that the ash residue of the food upon digestion is alkaline.)

* Berries
* Melons
* Lemons
* Oranges
* Limes
* Ripe Grapefruit
* Kale/Collards
* Romaine
* Spinach
* Beet Tops
* Asparagus
* Celery
* Carrots
* Ginger
* Garlic
* Peas
* Apples
* Grapes
* Cherries
* Mangoes
* Pears
* Apricots
* Avocados
* Kelp (and other seaweed)
* Parsley
* Wheatgrass
* Cayenne
* Figs and Dates
* Dandelion
* Chard
* Raw Honey
* Seeds
* Sprouts
* Herbs
* Broccoli

Breathwork, rest, kindness, love, prayer, meditation, smiling, laughing, yoga, walking and swimming are other activities that enhance body alkalinity.

Happy Fats

The topic of including a healthy amount of happy fats in our diets is always an evolving conversation. The most important piece of information to remember is to always trust your gut regardless of what you read. For some people, avocados and coconut oil work magic for their bodies. For others, these fats can be mucus-forming and not so in resonance with their Auric Body. A dose of healthy fats in the diet is important for cell membrane function and for lubricating the digestive tract. Hemp oil, olive oil, sunflower oil, grapeseed oil, avocado oil, and coconut oil (all organic) are popular options. Algae and seaweed are always great vegan options of Omega-3's and are sources of both Docosahexaenoic Acid (DHA) and Eicosapentaenoic Acid (EPA). For those who are not vegan, cod liver oil is a good option because it supports the reduction of inflammation in the body and has been shown to play a supportive role in autoimmune disorders. Sea buckthorn oil is currently one of my very favorites. This cosmic creation is not only packed with all the omega fatty acids (including Omega-7), but it is also loaded with over 190 bioactive nutrients. This oil is a topical beauty essential but does wonders upon ingestion, too. Evening primrose oil is another healing gem as it works to enhance the immune system, balance female hormones, and support skin radiance. Black seed oil is also a happy fat choice and has a small section devoted to it below. Nut and seed oils are also great choices both in terms of flavour and prana power. Organic pumpkin seed oil, hemp seed oil, and organic flax seed oil are among my favorites.

Although taking in happy fats is greatly beneficial to support cell membrane health, taking in too much is not ideal. Fats do have the lowest oxygen content of food families, which leads to them becoming oxygen stealers in the body when in excess amounts. Keep your fats happy and harmonious.

Minerals

Minerals should always be on your mind. These precious gems are the foundation of our structure and at the very core of our soul's manifestation into physical form. Our relationship with the divinity of our body should also inspire us to heighten our deep appreciation for the mineral kingdom. We are made up of minerals, and these minerals carry the vibrations of total life. Every mineral has a unique biosignature that resonates with a particular level of consciousness and speaks directly to certain areas of the physical and energy levels. Different minerals are therefore in greater resonance with different organs and chakras. Excess or deficiencies in certain minerals can therefore impact not only physical but emotional, mental, and spiritual wellbeing. It is important to note that mineral supplements are available almost everywhere today without much discussion about the source, manufacturing, and quality of them. It is vital to do your homework and even consider muscle and/or aura testing to help you select one that is in the best resonance with you. It is also important to remember that in nature, minerals work as a team. Each chemical reaction in the body impacts another. This is why, when we take mineral supplements, they typically don't perform best on their own as individual minerals. If you have had some testing done (such as a blood test, aura test, or muscle test) that identified a mineral deficiency, be sure to do your homework and ask someone you trust for a highly bioavailable brand that will actually work in the body. Most mineral supplements on the market today don't even dissolve in the body and have very low bioavailability. You can even test your mineral supplement by dropping it in a glass of room temperature water and timing how long it takes to dissolve. For bioavailability to be high, your body has to recognize it as pure and from the earth. If not, the cells will not welcome it in, and you will just excrete it out without any absorption or benefits. Cell salts are also great as they are homeopathic doses of mineral complexes and have a beautiful essence about them. I like to include both cell salts and select mineral supplements in my daily supplements. Fulvic and humic acid complexes are also ways for us to connect at the cellular level with prehistoric traces of plant minerals. Not only does this deeply ground us but it also connects us across the Auric Body to Mother Earth. These complexes are plant-based and available in liquid form.

Remember that being grounded as a being has a lot to do with mineral levels throughout our body being in harmony. Deficiencies will not only lead to physical body disfunction but will also impact the aura. Feeling ungrounded and disconnected from ourselves and the earth may be rooted in mineral deficiencies in the body.

Molecular Hydrogen

Molecular hydrogen gas (dihydrogen) is gaining traction in the medical science community. Hydrogen supports the body in many ways including inflammation reduction, hydration of lung surfaces, nutrient transfer, and body temperature regulation. Hydrogen is a key body nurturer and is soothing to the mind, body, and spirit. Water, of course, is one of the key hydrogen carriers. Too much or too little hydrogen can be harmful to the body, which is why homeostasis is key. Lemons, oranges, grapefruit, berries, cherries, lettuce, watermelon, chard, carrots, tomatoes, and fresh juices are all great sources of hydrogen. The hydration factor of a food is what makes it so magic for the body. These high-hydration-factor foods have hydrogen to thank for their radiance and juiciness. Research continues to take place into the benefits of hydrogen for inflammation reduction, surgery recovery, and chronic illness treatment. To date, hydrogen has been shown to have a therapeutic effect on more than 150 health conditions.

Niacin Flush

Elevated amounts of vitamin B3 can lead to what is called the "niacin flush," and is a wonderful way to relax the muscles inside the blood vessels (vasodilation). Niacin increases prostaglandins, which are fat compounds that have hormonal effects. There is a temporary reddening response of the skin with a niacin flush that can feel a little uncomfortable for some (especially when doing it for the first time). Therapeutically, niacin has been used for more than 50 years in holistic, nutritional, and naturopathic medicine. It is the most effective natural agent for increasing the body's natural levels of HDL (good cholesterol) by 20-40%. Niacin has also been shown to enhance mental and cardiovascular health as well as circulation and skin. Seek out support from an integrative health practitioner or naturopath to learn more about doing a niacin flush.

Sea Water

Drinking sea water is certainly not promoted in North America today but it is and has been a healing practice elsewhere around the globe. In Nicaragua, for example, the medicinal benefits of seawater are celebrated, and sea water clinics are located across the country. Not only is sea water deeply healing for the physical body, but it works at all levels of the Auric Body. In German New Medicine, Dr. Ryke Geerd Hammer discusses the healing benefits of sea water in greater detail. Although I am not endorsing it, it is worth doing your own research into the potential health benefits of drinking sea water.

Chlorine Dioxide

This is another touchy subject in the mainstream. It can be difficult to find information on the potential benefits of chlorine dioxide as well as getting your hands on it. Chlorine dioxide is what water purification tablets are made of, and the books written about its role in health and healing are worth at least a read. It has remarkable anti-parasitic properties and has been used in post-surgery treatment, wound healing, chronic disease management, and malaria treatment. There are many studies showing scientific promise for chlorine dioxide. It is inexpensive and easy to make, which is why many developing countries use it as a remedy. Again, I am not endorsing or promoting the use of chlorine dioxide other than for water purification, but you may wish to investigate this further if it intrigues you. We keep chlorine dioxide water treatment tablets on hand and ensure they are in our travel and home first aid kits. If you consider one theory that many illnesses (including many chronic illnesses) are parasitic in nature, it makes sense that an anti-parasitic such as chlorine dioxide would be beneficial.

Colloidal Silver

Topically, colloidal silver is a powerful anti-viral, anti-bacterial and anti-parasitic. Its biosignature is such that it deactivates and "puts to bed" anaerobic parasites without killing healthy bacteria and microorganisms. There is much evidence on the beneficial properties of colloidal silver for reducing pain, inflammation, infection, and parasites.

Good Karma Kitchen

On your healing journey, there is no room more worthy of sacred attention than the kitchen (other than, perhaps, the bedroom). The kitchen is the heart of the home and can act as portal to other realms. It is not only a place where our lives become interwoven with nature but a sacred space for creativity. In the kitchen, we become deeply connected with the circle of life and how deeply interconnected everything is. Our ability to create a joyful, peaceful, rhythmic, and spiritual life has much to do with our kitchen. The kitchen is at the very center of connection—connection with the earth, with all living things, and (of course) with our relationships. The energy of connection with all living things is always vibrant and present in the kitchen. As we've already discussed, how you eat is how you live. The kitchen can therefore be used as a beautiful sacred space to enhance spiritual living. How you feel when you walk into your kitchen has everything to do with your physical, emotional, mental, and spiritual wellbeing. Regardless of your abilities in the kitchen, everyone is a creator when they prepare food. Here are some simple suggestions to enhance the sacred biosignature of your kitchen:

1. Keep it clean and simple.
2. Strive for spaciousness.
3. Create beauty and order.
4. Make use of crystals.
5. Use incense and essential oils.
6. Keep it stocked with superfoods, spices, and herbs.
7. Fill it with lots of love.
8. Maintain your fridge in an orderly and clean way and filled with high-vibrating foods.
9. Opt for living foods.
10. Structure and love your water.
11. Remove (or unplug if you have a built in) your microwave.
12. Use natural materials, like clay and glass mugs and a glass teapot.
13. Keep it stocked with fresh fruit, flowers, and music.
14. Keep a good supply of dried flowers and herbs on hand.
15. Have an assortment of teas and glass water pitchers filled with water and lemon available for hydration.
16. Keep it well stocked with healthy cookware and tools, such as a juicer, dehydrator, blender, Mason jars, crockpot, and a high-quality sharp knife.
17. Use healthy cookware only that is toxin free and does not off-gas harmful chemicals.

I am often asked about dehydrated foods, and while we want to prioritize hydration in our diet, for travel snacks, kids snacks and tasty treats, a dehydrator is fun and a little addictive! Kale chips, seed crackers, dried fruit, and healthy cookies are just a few kid favorites for the dehydrator. Having a high-quality sharp knife stocked in the kitchen is also key. Symbolically this is very important! If all the knives in the kitchen are slightly dull or low quality, the creative energy will also be dulled. Removing microwaves from the home is also a key practice for Auric Nutrition. Keeping the kitchen as sacred and cosmically connected as possible will enhance integrous, whole, and healthy living.

Food Frequency Pyramid

Over future incarnations, we will be moving towards living off sunlight. We're obviously not there yet but understanding this can be helpful as we make more conscious and mindful choices today where nutrition and lifestyle are concerned. We are now meant to make lighter choices where food is concerned to keep our Light Bodies illuminated and free. When we are weighted down with too much density through food, it becomes difficult for our Light Bodies to emit highest vibrational energetic rays. We feel this effect of too much heaviness through our mindset and our mood. We are moving towards being full on beams of love and light by taking one small conscious step at a time. In *Auric Nutrition*, nourishing the body with breath is even more of a priority than food. This doesn't mean that you don't eat, but that optimal breath gets even more of our attention. When breath is taken in as spiritual food, our bodies require much less food. When we start and end our day with functional breath, we expand our auras and further transform into the Light Bodies we truly are. The core practices in Auric Nutrition include vibrational alignment exercises, seated eating, blessing, breath, hydration, moderate fasting and vital life enhancers. Auric Nutrition and Auric Health go hand in hand. In order to be able to effectively practice Auric Nutrition, healing must also be a committed practice. It is difficult to fuel the body well when trauma and discord reside in the body. For this reason, healing trauma is the soulmate to Auric Nutrition. When trauma is unprocessed, unhealthy and unwell relationships with the body and with food arise.

What is most important about the Auric Living food pyramid is to trust your intuition. There is no single way that works for everyone when it comes to nourishing the body. Our genetic makeup is unique and sacred, and our bioenergetic signature evolves as we do. Placing ourselves into physio-food prisons by way of labels hinders our ability to ascend past labels. Be leery of labelling the body and being with a label that hinders or limits expansion, expression or evolution in any way. Although sunlight, breath, and fruits are ideal in terms of biosignature and bio-resonance, we aren't all quite there yet in terms of frequency. The alternative is that we may be opening up our light channel to eat more raw fruit but taking a temporary detour to attune the body (including some heftier protein or gently steamed vegetables) may be given as intuitive guidance. It is true that the cleanest and highest-vibrational food on the planet is fresh organic fruit, but in many cases, we aren't quite clean and clear enough to actually benefit from the high levels of light they provide. Fresh, edible, and unsprayed flowers are also highest-light carriers in terms of biosignature. Eating edible flower petals is always nourishing for the cells and the soul. For this reason, you will notice bidirectional arrows on the food pyramid above between the fruit and vegetable category. This is to indicate that fruit may become more in resonance than vegetables in your daily nutrition based on your own biosignature and its resonance being more aligned with raw organic fruit. You may also alternate between raw and steamed vegetables/fruits depending on your own intuitive guidance. Remember to keep the intuitive channels open and optimal by way of meditation, prayer, and breathwork.

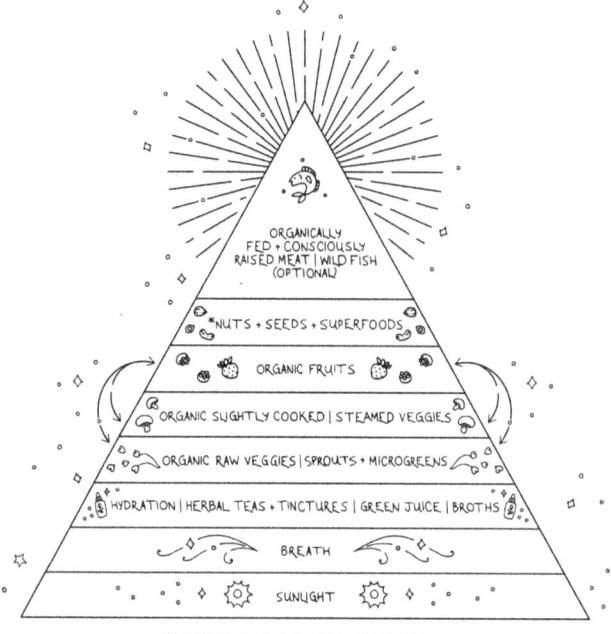

*SOME ORGANICALLY GROWN GRAIN IS OPTIONAL

Getting adequate sunlight is also highly important for this to occur. This typically happens at some point along the spiritual nutrition path—fruit becomes more of a priority than vegetables. Some spiritual teachers believe that the higher a fruit grows above the earth, the better it nourishes the soul and the body. You will therefore fluctuate between times of more fruits in your diet and times of more vegetables. This will also be dependant on how clean your body is and how well your microbiome is. If the body is clean and the microbiome is healthy and balanced, raw, ripe, and organic fruit intake will ultimately feel most intuitively right! As your frequency of light increases, it is therefore likely that more raw, organic fruit (over vegetables) will make up a significant portion of your nourishment intake. You may also feel intuitively called to eat a primarily raw diet for one season, followed by a diet of warm broths, steamed vegetables, and soothing teas for the next. You may even have a day where sipping herbal tea only for the day feels right and true. Roll like a wave and answer the intuitive call.

Blood type is also important to consider when it comes to food and nutrition. This is because proteins on the surface of blood have much to do with the immune and digestive systems of the body. It has also been shown that certain blood groups are more susceptible to different pathogens while others are more resistant. Parasites can also impact different blood types in different ways, which is why learning at least a little about your blood type is helpful. There is much evidence that certain blood types thrive better with some meat. It has also been hypothesized that those with rhesus factor negative (Rh-) blood have a different electrical charge to their blood, which changes their blood chemistry. In this case, a more alkaline-dominant diet is suggested. Breathwork and meditation may be particularly important for those with Rh negative blood. The impact blood type has on nutrition as well as optimal health is a fascinating and mysterious area of study that is continuing to unfold as more studies take place.

Some of my research has shown that even the Essenes had rituals for occasionally eating meat. If your intuition is guiding you to include some meat, put care and consideration into the farming practices of where your meat is raised and processed. The consciousness of the farmers as well as the farming practices are important here. From where you purchase your honey to where you get your eggs, poultry, and meat, the mindfulness factor is key. If you don't farm it yourself, ask friends for local organic suppliers who practice biodynamic farming or who put great care and mindfulness not only into their product but on caring for Mother Earth. Asking your local farm about their use of pesticides and chemicals is important, too. Even when purchasing land, my husband and I investigate past uses and activities on neighbouring lands to get a feel for chemical usage and the biosignature of the area. This investigation can also give you insight into practices you can do to heal the land on which you dwell. We must remember that we are not really here to own land but to honor, enjoy, and nurture it.

Climate is also very important to consider. If you're living in a tropical paradise, it's likely that fresh organic fruit, sea air, and sunshine are aligned with your highest vibration. In these climates, an ocean swim makes for a natural body cleanse and a perfect compliment to a diet rich in ripe raw fruits and farm fresh vegetables. Nuts, seeds, and occasional fresh fish are also in resonance for these climates. For those living in colder climates with long winters and less access to organic, farm fresh produce, making bread and consuming organic grains like spelt, millet, barley, buckwheat, rice, quinoa, and kamut may be beneficial to the body and to the soul. Should this be the case, purchasing your own grain mill is a beautiful Auric Living practice. I have many friends who have adopted the "If I don't grow it, I don't eat it" attitude, which is certainly a wise choice. If you aren't able to grow your own food, however, consider creating conscious greenhouse and farming co-ops in your area for living truly farm-to-table (or grow-to-table) as much as possible. Our foods are being poisoned, processed, and irradiated to such a degree that our bodies can no longer tolerate them—hence the massive incidence of gluten intolerance, grain intolerance, and even absolute intolerance of pretty much everything from a grocery store. If you're feeling inspired, perhaps it's your time to initiate a community collective around greenhouse growing, organic farming, or a local organic produce subscription service.

It is important to point out that many spiritual texts do indicate the healing benefits of a diet that is most comprised of fresh fruit. I believe that this is deeply healing, as fruits are the cleanest and highest vibrational choice when it comes to Auric Nutrition. The challenge comes when our bodies are not cleared of candida, parasites, and toxins. In this state, some bodies can be further aggravated by too much fruit. The other challenge where a fruit-rich diet is concerned is having access to fresh and organic fruit. When consuming grocery store fruit, there are many additives and sprays (even on organic produce) that alter the vibrational makeup and make it less healing upon consumption. If you are feeling a nudge to move towards more fruit in your daily diet, it is helpful to work with some of the detoxification practices mentioned in this chapter and consider colon hydrotherapy, ozone therapy, an herbal parasite cleanse, and perhaps a short, two-day fast. Adding a daily sauna and chi machine session will also help activate the lymphatic and circulatory system for nature's detoxification to be in high order. Chi machines can be purchased online for a few hundred dollars.

To summarize the Auric Nutrition food pyramid, this is to be used only as a guideline and will be ever evolving based on the spiritual stage of the individual. This is a general overview of where our bodies are right now in terms of spiritual evolution. There are some beings on the planet who are able to remove vegetables from the list and prioritize sunlight, meditation, breathwork, and fruit. As a collective, we aren't quite there yet, but Auric Nutrition is about listening on the inside to what feels right rather than listening to the thousands of trends, fads and opinions that are always happening on the outside.

Sprouts have always been a passion of mine due to their extreme nutritional power when it comes to micronutrients. The lifeforce packed into tiny sprouts is immense, making them true high-frequency food. These little powerhouses enhance the immune system and support detoxification as well as cellular repair and regeneration. Organic sprouts and microgreens of all sorts are often available at local organic farms. Some of my favorites include sunflower, broccoli, pea, clover, mustard, radish, and alfalfa I highly encourage you to consider sprouting yourself and/or searching out local markets for pickup and delivery options for sprouts and microgreens.

The Luminous Lymphatic System

As a former medical student, I was surprised to learn that the lymphatic system was not prioritized the same way the nervous or circulatory systems were. The lymphatic system is the sewer system of the body and should be sacredly cared for and nurtured. What typically happens after years of overwork and overtime (from eating poorly, excess trauma, chronic fear and/or chronic stress) is that the lymphatic system starts to get sluggish. Lymph stops flowing with radiance, and blockages occur so that drainage cannot take place as it should. This is often evident when it comes to bowel elimination. For many, a good poop hasn't happened for days, weeks, months, or even years. At the foundation of every luminous lymphatic system are healthy and happy kidneys. When kidneys underperform, so does the lymphatic system. This is just one of the reasons hydration (and the hydration quotient of food), is crucial. Nutrition is one of the most magnificent ways to transform a dull lymphatic system to a luminous one. And what does a luminous lymphatic system love most? LIGHT. Food that are rich in sunlight power are most beneficial to the lymphatic system. Fruits, vegetables, flowers, and herbs work wonders to restore lymphatic function. Flower essences and homeopathics can also be helpful. By incorporating green juice, berries, salads, and herbal teas as staples into the diet, luminosity can be restored. Green juicing will help to cleanse every cell in the body by way of lifeforce and restore good lymphatic flow. Edible flowers and herbs are like soulmates to the lymphatic system. Some other lymph-loving foods include watermelon, berries, lemons, pomegranates, mangoes, sprouts, dandelion, ginger, turmeric, seaweed, beets, parsley, cilantro, spinach, kale, cucumbers, celery, kiwi, and microgreens.

Detoxification

You always have an immune response when you consume food that is out of harmony with the human body. Excess mucus is then produced and excreted by the body, which indicates that the body us in a state of acidosis. The goal of Auric Nutrition is to nourish the body in a way that reduces the production of excess mucus. In this case, detoxification practices are helpful and healing. Detoxification can take on many forms, and there are thousands to choose from. When I speak of detoxification, I am referring to practices we can follow that activate the lymphatic system to do what it has been cosmically created to do—alkalize and detoxify the body. The liver is, of course, involved in the detoxification of chemicals, toxins, and ingested matter, but the lymphatic system is the true system of detoxification. There are things we can do to support the lymphatic system to get back to its natural state of greatness. I tend to leave detoxification protocols to my private and group detox sessions, but there are a few general practices that can be helpful for everyone. The role and goal of detoxification is to return the body to homeostasis and to slight alkalinity. Spiritual fasting can be a very effective way to achieve this goal, but we have to be ready for it throughout the Auric Body. All of our layers have to be on board for spiritual fasting to be possible and effective. There are many methods of fasting (including intermittent fasting), but spiritual fasting is unique in that it is a tool for total healing when one is ready for it.

We want to keep the kidneys filtering (which means the adrenals must be radiant) as well as keep all of the endocrine glands in tip-top shape. The liver is also a key organ for detoxification. It has 500 different functions, and when it is damaged due to excess alcohol, pharmaceuticals, stress, toxins, trauma, emotional distress, etc., it loses its ability to properly detoxify. When this occurs, excess levels of many hormones and toxins can spill back into the bloodstream without being processed. These include toxins, heavy metals, cortisol, estrogen, and cholesterol. This means that estrogen dominance and adrenal fatigue could actually be tied to liver health.

Detoxification protocols can be helpful in supporting the body's natural ability to detoxify waste matter and enhance lymphatic flow. Consider detoxification to be a lymphatic system tune-up with all the organs reaping a benefit. Typically, detoxification includes juicing, herbal protocols, herbal teas, a selection of superfoods, colon hydrotherapy, breathwork, and meditation. Prayer is also very powerful to enhance the detoxification process. During a detox, it is helpful to decrease physical activities and stick to yoga, stretching, swimming, and walking. Crystals such as shungite can also be used to draw toxic energies from the body further enhancing the detoxification process. Hydration also plays a key role in detoxification because it helps to flush out toxins and waste matter as the lymphatic system gears up. If you're going to do a detox, be sure to stay well hydrated throughout the entire process. For this reason, coffee, nutritional yeast, sugar, dairy, grains, gluten, meat, soy, processed foods, and carbonated water should be avoided. Some detoxes I know of do include some rice, but I prefer to leave rice out when detoxing. Herbal teas, green juices and broths are ideal during detoxification to give the digestive system a break so that etheric body vitalization can occur. For more active lifestyles, salads and fruits may also be included. For deeper cleansing to take place during detoxification, it is recommended to scale back physical fitness and enjoy a walk, swim, gentle yoga, or stretching. Resting the body plays a significant role during detoxification. I have attended detox programs where bentonite clay and other substances were used to help draw toxins out of the body, as well. Personally, I prefer activated coconut charcoal as a preferred detoxification tool. It is always wise to consult with a naturopath or detoxification specialist before you begin. It is also not wise nor recommended to do a detox while pregnant or breastfeeding. I am a living testament to this. I led myself through a detox when my son was only a few months old, and I was still breastfeeding him. My old "go big or go home" ways kicked into high gear and resulted in me being bedridden for 48-hours with a belly bug.

This list is not a complete detoxification protocol, nor should it be followed without professional supervision. This list is more of a starting point and educational tool. I highly encourage seeking out a practitioner (such as a naturopath, homeopathic nurse, nutritionist, or detoxification specialist) before embarking on your first detoxification. I also find having an aura scan done before and after a detox to be very revealing and insightful. It is a great tool as one progresses along a spiritual nutrition path. Here are a few items that often get included in my Auric Nutrition Detoxes:

* Castor oil (applied directly to hair and skin as well as packs)
* Cod liver oil (for some)
* Juicing (read on for my Auric Green Juice recipe)
* Ozone therapy
* Parasite protocol (herbs and others)
* Meditation
* Prayer
* Breathwork
* Yoga
* Seaweed
* Spirulina (source is critical)
* Colloidal silver
* Activated coconut charcoal
* Diatomaceous earth (food grade)
* Auric baths (detoxification baths)
* Essential oils
* Incense
* Smudge sticks
* Crystals
* Herbal teas, tinctures, and capsules
* Supplements (including magnesium, zinc, and N-acetyl cysteine)
* Superfoods (ashwaganda, triphala, and moringa are some favs)

* Cell salts
* Detoxing salts
* Bee pollen
* Structured water
* Aura scan (before and after detox)
* Ripe organic fruit (for some)
* Fresh organic vegetables (steamed for some, raw for others)
* Broths (vegetable and/or mineral bone broth)
* Sprouts and microgreens
* Nuts and seeds (for some and only if absolutely needed)
* Infrared sauna
* Colon hydrotherapy
* Chi machine
* Rebounder
* Cold plunge tub
* Dried eucalyptus for a steam shower
* Love, compassion, and kindness
* Wheatgrass
* Lemons (to be added to water, juices, and broths)
* Probiotics (for some)
* Zapper or microcurrent treatment
* Rife machine
* Tuning fork session
* Zeolite
* Blue green algae (such as spirulina and chlorella)
* Black seed oil
* Quercetin

Although mushrooms are highly beneficial and healing, I tend to leave them out during detoxification unless I know for certain the client is well alkalized throughout the body already. I also remind clients to set an intention to steer clear from nutritional yeast (and any other form of yeast), gluten, grains, sugars, and too much fruit during detoxification. Once the body is a clear channel of light, fruit can be increased. Making green juice and herbal teas staples in a detoxification diet is key. Detoxifying foods such as greens, microgreens, sprouts, citrus fruit, pomegranate, Brussels sprouts, parsley, ginger, turmeric, cilantro, beets, and dandelion greens can also be added. Interestingly, Brussels sprouts are powerful detoxifiers and have high levels of quercetin. Brussel sprouts work by increasing levels of glutathione-S-transferase (the enzyme that helps detoxify environmental toxins).

Some herbals that are helpful during detoxification include: horsetail, milk thistle, juniper berry, goldenrod, marshmallow root, uva ursi leaf, cleavers, graviola, fenugreek seed, bitter melon, dandelion, burdock root, Siberian ginseng, Oregon grape, chank Piedra, gotu kola, nettle, and red clover. These are just a few of the herbs most commonly included in detoxification teas and tinctures.

When it comes to heavy metal detoxification, infrared sauna, auric baths (see the Auric Beauty chapter), colon hydrotherapy, and a treatment with a reputable zapper instrument can be helpful. Other agents that work specifically to support heavy metal detoxification include blue green algae, olive leaf, zeolite, N-acetyl cysteine (NAC), melatonin, black seed oil, minerals, glutathione, selenium, flavonoids, taurine, activated charcoal, alpha lipoic acid, selenium, and modified citrus pectin (MPC). Zeolite, in particular, is a powerful chelating agent for removing heavy metals, effects from radiation, and other harsh environmental toxins. Herbs that are helpful in the detoxification of heavy metal include plantain leaf, cilantro leaf, parsley leaf, alfalfa leaf juice, cayenne, Irish moss, red clover, white oak bark, and echinacea root.

Nutrition and Hormones

I consider breath to be one of the pillars of harmonious hormones. When we breathe well, our hormones rhythmically set the tone for much of our body's radiance. There is so much magic we can do through our diets when it comes to hormones. The endocrine system is, in itself, a gateway to the cosmos. Each endocrine gland is associated with certain chakras in the body and plays pivotal roles in the opening and closing of energy portals within them. They are cosmic energy modulators and regulators.

Vibrationally, endocrine glands resonate strongly with sunlight, crystals, flowers, and herbs. This is why natural sunlight holds the key code for Auric Health. Flower essence, crystals, breathwork, herbs, Qigong, acupuncture, cognitive behavioral therapy, meditation, prayer, yoga, and adequate time in sunlight and in nature are all wonderful ways to support balancing hormone cycles by building an intimate and sacred connection with nature. This is a sure way to restore endocrine radiance. Green juicing, taking in herbs and herbal teas, spiritual fasting, flower essence, ayurveda, Traditional Chinese Medicine (TCM), body work, meditation, breathwork, and homeopathy are all helpful for overall hormone harmony. Many foods, spices, plants, roots, and mushrooms (such as reishi) also assist with hormone balancing. Ashwaganda, triphala, moringa, matcha tea, nature walks, sauna, bodywork, and daily detox baths have been staples in my own harmonious hormone journey. If your intuition is speaking to you when you hear the word hormones, consider seeking out the help of a naturopath or holistic health practitioner that specializes in hormones.

Microbiome

This topic could be its own book, but for our purposes here, it is being included to gently remind us all that our third chakra—the very center of our personal will, self-esteem, and emotional well-being—is a universe in itself. Of course, the microbiome impacts each and every aspect of the body and all chakras, but the third chakra is certainly a center point of this energy vortex. It is the energetic aspects and charge of the microbiome that is of primary importance when it comes to Auric Nutrition. You are what you eat physically, energetically, emotionally, and spiritually. Herbals that support the belly include licorice root, marshmallow root, slippery elm bark, aloe vera, ginger root, cinnamon bark, mullein leaf, camomile, comfrey, calendula, and fennel seed.

Consider the microbes that make up much of your microbiome to be feeding not only off of their physical environment but to also be micro versions of your emotional landscape. They feel what you feel and contract when you contract. They are feeding off of your emotional frequency. The microbiome is in desperate need of nurturing right now as the energetic currents of the world are being felt by the bugs in the belly. Perhaps it is time to offer a blessing to your microbiome or say a prayer for microbiome peace. As we find our center through spiritual activation, so does our microbiome. Instead of obsessively focusing on fixing the microbiome, focus on spiritual awakening and watch the microbiome find perfect grace. Probiotics, digestive enzymes, meditation, breathwork, broths, and fermented foods are among the physical realm assistants for the microbiome. Just remember that the emotional energy quotient is a much larger factor in microbiome health that most of us expect. When we hold emotional traumas, stresses, fears, and various types of resistance in our bellies, how can we have a healthy microbiome? Let go and let gut. Practice releasing the unwanted energies from the belly each day by placing your hands on your belly and watching it rise and fall with every healing breath. Speak only words of love and grace to your microbiome every single day.

Glutathione

Glutathione is a powerful antioxidant as well as a liver detoxifier. Glutathione helps open the liver pathways so that toxins and waste can be flushed out. Glutathione is made up of three different amino acids: glycine, cysteine, and glutamic acid. Your body needs healthy amounts of glutathione to keep the light shining. Spinach, avocados, and eggs are three great sources of the triple-threat amino acid team necessary for glutathione production. Selenium is also a cofactor to glutathione, so getting enough selenium in the diet is also key. There is growing research to indicate that supplementing with glutathione as we age is deeply beneficial for immune function, hormonal balance, detoxification, and radiant skin.

Shilajit
Shilajit is a black-brown complex mineral resin known as "mountain gold" because it is found high in the Himalayas. It is a prana enhancer and infuses lifeforce into your physical and energy body. It is an Ayurvedic powerhouse as well. It has been found to help with anemia, liver function, cardiovascular function, lymphatic flow, mental health, fertility, and immune function. It also acts as an anti-viral as well as a supportive supplement for autoimmune conditions.

Carbon 60
Carbon 60 (C60) is comprised of 60 carbon atoms in the form of a sphere, forming fullerenes (a kind of microscopic mesh). It is believed to be the most powerful antioxidant known and has also been shown to have an ability to repair DNA telomeres.

Black Seed Oil
Black seed oil is derived from the *nigella sativa* plant native to eastern Europe and western Asia and a member of the buttercup family. It is also commonly referred to as nigella and black cumin seed. Black seed oil is a common gem in Ayurveda as it has a multitude of benefits, including stabilizing blood sugar, improving skin, and reducing inflammation.

Spiritual Fasting
Spiritual fasting facilitates soul awakening and a return to wholeness. Spiritual fasting allows one to connect directly with the spiritual world. During deep fasting, the rational mind becomes quiet, still, and dormant. This facilitates the activation of a much higher form of soul intelligence that is housed in the heart. The activation of a much more powerful form of spiritual sight also takes place. The heart is the organ of high perception, and during spiritual fasting, it becomes activated and illuminated. The heart then begins to "see" and sense the hidden realms and all the beauty that lie within. Physical sight is limited to only a small fraction of all that

is. Fasting, therefore, can be used to develop this by way of heart illumination. Physical vision is only the very beginning of the path to true sight—spiritual insight.

Spiritual fasting is also a wonderful tool for removing emotional scar tissue from the heart. As illumination of the heart begins, this scar tissue is removed. This enables the heart to regain its flexibility, luminosity, and spiritual strength. The heart portal then opens. The lack of contact and connection with our own soul is what causes us to live a life that feels void of magnificence. The only true way to live a fully animated and joyful life is to fully and deeply experience the soul. A lack of direction or purpose in life is a great indicator that it is time to meet and greet the soul. The true purpose of spiritual fasting is not to transcend the body but to become more integrous, more whole and more alive. Spiritual fasting supports the weaving of soul and body. As the soul gains more power over the body, healing happens with much greater ease. The body can then become a pure and physical manifestation of soul-speak that guides us on our quest for living worthily and well. For people who have difficultly truly living in and feeling the sacredness of the body, spiritual fasting can be a gem. There's a reason why almost every spiritual tradition includes mentions of spiritual fasting. In ancient spiritual texts, the Essenes were known to prioritize highest health as a spiritual practice. Fasting, prayer and food blessing was a regular practice for them. Traditionally, many spiritual fasts were performed naked and in nature.

When it comes to living out our life's purpose, we spend much of our time trying to seek it on the outside. We sign up for courses, events, and seek out as many teachers as we can financially handle. We try this and try that, and when it doesn't work, we muster up the motivation to try something else. Eventually, we grow tired and wake up one morning wondering why we incarnated in the first place. Enter spiritual fasting. This practice can be used to find your bliss so that you can then follow it. Our highest life's purpose is contained in the soul, but it can be difficult to access when our world lacks spiritual contact. A busy and chaotic life is detrimental to discovering our true soul purpose, as the two work in opposition. The soul seeks simplicity, peace, connection, and wholeness, while society supports chaos, excess, addiction, and dis-ease. Let's not be too hard on ourselves; eventually, we all get stuck in a heartbreaking hamster wheel. We are now hungry more for soul food and less for physical food. For women, a spiritually sacred time takes place prior to pregnancy as well as during perimenopause/menopause years. Although spiritual fasting is deeply personal, age 25, 35, and 45 can act as cosmic center points in time to introduce shorter and less intense fasts. Over 45, spiritual fasting takes on a new strength, and you may be guided to engage in deeper and more frequent fasts. In the evening of our lives, we develop a yearning to have greater and more frequent contact with the soul. These can be ideal times for spiritual fasting as they are sacred bridges. When experiencing a dark night of the soul, spiritual fasting can help us gain insight into the lessons and the learnings that are taking place. The intention of a spiritual fast is to have a conversation with God; the side benefit is often body healing. When we get to a place in our lives where we can no longer seem to animate ourselves (I call this "spiritual limbo"), a spiritual fast just may pivot us into high harmonic gear.

In Auric Nutrition, mild to moderate fasting is a helpful way of enhancing and restoring rhythm to the Astral Body, which in turn brings the physical body back to order. Excess eating as well as the intake of acidic foods overstimulate the Astral Body, which results in a depleted and weighed-down physical body that cannot transmit as much light. When we fast, we quiet the Astral Body, enabling it to reorder and refuel the etheric body by restoring rhythm and harmony. When the etheric body is in harmony and full of vitality, so is the physical body. When this happens, we are in perfect harmony with the universe. It's that simple, but not that easy! A short fast can also be helpful to enhance practices such as meditation and prayer as well as the senses of higher perception. When our lifeforce doesn't have to be consumed by the digestive process, an entire cosmic world awakens. Just one to two days can be helpful for achieving this. Ancient spiritual fasts did not include any food or water, but we are learning the introductory principles to fasting and easing our way into eventual deeper fasting practices. With introductory fasting, broths, juicing, water, lemon water, herbal teas, maple syrup, and even some fruit is sometimes suggested. My preferred mini fast items are herbal teas and green juices when true fasting isn't what I need. Sometimes you have to meet the mind halfway! Some liquids may be helpful for those who are new to spiritual fasting. My very first fast was an intense 14-day fast. Needless to say, I wasn't at all ready or prepared for it. A deep fast should include preparation, knowledge, pre-fast practices, and mentorship.

Once we find our spiritual fasting feet, having a day each week for fasting is helpful. During this time, juicing and herbal teas may be preferred, but a dry fast or water fast for the day may also feel right. The goal of Auric Nutrition is to be a walking, breathing, transmitter of pure light and lifeforce. We simply cannot do this when we are weighted down with heavy food. Fasting should be intuitive, inspired, and a call from the soul.

Fasting is, of course, a popular physical body practice in nutrition but in the context of Auric Nutrition, it is a spiritual practice. This is why there are no rigid parameters, strict guidelines, or linear time constraints. Spiritual fasting goes by the cosmic clock. I will be dedicating an entire book to this sacred practice in the future, but for now, we will review and summarize key principles and practices. When the soul isn't fueled, the body and mind aren't either. Consider Auric Nutrition to be a new field of study that weaves spiritual, physical, emotional, and mental radiance. Guiding clients through spiritual nutrition mastery is my most cherished work. When we lack soul food, we crave dead food. If you're feeling like your aura is dull and your light is dim, a spiritual fast may be a call from your soul. If you're interested in joining one of our upcoming group spiritual fasts or detoxes, visit us at AuricLiving.com.

Food and the Light Body

An open heart and a quiet mind are the two key ingredients when it comes to Auric Nutrition. Prior to having practices that help us better hold higher frequencies of light, eating issues can arise. They can take all shapes and sizes, but as a rule of thumb, they are there for a reason. For many, food can act as a grounding tool for moments of highly ungrounded energy. For others, food can be used as a control mechanism to keep trauma buried and contained. Food can also be used as a powerful tool of light. Its divinity can bring a smile not only to the face but to the soul. Food is a juicy way to express creativity, nurturing, connection, love, appreciation, and joy. Food can heal the body as well as the soul.

We are also now in a particular phase in planetary and human evolution where we are better able to receive and animate the stored sunshine held in crystals, flowers, and herbs. Our frequencies now are not only better able to resonate with those things, but we hold the power to activate them as well. They are powerful tools for receiving and holding greater light. As previously mentioned, channeling light is now happening without much effort on our part. Holding light is our truest work. Here are some practices to help you:

1. Crystals (clear quartz, rose quartz, hematite)
2. Flower essences
3. Homeopathy
4. Cell salts, minerals, and supplements
5. Spiritual fasts
6. Prayer
7. Meditation
8. Nature walks
9. Tree hugging
10. Speaking to flowers and plants
11. Asking the angelic realm for assistance
12. Limiting how much jewelry is worn
13. Going watch-free as often as possible
14. Dressing the physical body with organic and natural fibers
15. Sleeping naked
16. Going undergarment free (at least at home)

17. Sound and music (singing bowls, spiritual, sacred, classical)
18. Chanting
19. Wind chimes
20. Essential oils and incense

Auric Nutrition Superfoods

The items on this list are also low mucus-forming and supercharged superfoods for helping inspire the lymphatic system and entire cellular structure to illuminate. These superfoods are wise and well for activating your highest-self pathways:

1. Lemons
2. Moringa
3. Tumeric
4. Ginger
5. Matcha
6. Ashwaganda
7. Hemp oil
8. Berries
9. Celery juice
10. Maca
11. Triphala
12. Green juice
13. Wheatgrass
14. Cilantro
15. Pomegranates
16. Watermelon
17. Chard
18. Collards
19. Brussels sprouts
20. Broccoli
21. Wild Norwegian cod liver oil
22. Fulvic and Humic acid complexes
23. Siberian ginseng
24. Gynostemma

25. Shilajit
26. Astaxanthin
27. Sea buckthorn oil
28. Mushroom Complexes (cordyceps, reishi, agaricus blazei, turkey tail, lion's mane, chaga)
29. Chlorella
30. Spirulina
31. He shou wu (fo-ti)
32. C60
33. Bee Pollen
34. Zeolite

When it comes to Auric Nutrition, graceful persistence is key. Don't be hard on yourself, don't lose faith, and don't give up. Highest-vibrational living is the greatest possibility for you at every single moment. I hope this book will inspire you to select and commit to this possibility today.

Auric Green Juice

Making a pitcher or large jug of green juice in the morning will help to support hydration and wellbeing throughout the day. Filling mason jars with juice and refrigerating them will help make juicing convenient and accessible. It is ideal to drink the jarred juice within the day, but if there are some leftovers for the next morning, that is fine (It just might not taste as good.). If you are juicing solo, a full juice container may be enough, but two containers full will give you some mason jars full for later. The amount of each ingredient also varies based on personal preference as well as juicer container size (we have an extra large one), so don't be afraid to play around with quantities for each. I prefer to include extra greens and celery while my husband likes to load on the ginger. Find what works for you, but our favorite ingredients include:

1. Heaps of kale/chard/spinach (whatever fresh organic greens you have)

2. 1-2 lemons
3. Handful of fresh organic cilantro
4. 6-10 celery stalks
5. Chunk of fresh organic ginger
6. 3-5 cucumbers

Note: Mint or turmeric can be substituted for cilantro. One half to a full apple can be added for children, but my kids like the juice as is and apple-free.

Auric Broth

Sipping broths during detoxes and through cold winter months is both nurturing and healing. Bone broth is a staple for two of my kids, while mineral vegetable broth is a favorite of mine.

You can use the following recipe for making both bone and vegetable broths. The only difference is that when I'm making bone broth, I give the broth several hours took cook before adding these ingredients. When I'm making mineral vegetable broth, I combine them all in the beginning, bring to a boil, and then leave on low for most of the day. When my vegetable broth has reached energetic alignment with my soul (and my taste buds), I remove the vegetables, lemon slices and ginger chunks to be used elsewhere. Any herbal leaves or stems can also be removed. I also like to wait until the broth is warm in temperature and not hot. This is helpful for healing the gut.

Whether you choose to make your broth with chicken, beef, fish, or vegetables, here is a starting point as you create your own version of Auric Broth. (Because I never follow recipes, I am providing you with the ingredients, but it will be up to you to play around with measurements. Everyone uses different pot sizes and has different taste so enjoy the journey.)

1. Structured water
2. Organic apple cider vinegar (start with a few teaspoons and add from there)
3. 1-2 organic ginger chunks

4. Organic lemon slices (peels off tend to be preferred for taste for children)
5. Himalayan Sea Salt
6. Vegetables of your choice (I add celery, collards, chard, kale, broccoli, spinach, and carrots)
7. (Optional) Organic sage, rosemary, cilantro, or herb mixes

Sensitives, Empaths, and Starseeds

For light workers, starseeds, empaths, and sensitives, nutrition must be understood and explored from a perspective of ascension and cosmic light. For these sensitive souls, food has an ever more significant and immediate impact on the body. Too much food can literally shut down their light channel. Eating live and light is key. Regular, short fasts are also highly encouraged as these types of bodies are learning to live less on food and more on light with every soul incarnation. These individuals should also prioritize meditation, daily detox baths, sunlight, juicing, short fasts, walks, and yoga. Grains can also have a less-than-optimal effect and should be minimized in the diet. Should grains be included, making homemade bread and other items using a grain mill is best. Sensitives, empaths, and starseeds should also consider colon hydrotherapy, sauna, daily herbs, rebounding, and a home chi-machine. EMF protection, including shungite stones throughout the home, is also helpful. For these individuals, clothing is also extremely important. To be honest, going undergarment free is ideal but not always possible, so use your own discretion. Elastics and restrictive fabrics significantly hinder prana and light flow throughout the body for everyone but particularly for sensitives. Wearing loose organic fiber clothing such as organic cotton or hemp is preferred. Wearing jewelry and watches can also significantly hinder prana flow, which is why they should be avoided or kept to a minimum. Wearing crystals would be an exception here. These individuals should also be as mindful as possible when it comes to the water they drink. Wherever possible, natural spring water from clean wells or sources is preferred. Creating a natural vortex for your water is also a wonderful idea unless it comes from a naturally vortexed source. Begin to develop intuitive abilities to such a level that even a single drop of water on the tongue signals to your intuitive nature. Here is where your outer senses come in so very handy—when they dance in beautiful harmony with your inner wisdom and guiding light, magic happens!

When I create stillness and present-moment awareness, I cannot stop the downloads and divine guidance from entering my energetic channel. I typically get my most creative insights when walking. For me, silent walks are walks with the divine. The reason they are so full of light and life is because they create complete present moment awareness. When we are fully present, we cannot stop being light. We are pure creative channels moving light throughout our bodies at cosmic speeds. This is why so many people who have experienced miraculous healings explain their journey as one of coming back to present. In the present, your cosmic abilities are far greater than you know. It is my hope that throughout this healing journey, you are reminded that in this very moment, you are infinite possibility and have the potential to create all that you desire.

We have reached a very sacred time in human and planetary ascension. Healing trauma and feeding the soul is going to revolutionize nutrition. Spiritual nutrition is now the way to an integrated, whole, healthy, and soulful life. It's time to gain the spiritual lightness so many of us seek while appreciating, connecting, and grounding to Mother Earth at the same time. Stretch your crown to the stars and plant your feet firmly to the ground—this is what spiritual nutrition can do for you. We absolutely can spread our wings while walking. To join one of our upcoming spiritual fast groups, visit AuricLiving.com.

Chapter 8: Auric Beauty

You are sound that has been shaped by the divine to carry light. Auric Beauty is an expression of harmonious exchange between the physical body and the universe. When this is expressed, an expansive light transmits from the human aura. As we inch closer towards full being integrity and order, expansive light illuminates both the physical body and auric field. When the auric field is fully of integrity, so is the physical body; there is balance between the body and the universe. This is an expression of auric beauty.

In order to achieve this full creative expression of beauty, it is essential that harmony, order, and balance be reinstated in daily life. The practice of Auric Beauty is a divine contract between inner and outer temple. We truly can shine from the inside out and a deepened spiritual practice will transform your light beyond belief. In today's quantum reality, authenticity and wellbeing are foundational for beauty. In this chapter, we will discuss daily practices and rituals that enhance life force energy throughout your being on the physical level but also on the levels of the aura. Remember that to radically transform the physical body, nurturing and healing the aura is necessary.

We have been disconnected from truth from all institutional angles and have lost touch with beauty as a whole. What is beauty? It's the manifestation of creative express and divine light. The heart chakra is the portal where this exchange takes place. The heart is therefore the primary tool for Auric Beauty. This spiritual synching activates our aura and brings us into harmonious order. In this chapter, we will discuss practical ways to enhance beauty in your physical and spiritual world. As the flower petals of your heart open wide, illumination throughout the body will occur. When given permission (often through surrender), the heart uses its infinite reach and power to marry mind and soul. When this occurs, the soul takes the reigns of life. This can often be seen in people through a shine and clarity in the eyes as well as an inexplicable physical transformation. I have personally witnessed this truth transformation take place in several people, and it is miraculous.

The path to Auric Beauty is twofold: 1) patiently practice opening the flower petals of the heart more often and widely with every day, and 2) transfer as much sunlight frequencies into the body as possible. Inhaling and ingesting sunlight can happen in a variety of ways. Drinking living water and auric green juice is a great place to begin. Other methods include using flower essences, herbs, sea water, and air, flowers, plants, crystals, living foods, essential oils, homeopathy, time in nature, sunbathing (more on this shortly), prayer, breathwork, meditation, and superfoods. All of these methods support bringing our bodies in resonance with the highest light order of the sun.

We have spent so much of our lives resisting, constricting, and cutting off from energetic flow and freedom, and it's time to significantly synch up to source. This means that anything that constricts and restricts the body and the aura should be avoided or limited in use. Not only do these energy constrictors block lifeforce flow, but they also block lymphatic flow and circulation. These inhibitors include constrictive clothing and tight undergarments, synthetic fibers, wires, metals, artificial scents, watches, hats, scarves, socks, nylons, jewelry, and accessories. Going barefoot and naked is obviously the highest vibrational choice but may not be an ideal choice for a variety of reasons. The next best option is to wear natural fibers as much as possible and limit undergarment use at least around the home. Keeping your body fluids and energies flowing without any hesitation is the key. This is likely why it feels so deeply healing and restorative to spend a few nights at a spa where a cotton bathrobe is the only thing you put on. Metals and watches can have a less than optimal effect on the aura as well. On a personal note, as much as I value all of my time going undergarment free and wearing only organic cotton clothing, I do still feel happy having my fashion days. I believe in avoiding extremes and give myself permission to have days where I don't shower myself in guilt if I put on a non-organic cotton dress. Still, I find that most of the time, feeling unrestricted and free is so much better than wearing tight, high-fashion clothing. I would not have said that 10 years ago. Keep your body as free as possible, as much of the time as possible. The rest of the time, enjoy your fashion and seek out eco-friendly brands that synch up to your soul. Bras and underwear have been sporadic choices in my life for decades and used only when absolutely necessary, like speaking events! My soul just feels most free when my body is undergarment-free. I am mindfully aware that this is not possible for every body type. Where undergarments are required or preferred, seek out natural fibers that are crafted in a way that enhance body fluid flow as well as energy flow. Try your best to avoid metal wiring, elastics, and overly tight undergarments. With underwear, if bikini or brief style is a favorite, select one size up so things are loose and flexible. Find 100% organic cotton when possible and select options without elastics or that are ultra-tight fitting. Again, if you're splurging on a date night, travel, or fashion event, do whatever moves you to a state of joy (including your undergarment and clothing choices). Just be mindful to keep your body free as much as you can. Support is great when it comes to clothing, but suppression is not.

Auric Beauty is an exploration and journey into one's ability to self-nurture and receive. There is direct correlation between these abilities and belly and womb wellness. As we are in a phase of rebalancing yin, practices that enhance and awaken the feminine are calling us all. Our bellies are speaking loudly as our third chakras awaken to new dimensions of courage, will, self, and soul. Dr. Edward Bach believed that all disease begins in the stomach as the stomach is the emotional center, and that emotions are the language of the soul. This is one of the reasons that self-nurturing (especially when centered around womb and belly wellness) is a cosmic calling today. This is also the cosmic reason behind the prevalence of womb and stomach dis-ease being experienced today. The beauty in all of this as that we are being called back to emotional center, to the self and to the soul. As we return, our eyes will gain a sparkle beyond language. Our hearts will illuminate our entire body and our skin will glow with a radiance that only the soul can provide. Returning to simplicity is an important and necessary practice for Auric Beauty as it breaks down our personality-built fortress and creates a naked and raw beauty that is rooted within. Returning to simplicity lovingly nudges us to prioritize the soul over the outer experience.

Rhythm and ritual are keys to Auric Beauty. In a society that is addicted to rushing, hustling, and more, beauty has become something we chase in the physical realm instead of something we hold sacred within the inner temple. We must rekindle a spiritual romance with our inner god/goddess and hold ourselves in high divine order. Auric Beauty is an art form.

Auric beauty predominantly centers around harmonizing the Auric Body (physical body and subtle bodies) with nature. It is therefore a core principle to center life as a whole around the healing power of flowers, plants, crystals, and herbs.

The following processes are the fundamentals that make up Auric Beauty:

Heart Harmonics

When opened, the flower petals of the heart illuminate the entire body more than any beauty tool can. True beauty shines when the heart is open, appreciative, and ready to serve. When we shelter the heart or let energetic scar tissue accumulate, our authentic beauty can only partially shine. As we heal our trauma and open our hearts, cosmic light shines from the heart, the eyes, and the entire Auric Body. This is not an easy process, and angelic support is often essential. But with intention and commitment, those heart petals open and shine.

Breath Beauty

Breath is beauty. Breath is not only transformative for the spiritual body but also for the physical body. You can absolutely transform your physical body through breath. A regular breathwork practice can reorder the very carbon structure of the physical body. Instead of creating attachments to too many beauty tools and gadgets, give breathwork a try first and watch the inner and outer transformation unfold before your very eyes.

Spiritual Practices

Spiritual practices are at the very foundation of Auric Beauty. Without them, fear and stress will steal not only beauty but life force from the body. There is nothing that sucks the life force out of us more than fear and stress. Unfortunately, trying too hard to combat stress and fear only makes matters worse. The way through fear and stress terrain is a complete surrender to soul. This may not happen overnight but eventually; the soul takes charge. Prayer and meditation have incredible effects on the physical body as they soften us, fuel us, and shake out all the energy wrinkles out of us. As an added benefit, spiritual practices can return the body to harmony and inner peace. These are keys to graceful aging rather than stress and fear-induced accelerated aging.

Strengthening the Auric Field

In order to keep the physical body ordered and integrous, the auric field must be strong. For empaths and sensitives, this can be challenging and should be prioritized every single day. The aura weakens through a variety of factors but can be strengthened back to whole. A weakened aura can appear cloudy, milky, porous, and/or dark. Because each layer of the aura corresponds and interconnects with the energy centers within the body, physical strength, flexibility, and balance are key. It is also important to seek wholeness and integrity from an emotional, mental, and spiritual perspective. This is, of course, a lifelong journey with many twists and turns. When the auric field is damaged or weakened, the physical body eventually loses strength and integrity as well. Auric Beauty has everything to do with a strong, radiant, and expansive aura. Here are a few ways to keep the aura strong as well to repair it:

* Tuning fork session and sound therapy
* Crystals (wearing them and setting up grids)
* Chromatherapy
* Meditation
* Prayer
* Aura brushing
* Qigong and tai chi
* Yoga
* Energy work and healing
* Eating alive foods and full-color-spectrum eating
* Healing trauma
* EFT
* Cold plunge
* Forest bathing and nature walks
* Homeopathy
* Flower essences and herbs
* Vaastu
* Art therapy
* Cell salts
* Sun bathing
* Heart harmonics
* Vogel crystals

I highly encourage my clients to get a Vogel crystal for self-healing. It is one of my most sacred and cherished healing tools and I never travel without it.

Beauty Rhythm

Setting a tone and rhythm each day is always a good idea, but when it comes to Auric Beauty, it is essential. Auric Beauty happens when we learn to deeply love and nurture ourselves spiritually, mentally, emotionally, and physically. Whole-hearted self-love benefits from sacred rhythm in daily life. Although not every practice in this chapter can be done every day, select a few that intuitively feel most beneficial for your right now. Create space for the beauty you desire and set a rhythm. This may mean having your Auric Baths at the same time every day, body brushing at a specific time each day, and sticking to a similar sleep cycle each night. Going to bed and awaking at a similar time each day is extremely beneficial to the physical and energy body. Each morning, consider keeping the same ritual at roughly the same time to help the body dance through the cadence of life. Although you may not always be physically dancing, set your life up so you are rhythmically dancing each day. Having an oral care practice each morning and night at roughly the same time is also wise. It may take some time to set sacred rhythms into your days and evening but once you have them set, you will hold them sacred. To do this, you may also have to let go of things that no longer serve you in order to make space for these rhythmic beautifiers. Let go and let glow.

Sunbathing and Sun Gazing

In the book, *Angel Medicine: How to Heal the Body and Mind with The Help of Angels* by Doreen Virtue, I came across an Italian saying that reads: "*Dove il sole non entra il dottore,*" which translates to "Where the sun doesn't enter, the doctor does."

Low sun exposure is linked to physical dis-ease. It's a wonder why society is obsessed with sunscreen and shielding our beautiful bodies from the sun. Not only is there evidence of autoimmune, mental, circulatory, and lymphatic sub-optimization being linked to lack of sun exposure, but so much of our emotional wellbeing is linked to the sun. We are suffocating our skin and harming our bodies by shielding ourselves from the sun. The sun has become an enemy where is should be held as healing and sacred. Not only do we block our bodies from the sun, but we then try to overcompensate by consuming vitamin D in supplement form. There is of course a place for vitamin D supplementation, but it doesn't make up for a complete lack of sunlight exposure. Nothing can replace the healing powers of the sun.

I've never obsessed over sunscreens and sun blocks This is not to say that there isn't a place for a mindfully made mineral sunblock, but slathering the skin with toxic chemicals has just never felt like highest health to me. Excess chemical sunscreen use has been linked to increased estrogen levels in the body and also wreaks havoc on the oceans.

I know my opinion is not a popular one in the mainstream, but I have always had an intuitive nudge to keep my body and skin connected with sunlight. Moderation is key, of course, and training the skin to lovingly accept the rays of the sun is important. There are also skin types that are much more sensitive to the sun, which is why I am not suggesting we banish sunscreens, just that we be mindful when selecting them. To avoid sunburns, there are many things we can do to support how our bodies interact with the sun optimally, like using clothing and mineral based sunscreens (such as zinc oxide), eating pure and unprocessed chocolate, eating the color spectrum (especially foods that are rich in chlorophyl), consuming healthy fats, and ensuring our diet is rich in vitamin C. Keeping the skin hydrated and healthy also plays a key role in sunbathing as well as body brushing, and hydrating the skin with natural and essential oils. Sunbathing is about moderation, care, and mindfulness when it comes to how much time is spent in the sun. Early morning is a wonderful time to sunbathe, and most sunbathing advocates select times before noon and limiting it to intervals of 10-15 minutes. Sunbathing is not about excessive exposure to sunlight. It takes great care and is a fabulous way to begin to have an intimate and sacred relationship with the sun. You will also likely find that as you practice mindful sunbathing, the sun begins to speak to you. It's as if the sun literally illuminates the soul—you won't be able to stop the divine downloads! You'll quickly find out why ancient civilizations worshipped the sun. Our private parts as well as our eyes also benefit from mindful and conscious sun exposure so don't forget them too. Shielding skin, bodies, and eyes completely from the sun harms the auric body from head to toe.

Exposing the body to sunrises and sunsets is a key practice for Auric Beauty. Why? Because they harmonize us back to natural body rhythms and act as rejuvenation resets. There is nothing better for a body rhythm reset than a barefoot walk or mountain pose stance at sunrise and/or sunset. The ancient practice of sun gazing took place at sunrise (within the hour after) or sunset (within the hour before). Gazing at the sun during these times has been done since ancient times, as ultraviolet levels are extremely low during these periods. This practice has the power to regenerate and restore Auric Health, and after having sun gazed for years, I firmly believe this is true. Avoiding excess use of glasses and sunglasses whenever possible is key for optimal eye function and health. Bare is better!

Moon Beauty

The mystery surrounding the moon and its many unusual properties have always fascinated me because of its very powerful impact on the Auric Body. Vedic Astrology is just one of the incredible tools we have access to when seeking a more intimate relationship with the moon and its influence. The day prior, the day of, and the day after a full moon is a powerful and sacred window of time that is perfect for moon bathing. You can, of course, take a bath or swim during that time, but you can also just sit and take in the moonlight. Having an outdoor tub not only for cold plunges but also for moon baths is a treat! The evening prior to a full moon is a perfect time to recharge and infuse our bodies, crystals, and oils. The full moon is a great for releasing unwanted energies and experiences. Many practitioners and healers suggest writing out what exactly it is you want to release and then burying or burning the paper. The new moon is a beautiful time to attune to what exactly it is that you want to manifest. This should be a whole-body experience. Every cell of your body should attune to your greatest desires and highest vibrational vision.

It is a wonderful practice to work with angels and archangels always but in particular during the new moon. The half-moon is also infused with mystery and potential. This moon phase is ideal for connecting with your third chakra and calling on your absolute power to work your magic in the world. The half-moon is a perfect time for moving through fear and choosing love, courage, and commitment. Consider the half-moon to be a time of highest self as self-will and divine-will merge. Archangel Michael can be of great assistance during this time. The portal to courageously making magic happen through commitment is open during the half moon.

Your Beauty Bathroom

The bathroom is a ritual room. It should feel healthy, spacious, healing, and harmonious. Keeping the bathroom simple and clean (using natural cleaners and essential oils) and beautiful (using flowers, crystals, and herbs) is key. Stocking your bathroom with your favorite salts (Dead Sea, Himalayan, Epsom), clays, body oils, essential oils, flowers, and herbs is important. An Auric Beauty bathroom should ideally have a tub and a shower as well as your favorite healing beauty enhancers. Use organic cotton bath towels, there is no room in this consciously curated bathroom for harmful toxins and chemicals. From soaps to shampoos to cleaning products, everything that enters the bathroom should be highest healing vibration. Energetically clearing the bathroom on a regular basis is key as well, which is why using essential oils, incense, crystals, herbs, and smudge sticks in the bathroom is a good choice. It is also important to remember that as we evolve, so will our bathroom. We may notice that as our spiritual wings expand, our bathroom takes on a new energetic signature. Keeping a little bit of fresh air (even a slight slice of a window opening) at all times in the bathroom is also wise. Many of my friends are taking their bathrooms outdoors these days with cold plunge pools, outdoor showers, mineral pools, and moon bathtubs. It's so lovely!

Beauty and order should emanate from the bathroom as much as possible (without any mom-guilt or shame). Setting the intention is what is important, the rest will come. Remember to stock your beauty bathroom with a body brush, facial brush, facial roller, tongue scraper, holistic oral care kit, and natural sea sponge. There are also red-light therapy and microcurrent wands on the market today that can enhance a skincare and beauty routine.

Self-Love and Self-Nurturing

We often speak of self-love but not often enough about self-nurturing. For empaths and sensitives, nurturing others is effortless while nurturing the self is a struggle. Auric beauty seeks to bring the energetic direction back to the self when it comes to nurturing. This topic doesn't need to be wordy or lengthy. Simply put, self-nurturing is now the order of each and every day. As we slow down, self-nurture, and simplify, we awaken and unleash the soul. This animates every detail of every day to such a cosmic brilliance that you will wonder what you were doing with all of your time previous to this point.

Hydration

The most important and meaningful physical process in Auric Beauty is hydration. Eating our water and drinking our food is a great methodology. We still want to shower our bodies inside and out with living and structured water, but the more hydration we can take in through food (juicing, smoothies, broths, soups), the better. Our cells crave hydration, and it unlocks the key code to inside out beauty rays. Using organic body oils as well as taking in healthy fats are also important to keep skin luminous and cells integral. Healthy fats will help to lock the moisture in. Drinking spring water throughout the day (vortexed and structured, if you want to get fancy) and drinking green juice will ensure every cell in your body emits light. Adding some edible flowers and fruits to your water will link you up with the frequencies of the sun. For optimal hydration, keep a large glass pitcher or jar filled with water. Add some edible flowers and fruits and make it a daily practice to refill the jar regularly throughout the day. This will enhance the daily habit of gorgeous hydration for you and your family. Make it as easy as possible to stay hydrated and happy! Hydration and happiness go hand in hand.

Get Naked

Covering ourselves up has become normal. We cover up our skin, cover up our bodies, and weight ourselves down with so many accessories, jewels, etc. A return to nude is happening, and it is sourced in the spiritual realm. Our bodies and our souls want to be free. I always appreciate fashion as an art form, but as I awaken to my soul, I no longer want to wear clothing that is tight, restrictive, chemical-dipped or chemically dyed, or artificial. As previously mentioned, even watches, chains, and jewelry can alter your resonance with nature and with the soul. This is not to say that these items are bad, but just be mindful what intuitive messages you get when loading up the body with any metals, constrictive gear, etc. The aura wants to shine, and this can be enhanced by more time outdoors, embracing the *au naturel*, going undergarment-free, naked sleep, organic cotton or hemp clothing, body brushing, auric baths, and sunshine. A good place to start is to make a habit of going undergarment free at home and slipping into comfy loose organic cotton clothing. Taking off watches and jewelry in the home is also a suggestion. There is a reason why spiritual fasting traditionally took place in the wilderness naked.

Auric Intimacy

Returning to sacred intimacy as a means of opening up portals of light throughout the body is a spiritual practice. It is also helpful to understand that there may be moments during spiritual transformation and transformational healing when intimacy takes a back seat or doesn't even have a seat. For many of my clients, they feel tremendous guilt when this happens, but I want them to feel free. These temporary phases can be indicative of someone using life-force for other processes of the spiritual kind that cannot be seen or diagnosed in physical reality. If you are in the spiritual body shop, it is possible that you may feel turned off in the intimacy department. This can be difficult for a partner to understand or not take personally. For this reason, honest and authentic conversation must be continuous. Many women have also expressed in recent years that physical intimacy feels uncomfortable or painful, and many try to avoid it all together. This seems to be happening as a collective and not only for those with physical factors as the cause. Although womb grief is not often discussed today, it is being processed by Mother Earth herself and being felt by women within their individual lives. Everything is being heightened, sped up, and amplified today, including the processing of womb grief. We are grieving alongside our planet. It is very likely that what you are feeling, others are feeling too. The womb of Mother Earth is in a grieving phase and so are our own wombs. This is a natural stage in the healing process and should be honored and expressed. The womb is healing and awakening and feeling all the feelings right now in preparation for higher stages of consciousness. This is an energetic shedding and letting go of all of the old to make sacred space for the new. On an individual level, wombs are grieving from many physical world experiences from the past including abortion, infertility, miscarriage, trauma, surgery, medications, abuse, etc. We have all had our own individual experiences that the womb is processing right now, just like the womb of the earth. This is a time for trauma healing and integration, on all levels and as a collective. We are in this together. If you are currently in a grieving period and intimacy isn't what it once was, make self-nurturing your priority. How can we experience true connection and intimacy with another if we haven't developed it with ourselves? We are graduating to levels of intimacy that we have yet to experience—sacred intimacy. When we are integrous, whole, and complete, the true spiritual animation that takes place during physical intimacy is on a cosmic level. At this level of sacred physical intimacy, a portal to other dimensions is activated which can lead to the channeling of cosmic creativity like never before. Healing can also take place when the sacred intimacy portal is activated.

Intimacy is at its most powerful when the Auric Bodies of two whole beings come together. Before this time, intimate connection occurs mostly on the physical plane, which is fine, but there are so many more planes to explore. When two whole beings sacredly connect physically, there is no energy vampire in the room, and prana flows in circular fashion up and down the auric field of the couple. This energy vortex of sorts is what leads to the opening of a gateway or portal into the cosmic realm where a great deal of healing, insight, and ascension takes place.

If you're experiencing physical discomforts associated with womb grief or discomfort during intimacy, here are a few things that can be helpful:

- Auric baths (let the salts do the cleansing rather than soaps)
- Green juicing
- Probiotics
- Vaginal ozone therapy
- All-natural vaginal oils and serums (find some at AuricLiving.com)
- Herbs and supplements
- Essential oils
- Flower essences
- Spiritual psychology session
- Naturopathic care
- Hydration (water, broths, juicing, living foods)
- Bathing in herbal tea (adding herbals to your bath)
- Prayer and meditation
- Cold plunging
- Infrared sauna
- Yin yoga, restorative yoga
- Forest bathing
- Gardening
- Earthing
- Vogel crystal healing
- Sound healing

- Organic cotton underwear (or no underwear at all)
- Sleeping naked
- Pelvic floor therapy
- Auric Nutrition (including a short spiritual fast)
- Leaving some hair down there (this is important for the vaginal microbiome)

Vaginal microbiome health is absolutely as important as gut microbiome health (and of course intimately connected). Our mouth, gut and vaginal microbiome are delicate forests and must be nurtured, loved, and cared for. They must all get the attention they need and have the friendly bugs nestled within them to keep things working harmonious and well. For vaginal discomfort (especially during intimacy), consider adding herbal teas to your bath, including teas made from the following: slippery elm bark, mullein leaf, ginger root, maca, wild yam root, burdock root, chamomile flower, calendula flower, goldenseal root, and/or marshmallow root. You can make your own herbal tea blend or purchase it at your local herb apothecary or natural health store.

When it comes to healing through intimacy and amping up cosmic sex practices, there are many enhancers that can be helpful. Communication is key when it comes to cosmic sex, especially in long-term relationships. For parents, the topic of sex can be a windy, curvy, mountainous, and cavernous trek. For women especially, if there are hidden emotional blocks, there will eventually be sexual blocks. Practices including orgasmic breathing, orgasmic meditation, massage, tantra, and touch are all healing and helpful. Enhancers and herbs that have the ability to transform 3D sex to cosmic sex include ashwaganda, goji berries, pomegranate, cacao, schisandra, maca, shilijit, shatavari, saffron, damiana, guarana, cinnamon, vanilla, and rose oils. Great essential oil options for cosmic sex include vanilla, cinnamon, bergamot, cacao, rose, jasmine, clary sage, hibiscus, sandalwood, and ylang ylang. Studying Tantra Yoga can be a beautiful journey to discovering a more intimate and divine relationship with the self, as well as deeply healing when it comes to practicing intimacy in relationship. The self must be intimately explored if cosmic sex is the intention.

What I have found to be most beneficial for vaginal healing is to heal and integrate trauma. As we learn to integrate all layers of ourselves (flower essences are wonderful for this), we learn to surrender to soul. When this happens, miraculous transformation happens within the vaginal walls as well. In the physical realm, I found kicking gluten, nutritional yeast, and sugar out of my diet to be extremely healing. Nutritional yeast does get added to many health food products, so be sure to look for it on the label. Vaginal ozone therapy as well as all natural flower essence oils and lubricants are beneficial. In many cases, diet can be a culprit in vaginal inflammation or discomfort. It may take some patience but with a little stillness, your intuition will lead you to exactly where you need to be (and what that food might be). Stress plays a big role on vaginal wellness, too, which is why daily breathwork and meditation is key for vaginal radiance. Getting some sunshine is also fundamental for vaginal wellbeing.

Womb Healing

We have discussed this topic already, but a slight expansion emphasizes its importance. As women, we are returning home to the womb. We are healing the trauma from this lifetime and previous ones. This can be greatly facilitated through pelvic floor therapy, herbs, tantra yoga, Vedic astrology, meditation, prayer, slowing down, yin yoga, spiritual psychology, and naturopathy. Homeopathy is also a wonderful supportive practice.

Herbs that are helpful for womb healing include moringa, nettles, red clover, chasteberry, ashwaganda, wild yam, maca, black cohosh, marigold, motherwort, dong quai, shatavari, ginseng, adaptogenic mushrooms, and ginger. Self-massage, flower essences, cold plunging, breathwork, body oils, and reiki can also be very nourishing for healing the womb. Applying warm sesame oil to the lower abdomen as well as the use of castor oil packs can enhance healing. The most effective and transformative way to heal the womb is by developing a self-nurturing rhythm in one's life and through heart activation.

Healing the mother wound is also pivotal for healing the womb. Guilt, shame, fear, unhealed trauma, and unprocessed grief are often passed down generationally from mother to daughter. Overall, unresolved trauma is at the root of a mother wound. Here are a few indications that a mother wound may be worthy of healing right now:

* Having difficulty experiencing joy or happiness
* Feeling guilty experiencing joy
* People-pleasing and have difficulty saying no
* Lowering your vibration and self-expression to fit in and be liked
* Seeking your mother's approval even as an adult (or thinking about her approval)
* Comparing yourself to others and feeling envy or competitiveness
* Feeling there is something wrong with you
* Codependence in relationships

One doesn't have to overfocus or even talk about the issue to heal the mother wound. This experience has been carefully and purposefully crafted by the Universe to train and teach you to powerfully step closer towards a full expression of unconditional love. If, with every incarnation we get closer and closer to fully expressing unconditional love, then every incarnation is a whole and complete blessing. Identifying that there may be a mother wound lingering in the body and auric field is not to be feared but to be nurtured, loved, and integrated. When we speak to this wound with great compassion and care, it tends to begin to heal effortlessly. Every mother is doing her very best, regardless of how much trauma she experienced. At this very moment, we are collectively healing the mother womb within ourselves and within Mother Earth. This is a collective healing process right now. Consciously opening the flower petals of the heart every morning and throughout the day will have a divine domino effect across the planet. When opening the heart-flower petals feels most difficult, that is when it is most needed and most healing.

Art
Surrounding our life with art is a sure way to feel the energy of beauty. Books, paintings, sculptures, design, movement, song, kid creations—art is beauty and beauty is art. Discover new ways within the home as well as throughout the day where art can be infused into your life. Artistically move the body throughout the day as a loving reminder to rhythmically flow through this lifetime. This is one of the great benefits for those who grew up dancing—all movement should be appreciated as art. Find your unique way of artistically expressing yourself and watch your true beauty shine. Art makes the soul sing.

Earthing
Earthing is a key practice for Auric Beauty. Try walking barefoot, strolling beaches and forests, and even digging out an earthing hollow for yourself. If you have some land, you can do this on your property by digging a sizable hole that you can sit or lay in. This is an ideal way to experience earthing. At the beach, dig yourself a hollow in the sand and enjoy the healing benefits. Placing your hands and feeling the dirt is a perfect way to get earthing. Earthing mats are also available on the market, but I prefer going directly to the source for earthing. (Earthing mats can be helpful for anyone living in a condo or high-rise, of course.) Bringing as much nature indoors as possible and even building a greenhouse is encouraged. Greenhouses will be the new walk-in pantry in the coming years!

Creative Expression
When we block or limit the flow of creative energy in and throughout the body, we lose luster and shine. Creative energy is beauty in motion. For some people, getting downloads of creativity happens

easily and often, but it is acting on them that can become a challenge. Creative energy comes into our beings to be expressed in some way. When we block this expression, our health eventually suffers. Consider where you may be blocking creative expression (especially because of lower vibrational self-talk). When we don't have enough time, we aren't good enough yet, we aren't sure what people will think, etc. we block the movement and full expression of divinity. Creative energy is sacred, and divine communication being infused into us. It is ours to mold, work with, use and share with the world. As we will discuss in our Auric Wealth chapter, when creative energy is blocked, so is the flow of money. The key to full and radiant creative expression is the harmonizing of self-will and divine-will. Awakened self-will requires confident and courageous communication with ourselves, while awakened divine-will requires faithful and frequent communication with the divine.

The Goddess

In her book *The Living Goddess*, Marija Gimbutas writes that the interlink between hydration, life, and the life-giving goddess is cosmic in nature. As human life begins in the watery realm of the female womb, the goddess was the symbolic source of all human, plant, and animal life. In many traditions, the goddess often incarnated as a deer or a bear in order to offer support and assistance through the birthing and nursing process. Ancient agriculturists clearly understood the cosmic connection between grain seeds germinating in the fields and new life maturing in the womb. The earth goddess (or Mother Earth) is one of the most-represented female figures in history.

The role of the goddess from an Auric Living perspective is to reconnect with sacred life. Instead of fighting with the body, transition to a daily practice of deep appreciation and love. Studying goddess mythology and archaeology can be very healing for awakening the goddess within. When we resist or suppress the sacredness of who we are, we are only partially living. An appreciation for biodynamic farming practices and all of the wise ones who weave their lives with Mother Earth is due. These individuals are teaching far more than optimal farming practices—they are awakening the goddess within.

Beauty Sleep

Stay in a similar cycle each night. Keep the bedroom simple, calming, and deeply healing. Avoid keeping electronics in the bedroom. Bedding should be organic and natural fibers only. Colors should be calming, and try to bring in nature as much as possible. A coil-free, naturally sourced mattress is ideal. A clock-free bedroom is ideal but if you need a clock or alarm clock, consider a battery operated, old-school alarm clock. Natural lighting is best in the bedroom so that you wake up with the sun and go to bed with the sun. If it gets dark later near you, having some natural fiber draping on the windows is helpful. Keeping your room as organic and earthy as possible will go a long way for a healing and rejuvenating sleep cycle. Placing sacred geometry prints and wall art in the bedroom is also suggested. Keeping the bedroom minimalist and peaceful is the intention. Air quality and circulation should be optimized along with a constant flow of fresh air. (Even if full open windows are not possible, a little fresh air goes a long way). Fresh air is always best. Choosing fans over air conditioning is also better. Keeping a few books in the bedroom that exude highest vibrational qualities do a lot for enhancing the energy signature of the bedroom. Spritzing pillows and sheets with organic essential oils to suit your highest health is also a wonderful healing ritual. Rose quartz and clear quartz in the bedroom enhance not only high heart living but total body healing during sleep and while awake. Shungite and hematite can also be used for protection in the bedroom to protect from lower-level energies such as EMFs, geopathic stress, etc. Use your intuition and play around with creating a crystal grid. You may choose to place crystals in the corners of the room, around your bed or in a geometric form (such as a triangle). If there is a specific chakra that could use extra care and nurturing, including healing crystals for this particular chakra is helpful. Use as much natural light as possible and limit the need for artificial light in the bedroom. When extra lighting is necessary, consider beeswax or coconut wax candles or salt lamps. 100% natural and clean soy candles are also good options; however, it is worth doing some ingredient research (such as wick ingredients and soy sourcing).

Yin Balancing

Yin balancing practices are keys to reconnecting with our divine beauty. Gentle movement practices such as dancing, swimming, yin or restorative yoga, tai chi, stretching, rebounding, and walking are wonderful. Slowing down the pace of each day is also soothing and healing to the soul. Creative expression through art, journaling, writing, and movement is a true beauty enhancer. Balancing yin is something we can all benefit from right now. Cooling herbs and foods can also support this practice, including cucumbers, mint, eggs, berries, seaweed, grapes, celery, mango, kiwi, asparagus, cilantro, watermelon, bananas, pomegranate, chlorella, spirulina, lemon balm, chamomile, and valerian. Herbal teas and bone broths are also wonderful yin optimizers.

Happy Hair

I had a phase in my life post-babies, where my hair was less than radiant and—wow! After so many decades where hair was my "thing," it was a difficult emotional process to go through. Even in high school, I was known for my hair (and hairspray) and suddenly, my defining physical trait that was once a source of so much pride was now the bane of my existence. I can absolutely relate to anyone reading this who is also experiencing hair grief. It is a difficult journey, yet there is so much self-love goodness being developed. Instead of fearing and avoiding doing my hair, I began to create a morning and evening ritual where I brushed my hair with love and compassion and applied an organic oil serum.

Have you noticed that hair and hair loss seem to be a major topic of concern in the collective today? This is a physical manifestation of total transformation and trauma processing going on. I personally prefer to not blame everything on hormones; what if something more spiritual and cosmic is going on? There is, of course, a direct link between womb healing and hair loss. I'm sure there are many factors you already know about linked to hair loss, like EMF exposure and radiation, stress, fear, adrenal exhaustion, hormones, heavy metal toxicity, post-partum changes, mineral deficiency, toxins, and chemicals. You can grab some tools to help heal the hair that you see, but don't neglect the power of inner healing when it comes to hair. Here are a few things that can support radiant hair renewal:

* Nettle tea rinse (make a big pot and drain the water for hair rinsing)
* Rosemary essential oil (add a few drops to shampoo and lather in)
* Herbs (including nettles, gingko, peppermint, lavender, Siberian ginseng, saw palmetto, horsetail, and burdock root)
* Cell salts
* Minerals (supplements, cell salts, bone broth, living foods, and humeric and fulvic acids)
* Hemp oil
* Castor oil
* Coconut oil
* Aloe vera
* Auric green juice
* EMF protection (such as shungite crystals, shielding fabrics, EMF protection coins)
* Silica (one of the great minerals for hair health)
* Vitamin D
* Vitamin C
* Vitamin B12
* Shilajit
* Collagen
* Mushrooms (such as reishi, chaga, and lion's mane)
* Time in Nature
* Sunshine

My favorite hair-healer sprays include witch hazel, hemp oil, camellia oil, moringa oil, castor oil, rosemary, peppermint, and lavender. I also love making a hair serum using coconut oil, avocado oil, jojoba oils, and essential oils.

Increases in DHT in the blood stream can also lead to a less harmonious hair situation (including hair loss), which is why it can be beneficial to have DHT levels checked by a functional medicine practitioner to ensure the harmonious hair button is switched on. Hormones, of course, play a key role for happy hair, as does a healthy microbiome, which is why fermented foods, broths, green juices, and probiotics are great for hair, too!

The Cosmic Core

It is easy to see the symbolic connection between beauty and the core. The stomach region and third chakra area are at the very center of our being and self-nurturing. As we learn to nurture ourselves, we are better able to then nurture our children, our elders, and Mother Earth. Stomach soothing happens when we self-nurture. Microbiome health is, of course, a physical body way of approaching the cosmic core, but the energetic nourishment comes with healing trauma, nurturing the self, and committing to highest-vibrational living. Physical core strength also goes hand in hand with energetic core strength. Remember not to overprioritize physical practices over energetic ones as the cosmic core seeks a return to yin, to simplicity, and to loving energetic nourishment. As we reunite with the soul, the cosmic core will heal and shine. The stomach meridian is also of great importance for a cosmic core because it works closely with the spleen meridian to rule energetic optimization for digestion and absorption.

Color Therapy

We have already introduced color therapy for Auric Health, but because of its magnificence, I wanted to touch on it once again as it relates to Auric Beauty. Not only is color therapy brilliant for Auric Beauty but is also an incredible way to eat. Full spectrum color in nutrition is key for enhancing inner *and* outer beauty. If the inside of the body isn't feeling beautiful, it doesn't matter how much manipulation you do to the outside—beauty simply won't animate. Beauty animates from within, and color has much to do with this. When you feel beautiful, you look beautiful. Consider color as a magnificent tool for animating all of the beauty within that will then shine rays of color and light out of your entire body. The sun is the fundamental practice for this, but color therapy through food and light is also very beneficial. Here are a few simple indications for color as a starting point:

Rose: Relaxation of the body and nervous system

Magenta: Emotional wellbeing and harmony

Violet: Connecting to creativity, inspiration, giving, and divine guidance

Indigo: Deep peace, stillness, and serenity

Blue: Divine-will activation and enhanced communication

Green: Peace, love, and harmony

Yellow: Courage, creativity, self-will, and confidence

Orange: Joy, happiness, and community

Red: Body healing, lifeforce flow, circulation, safety, and feeling secure

Chromotherapy today is more widely offered at many holistic and naturopathic clinics. Many infrared saunas come with a chromotherapy device. Chromotherapy devices are also widely available for home as well as professional clinic use.

Eating in color is also key, which is why generous amounts of fruits and vegetables in the diet is essential. Juicing as well as cold and warm soups are fabulous ways to make eating in color a daily devotion. Chlorophyl, berries, beets, turmeric, parsley, cilantro, lemons, red peppers, raw dark chocolate, seaweed, tomatoes, spirulina, and chlorella contain the color codes for Auric Beauty within them. There are, of course, so many others but these are a few of my favorites.

Mindful Movement

Movement and fitness should be less about rigidity and time and more about feeling and flow. What is most important is the care and mindfulness that goes into body movement. Just imagine doing a walk around the block where every step is nurtured with heart and every moment is appreciated. This would not have been something I could have successfully done even a few years ago. This is not to say that high performance sport doesn't have a beautiful place in the world, but more people are being drawn to moving the body just for the feel of it. The days of timing a cardio workout are simply of less interest for more and more people. This is because we are now on the cosmic clock, and the cosmos want us to move our bodies in a way that intertwine us with our souls. Dance, nature walks, stretching, yoga, and Qigong are just a few examples. There are certain ways of moving the body that enhance lifeforce to a higher degree. Yoga is just one example. It has a certain prana activation power that may not be the case in another more common form of fitness. Fitness is wonderful for enhancing lymphatic flow, mental wellbeing, and cardio strength, but adding on a few movement practices that are curated specifically for life force activation is ideal. Swimming, dance, nature walks, labyrinth walks, forest bathing, yoga, and martial arts (including Tai Chi and Qigong) are examples. They connect us with the soul in a special way. A home chi machine and a rebounder are two lymphatic movers that greatly enhance Auric Beauty. What I love most about yoga is the way it places and positions your body into sacred geometry shapes. This is one of the reasons it just feels right and true. This is an outcome of the mindfulness and care that went into the creation of the postures and the sequencing.

Auric Baths

This is a daily ritual (sometimes twice or even three times a day) in my home. Auric baths are aura cleansers and healers. Not only are auric baths intended to cleanse and clean the physical body, but they also draw out any energies that are less than optimal for highest self and highest life. The intention with an auric bath is to treat your bath as if you were creating the most delicious energy recipe. Feel free to mix and match ingredients based on the intention with which you seek to be in perfect resonance. For example, if your intention is to detoxify, you may wish to add a variety of salts or detoxifying agents such as charcoal and clay. If you seeking to illuminate the heart through the senses, adding flowers, flower essences, herbs, and essential oils may be most appropriate. This is an intuitive and heart-led experience. Every Auric Bath should be a sacred one. Remember that there is no wrong choice when it comes to an auric bath. Add whatever you feel called to add! Here are some examples:

* Activated coconut charcoal
* Essential oils
* Organic baking soda
* Clays
* Epsom salts, Himalayan salts, Dead Sea salts
* Crystals
* Flowers
* Herbs
* Organic body oils
* Flower essences
* Vanilla beans
* Coffee beans
* Coffee grounds
* Cacao beans
* Turmeric

If your intention is specifically body detoxification, here are a few suggestions:

* Coffee grounds
* Activated charcoal
* Bentonite clay (and other clays)
* Apple cider vinegar
* Himalayan sea salts
* Dead Sea salts

* Epsom salts
* Turmeric
* Baking Soda

Beauty Herbs and Flowers

All herbs are beautiful, but there are a few that should be staples in our daily Auric Beauty regime. These include rosemary, lavender, cedarwood, sage, peppermint, ashwaganda, holy basil, siberian ginseng, calendula, chamomile, turmeric, bergamot, ylang ylang, rose, honeysuckle, vanilla, and lilac. Amber is resin, not a flower or herb, but it is a beauty staple that functions in a similar manner.

Beauty Oils

Sea buckthorn is my absolute favorite oil at the moment, but apricot oil is also a cosmic crush. Body oils and essential oils are daily dos for Auric Beauty. A few of the top beauty enhancing essential oils include rosemary, jasmine, rose, amber, cacao, lavender, lilac, vanilla, honeysuckle, mint, holy basil, bergamot, cedarwood, grapefruit, lemon, orange, cinnamon, geranium, tea tree, sandalwood, and ylang ylang.

In terms of body oils, camellia oil and moringa oil are my favorites after sea buckthorn. Sweet almond oil, kukui nut oil, pomegranate oil, rosehip oil, jojoba oil, and apricot kernel oil are also on my happy hit list. Listen with your heart as to which oils pull on your intuition strings and guide you to get more acquainted with them. Castor oil and coconut oil are also healers that I always have handy for hair and body nurturing.

Oral Caregiving

Oil pulling, tooth and gum serums, essential oils, and natural bristle toothbrushes are vital! My greatest mentor when it comes to oral caregiving is Nadine Artemis. Her books *Renegade Beauty* and *Holistic Dental Care* are must-haves in every home library. The mouth is a living ecosystem, and the over-obsession with perfect-looking teeth rather than a thriving oral health ecosystem is finally crumbling. For people with acidosis throughout the body, oral health and gum health is deeply important. Alkalinity restored in the body will greatly benefit the oral ecosystem. Nutrition plays a key role in oral health, which is why eating alkaline foods as well as the full color spectrum of foods is key. I have personally found bone broth (in combination with green juicing) to be helpful in restoring my own oral health ecosystem. Too much lemon can be damaging to the enamel, which is where reusable straws come in handy. Bamboo, glass, grass, silicon, and metal straws are all good options.

Consider a daily oral health ritual to be an integral gateway towards true self-nurturing. Not only will your mouth and body thank you, but you will feel so much appreciation and gratitude for the ritual love you are offering yourself. Here is a simple oral care ritual that can be practiced twice or even three times a day. This simplified routine is a good starting point (and great to teach kids,) but I also encourage expanding your knowledge and practice through reading *Holistic Dental Care* by Nadine Artemis.

A simple oral health practice:

1) Salt rinse
2) Tongue scraping
3) Tooth polishing (baking soda and activated charcoal pastes are great)
4) Floss
5) Essential oils and serums (naturally, organically, and ethically sourced)

Water flossing as well as oil pulling are also wonderful additions to any oral health routine. An oral probiotic is also a great addition to an evening oral health ritual and can be taken after following the oral healthcare steps mentioned above.

Finding a biological or holistic dentist can be tricky in some parts of the world but worth the research. When it comes to orthodontics, I believe that less is more and that choosing an orthodontist for children and adults should be done with great care and mindfulness. Finding a dentist (and orthodontist) that is holistically minded and offers healthier choices when it comes to what substances and fillers are being added to the mouth is key. Consider seeking out an orthotropist, biological dentist, and/or holistic dentist. There are a few rare gems who are certified in naturopathy and dentistry, if you happen to find one in your area. For parents of children who breath primarily through their mouths, a holistic or biological dentist can be truly cosmic as these children tend to need a little more oral nurturing and care.

Cosmic Coffee

Coffee is absolutely cosmic, not only as an aura and physical body awakener, but as a beauty body scrub. I typically start my day with a cup of coffee and then switch to herbal tea after that. Coffee grounds are my go-to gems for body exfoliation. A coffee scrub in the bath and shower is wonderful (although you may spend just as much time cleaning your tub if you use it in the bath). For this reason, I typically do my coffee scrubs in the shower and use my tub for Auric Baths. Coffee enemas and colon hydrotherapy can also be used to dilate bile ducts for enhanced toxin removal. Coffee enemas are also helpful for parasite and candida removal. Drinking some coffee has been shown to enhance cardiovascular function, prevent insulin resistance, and support liver health. When practicing detoxifications, spiritual fasts, or naturopathic protocols, however, it is helpful to temporarily limit or avoid coffee. Coffee is a stimulant, and when we are healing the endocrine and lymphatic system or simply wanting to calm the nervous system, herbal tea is a better choice.

Aura and Body Brushing

Every day, remember to brush your aura as well as your body! I have found using a selenite wand helpful for brushing my aura. I also use one to brush the auras of my kids. They love the practice and find it very calming and soothing. Sometimes I get my children to brush my aura to ensure I get a good cleanse. You can, of course, brush your own aura, but having your kids do it is a treat. Starting at the crown, hold the selenite wand about five inches away from your body and simply comb the body from head to toe just like you are brushing energetic hair. You can also do a little stroke away from the body with the wand to brush the unwanted energies away from the body. Selenite crystals also balance the chakras, connect you with the divine, and don't need to be cleared or charged. Barbara Brennan, author of *Hands of Light* and *Light Emerging*, is one of my very favorite mentors and writes about the benefits of aura brushing.

When it comes to body brushing, having a wood-handled body brush and facial brush for daily use is encouraged. I like to do my body brushing in the evenings, but morning body brushing is fabulous, too. Body brushing encourages circulation, lymphatic flow, cellulite reduction, and glowing skin.

Flower Essences

This is by far one of my most passionate topics. Flower essences will continue to grow in popularity over upcoming years. Because our work on the planet right now is to heal multigenerational trauma (as well as deeply connecting with Mother Earth), emotional body integration is key. Flower essences work on the emotional body, which makes them gorgeous gems for healing. I am so grateful to be enhancing my studies right now to be able to offer more workshops on this topic. Here are just a few essences that can be helpful along your emotional radiance (and Auric Beauty) journey:

Lilac- alignment

Matilija Poppy- physical grace

Lovage- divine feminine

Chicory- unconditional love

California Poppy- inner beauty

Daphne- illumination

Jerusalem Artichoke- joy and radiance

Dayflower- light therapy

Calla Lily- forgiveness

Bougainvillea- grace and beauty
Calendula- inner light
Burdock- integration
Cherry Plum- openness and higher-self guidance

Crystal Care

Crushed crystals in body scrubs, crystal charged water, Vogel crystals, quartz crystals, and crystal grids are powerful tools for Auric Beauty. Quartz crystals carry with them special healing properties that can both protect and heal the Auric Body.

Quartz crystals vibrate the aura at such a rate that lower unwanted and heavier energies get energetically shaken out of the body. They are the true Auric Beauty gems. It's just like having your own energetic chi machine. Quartz crystals are excellent for supporting auric beauty and an overall showering of love, healing, health, protection, and radiance.

Rose Quartz: This quartz is the cornerstone and master gem for the heart chakra. This quartz will infuse your body and life with love, beauty, healing, and fulfillment. This is the master love gem promoting self-love and self-nurturing. Rose quartz beauty tools such as a Gua Sha, face roller, and razor will infuse love and nurturing frequencies into your Auric Body as you use them. Bring in and on the love!

Smoky Quartz: Drawing the love from the heart chakra down to the root chakra to support grounding, security, and protection, it is ideal for detoxification and grounding. Cleansing the physical and Auric Body is enhanced when smoky quartz is around.

Citrine Quartz: This quartz holds within it the healing powers of the sun and supports activation and integrity of the third chakra. It will infuse your being with confidence, resilience, will, and commitment. Citrine quartz is a powerful stomach soother that will both sooth the belly as well as manifest and make things happen!

Amethyst Quartz: Amethyst Quartz is helpful for soothing the mind and trust in the greater cosmic order of things. amethyst quartz helps you to let go, to be still and to gain greater wisdom and understanding of higher realm order.

Clear Quartz: The master healer quartz, this gem promotes integrity, clarity harmony, and order throughout all layers of the Auric Body. It is also one of the greats for spiritual growth and activating the light body.

Love is the state of consciousness that illuminates and transforms the physical body. Love is a state of beingness that shines bright like the sun. Auric Beauty inspires each and every one of us to light up and animate our entire life and being—from the inside out. Once we consciously decide to live a soul-guided life, the lotus petals of the heart activate and open. When this occurs, every cell in the body begins to emit light. This is when Auric Beauty shines. Every cell is the body has the capacity and ability to act as a mini sun. When every cell in the body is loved and supported to emit this sunlight, we really do glow from the inside out. This can only occur when the flower petals of the heart are open and activated, and when the soul is in charge.

Chapter 9: Auric Home

Good-bye real estate, hello *heal* estate! Beauty, home, and health go hand in hand, and for Auric Living, they must be in synch and energetically intertwined.

When we think of home, we often first think of our actual physical home address rather than the energetic signature it carries. For this reason, the energetic factors associated with our home amongst the cosmos and on the planet will be just as important as our actual mailing address! We must remember that everything is connected and "as above, so below" always applies. While this chapter will focus primarily on the physical home, always remember that our place amongst the cosmos is a much more mysterious and divinely ordered locale.

This is where Vedic astrology and Vaastu can come in handy. As we learn to deepen our connection with the cosmos, we will also have a greater appreciation for the divine connection of all things—the divine matrix. Regardless of what is happening to us at the physical level, there is divine beauty and order to everything. As we open the portals through our heart, we will begin to channel and bring in more light, but we must also develop the skills to hold and ground this higher order light. This is where the Auric Home comes in. Our relationship with the cosmos as our soul's playground is key as well as our relationship with Mother Earth, which provides us with the tools to ground and hold the light. Developing a relationship with the sun is also critical to this process as we come from and return to the sun in the cycle of life.

Although health and healing retreats are magnificent, what if your home could reorder your body every single day? One of the most important aspects of Auric Living is to make one's home as bioenergetically healthy as possible. In our new reality, the shapes, colors, sounds, spaces, architecture, smells, beauty, and light must all be taken into energetic consideration. For our bodies to manifest the highest possibilities for ourselves, a sound heart and mind must be optimized. The home is where we spend so much of our time and impacts this heart-mind synergy far more than we realize. To activate the portal opening power of an open heart, the environment in which you dwell must be of the highest vibrational order. I anticipate a surge in demand for stagers, designers, decorators, builders, building biologists, and architects who are training in sacred geometry, Vaastu, astrology, feng shui, and bioenergetics. Studying ancient civilizations and architecture is highly valuable as you will begin to understand that these structures were impeccably designed structures for optimizing and enhancing energy.

How a home is energetically optimized is also very important for children. Children want to feel safe, grounded, happy, healthy, and creative in their home. If homes are overly large, have restrictive air flow, or very high ceilings, a child's nervous system and emotional wellbeing can be hindered. Homes that are perfectly pretty but institutionally stale when it comes to energy flow also impact a child's bioenergetics. Cognitive function, emotional resilience, and energetic balance are all impacted significantly by the home in which a child dwells. Allergies, attention, and digestion can all be impacted by the energetics of the home. Pets are also extremely sensitive to the bioenergetics of a home. Their health can be hindered by poor bioenergetics and greatly enhanced by harmonized bioenergetics.

The purpose of this chapter is to offer simple strategies and steps that can be easily implemented to transform your house into an Auric Home. An Auric Home is one that is bioenergetically optimized, harmonized, and balanced. When you walk into an Auric

Home, there is peace in your heart and a sense of joy throughout the body. You just know something is absolutely right with the home. Consider your home to be a living and breathing being with emotions and an energy system that gives constant feedback. A home that is always leaking water and growing mold for example, is trying to tell you something. The home is bioenergetically unwell.

Healing should be continuously happening in the home. Your body should feel expansive, free, and flowing. Moving through the home should feel like a dance. This chapter will emphasize Vaastu (or Vaastu Shastra) inspired principles for enhancing the bioenergetics of the home in simple and easy to implement ways. Vaastu is the ancient Indian science of architecture and building biology that incorporates science, art, astronomy, and astrology. It enhances physical, mental, emotional, and spiritual health as well as property and longevity. Vaastu is also the science of directions, which means it incorporates all of the five elements of nature (fire, air, earth, water, space) as well as magnetism and gravity. Vaastu then balances the energetics of the home with the individuals who dwell in the home as well as those who visit. The intensity of rainfall, sunrays, and wind are all taken into consideration. I am deeply grateful for biofield expert Rev. Jayme Westrom (also a member of our Auric Angels and Advisory Team) for inspiring and consulting on this chapter. Jayme is one of the very few experts I have met in this field who seamlessly weaves the health of the physical body, spirituality, and energy body with the health of the home. We share a similar passion for auric Health, and she has become my go-to expert for all things biofield! Her expertise and wisdom infused in this chapter is a blessing.

As an Auric Home starting point, consider the actual energetic feel of your home. The most important factor to consider is how well you can breathe in your home. Does your home feel airy and light or burdened with constrictive air flow and density? Feeling energetically weighted down in a home will eventually lead to feeling physically weighted down in life. Take a moment to walk through your home. How does your body feel in each room? How does your breath change? How light or heavy do you feel as you move from space to space? The goal of an Auric Home is to feel fluid, inspired, happy, healthy, light, and full of flow. Regardless of physical size, the home caries an energetic signature that can be easily elevated and transformed with a few simple steps. These include keeping clutter to a minimum; maximizing air flow; purifying air and water; working with natural light; infusing nature into the home; and using healing sounds, colors, and scents throughout the home. Sunlight plays one of the most crucial roles in transforming an ordinary home to an auric one. In an Auric Home, you breath in lifeforce and breath out all that no longer serves.

Our home plays a vital role in vital body health. Our chakra health (especially our lower three) is significantly impacted by the home in which we dwell. I have travelled significantly with my children, which has given them a flare for adventure and culture but has also taught them to appreciate the grounding and coziness of home. I like to consider my home as a living, breathing being that wants to feel healthy and healed—just like us!

First Things First

One of my favorite philosophies for arranging a home is this: Create space for the beauty you desire. Prior to getting too ambitious about transforming a home into a healing sanctuary, make sure it isn't hoarded up or overspilling with matter. It is important for us to always remember that every single piece of physical matter in a home (every piece of furniture, frame, accessory, appliance, nicknack, etc.) holds a fragment of your lifeforce. The more stuff we collect, the more weighted down our energy is. Spend a few moments right now to contemplate how energetically heavy you feel and how much cleansing may be beneficial for the light body within the home. Too much physical weight around us can eventually impact physical weight within us. Take a moment to contemplate and consider if the amount of clearing and cleansing needed in the home is minor, medium, or major. There is no wrong answer but knowing the appropriate amount will be helpful to block out a window of time with some health first urgency. This is not to create pressure but to prioritize personal health and highest-vibrational living as soon as humanly possible. Clearing and cleansing are at the very top of the cosmic check list.

Building Biology

A new and emerging field of brilliance is building biology. This field of study and practice is the study of the holistic relationship between people and their homes. The objective is to create an optimized energy signature for a home. Building biologists work to create the healthiest, most natural, sustainable and beauty enhanced living environment possible. The focus is on healthy air, healthy lighting, healthy water, healthy sound, healthy materials, EMF reduction and mold elimination. The energy flow and feeling of a home is priority. How much or how little natural sunlight shines upon a home throughout the day is also taken into serious consideration. Not only can building biologists consult on an existing home but they can also be included in the team for a new home build. Building biologists can also offer suggestions for available technologies that can optimize health within a home. Human health and Mother Earth are sacred priorities in building biology as well as how they relationship and interact with a home. Here are just a few principles involved in building biology:

* Create an optimally healthy and toxin free environment
* Minimize harmful effects of EMF sources (cell towers, home appliances, electrical towers, etc.)
* Optimize amount of natural light within the home
* Minimize building material interference with the earth's natural healing frequencies
* Create EMF strategies for the home and lot
* Eliminate the use of building materials that have elevated radioactivity levels
* Maximize ventilation
* Minimize and manage moisture content

* Optimize water quality and structuring throughout the home (for drinking, bathing, and cleaning)
* Optimize air quality and flow throughout the home
* Prevent interior growth of fungus, bacteria, and dust mites
* Ensure sound quality within the home optimizes health (as well as provide acoustical protection)
* Interior design and staging principles for enhancing the energetic signature of a home
* Consider and consult on proportion, measurements, harmonics, shape, and flow of a home
* Ensure non-toxic building materials, cleaning products, and other home products are used
* Ensure materials and methods promote highest human health
* Ensure rhythm and order are optimized between a home and its residents
* Create optimal relationship with nature and natural cycles for new and existing homes

Vaastu

Vaastu is an incredibly detailed and sacred science. To summarize Vaastu is to dimmish its very essence, yet for the purpose of this introduction, I will do my best to honor its beauty in summary form. Vaastu Shastra is thought to have been formulated somewhere between 6,000 BC and 3,000 BC in India, but its roots are likely even older. Vaastu is a branch of the Vedas and an area of study all on its own as documented in ancient Vedic texts. The most basic principle of Vaastu is to honor and observe nature. Traditionally, Vaastu experts would spend significant time in an area before any design or construction was done. It wasn't uncommon for them to spend a year observing nature's rhythm, movement, and flow, observing all the seasons and qualities of nature in the area before doing any architectural drawings. Vaastu is the organization and systemization between form and space. Direction plays a foundational role in Vaastu including the spiritual order and association for each of them. Sundials were used with great precision to locate sacred directions beginning with perfect east. There is a 12.3° difference between a sun dial and a magnetic compass, which is why Vaastu traditionally uses the sun dial. (The magnetic compass was traditionally used in Feng Shui while the sun dial was used in Vaastu.) In Vaastu Shastra, the three anchors of design are usefulness, beauty (outer delight), and spiritual satisfaction (inner delight). One must also be sensitive to the dynamics of the natural surroundings and space before being able to achieve all three anchors of Vaastu. Even the water of the property would be checked for clockwise or counterclockwise movement. A clockwise energy movement is aligned with nature, the cosmos and with inner peace and harmony. Breeze direction, sloping of the land, and sunlight movement is also critical. Vaastu teaches that everything in the physical realm is a manifestation of rhythm and order. When you see a temple or building created using Vaastu principles, you are looking at visual music.

Here are a few simple Vaastu principles:

1. The very center point of the home as well as the space around the center point is sacred. This should feel harmonizing, life-force filled, and healing to the body and soul. This is the very location in the home where the cosmos connect in communication with the earth. This area should be spacious and free.
2. Practicing yoga is helpful for tapping into the spiritual wisdom of Vaastu as it trains one to connect with and feel the relationship between one's inner space and outer space. Having a yoga mat set out in the home will inspire you to start and end your day with a sun salutation as well as to take a few moments throughout the day to move with the energy of your home.
3. A residential home is ideally square or rectangular in shape for optimal life force and harmony.
4. Your front door is not only the main physical entry but is also the main energetic entry, which makes it a top priority in Vaastu.

Your front door should be the grandest door in your home and should also be the most well-lit.

5. For areas that feel energetically off, it is possible to enhance the area by combining three aspects: a sacred object, a prayer, and a mantra. The mantra is a method of using mind and sound to enhance the energy signature of the space. These three aspects are referred to as yantra, mantra, and tantra. When incorporating these three aspects, energy optimization takes place within approximately 45 days.
6. A home should ideally be built facing one of the cardinal directions (north, east, south, west) rather than ordinal directions (northeast, southeast, northwest, and southwest). This is because of the amount of energetic strength associated with the directions. The cardinal directions hold much more energy force and have greater influences on health, prosperity, wellbeing, and manifestation than the ordinal directions do.
7. Every home should include a room or space dedicated to meditation or prayer. This room does not have to be large but should be used to reconnect with the higher self. Facing east when you meditate will enhance spiritual growth, which is why this room in the home should face either east or northeast. White, beige, light yellow, or green are beneficial colors for this room. Creating a sacred alter in this room including herbs, candles, and incense is bioenergetically beneficial.
8. The main living room of the home must be clutter free and energetically harmonious. This room is a room where many blessings and offerings take place as we entertain, laugh, communicate, and enjoy life.
9. In the bedroom, energy is everything. It is ideal to avoid placing a television or mirror in front of the bed (or in the bedroom at all). This room should be absolutely clutter free the room should feel peaceful and healing. Neutral or earthy paint colors should be used, as well as essential oil diffusers, natural aromas, and incense. Organic and natural fiber bedding and mattresses are important as well as eliminating EMFs in this room as much

as possible. Try to keep this room wifi, electronic, and plug-in appliance free. Earthing this room as much as possible is also wonderful by bringing in plants, herbs, and incense. Lighting is very important as the bedroom should be calming and mood-enhancing. If you are going to incorporate plug-in lighting, consider a salt lamp. Clear quartz or rose quartz crystals in the bedroom will also enhance the heart and body harmony when it comes to Auric Health. Shungite can also be used should the home be located near cell towers, electrical towers, or if you live in an apartment building or condo.
10. Asking higher realm beings for support and assistance for enhancing the energy of a room or area in the home is highly encouraged. Calling on divinities through prayer and chanting is a sacred Vaastu practice.

There are varying recommendations when it comes to placement and direction in the home. The weaving of energy and form within a home is deeply rooted in direction, so suggestions and recommendations to enhance a home will be plenty. Vaastu tips given should be offerings to enhance, welcome and befriend all energies of the home rather than playing on fears or warnings.

Planetary Grid

The planetary grid is a naturally occurring electromagnetic grid system that goes by many names. This grid is also referred to as the electromagnetic grid or Christ Consciousness Grid. This grid contains within it all of the patterns we find in the flower of life and in all sacred geometry. This grid holds the consciousness for the planet through an etheric crystalline structure and has influence over all aspects of our lives even if we aren't aware. It is believed that this Divine grid was constructed with the help of the Archangels to bind collective human consciousness. This grid also regulates the electromagnetic systems such as ley lines and vortex systems. It is also referred to as the earth's nervous system.

Several fields have been discovered and researched throughout history all across the globe including geopathic stress, the vivaxis, black streams, Hartmann lines, the Benker cubical system, curry lines, black lines, and ley lines.

Ley Lines

Ley Lines are energetic lines on or within the earth that are electromagnetic in nature, much like the nadis or meridians of the body. They are lines of energetic power. Ley lines are also dotted with energetic points similar to chakras or acupuncture points in the physical body. Each point can be electromagnetic, magnetic, or electrical. Many sacred and ancient sites were built on ley lines, which tend to flow along natural paths of conductive minerology such as quartz, water, or metal.

One of the most discussed ley lines is the Saint Michael's Line, which encircles the earth and is dedicated to the Archangel Michael. This line connects many sacred places that were strategically built along the line. This ley line perfectly aligns with the sunset on the day of the northern hemisphere's summer solstice. Many sacred sites are included on this line in Europe and the Middle East, including Mount Carmel, which was sacred to many ancient peoples and traditions.

Portals

Portals are created based upon the magnetism, crystalline energy, and planetary consciousness. When synergized, these three factors (along with the time factor) impact the opening and closing of portal windows. It is theorized that portals appear all over the planet, even under water. When you live near a portal or travel to one, you cannot ignore the intense energy that you feel within your body. Many sacred sites were built on or in close proximity to portals.

Energy Vortexes

An energy vortex is a specific location on the planet that acts as a swirling center of energy containing enhanced energy as compared to a non-vortex location. Ancient sites such as the pyramids and Stonehenge are just a few examples. Other examples include Sedona, AZ; Mount Shasta, CA; Mayan Ruins in Central America; Mount Kailash; the Hawaiian island of Maui; and Table Mountain in South Africa. It is helpful to energetically prepare oneself prior to visiting an energy vortex site, as the experience can be incredibly intense for the body. With regard to creating an Auric Home, however, this is likely not a major concern.

Geopathic Stress

Too much charge on the body can disrupt it. The Auric Body is extremely sensitive to all energetic influences. Geopathic stress (or geopathic radiation) is the non-optimal impact of natural and artificial fields of radiation on the Auric Body. Many people experience physical symptoms and feelings of dis-ease when exposed to high levels of geopathic stress. As this stress can disrupt the auric field, it therefore can also disrupt the physical body. Geomagnetism is important for life, but disruptions (either natural or manmade) can increase geopathic stress.

Geopathic stress is natural radiation that rises up through the earth and can disrupt the physical and energetic body. Geopathic stress can be created by subterranean running water, certain mineral concentrations, fault lines, and underground cavities. The wavelengths of the natural radiation disturbed in this way become harmful to living organisms. A simple way of detecting geopathic stress can be through radiesthesia or using the Lecher antenna. Radiesthesia is the principle behind dowsing, which uses a variety of instruments such as pendulums and dowsing rods to test electromagnetic fields in the body or earth. The Lecher antenna was developed by Dr Ernest Lecher and also functions off of resonance to test for geopathic stress.

There are several ways to protect oneself against geopathic stress, including paints, clothing, shields, coins, chips, and instrumentation.

Black Lines and Sha Lines

There are also lines that draw on our lifeforce energy. In Feng Shui, this is referred to *Sha Chi* or "Sha lines." Black lines appear to be naturally produced but there are also artificial lines that can invert lifeforce and reduce vital life energy. As in Vaastu, rather than making these energies your enemy, make friends with them and enhance them if you can.

Artificial ley lines, rebar grids, cell towers, cell phones, smart meters, appliances, and car batteries all impact our Auric Body. Too much energy received too fast can depleted the human energy field. Sacred sites, vortexes, and electrical towers are just a few examples of structures that can overwhelm the auric field. We can't really avoid them all (nor would we want to, in the case of sacred sites) but we can tune into when our energy system is in need of balancing. Not only can the heart chakra be developed to finely tune into the impacts of energy-draining fields, but it can be used to harmonize it as well. There is no need to fear all of this but to become mindfully aware that there are choices we can make to limit exposure to the negative and enhance any exposure from which we cannot physically distance.

The Vivaxis

In her book *Vivaxis: The Spiral of Life*, Frances Nixon shares that there is an energetic cord linking the human and the earth—our umbilical cord to the planet that acts like a center point or sphere of energy and is located where our mother spent the last few weeks of pregnancy. Consider it as an energetic center that we are linked to throughout our lives. It then remains as a two-way energetic cord throughout one's life. Disturbances in the location of the vivaxis center can disrupt the Auric Body of a person. This is a possible reason behind why we feel so energetically drawn, connected, and often called to return to our place of birth. Understanding our vivaxis and how it impacts our lives and our energy bodies has been a significant area of study for me. It is truly fascinating. If the town where our vivaxis is planted becomes energetically harmed in any way (such as overdevelopment, environmental toxicity, or excess cell towers), we will feel it in our energy bodies and eventually at the physical level as well. It is also common to be called or directed to replant your vivaxis in a new location later in life, which was the case for me. This is often felt as an energetic intuitive nudge to move somewhere, visit a specific location often, or call a new town home. You may find that nestling in a new town later in life just feels like home. This is what it feels like to replant your vivaxis. It feels homy, cozy, and right. You may also choose to select a power center as your new point of anchoring for your vivaxis. This could include a magical forest, mountain range, or favorite meadow. Nature always knows best and will guide you to your new anchor point.

Healing the Home Grid

We can't always uproot or move when electromagnetic forces throw us energetically and physically off center. What we can do is learn centering and harmonizing practices that can support our greatest good both inside and outside of the home. Here are a few suggestions:

1. Ground the house using llanite rocks to ground any geopathic stress in the home and cancel out the rebar grid and cement foundation of the home. This helps to calm the nervous system, accelerates recovery, improves heart rhythm, reduces anxiety, reduces inflammation, and aids focus. Place small bags of three or four rocks in each corner of the house. You can bury these rocks in corners of your home. I have also used hematite, rose quartz, and shungite as grid stones for both body and home. Whenever I move into a new home, I create a rose quartz grid around my home not only as a healing grid but also as a high heart grid to protect and uplift.
2. Fast moving Sha Chi can impacts health and wellbeing. It is often felt at vortexes, power centers, and sacred sites but can also occur due to large mirrors, fast moving water, big windows,

sharp corners, high ceilings, placement of windows, and L-shaped homes. Homes have ideal energetics in a rectangle shape. Many architects use rectangles for building structures and the golden ratio used (1.618) is often why many government buildings are rectangle in shape with two large pillars at the front. These buildings often include lots of granite and stone and have complete symmetry.

3. Placing llanite under or at the center of smart meters, rebar grids, cell towers, traffic circles, electrical towers can help to reduce sha chi. Traffic circles create cha chi and mess up your energy! Anything that creates a vortex in the environment can throw off your energy system. Vortex generators going around in circles creates a very chaotic energetic environment. Bury rocks in the center of the traffic circle. These stones are helpful due to their molecular structure and their ability to harmonize fields. Hematite and shungite can also be protective and supportive. These stones also help to cancel out the frequencies in the rebar grid of the home so it can reconnect and reunite with the Schuman resonance.

4. You can purchase biofield protection and shielding paints where only a brushstroke or two is sufficient. Just a dab on cell phones, smart meters, water lines, car engines, and routers to harmonize the field. There are a variety of shielding paints, clothing, and fabrics on the market today. Shielding fibers, drapes, and nets are also available for EMF protection within the home. These are especially important for anyone living in high rises, condos, or near cell phone towers.

5. Biofield shields, chips, and coins are also available that can be attached to a variety of items including rooms, cell phones, computers, appliances, and meters. As a starter, it is helpful to reduce natural or artificial frequencies that may be hindering your vibe. Tour your home first and make any minor (or major) changes that can enhance your biofield. Keeping all bedrooms in the home as biofield enhancing as possible is top of the list.

6. Sky harmonics is an emerging field where we use tools and techniques to harmonize the sky above our homes. Copper rods and leads can be used and are being researched as effective tools for this. As more and more satellite frequencies are showered upon us, some shielding advocates are also creating Faraday cages around their homes as protection. (This is one bonus of having a metal roof.)
7. Vaastu practices and principles are very helpful for harmonizing all grids and fields within, above, and around the home. Simple practices include an infusion of love, which goes a long way toward creating resonance.

As Rev. Jayme Westrom points out, all energy is good energy. You can use any type of energy by flipping the switch for its beneficial advantage. It's what is being done to energy that causes the drain on our bodies. I have learned from personal experience that fearing the bad energy does not enhance personal life force or joy. What is important is to mindfully protect your body, aura and as best you can without living in a constant state of obsession or fear. If you can leverage whatever energy is around you for good, you will be doing a tremendous service to your Auric Body and Auric Home.

Structured Water

We spoke about the importance of structured water in chapter 7 (Auric Nutrition), so I won't rehash that here except to say that collecting water directly from its natural source ideal, but one must also work within the boundaries and frameworks of what is available and safe when it comes to drinking water for the home. If water is treated, the highest vibrational intention would be to reproduce the water to be in a form most closely related to how it naturally occurs in nature.

Water can be structured using sunlight, prisms, color, technology and crystals. Blue and green light will actuate water in a way that is alkaline and healing for the body. A magnet will also structure water in an alkaline way with its north pole. North pole water is also an antibiotic quality-type water because the north pole of a magnet can support the healing of bacterial infections. Silica has also shown to be beneficial for structuring water, and you can find activated silica drops for water structuring as well as structuring stones (such as opal flint) that naturally release healthy amounts of silica into the water. Silica is also a wonderful alkalizer. It is important to do your research in terms of the stones and/or drops you are purchasing to ensure they are from pure and natural sources and are free from toxins. My favorite way to structure water is using crystals as outlined in chapter 7.

Chemicals and Toxins

If you're reading this book, you're likely already aware of the harmful effects of chemicals and toxins in the home. Replacing chemical cleaners with all-natural ones is one simple step towards creating an Auric Home. Avoiding the use of artificial fragrances, air fresheners, and aerosol freshening sprays is key. Avoiding using toxin-induced cookware, chemically sprayed home furnishings and dry cleaning are also worthy of consideration. Using non-toxic laundry and dish detergents is also very wise. Keep plastics in the home to a minimum (or gear up for a plastic-free home) and avoid drinking from plastic water bottles. When it comes to sprucing up your home, look for healthy and eco options for paints and stains. Always keep at least a little fresh air flowing throughout the home! Outside air is always healthier than inside-the-home air. It is worth considering purchasing furniture that is toxin and chemical free (most contain a chemical spray coating) or purchasing gently used furniture that has been worn in and off-gassed already. If you do have to purchase new furniture, it is a good idea to air it out in a garage or outdoors to allow off-gassing to happen outside rather than in. Little by little, having a philosophy of reducing toxins and chemicals in the home a little more every day is fabulous. With every day, feel the healthy energy signature of your home enhance and take flight.

Purifying Plants

Air quality in the home is key. Plants that circulate and detoxify the air should be prioritized. Growing as many plants indoors is very auric! Turning your home into a gorgeous greenhouse is necessary not only for air purification but for home resonance, spiritual sacredness, inner peace, emotional wellbeing, and solar frequencies within the home. Scent is also very important when it comes to transforming your house into an Auric Home. In terms of toxin reduction and purification, plants from the list below are wonderful for removing tricholorethylene, formaldehyde, benzene, ammonia, and xylene from the home. Here is a short list of some home healers should you be inspired to turn your home into a secret garden:

* Holy Basil
* Jade (a personal favorite)
* Mint
* Rosemary
* Thyme
* Lavender
* Sage
* Aloe Vera
* Spider plants
* Ficus
* Snake plants
* Aloe
* Dracaena
* ZZ Plant (Zamioculcas Zamiifolia)
* Watermelon Peperomia
* Peace Lily
* Dwarf Date Palm
* Weeping Fig
* Flamingo Lily
* English Ivy
* Broadleaf Lady Palm
* Variegated Snake plant

* Florists Chrysanthemum
* Red-Edged Dracaena
* Barberton Daisy
* Cornstalk Dracaena
* Devil's Ivy
* Flamingo Lily
* Lily Turf
* Boston Fern
* Kimberley Queen Fern
* Chinese Evergreen

When your home feels, looks and smells like a garden, you're absolutely practicing Auric Living!

Cosmic Canaries

Chemical and electrical sensitivity has become common today. Smells, electrical appliances, wifi routers, cell phones, fluorescent lighting, EMFs, foods, clothing, mold, and toxins can give the body the blues. Although much of this can be correlated with a sluggish and underperforming lymphatic system and unhappy adrenals, there is also the cosmic cause. As our Light Bodies emerge, we become pendulums for that which is true and that which is not. It is interesting that women report multiple chemical sensitivity (MCS) twice as often as men. Our bodies know that cell towers and toxins are harmful. Our bodies also know that herbs, green tea, green juice, and nature lead to peace and positivity. Other helpful practices include:

* Sauna treatments
* Cold plunge
* Auric baths
* Herbs
* Time in nature
* Lymphatic support
* Detoxification

* Using a chi machine
* Colon hydrotherapy
* Ozone therapy
* Amalgam filling removal
* Removing toxins from the home
* Meditation
* Sunlight
* Earthing (barefoot outdoor activities as much as possible)

As the immune system heals and optimizes, sensitivities will decrease and may even disappear. Spiritual practices are vital for optimizing the immune system as it is gateway to the spirit world.

Smudging

I have learned so much herbal goodness from Adriana Ayales, author of *Adaptogens: Herbs for Longevity and Everyday Wellness*. Adriana offers the following herbal insights when it comes to smudging. For protection, several herbs including palo santo, basil, nettle, and cedar are wonderful. For abundance, use bay, marigold, and marjoram. For happiness, try cinnamon, rose, sweetgrass, and St. John's Wort. For love, use rose, hibiscus and coriander. For intuition and high perception, smudge with clary sage, blue lotus, and rosemary. For clarity, use sage, mint, and rosemary.

Mold

For those who are environmental canaries in the proverbial coalmine, you will likely be able to sense mold in a home as soon as you step into it. Over the years, I have learned much about the harmful impacts of mold from Dr. Lisa Nagy, MD. It was fascinating to me that certain addictions and behaviors could be possible symptoms of mold toxicity. For women, Dr. Nagy explains, migraines and excessive red wine consumption have both been linked to mold toxicity. For men, excess anger can be linked to mold. Having your home tested for mold is a good idea as well as doing what you can to prevent any further mold from taking over your gorgeous space.

For canaries like myself, mold can be instantly felt as soon as the front door opens. This is a gift when purchasing a home but not always ideal when residing or visiting a home where mold is present. Air flow and movement within the home is very important to keep mold away. Plumbing should be checked regularly and regular repairs of cracks, leaks, and damage is a must. Drying any wet areas in the home immediately is also a healing practice. Increasing ventilation throughout the home (especially mold-loving nooks and crannies) is key. Dehumidifiers and plasma air purifiers are very helpful for mold prevention. Mold-resistant building materials are widely available but be sure to do your research for any toxic chemicals used in the product line. Any condensation showing up on windows, walls, or pipes is a possible sign that mold spores could find a cozy environment. It is also important to ensure water directs away from your home.

Numerology and astrology

Numerology and astrology can be very helpful when it comes to healing your home. As a starting point, consider the physical numeric address of your home. If you have a single digit numerical address, research what that may correspond to in terms of numerology. For double- or triple-digit numerical addresses, simply total up the individual digits to get the total sum. For 132 Lilac Way, the house number would be 6 (1+2+3=6). For numbers totaling more than 9, keep adding until you reach a single-digit number; for example, 3219 Arbor Way would also be 6 (3+2+1+9=15, then 1+5=6). Home astrology can also be helpful to enhance not only the biosignature of your home but harmonize your relationship to it.

Holistic Home First Aid

I am obsessed with making first aid kits. This could have a pinch of fear energy behind it, but it makes me feel happy and complete. As soon as I had kids, I started putting first aid kits everywhere—in each vehicle, throughout the home—and truly love putting them together. Many clients have asked me what to put in a more holistically-minded home first aid kit. You are always encouraged to add and modify but here is a list of items to consider for your own home or travel needs:

1. Crystals (such as hematite, quartz and shungite)
2. Matches/lighter
3. Beeswax tealights
4. Calendula oil, cream, tincture
5. Witch hazel
6. Aloe vera
7. Lavender
8. Activated charcoal tablets as well as loose activated charcoal
9. Stitch tape
10. Tweezers
11. Adhesive bandages/Gauze/Organic cotton or hemp cloths
12. Essential oils (such as lavender, tea tree, eucalyptus, thieves blend)
13. Echinacea tincture
14. Dried chamomile
15. Dried ginger
16. Slippery elm lozenges
17. Elderberry syrup
18. Dried eucalyptus
19. Comfrey leaves
20. Homeopathic healing creams
21. Enema kit
22. Iodine
23. Epsom salts
24. Hydrogen peroxide
25. Baking soda
26. Rubbing alcohol
27. Water purification tabs (chlorine dioxide)
28. Anti-parasitics
29. Magnifying glass
30. Splint

31. Tensor bandage
32. Coconut oil
33. Probiotics
34. Cayenne tablets and loose powder
35. Dried plantain
36. Apple cider vinegar
37. Cell salts
38. Flower essences
39. Castor oil
40. Colloidal silver
41. Diatomaceous earth (food-grade)
42. Borax
43. Fennel Seed (for indigestion, breast milk production)
44. Oatmeal (rashes, anxiousness)
45. Marshmallow root (indigestion, heartburn)
46. Peppermint (gas, indigestion and nausea)

Home Energy Signature

My husband and I feel our way through the house-hunting process. We are typically less focused on the home and more focused on the land. We don't even have to step on the land to be able to feel its energy as we can typically sense it with just a drive-by. We don't even purchase investment real estate unless we can feel out the land, either. There is one exception when we purchased a property that radiated such a high vibration that it jumped out of my computer screen and touched my soul. As you play more in the higher dimensional realms, you will develop abilities to feel your way through most of life. We have often called ourselves "house healers" because we purchase homes on high vibrational land, but the homes themselves have usually suffered a little physical or energetic trauma. It's as if homes call us in for healing. We come in with energetic magic wands and mindfully makeover physical and energetic layers of a home. Don't forget, homes have auras, too—everything is energy! Our favorite is when we find a home that sits on a vortex or power center. When you find land like this, don't worry so much about the home. As we evolve, the cosmic coding of the land will be more important than the home. You can always vibe up a home, but you can't always vibe up land. There are, of course, ways to heal land that has been harmed or traumatized, but you typically need very well-trained healers with decades of experience to do this work. We have purchased a few homes that have taken on the responsibility of holding the trauma of the residents. This is a heavy task for a home, and the energy held in the home can be dense and dark. Later in the chapter, there will be a list of things you can do to nurture and heal your home if you can feel it has been wounded. When a home has excessive leaking, foundation cracking, electrical issues, mold, rodents, wasps, insects, etc., the root cause may an energetic one more so than a physical one.

If you're house hunting, start feeling your way through a home and property to pick up on earth intelligence. You'll surely get some downloads! For my husband and me, being mindful with the energy of rental properties is also important. If the energy is off and I couldn't live there myself, it feels wrong to make money off of the exchange. Even if it isn't my dream home, I want the renters to feel high vibrational and well in the home. What they do once they move in is on them, but I want to ensure it has an energetic beauty and signature to it. Every home has an energy signature. As you connect more with your spiritual forces within (such as intuition), you will become highly sensitized to the energy signature of a home.

Radiesthesia

This is the practice of using the human biofield as a tool for gaining insight and information about other surroundings or objects as either enhancing or potentially harmful to the auric field. There are qualitative and quantitative instruments available on the market today including rods, pendulums, muscle testing, and devices.

Biogeometry®

Dr. Ibrahim Karim is the author of *Back to a Future for Mankind: Biogeometry®*. In his book, he studies how geometry can impact our environment and our bodies. Geometrical shapes can produce living energy and emit multidimensional energy. We can use this energy to then optimize our immune systems, energetic systems, and physical bodies. It is a design language based on the physics of quality that uses geometry to restore balance and increase vitality, which is how we exchange energy with our environment. His work demonstrates that the impact geometric shapes have on the human body are similar to those produced by power centers around the world. His work can be used to raise chickens and cows without antibiotics as well as protect towns from the negative health effects of EMFs. It can also be used to enhance personal and community emotional resilience and wellbeing.

The ancients did this with statues placed on power spots to enhance lifeforce and connect to higher dimensions of consciousness. The ancients invited lifeforce into every activity they did.

Sacred Geometry

Sacred geometry holds within it the key codes for all of life. We've already discussed the power of sacred form on health. Sacred geometry has the power to fully open the heart portal. Sacred geometry the physical expression of divinity through mathematics and geometry. As mentioned previously, these forms already exist in higher realms of consciousness even before they work their way into our physical consciousness. We invite them into our physical reality through light and sound. This is demonstrated in many experiments including Dr. Masaru Emoto's water experiment as well as sand experiments performed in cymatics. In early experiments, a Chladni plate was used to demonstrate how sand could be ordered into beautiful sacred geometry patterns using only sound. In early cymatics experiments, every audio frequency was tested to see what repeatable pattern would be created. Cymatics is a growing and fascinating area of study. One of my very favorite reads is *The New Energy Body* by Natalia Rose. I highly recommend getting your hands on a copy of this e-book. She reminds us that, "All creation is moving light" and that "you are a sound that has become a shape that carries light."

Sacred geometry is the blueprint of divine form. These forms express within them divine order and organization. Flower petals, the cornea of the eye, and shells are all examples of divine expression through form (sacred geometry). The flower of life, seed of life, vesica piscis, and tree of life are examples of sacred geometry patterns. Simple triangles throughout the home are highly effective for invoking this energy. As you become more allured with sacred geometry, you will become more mindful of how you place furniture, shapes of items in your home, and architecture when you build or renovate. I have enjoyed finding wall art of sacred geometry patterns to place throughout my home. If you're an artist, simply drawing sacred geometry forms has a deeply healing effect. Sacred geometry coloring books for children are great tools for calming the nervous system and enhancing energy centers. Sacred patterns hold the key codes for all life—divine intelligence expressed through form. The mathematical essence of this patterning is referred to as the Fibonacci Sequence. This is the mathematical formula behind my favorite expression: "As above so below." All cosmic creation is routed in this mathematical mystery containing the key codes of all of life. Our bodies are divine expressions of these sacred forms. Throughout the body, we find sacred geometry patterns. When we truly understand how mathematics and geometry govern the design of all of creation, we simply want more sacred geometry in our daily life! This is why a simple gaze at a sacred geometry pattern has healing benefits. These patterns exist all around us in the ether, even before we can see them with our physical eyes.

The golden ratio (approximately 1:1.618) is yet another example of sacred mathematics as coding for divine beauty and order. This mystical ratio contains within it the sacred coding clearly understood by ancient civilizations. The golden ratio is found throughout nature, ancient architectural sites and monuments, art, as well as throughout the body. These mystical numerical sequences and ratios represent the divine beauty and order found throughout nature. The Fibonacci sequence, golden ratio, and sacred geometry are all interconnected and contain within them nature's sacred coding and mystery school wisdom.

Visible sacred geometry patterns are physical manifestations of vibrations that already exist in higher planes of consciousness. Many ancient cultures clearly understood that we can invite them (and their divine properties) into our physical reality through sound. These patterns contain within them the very key codes of life and of optimal health. Sound, vibration, light, and form are the very pillars of creation.

The more we understand the power contained within sacred geometries, the more we hold them sacred. Inviting sacred geometry forms into your home is a daily practice for Auric Living. As you activate and open the very petals of your heart, you are activating these sacred patterns within your very DNA. When this happens, your body takes on new form, your voice takes on new sound, and your very life animates with divinity. You activate highest order sacred geometry within your very DNA. This is true rebirthing; you have activated they very divinity within you in highest form. This is because love is a state of being that activates highest order form and instructs every cell in the body to emit the very highest light. This isn't always an easy process, as it can bring with it the death of the old. Often times, our old life seems to crumble in front of our very eyes. Relationships may crumble, careers may vanish, and uprooting may take place. This experience is often referred to as the "Dark Night of the Soul." The divine may reorder your entire life. It is okay to grieve and to cry during this experience; it is part of the divine order of all things.

Simplicity

Simplicity in the home corresponds with beauty, order, and alignment. When our external environment is held sacred, it becomes much simpler to prioritize and focus on inner healing and wellbeing. A simple and orderly home environment results in an aligned and ordered mind. One of the reasons that truth- thinking isn't more prevalent is because our lives and environments are so chaotic and lack space. The most beneficial question we can ask ourselves daily is "How can I simplify my life and my home today?" Asking ourselves this question on a daily basis will enhance joy, wellbeing, and healing. Look to nature for clues and guidance.

Sunlight

Many cultures around the world are masters when it comes to how sunlight activates and animates structure. Windows and highways of light within the structure are architecturally designed with great care and precision. If your home isn't able to receive the sun's divine light data, those who inhabit or visit the structure will feel less-than-optimal. Homes that aren't well sunlit seriously dim the Auric Body and lead to all kinds of health hindrances. In terms of health and healing, using natural light as much as possible is ideal. Waking up with the sun and going to bed with the sun is nature's way of taking highest health care of you. Depending on where in the world you live, using blackout blinds at night can be very effective and helpful for promoting the body's natural rhythms especially where sleep is concerned.

Music and Sound

There are times when silence in a home is important and others when music is needed. Be mindful of the frequency emitted by the music you select when it comes to making your home a zenscape. The frequency emitted by the music you listen to has profound effects on the Auric Body. The modern standard of 440 Hz in music is not supportive of Auric Body expansion. A much better choice would be 432 Hz music. Scientific studies have shown that 432 Hz-tuned music enhances creativity, insight, health, and intuition. Studies have also shown that this frequency resonates with the 8 Hz heartbeat of the earth (the Schumann Resonance). 432 Hz-tuned music creates coherence and harmony between both hemispheres of the brain and was used in many ancient civilizations around the planet. Ancient healing and sound instruments such as Tibetan singing bowls produce a tone that vibrates at 432 cycles per second.

This sacred number was the keystone for ancient instrument tuning. 432 Hz is considered to be the pure tone of mathematics in nature and vibrates with the golden ratio. 528 Hz has also been studied and said to enhance chakra opening, spiritual ascension and higher dimensional abilities. "Imagine," John Lennon's song about healing the world, is 528 Hz. 528 Hz is also one of the original six Solfeggio frequencies and is known as the love and wellbeing tone for its beneficial impact on health.

Crystal Grids

Creating crystal grids around your home and body is a staple for Auric Living. This does not have to be done every day or even every week, but when you get the intuitive nudge, crystal grids are very healing for the home and for the body. I personally prefer to use quartz crystals for my home crystal grid, but as mentioned previously, llanite, shungite, and hematite are also wonderful stones to use. If you have a favorite stone that calls to you, by all means take the call. Making use of crystals in the corners of your home (outdoors and indoors), in gardens, and even on the perimeter of your property is healing and helpful. Using crushed quartz in gardens is a great way to enhance yield and wellbeing of any garden.

Air Quality and Flow

There are many natural and technical ways to enhance air quality and flow throughout the home. First and foremost, adequate ventilation is key. Stale air creates stale living. Hiring a building biologist is a great way to get some simple and effective tips for enhancing not only healthy air flow in the home but also a buffet of healthy home strategies. Air quality in a home can be greatly enhanced by simply inviting in fresh air. If you can do without air conditioning and opt for open windows, this is ideal. Plasma filters and air filters are also very helpful in purifying air within the home. Plasma filtration is an emerging field and is very effective for purifying viruses, bacteria, and mold from the air inside the home. Plasma technology in general is an emerging field that is gaining significant traction in home and body health industries. So many products today (including many air filtration systems) do more harm than good as they off gas for days, weeks, months, and even years. If you do purchase items that have been treated with chemicals, plastics, and wrapping, it is helpful to let them off-gas for a day or two in a garage or outdoors before bringing them into your home. If you can make healthy selections for your home and avoid items (including furniture) that is not treated with toxic chemicals and dyes, go for it! Chemically waterproofed and stain-proofed fabrics hinder the auric quality of the home and the body.

Home Detoxing

Just like we need to optimally breathe, so does our home. A good home detox just might be a high calling for your right now. Airing out and detoxing a home is a great regular ritual. A good home detox can include a good smudging, an incense burn, an essential oil infusion, and a half- or full day of working with a natural cleaner. A good home detox is typically a full-day ceremony but is so worth the time and energy. This is one of the quickest and most effective ways to also enhance Auric Health almost instantly! When your home vibes high, so does your body. Water, baking soda, castile soap, lemon juice, white distilled vinegar, baking soda, borax, essential oils, and club soda are all wonderful ingredients for a good home detox. As you get into it, home detoxing will become a daily thing. You may not totally have the desire to go dishwasher-, dryer-, and microwave-free just yet, but it is certainly in the realm of possibility. A great house cleaner is often on the wish list, but there is nothing more delicious for the first chakra than to do the home cleansing and detoxing yourself once in a while. Cleaning the home is a grounding ritual and does more for your health than you know. You may still wish to book a great house cleaner but doing your own home detoxing is a very grounding and wise decision.

Gardens and Greenhouses

This is the to-do list priority for our family as well as for most of our friends: Grow as much organic goodness as possible right now. Biodynamic farming is a personal interest, and although I am far from an expert, I have been learning simple and beginner practices such as using crushed quartz in soil. If you can team up with friends or family, or even want to go out on your own and grab some land over the next few months or years, it is well worth the effort. Getting your hands on organically-sourced seeds is also a brilliant practice right now. I am stocking up. A priority today is to grow organic food. If growing on your own is not feasible, team up with others to get a local co-op or greenhouse going. As a global family, we must support each other when it comes to growing healthy and organic food. This is an absolute necessity today. Healthy food is one of the most essential and fundamental practices for Auric Living, and this is not an individual task—it is a collective one. Dream up, team up, and grow up. Whether its vertical gardening, greenhouse gardening, sprouting, or microgreen growing, we need it all! If you've been feeling called to start a greenhouse or farm co-op, perhaps this book is yet another intuitive nudge to just do it! If you can get even a little greenhouse going on your property, now is the time! Getting together with others in your community to start up a food coop or organic produce collective is a wise idea right now.

EMFs

One of my biggest areas of concern is the rising number of cell towers installed on or around schools and playgrounds. Some of the most beautiful schools I have found seems to have brand new cell towers installed directly on or across from the playground, which breaks my heart. We may not be able to do away with cell towers and EMFs, but there are many things we can do to enhance our body's ability to deal with them as well as ways to lower exposure. There are many products already available on the market to shield the body and home from harmful levels of EMF exposure. We currently use cell phone Faraday bags and shield our home as much as possible. Shielding paints, shungite crystals, EMF protection coins, and Faraday cages are all great resources for this. Environmental home builders are also starting to create Faraday cage homes for clients who are particularly concerned about EMF exposure from satellites and cell towers. A simple place to start is to use shielding paints (just a little will do), shielding fibers, and a home EMF audit. Calcium and possible magnesium ions can be removed from cell membranes by electromagnetic fields. This, in turn, can cause cell membranes to be more porous and create a sort of leaky cell syndrome (similar to leaky gut but at the cellular level throughout the body). DNA fragmentation can also occur in cells when exposed to EMFs over periods of time (such as daily cell phone use). This may lead to cells leaking enzymes vital for optimal health. There is also evidence that chronic EMF exposure can lead to genetic disorders and reduction in fertility. To access many scientific papers, visit Dr. Magda Havas's website at MagdaHavas.com.

Some tips for reducing your EMF exposure are:

* Unplug appliances when not in use.
* Reduce cell phone use.
* Avoid Bluetooth technology.
* Avoid wireless headphones and speakers (as much as possible).
* Remove microwaves from the home.
* Keep bedrooms as appliance- and electronic-free as possible. (Nothing plugged in is the ideal.)
* Hardwire internet if possible.
* If you need a wifi router, put it on a timer or turn it off at night.
* Purchase an EMF reader for your home and work on reducing readings in bedrooms.
* If possible, avoid installing a smart meter on your home.
* Naturally light a home as much as possible.

* Keep windows open as much as possible (even a smidge in cold months).
* Use a clothesline as much as possible rather than an automatic clothes dryer.
* Clean your own home at least some of the time rather than hiring someone.
* Learn about building simple Faraday cages.

For me, these are these additional factors come into play when considering a home for my family:

* No cell towers in sight (and ideally more than 10km or 6.2 miles away)
* No smart meter
* Clean natural water source (An artesian well is ideal.)
* No chemical plants in vicinity
* Lots of trees (some forest on property)
* Land (Selecting properties with more land will come in handy.)
* Area to garden and grow food on the land
* No air conditioning (This is a personal preference.)
* Alternative heat source (Wood-burning stoves are great.)

It is also important to educate children and teens on being mindful where EMF exposure is concerned. This is not to instill fear but rather to educate them on simple things they can do to provide their growing bodies with some EMF recesses. Teaching children to unplug DVD players, gaming consoles, and televisions when not in use are simple examples. It is also important to teach them not to sleep with cell phones or devices beside their beds and to unplug reading lamps or electrical devices around their bed before they go to sleep. The next generation will likely have much higher EMF exposure through their lifetime than we have had, but that does not mean we can teach mindfulness in this area.

Earthing

"Do nature" as much as possible throughout the day, especially in your home. The more you connect your home to nature, the healthier you will feel and will be. This can be done by reducing EMF exposure in the home, enhancing natural air flow and fresh air, maximizing natural light in the day, filling a home with plants and herbs, and bringing in as many naturally invigorating scents as possible. Make use of as many natural fibers as possible within the home, too. Wood is a very grounding element both for construction material as well as for furniture. There are more and more lumber companies that only use naturally fallen trees for their construction, which is beautiful to see. Walking barefoot as much as possible in the home and on the land is the easiest and most powerful techniques for earthing. Earthing mats are also available on the market for anyone who lives in an apartment or condo.

Earthing pits can also be dug out on your property (just large enough to sit in). These pits can be used to sit in just minutes a day and have been shown to have a very beneficial effect on circulation, body rhythm, digestive system, and nervous system. Fifteen minutes sitting in an earthing pit followed by a sauna and a cold plunge is a dream! When it comes to earthing, finding simple ways to connect with nature inside the home is the intention. Bring as much nature inside as possible so that you can see, hear, smell, taste, and feel the healing properties of nature. Limiting toxins and chemicals inside the home is truly a healing journey. Replacing cleaning products and personal care products with all-natural alternatives is an Auric Living priority. Making your own healing cleaners and self-care products is next-level goodness.

The home is where the heart is and where health is. There is nothing more nurturing to the body and soul than to create a home that is worthy of highest-self living.

Auric Living

As we part, here are some simple ways to enhance your Auric Home:

* Hang wind chimes outdoors.
* Infuse the home with flowers (dried and fresh).
* Place herbs in each room for scent, frequency, and décor.
* Burn incense.
* Enhance the amount of natural sunlight your home gets.
* Use artificial lighting less.
* Book a Vaastu/Feng Shui/shamanic clearing session for your home.
* Get an essential oil diffuser (or several).
* Place at least one crystal in every room in your home.
* Toss toxic chemical cleaners and commit to make your own or go 100% natural.
* Use only organic, natural-fiber bedding.
* Go through every room in your home and cleanse it using dried herbs.
* Walk through your entire home in complete silence and note which rooms and spaces feel off.
* Create a space in your home (you don't need much) for a yoga mat, altar, meditation pillow, and crystal grid.
* Get a sound bowl or two. (Large quartz crystal ones are beautiful)
* Consider replacing your mattress with an all-natural, coil free organic one. (Be sure to do your homework!)
* Use essential oils and wool dryer balls if you cannot dry your clothes outdoors year-round.
* Hang your laundry outdoors to dry.
* Avoid using (or even having) a microwave.
* Remove electronic appliances as well as wireless tech from your bedroom.
* Shield your bedroom from EMFs. (If you can Faraday cage your home, even better! This can be done with shielding tents, bedding, mineral paints, drapes, coins, etc.)

* Feed your home with fresh air. (We choose fans over air conditioning).
* Unplug appliances when not in use.
* Make use of natural stains and paints as much as possible.
* Fill your home with natural fibers and materials.
* Enhance your home with art, beauty, and simplicity.
* Be mindful of sounds in your home and their impact on wellbeing (e.g., tech buzzing and hums).
* Fill your home with silence and stillness as well as with beautiful music and healing sounds.
* Take deep breaths in your home throughout the day.

Transforming your real estate into heal estate is a spiritual practice. As you let your feelings guide you through your home, you will be intuitively guided as to what small changes can have big impacts on your health as well as the health of your family. The home in which we dwell has a profound impact on our health.

Chapter 10: Auric Wealth

"I surrender my body to be ruled by my mind; I surrender my mind to be governed by my soul, and I surrender my soul to the guidance of God"

-Wallace D. Wattles

Auric Wealth is a frequency of total abundance and faith. To practice auric wealth, one transcends fear. In our new quantum reality, creating lasting and meaningful abundance and prosperity is highly probable if not certain to manifest through an open heart. The heart is now more than ever, the prosperity portal. The days of hoarding and imprisoning money in locked up accounts are quickly dwindling as these practices do not align with universal law. Our relationship with money will become healthy and faith filled when fear and trauma are healed and released. Money acts as a trigger button that perfectly activates fears, traumas and wounds that lie dormant beneath the surface or our 'looking good' personality. What we are seeing now is that the global narrative around money is activating fear and trauma buttons around the globe simultaneously which is creating the circulation of fear, trauma and scarcity in the ether. For many, regardless of how much money is in one's bank account, there is an underlying chronic feeling of fear and panic that is bubbling to the surface. Money is just one of the many triggers that activates the 'never enough' conditioning that we have all been exposed to since childhood.

For many, the fear of losing security resides within the cellular structure of the body and mind. It may lie dormant for a season or for years at a time, but when a certain set of conditions express themselves in physical reality, this fear awakens as if it were a waking giant within. When awakened, this fear has the potential to consume the mind and control the body. It has the power to manipulate hormone levels, sleep patterns and personality traits. It can absolutely take charge of the entire Auric Body if one is not conscious of what is taking place. Fear can easily transform into a paranoia if one is not trained on how to take charge and control. If the auric body is not calibrated to lead from faith, it will, through its very conditioning, lead from fear. When we don't clearly see and understand this fear, we can spend a lifetime projecting this fear onto others never realizing that it is our very self that is in need of love, nurturing and healing. As Shakti Gawain shares in her book *Awakening: A Daily Guide to Conscious Living*, 'Many people have gotten safety and security mixed up with money. Most of us, to some degree, are motivated by fear when it comes to money. We feel that somehow money can give us security. Whether we have little money or a lot of money doesn't matter. We feel that if we could only have more, we would feel safe and secure. But underneath, we are basically trying to take care of our inner child. Money is a way of trying to make the child feel safe when we're not in touch with the child's real needs. But money is not necessarily what the child wants. We need to be in communication with the child and find out what the child really needs, and give it". Sacred self-nurturing is the only true path to Auric Wealth. Regardless of the amount of money we have, when we practice Auric Wealth, we always feel secure, safe and held. Not only are we provided with everything we need at exactly the right time, but we are given the divine keys to unlocking Auric Wealth- creativity, intuition, grace and resourcefulness. If one is not kind during the pursuit of money, one does not understand the keys to the cosmos. Money can be accumulated without being kind but happiness cannot. When money is accumulated without grace and kindness, the soul starves and the personality is in discord. This is always the outcome. If the accumulation of money isn't aligned with cosmic truth, it will not be lasting nor will it lead to any sort of joy or fulfillment. This is one of the reasons you see so many people with heaps of money live unfulfilled and unhappy lives. Every moment of the journey towards Auric Wealth must be held sacred. Along our Auric Wealth journey, it is important to take many prosperity pauses. These pauses are to be used as mindfulness moments to check in with the self and the soul. These pauses are also meant to be used for contemplation to ask yourself questions such as; 'How am I feeling about my choices? How well am I serving others? How grateful and generous am I? How open is my heart? What compromises aren't feeling aligned with my soul in the pursuit of money? Am I living in deep alignment with my most sacred values?'. Too often, people get addicted to pursuing money and assume that they will eventually reach a finish line when they will then pause, relax, spend time with family and live a fully aligned life. The trouble is that this addictive race never ends and becomes even more entangled with the ego along the way. What was originally a straight forward financial plan turned into a spider web of obsession, addiction and lost time. This can easily be avoided by taking frequent prosperity pauses in life. These are used and soul check-ins to ensure the pursuit of money feels true and right to you. These pauses are also used to ensure you are not swaying too far off from soulful center.

Faith vs. fear
Conditioning the body to lead from faith instead of fear when it comes to money, does take time, love and patience. This is because the very lower energy centers (1st, 2nd and 3rd Chakras) contain an entire energetic database of our history when it comes to safety, security, nurturing, money, self-confidence, responsibility, etc. These energy centers hold the keys and patterns that play our in our lives and we are often completely oblivious to the relationship our lower three chakras have with money and security. This is why we must take an observer approach to our lives. We must stop holding others accountable for the theatre that is playing out in our lives and begin to reclaim our personal power. This is definitely not an

easy or speedy process but at a certain spiritual stage in our lives, blaming others becomes just too exhausting and draining. The moment we take absolute and full responsibility for our lives, the 1st, 2nd and 3rd chakras undergo a miraculous rebirth. It's as if they harmonize, recharge and activate with a pranic power that was simply non-existent before. The lower three chakras are responsible for running our physical world. When they are healthy and harmonious, our physical reality expresses just that. When our lower three chakras are impaired and dysfunctional due to fear, trauma and feeling victimized, our physical reality also expresses just that. When we operate from fear (whether we are aware of this or not), our lower three chakras are not spinning success or synchronicity in our lives. A majority of the population is not even aware that fear is keeping their lower three chakras in states of disfunction which is why life feels repetitive, limited and dull. Many healing modalities already mentioned throughout this book are very helpful in harmonizing and animating the lower three chakras but the best calls to action are; heart opening and self-nurturing. These two practices are authentic and true to our higher self but we have been conditioned away from them. This is also why a near death experience or difficult medical prognosis can be so very freeing- the body and mind surrender to the soul. The soul instructs the heart to open wide and inner freedom shines. The beautiful news is that we don't have to wait for a 'near-deather' or difficult medical prognosis, the soul has been waiting for you all along to hand over the reigns so that it can set you free to BE. When this occurs, fear becomes a thing of the past. You simply no longer attach to fear nor do you align with it in any way. This is where happy lives.

Cosmic Cash

Wealth creation in today's cosmic reality is about opening up the energy portals throughout the body so that energy can continuously flow throughout the body in an expansive and creative way. Money is to be shared and circulated and not to be hoarded and obsessively accumulated. Money is movement. Auric wealth is activated when we learn how to effectively pull down higher dimensional consciousness associated with love, light, sound and form and use our bodies as transformers to then manifest it as currency and prosperity in three-dimensional reality. Creative expression is the key. When we pull in higher dimensional consciousness into our auric field and receive the downloads but don't act on them, we simply cannot process and manifest abundance in the 3rd dimension. Auric wealth is less about money and more about intentional creative expression. Remember that the choices we make are of the highest spiritual significance and the intentions behind our choices are what moves us closer or further away from auric wealth. It doesn't take much spiritual strength to make a quick decision that will make us money in the moment, but if the intention behind that action is not aligned with high heart, something's going to backfire. It is absolutely now our cosmic reality that Auric Wealth occurs when we transition to a state of being that prioritizes 'how can I serve' rather than 'how can I get'. When we lovingly and compassionately become aware of our collective addiction to not having enough and not being enough, we see the greater picture where money is concerned. We have been conditioned since before birth to be addicted to consuming and to seeking more on the outside because we don't feel like enough on the inside.

Our relationship with money always tells a spiritual story. Consider your own relationship with money and contemplate the pattern it reveals. How in alignment with or out of alignment with your own truth and integrity are you for the purpose of financial gain. Where does the prostitute archetype show up in hopes of making financial gain? We have all come victim to our prostitute archetype when it comes to money. This can manifest in our reality when the intention behind our choices prioritize money. As an example, when we choose a career, partner or business based on money as the top priority spot. It's not that these choices are bad or good but they do signal to the cosmos that paper pieces of currency have been given incredible power and priority over one's life. If we aren't careful, we can wake up one morning wondering why we feel dull, stale and void of heart illuminated joy in our lives. When our choices are made from money first, we get spiritually stuck in our lives. The time has come to surrender to the higher order of things in our lives and give in to creative cosmic forces. Faith and trust is quickly becoming a significant player in the new money management strategy. We must learn to deeply trust that when our intention is strong and our heart and mind are working with high coherence, the resources will show up. We were taught to hoard the bank accounts, the insurance policies and micromanage our money. What if all of this was not only creating dis-ease but a misalignment with soul? Most of these strategies are fear based and life force leaking. Our work in Auric Living is to live each day releasing fear energy from our cells. This means that we may still have fear and notice fear, but we consciously choose to create a rhythm in our lives where choices are not made from fear. This includes money choices. I cannot tell you the amount of people I know whose heart spoke to them that having more children was deeply desired but was not brought into their physical reality because of a fear of not enough money. They consciously chose to not have another child in the chance that they didn't have enough money. As we shift our perspectives and illuminate our hearts, we begin to expand our awareness that if it is the hearts desire, the resources will show up. One of my mentors used to always say to me 'create the problem and then worry about that'. What she meant by this was that we often worry and create fear around things that we really want but then obsess about the problems and issues that might arise. She reminded me early in life to create the 'passion problem' first. Run with the passion to make it a problem and then deal with it. As an example, if it is the book you want to write but you are worries that it is too expensive to write and market, just write the book! Once it is written, you never know what magic might show up to cosmically solve the problems for you. If you want to pursue you dream career but are worried about costs, commit to the dream career with all of your heart and you will with certainty figure out a way to make the money happen. This may consist of asking the institution for an extended payment plan or other creative ways to make payments. There is always a way when you infuse creativity and imagination- the voice of the divine.

Wealth creation in the quantum field is about opening up the energy portals throughout the body so that energy can continuously flow throughout the body in an expansive and creative way.

It's not uncommon for spiritual teachers and healers to struggle with finances. The reason for this is that in most cases the financial flow is very healthy and strong with the higher dimensions of consciousness but once it is pulled into the aura, the information scatters, deflects and dissipates into the ether for others to then effectively make use of. Being well aligned to receive the higher dimensional information is only part of the equation. We must also be successfully able to transform this information through the many energy portals in the body and then pull this information down and into the 3rd dimension. Pulling the information down into the 3rd dimension requires us to be well linked and connected with the 2nd dimension- mother earth. In other words, we must be well grounded with the earth. When we're not grounded, we may get the downloads and intuitive nudges but we struggle to order the information and act on it.

In the quantum field, here are the cosmic key codes that activate Auric Wealth:

* Creativity
* Authenticity
* Connection with Soul/Source
* Inspiration
* Auric Beauty
* Order
* Rhythm
* Harmony + Balance

* Space
* Connection (with earth and others)
* Healing
* Self-Esteem + Personal Power
* Will
* Fluidity + Flexibility
* Strength

Here's where the very portals within the body play a critical role in one's financial world and beyond. Our lower chakras (1st, 2nd, 3rd) must be transforming energy well in the physical world while our higher chakras (4th, 5th, 6th and 7th and higher) fluidly function to receive the very inspiration that our bodies can then transform into auric wealth. Consider our lower chakras to be our physical world energy portals while our higher chakras act as our spiritual world portals.

Outer Freedom vs Inner Freedom

We are trained and conditioned to believe that a good job, nice car, good neighbourhood, nice home, healthy savings account, insurance plans, etc. lead to freedom. This was what I thought too! I spent much of my life sticking to the book when it came to what sets you up for success and freedom. As I filled and fueled up on most of these, I discovered that regardless of how much or little I had in the bank, a true feeling of inner freedom didn't seem to be happening. I become fascinated with the psychology of safety and security as well as how it impacts our relationship with money. I pretty quickly realized that it is never about the money but what data is stored in the chakras that oversee money. The second chakra is often most associated with money but it is truly the symphonic relationship between several chakras that manifests our financial reality. As much as we financially frill up the outside world, we cannot express and experience freedom unless we seek it on the inside first. It doesn't matter how much money we have, if we have a deep-rooted fear of losing security or not feeling safe, we will never feel happy and free. Instead, we will spend our entire life obsessing about making money and being addicted to money and more. When we discover that our outer relationship with money has everything to do with how safe and secure we feel on the inside, as well as how deeply we love and nurture ourselves, we can release all resistance. This understanding unlocks divine compassion towards ourselves. As we spiritually mature, we begin to release the hold the ego has on our lives and let the soul settle in. Little by little, we begin to breath frequent sighs of relief that there is a greater power overseeing our path. As the heart opens and awakens, the cells literally release fear just as they do toxins. This physically and energetically transforms the body. As the cells release this fear and replace this space with faith, an immeasurable amount of wealth and abundance will be discovered in our lives. When this occurs, the gates to Auric Wealth open wide.

Peaceful Prosperity

It is an absolute possibility to create Auric Wealth in a peaceful and powerful way. The secret to peaceful prosperity is clarity. We leak much prosperity power when we lack vision, clarity and faith. When we are scattered in our daily work and thinking, it is as if conscious cash is leaking from our very bodies. To become a money magnet, one must get crystal clear on what it is we want to craft and create. When we lack clarity, we often lack confidence as well. The default in our physically constructed world is one of chaos, disorder and busyness. Our work is to connect and align with nature and the natural order of all things abundant and alive. When we synch up with natural law, effortless effort happens. Effortless effort is when we apply our gifts and act on creative downloads as well as allow ourselves to be carried towards aligned abundance. There is action-Yes, but the action feels aligned with universal law and feels true in our heart. You'll know when you're being carried towards aligned abundance because you'll be rising others up along the way. The Auric Bodies of others will also illuminate along your own peaceful prosperity path. There may be short stints of hustle or busy on this path as well, but for the most part, it will feel like a conscious cash continuum. On this path, the heart remains open and activated. It is a completely different feeling than the ego led and addictive path of fear-filled financial gain. On days where one might be feeling 'less than' where money is concerned, taking a meditation moment can be very healing and helpful. I have created a Beautiful Money Meditation as a supportive tool for peaceful prosperity (available on insighttimer.com). As you practice peaceful prosperity on more days than not, you will feel the difference in your soul.

Money is Movement

During this cosmic time in human history, money is meant to be circulated not stored or hoarded. Money is energy and it wants to move, support and serve. It's very important to understand how important circulation (rotation) is when it comes to money. Consider the torus energy pattern when it comes to money flow. In the world of form, rotation creates a center and a center creates a vortex. When things move in a circular pattern, they draw in life force. If we use money as an example, the more we circulate money, the more we invite in abundant life force. Rotation of the 2nd chakra also draws in abundance as this is your money power center. I personally love supported bridge in yoga (using a block) several times a week to invite abundance in. The more you surround your home, office and environment with highly ordered design patterns, the more in resonance with prosperity you will also be. Sacred geometry patterns are examples of highly ordered forms that harmonize your body and environment. This is a great example of a simple thing you can do to put your 2nd chakra (and all chakras) in resonance with higher realms of consciousness which then leads to abundant flow of life force.

When we live from a frequency of faith (and not fear), we simply trust this truth without question and move through our day serving as many people as we possibly can. Having some extra funds on hand as well as valuable assets is always helpful as long as we develop a sense of security within that is not obsessively attached with addictively pursuing them. One should feel guided and supported from the higher realms while being strategic, resourceful and creative in the lower realms (and in this reality). This means that it is absolutely worthy to act each day from a place of excellence while always remembering that we are energy first, physical second. We must always stay centered in spiritual principles that maintain our healthy state of inner freedom. When we do this, we will always be taken care of and provided for in this physical reality.

Wealthy Will

Auric Wealth and gorgeous legacy go hand in hand. This doesn't require a full decade or two of study but a simple understanding when it comes to cosmic law. Before this cosmic nodal point in human history, we could get away with much more selfishness and silliness. Today, we are all experiencing instant karma as the cosmos reset us back on track with divine law. As the veil lifts for so much of humanity during this time, we will begin to experience in our bodies and in our daily life what is meant by 'the illusion of time'. Opening the portals to Auric Wealth begins when we have a deep and honest conversation with our soul. Time as we know it is not as relevant today. What may have taken years if not decades to create before, can now be done in months if not weeks. The very concept of time is accelerating at such a speed that many are feeling the strangeness of this shift. It is difficult to describe but the strangeness of it is very real. It's as if we're in one timeline in the morning while on a completely different one in the afternoon. Bizarre and beautiful at the same time. What this means for your money is that there has never been a more extraordinary time to tap into those creative juices and transform them into conscious cash! You now have all the power within you to create as much abundance as you desire for yourself in all aspects of life- you simply have to believe in YOU right this very moment.

Here are the 3 personal pillars of self-mastery that activate portal opening for Auric Wealth: Will, Love and Wisdom The wisdom pillar refers to universal law, cosmic truth and spiritual knowledge about how things really work in the physical realm. The will portal is associated very much with the 3rd and 6th chakra health. The 3rd Chakra is associated with self-will while the 6th chakra is associated with divine will. In order for this pillar to be strong in a person, self-esteem must be strong and healthy. The ground for healthy self-esteem is laid during childhood. It is, however, important to understand that it can always be strengthened (at any age). Affirmations, Action and Strengthening the Physical core are all very helpful when it comes to balancing the 3rd chakra. Opening the 6th chakra happens as we gain spiritual maturity and peel all layers not associated with deep authenticity. As we do this, this portal opens and the soul can deliver us our true calling in this lifetime. For this reason, strengthening self-will (3rd chakra) typically gets us a good job while strengthening the 6th chakra connects us with our calling.

LOVE

WISDOM   **WILL**

They key to bringing in auric wealth into the 3rd dimension from higher ones is that you open your heart, strengthen your mind and consciously commit to taking aligned action. Remember that abundance is ever flowing but it cannot make its way to you if the portal is closed. Many believe the portal of money to be the 2nd chakra (the money, sex and power chakra) but always remember that it's not only about the health of individual chakras, it's how to play together. Auric wealth flows in when all chakras are in synch and make magnificent music. It's sound that creates form remember so tune your chakras to higher realm consciousness where money music is always playing. Money music is the sweet sound of spiritually directly intention connected with authentic and aligned action.

Feminine Flow

To recalibrate our bodies and beings with divine harmony, feminine essence is now necessary. We have stepped out of harmonious flow for far too long. The masculine dominant hustle not only messed up the planet but greatly messed up our Auric Bodies. What is needed right now is a harmonization of how one creates money as well as circulates it. This is done by infusing feminine energy flow into daily life. Intuition, creativity, feeling and movement are all elements of feminine financial flow. It's not that the masculine energy elements are now done and void but that we must embrace and invite feminine energy forces to rebalance the masculine energy dominance that has ruled over finances for far too long. There must now be more kindness, grace, generosity, nurturing and natural flow in all aspects of money management, money movement and money education. Natural laws must weave with financial strategies for human and planetary healing to take place. Simple things that can be done to begin this process is to act more on intuitive hunches on a daily basis as well as let creative energy take shape into conscious cash. Allow and expect money to flow into your life as you commit to doing so much good and service to those around you and to the planet. There must be a balance between male and female energies for Auric Wealth to manifest. This means that we must be responsible, integrous and resourceful while always expressing generosity, gratitude and kindness. Allow abundance to flow into your life by releasing the excess male dominant energy traits. Settle into the feminine energies that want to express and circulate.

The Creativity Continuum

Creativity is conscious cash. This is why when we block creativity, we block financial flow. When we get a creative download or inspiration, we are meant to act on it. It doesn't always have to be that exact day but when we delay creative doses of inspiration for too long, they dwindle in force. Creative energy is meant to be expressed, not held in the body. Our creative energy is not only our gift to the planet but the key code to conscious cash flow in our lives. It is sometimes necessary to roll with the universe by downsizing, selling assets and/or being mindful of spending but not at the expense of expressing creativity (as this is the key to increasing cash flow). There should always be a balance between being mindful and creatively creating cash. I often find when clients get overly focused on reducing spending in their lives, they completely neglect to keep on creating cash flow by way of creative gifts and inspiration. Being mindful on spending is good but being a master cash flow creator is great. Mindfulness must always be present for Auric Wealth to manifest but never forget to act on creative inspiration as it just might be the magnificent money manifestation you have been dreaming of! When we block creative flow, we absolutely block money flow. Creativity is the master key to Auric Wealth.

Spiritual Serving

Self-Will is the will to act that helps us to gain the things we want and desire in life. This is a helpful and necessary practice to master on the path to spiritual maturation. We learn much from strengthening self-will including healthy habits that help us thrive and succeed in personal and professional. Self-will success has been the focus and priority for most training programs up until this point when it comes to business, money, finances, etc. What is now taking center stage is the development of divine will. This is the will of the soul and of source for our life. Developing strength in divine will connects us to our true purpose in this lifetime and our destiny. When we are cut off from communication with our soul, we get stuck in self-will practices for far too long in our lives which is why so many people feel confused as to what their true purpose in life is. To gain clarity on one's true purpose in life, divine will must be activated and animated. To do this, one must train the ego to be resilient and healthy but to give full permission to the soul to be in charge. We must begin to train our children to do this earlier in life than we have been taught. When we have activated divine will in our lives (and animated the 6th chakra), we won't be able to stop seeking how to spiritually serve. Our focus moves away from serving the self (although taking care of ourselves and our families will remain important) and towards spiritually serving. We become deeply aware that we are here with a much greater purpose than to accumulate material frills like houses, trips, boats and cars. When we become emotional at the very thought of serving others and the planet with greater depth, we have activated divine will. Divine will is activating in millions of people across the planet at this very moment in time, and at speeds never experienced on earth ever before. When we activate divine will, it is as if the angelic realm takes over our life and we are left wondering who or what was in charge up to this sacred time. It's as if we leap into a completely new reality- and we do. Something spiritually strange is going on right now on the planet and it is absolutely divinely timed. Can you feel it?

Aligned Abundance

Aligned abundance is key in the quantum realm. Making money from doing things that aren't in alignment with the soul or higher consciousness is no longer of highest order (not that it ever was but it was somewhat tolerated as we found our feet in the 3rd dimension). So don't be surprised if aura contracting activities don't bring much cash. Many people are reporting that activities that used to bring them lots of cash before simply aren't working anymore- no matter how hard they try. It's not that you can't make money from things that don't elevate the planet but it will just take so much more life force to animate this kind of work into abundance. It will be even more exhausting and leave you feeling dull and dead inside.

Here are some business ideas that will be gaining great momentum:

* Food Coops
* Community Greenhouses

* Gardens + Food Production
* Gold and Silver Depot
* Real Estate
* Land
* Crypto
* Detox Clinics
* Integrative Wellness Clinics
* Naturopathic Clinics
* Healing Clinics + Spas
* Healing Retreats
* Quartz Business/Retail
* Crystal Business/Retail
* Water Purification Business
* Home Purification Business
* Off Grid Living Technology
* Off Grid Living Installation/Repair/Retail
* Home Healing Business (air, water, mold, sound, emf, light)
* Spiritual Psychology Practice
* Grief Counselling Clinic
* Funeral Business
* Retreat and Detox Center
* Biodesign (healing home design)
* BioBuilding/BioConstruction
* Technology
* Space/Space Travel/Space Medicine
* Home Healthcare Business
* Property Management Company
* Zero Point Energy Technology
* Plasma Technology
* Biotechnology
* Technology
* Natural Medicine
* Herbal Medicine
* Herb Apothecaries
* Eco Home Business

- * Colon Hydrotherapy Clinic
- * Light + Sound Clinic

Here are some career ideas that will be gaining great momentum:

- * Energy Healer
- * Farming
- * Foraging
- * Greenhouse Farming
- * Sprouting + Microgreen Growing
- * Trades
- * Carpentry
- * Spiritual Coach
- * Spiritual Psychologist
- * Funeral Direction
- * Grief Counsellor
- * Death Doula
- * Building Biologist
- * Home Design (specializing in home biosignature and energetics)
- * Naturopath
- * Home Health Care Worker
- * EMF Specialist
- * Mold Specialist
- * Spiritual Nutritionist
- * Homeopath
- * Herbalist
- * Crystal Healer
- * Sound + Light Healer
- * Colon Hydrotherapist
- * Flower Essence Therapist
- * First Responder
- * Health Care Worker/Alternative Health Care Worker
- * Detox Specialists
- * Mental Health Worker/Therapist

* Property Manager
* Doula
* Midwife
* Etheric Healers/Channelers
* Child Psychologist/Therapist
* Personal Support Worker
* Microcurrent medicine therapist
* WaldorfEducator/OutdoorEducationEducators/Alternative Educators)
* Early Childhood Educators
* Alternative Education Specialist
* Homestead Specialist/Educator
* Survival and Outdoor Living Specialists
* Akashic Record Practitioner

Multidimensional Money

Regardless of how much or little one understands quantum physics, we are all multidimensional beings and we must start living and acting from this cosmic reality. When you fully embrace multidimensional beingness, you are able to warp time and space. This means that you can quickly and easily transform creativity into cash- at the drop of a hat. You are being showered 24-7 with creativity that is at your disposal to transform into conscious cash.

When you live from higher realms of consciousness, the law of causality (cause and effect) is replaced by the law of resonance. This is where quantum money leaps happen. What this means is that even if it took you 15 years to build a healthy income stream for yourself in the past, this doesn't have to be the case anymore. You can experience quantum prosperity leaps overnight, as long as you make highest vibrational choices in your life and work each day to maintain resonance with higher consciousness realms (4th, 5th, 6th and beyond). My daily mantra is 'highest vibrational choices only today'.

Here are some multidimensional money tips:

* Every morning, say out loud 'highest vibrational choices only today'
* Do one thing every day to bring more beauty and order into your physical environment
* Increase rhythm in your life (as if you are dancing daily)
* Circulate money without feeling stressed about it or looking at it as a loss
* Have faith and be reminded that your work is to live from highest consciousness realms possible, the divine is in charge of the rest
* Make mindful money choices throughout your day. Make sure your spending is aligned with your greatest values. If a forest school and organic groceries are at the top of your list, trust the money will come.
* Always remember that everything is energy first, matter second. Craft your highest vision in the energy realm.
* Work towards 10 income streams (as many passive ones as possible!)
* Authenticity and Wellbeing are your greatest money magnets
* Hustle backfires! Aligned action is where it's at.
* Work like water- be fluid and flexible while staying strong and resilient.
* Become a pivot master. Be able to pivot in an instant and upgrade a choice when you're called to

It's wonderful to have a career you love or work that is deeply fulfilling and rich with service but you are only one person and there are only so many hours in a day. For this reason, set as an absolute possibility for yourself to make as many as 10 income streams (or more!) in your life. Aim for at least one of these income streams to be a passive one that isn't directly dependent on your time (such as a rental property, royalty income, direct sales business, recurring revenue, etc.).

Here are some incredible asset options that will serve you well:

* Food
* Art
* Energy Production Equipment
* Purification supplies and equipment (water, air, earth)
* Collectibles
* Health Care equipment/Healing Equipment
* Holistic Healing Supplies and Treatments
* Farming equipment and supplies
* First aid equipment and supplies
* Building supplies
* Electronics
* Land + Real Estate
* Off grid equipment
* Batteries
* Greenhouses
* Plants + Herbs
* Medicinals
* Flower Essences
* Homeopathics
* Supplements
* Gold + Silver
* Copper
* Quartz Crystals
* Cryptocurrency

These are Auric Wealth assets!

Fearless faith is our work right now. As we integrate, heal and release fear from our cells, attunement with abundance will occur. 'Auric Wealth' used as a money mantra will stimulate creative flow, inspirational insights and mindful money practices. Finances is just one dimension of life where conditioning is rooted in fear. It is time to make money peace with our path and acknowledge the cosmic abundance that lies dormant within our cells. When fear is released, great abundance illuminates. The heart chakra plays a vital role in prosperity power right now. As the heart opens and activates, great self-compassion, self-love self-nurturing takes shape. Not only does this take shape through an illuminated and vibrant Auric Body but through the activation of Auric Wealth.

Soul Leader

As we continue to expand and awaken to higher realm wisdom, we have a sacred responsibility right now to mindfully move through every moment of every day. May practicing Auric Living bring you closer to living intimately with the law of one at every moment. May you listen at every moment to the guidance you are receiving from higher realm truth. Nature delivers intimate secrets and absolute grace to all who are open hearted enough to pause, to be patient and to be kind. May you know at every moment of every day that you are here with great purpose and that you are infinitely loved. Here are three simple intentions for Auric Living:

1) Embody love expecting nothing in return
2) Be kind towards yourself and others
3) Be a luminous listener

Being a luminous listener means that you have a sacred understanding that when your Auric Body is resilient and well, you really don't have to talk much. A luminous listener is spiritually strong and flowing with lifeforce energy allowing them to hold space for others (often through listening) without diminishing their love and light. They hold their frequency high, regardless of who they are surrounded by. This takes place when Auric Living is a daily practice. Luminous listeners do not lower their own frequency to meet another's- they hold themselves vibrationally high because of the high level of light they transmit. Every cell in their body shines divine light.

Never in the history of humanity has there ever been a more spiritual significant time to say YES to life, YES to love, and YES to your soul. At this very moment, you soul is asking you to surrender and let go—and to let it take charge of this physical reality. As you complete this book, it is the perfect time to pass the torch to your soul and master within. Simply release and allow yourself to be well, be happy, be guided and be you. Enjoy the unfolding and mystical unravelling of soul leadership.

Now go and do your destiny.

References:

Apelian, Nicole, and Claude Davis. *The Lost Book of Herbal Remedies: The Healing Power of Plant Medicine.* Capital Printing Co, 2021.

Artemis, Nadine. *Holistic Dental Care: The Complete Guide to Healthy Teeth and Gums.* North Atlantic Books, 2013.

Artemis, Nadine. *Renegade Beauty: Reveal and Revive Your Natural Radiance: Beauty Secrets, Solutions and Preparations.* North Atlantic Books, 2017.

Auken, Van John, and Ruben Miller. *Edgar Cayce on the Mysterious Essenes: Lessons from Our Sacred Past.* A.R.E. Press, 2016.

Ayales, Adriana. *Adaptogens: Herbs for Longevity and Everyday Wellness.* Sterling Publishing Co., Inc., 2019.

Babbitt, Edwin D., and Faber Birren. *The Principles of Light and Color; the Classic Study of the Healing Power of Color by Edwin D. Babbitt. Edited and Annotated by Faber Birren.* University Books, 1967.

Bach, Edward. *The Essential Writings of Dr Edward Bach: The Twelve Healers and Other Remedies & Heal Thyself.* Vermillion, 2005.

Banis, Reimar. *New Life Through Energy Healing: The Atlas of Psychosomatic Energetics.* Artemis Books, 2008.

Banis, Reimar. *Psychosomatic Energetics Textbook.* Books ON DEMAND, 2017.

Barbour, Julian B. *The Discovery of Dynamics.* Oxford University Press, 2001.

Becker, Robert O., and Gary Selden. *The Body Electric: Electromagnetism and the Foundation of Life.* Quill, 2005.

Bigelsen, Harvey. *Holographic Blood: A New Dimension in Medicine.* Hemobiographic Publications, 2006.

Boericke, William, and Willis A. Dewey. *The Twelve Tissue Remedies of Schüssler: Comprising the Theory, Therapeutic Application, Materia Medica, and a Complete Repertory of These Remedies.* Jain, 1973.

Braden, Greg. *The Divine Matrix.* Hay House. 2008

Brennan, Barbara Ann. *Hands of Light: A Guide to Healing through the Human Energy Field: A New Paradigm for the Human Being in Health, Relationship, and Disease.* Bantam Books, 1993.

Brennan, Barbara Ann. *Light Emerging: The Journey of Personal Healing.* Transworld Digital, 2011.
Brulé Dan. *Just Breathe: Mastering Breathwork.* Atria/Enliven Books, 2020.
Buhner, Stephen Harrod. *Transformational Power of Fasting: The Way to Spiritual, Physical, and Emotional Rejuvenation.* Healing Arts, 2012.
Castro, Miranda. *The Complete Homeopathy Handbook: A Guide to Everyday Health Care.* Macmillan, 1995.
Cayce, Edgar Evans, and John Van Auken. *Atlantis.* A.R.E. Press, 2021.
Cayce, Edgar, and Hugh Lynn Cayce. *Edgar Cayce on Atlantis.* Warner Books, 1968.
Cleary, Thomas F. *Wen-Zi: Understanding the Mysteries.* Shambhala, 1992.
Clow, Barbara Hand, and Gerry Clow. *Alchemy of Nine Dimensions: The 2011/2012 Prophecies and Nine Dimensions of Consciousness.* Hampton Roads Pub. Co., 2010.
Cousens, Gabriel. *Spiritual Nutrition: Six Foundations for Spiritual Life and the Awakening of Kundalini.* North Atlantic Books, 2005.
Cowan, Thomas S., et al. *The Fourfold Path to Healing: Working with the Laws of Nutrition, Therapeutics, Movement and Meditation in the Art of Medicine.* NewTrends Pub., 2004.
Currivan, Jude. *The 8th Chakra: What It Is and How It Can Transform Your Life.* Hay House, Inc., 2008.
Dyer, Wayne W. *The Power of Intention: Learning to Co-Create Your World Your Way.* Hay House, 2008.
Ehret, Arnold. *Mucusless Diet Healing System - Scientific Method of Eating Your Way to Health.* Ehret Literature Publishing Co, 2011.
Easwaran, Eknath and Michael N. Nagler. *The Upanishads.* Nilgiri Press, 2007.
Easwaran, Eknath. *Mantram Handbook.* Nilgiri Press, 2001.
Gawain, Shakti. *Awakening: A Daily Guide to Conscious Living.* Nataraj, 2006.
Gawain, Shakti. *Living in the Light: A Guide To Personal And Planetary Transformation.* 25th Anniversary Edition ed., New World Library, 2011.
Gerber, Richard. *Vibrational Medicine - Revised and Updated 3rd Edition.* 3rd ed., Inner Traditions Bear And Comp, 2001.
Gimbutas, Marija Alseikaite, and Miriam Robbins Dexter. *The Living Goddesses.* University of California Press, 2006.
Goddard, Neville. *Feeling is the Secret.* General Press. 2019.
Gold, Thomas. *The Deep Hot Biosphere: The Myth of Fossil Fuels.* Copernicus Books, 2010.
Goswami, Amit. *The Quantum Doctor: A Quantum Physicist Explains the Healing Power of Integrative Medicine.* Hampton Roads, 2011.

Greer, Beth. *Super Natural Home: Improve Your Health, Home, and Planet-- One Room at a Time*. Rodale, 2009.

Gurudas. *Flower Essences and Vibrational Healing*. Cassandra Press, 1989.

Hall, Manly, P. *Pineal Gland: The Eye of God*. WWW BNPUBLISHING COM, 2015.

Hawkins, David R. *Power vs. Force: The Hidden Determinants of Human Behavior*. Hay House, Inc., 2014.

Hay, Louise L. *You Can Heal Your Life*. Hay House, 2008.

Heline, Corinne. *Healing and Regeneration through Color*. DeVorss, 1980.

Hill, Napoleon. *Outwitting the Devil: The Secret to Freedom and Success*. Sound Wisdom, 2020.

Hofstadter, Douglas R. *Godel, Escher, Bach*. Penguin, 2000.

The Holy Bible English Standard Version, Trutone, Berry, Floral Design. Crossway Books, 2015.

Jones, Betty. *A Child's Seasonal Treasury*. Lulu.com, 2012.

Jung, C. G., et al. *Collected Works of C.G. Jung, Volume 9 (Part 1)*. Princeton University Press, 2014.

Jung, C. G. *Synchronicity*. Taylor & Francis Ltd, 1985.

Karim, Ibrahim. *Back to a Future for Mankind: Biogeometry, Solutions to the Global Environmental Crisis New Energy Secrets of Ancient Egypt and the Great Pyramid Revealed*. Biogemetry Consulting Ltd., 2010.

Karim, Ibrahim. *Biogeometry Signatures: Harmonizing the Body's Subtle Energy Exchange with the Environment*. BioGeometry Energy Systems, Ltd., 2016.

Lao-tzu, and Thomas F. Cleary. *Wen-Tzu: Understanding the Mysteries*. Shambhala, 1992.

Laszlo, Ervin. *Science and the Akashic Field: An Integral Theory of Everything*. Inner Traditions International, 2007.

Liberman, Jacob. *Light: Medicine of the Future: How We Can Use It to Heal Ourselves Now*. illustrated ed., Bear & Company, 1991.

Maté Gabor. *When the Body Says No*. Scribe Publications, 2019.

McMakin, Carolyn. *Resonance Effect*. Illustrated ed., North Atlantic Books, 2017.

Meyers, Bryant A. *PEMF - the Fifth Element of Health: Learn Why Pulsed Electromagnetic Field Therapy (PEMF) Supercharges Your Health like Nothing Else!* Balboa Press, a Division of Hay House, 2014.

Milanovich, Dr. Norma J, and Dr. Shirley McCune. *The Light Shall Set You Free*. Athena Publishing, 1996.

Morse, Robert. *The Detox Miracle Sourcebook: Raw Foods and Herbs for Complete Cellular Regeneration*. Kalindi Press, 2004.

Myss, Caroline M. *Advanced Energy Anatomy*. Sounds True, 2001.

Myss, Caroline, et al. *Entering the Castle: An Inner Path to God and Your Soul.* Atria Paperback, a Division of Simon & Schuster, Inc., 2013.

Neufeld, Gordon, and Maté Gabor. *Hold on to Your Kids: Why Parents Need to Matter More than Peers.* Vermilion, 2019.

Nightingale, Earl. *The Strangest Secret: For Succeeding in the World Today.* Nightingale-Conant Corp., 1998.

Nixon, Frances, and Bessie O'Connor. *Vivaxis: The Spiral of Life.* Abbey Book Publishers, 1969.

Orloff, Judith. *The Empath's Survival Guide: Life Strategies for Sensitive People.* Sounds True, 2020.

Pearce, Joseph Chilton. *The Biology of Transcendence: A Blueprint of the Human Spirit.* Park Street Press, 2004.

Proctor, Bob. *You Were Born Rich: Now You Can Discover and Develop Those Riches.* Proctor Gallagher Institute, 2014.

Rakel, David. *Integrative Medicine.* 4th ed., Elsevier, 2017.

Rose, Natalia. *The New Energy Body: Discover a Hidden Source of Energy That Will Amaze You.* Ebook. 2007.

Russell, Walter. *The Secret of Light.* Illustrated ed., Bridger House Publishers, 2018.

Russell, Walter. *The Universal One.* University of Science and Philosophy, 1974.

Sagan, Samuel. *Awakening the Third Eye.* 3rd ed., Clairvision School Foundation, 2013.

Scheffer, Mechthild. *Bach Flower Therapy: Theory and Practice.* Healing Arts Press, 1988.

Scheffer, Mechthild. *The Encyclopedia of Bach Flower Therapy.* Healing Arts Press, 2001.

Siegel, Daniel J. *Mind: A Journey to the Heart of Being Human.* W.W. Norton & Company, 2017.

St. John of the Cross. *Dark Night of the Soul.* Dover Publications, 2003.

St. Teresa of Avila, and Mirabai Starr. *The Interior Castle.* Riverhead Books, 2004.

Steiner, Rudolf. *Atlantis and Lemuria.* Fredonia Books, 2002.

Steiner, Rudolf. *Theosophy: An Introduction to the Supersensible Knowledge of the World and the Destination of Man.* CreateSpace Independent Publishing Platform, 2008.

Steiner, Rudolf, and J. Wood. *From the History and Contents of the First Section of the Esoteric School 1.* Anthroposophic Press Inc, 2010.

Steiner, Rudolf. *Esoteric Lessons, 1910-1912: Notes Written from Memory by the Participants and Meditation Verses by Rudolf Steiner.* SteinerBooks, 2012.

Strom, Max. *Life Worth Breathing: A Yoga Master's Handbook of Strength, Grace, and Healing.* W W Norton, 2012.
Virtue, Doreen. *Angel Medicine: How to Heal the Body and Mind with the Help of the Angels.* Hay House, 2004.
Vranich, Belisa. *Breathe: The Simple, Revolutionary 14-Day Program to Improve Your Mental and Physical Health.* Hay House, 2016.
Wattles, W. D. *The Science of Getting Rich: Attracting Financial Success through Creative Thought.* Destiny Books, 2007.
Wentz, Dave, et al. *The Healthy Home: Simple Truths to Protect Your Family from Hidden Household Dangers.* Vanguard Press, 2011.

Websites:

"About Us." *Biofield Expert*, Rev. Jayme Westrom. https://biofieldexpert.com/pages/about-me.
"A School of Higher Learning." *International School of the Healing Arts and Sciences*, https://internationalschoolofthehealingarts.com/.
"Beyond Organic for a Healthy Terrain." *Alfa Vedic™*, 14 Apr. 2021, https://www.alfavedic.com/.
"Edgar Cayce's Association for Research and Enlightenment: Edgar Cayce's A.R.E." *Edgar Cayce's Association for Research and Enlightenment | Edgar Cayce's A.R.E. | Edgar Cayce's A.R.E.*, https://www.edgarcayce.org/.
"Experiential Expanded Consciousness Meditation Programs and Research." *The Monroe Institute*, https://www.monroeinstitute.org/.
"Dr. Magda Havas, Phd. – Electromagnetic Field News." *Dr Magda Havas PhD*, 20 Feb. 2022, https://magdahavas.com/.
"Dr. Lisa Nagy. "Home." *Environmental Health Center of Martha's Vineyard.* 10 Aug. 2022, https://lisanagy.com/.
"Home of Dr Edward Bach and the Bach Flower Remedy System." *The Bach Centre*, 13 July 2020, https://www.bachcentre.com/en/.
"Heartmath Institute." *HeartMath Institute*, http://www.heartmath.org/.
"Marcel Vogel's Groundbreaking Work." *Marcel Vogel Legacy*, https://marcelvogellegacy.com/.
Nelson, Mika. "Mika Nelson." *Academy For Healing Arts*, 27 Aug. 2020, https://www.academyforhealingarts.com/author/mika-nelson/.
"Plant Medicines." *Anima Mundi Herbals*, https://animamundiherbals.com/.
"Researchers of Truth.". *RESEARCHERS OF TRUTH Archives*, 7 June 2021, https://archive.researchersoftruth.com/.
"Rudolf Steiner Archive." *GA 212. The Human Heart - Rudolf Steiner Archive*, https://rsarchive.org/Lectures/HumHrt_index.html.

"The Heart of Healing." *Klinghardt Institute*, https://klinghardtinstitute.com/.
"Tiny Rituals Blog." *Tiny Rituals*, https://tinyrituals.co/blogs/tiny-rituals.
Transformational Breath Foundation, https://www.transformationalbreath.com/.
"*Vesica Institute.*". *Vesica Institute for Holistic Studies in Biogeometry + Vibrational Science.*
https://vesica.org/.
"Water Filtration, Air Purification, EMF Protection & Earthing Solutions: Niagara, Ontario." *Purahome*, https://www.purahome.com/.

Research Papers:
Noszticzius, Zoltán, et al. "Chlorine Dioxide Is a Size-Selective Antimicrobial Agent." *PLoS ONE*, vol. 8, no. 11, 2013, https://doi.org/10.1371/journal.pone.0079157.

www.ingramcontent.com/pod-product-compliance
Lightning Source LLC
Chambersburg PA
CBHW071646090426
42738CB00009B/1436